CONSUMER ECONOMIC PROBLEMS

(*Abridged Volume*)

By

H. G. SHIELDS

Associate Professor of Business Education
The School of Business
The University of Chicago

AND

W. HARMON WILSON

Lecturer, University of Cincinnati
and Editor of The Balance Sheet

Published by

SOUTH-WESTERN PUBLISHING COMPANY

Cincinnati New York Chicago San Francisco Dallas

G13

H341

Printed in the United States of America

PREFACE

Development of the Book. CONSUMER ECONOMIC PROBLEMS is recommended for a course in consumer education, whether it is offered as a single isolated course or as a part of a school-wide program.

This book is the outgrowth of a book originally published under the title of BUSINESS-ECONOMIC PROBLEMS. At the time the original book was published, there were many different types of courses emphasizing consumer education. Great strides have been made in the development of courses in consumer education. As a result, opinions have been crystallized as to what should be covered in courses in consumer business education and other types of consumer courses. On the basis of this crystallized opinion, the book has been completely revised. Some subject matter has been omitted, and considerable new subject matter has been added. As a result of these changes the title of the book has been changed to conform more definitely with the contents.

The book provides a well-rounded treatment of consumer education, the plan of which is as follows:

Objectives. The objectives of the abridged volume of CONSUMER ECONOMIC PROBLEMS can be briefly summarized as follows:

1. To provide the general information that a consumer needs in solving his problems
2. To provide specific techniques that may be used by the consumer in satisfying his wants
3. To provide a general understanding of how the consumer can use to his best advantage the services offered by business

General Problems of the Consumer. Before it is possible to determine how to solve the problems of the individual, we must recognize that the basic consumer problems of the individual center around the following:

1. Obtaining food
2. Obtaining clothing
3. Obtaining shelter
4. Obtaining economic services

Specific Problems of the Consumer. There are many other problems that are the outgrowth of these four larger problems. The consumer must, of course, earn an income and know what to do with it. He not only has to provide the necessaries of life, but he must also protect what he has acquired and build up a plan whereby he can be sure that he will be able to provide those necessaries in the future. The following is a rather brief classification of the specific consumer problems covered in this course:

1. Earning a living
2. Budgeting and planning
3. Saving
4. Investing part of the savings
5. Acquiring protection through insurance
6. Borrowing and other financial relations
7. Buying and spending
8. Providing a home
9. Practical business relations

Integration of the Subject Matter. It is possible in a course in consumer education to treat each topic separately without showing its relation to other topics. The authors are of the opinion, however, that the best results can be obtained by an integration of the subject matter. Therefore, mathematics, business principles, general principles of buying, specific principles of buying, and legal principles are woven into the discussions wherever they help to complete the picture.

Nature of the Subject Matter. An examination of the Table of Contents and the individual chapters will show that abstract principles and theories have been avoided. A student is not expected to memorize rules and theories. He studies practical applications as they occur in everyday life. Every principle is presented through concrete examples. Numerous questions, problems, and projects provide adequate means of applying the knowledge gained from the various chapters.

Scope of the Content. Every available state course of study and city course of study in consumer education has been studied to determine the most generally accepted content of a course of this nature. The abridged volume of CONSUMER ECONOMIC PROBLEMS is designed specifically to fit the requirements of a rather comprehensive course offered by a single department. No attempt is made in this book to present any economic theories as they are applied to the consumer. In that respect the book avoids overlapping the work that may be offered in another course or in another department. It is possible that some of the topics in this book may also be covered in another course. These may be omitted if desired. For instance, if the home economics department covers the buying of clothing and foods satisfactorily, these topics may be omitted. However, many courses in home economics are not available to boys. It is therefore considered essential to include this type of training in CONSUMER ECONOMIC PROBLEMS.

The authors are particularly thankful to the many teachers who offered suggestions and to those who read and criticized the manuscript.

H. G. SHIELDS
W. HARMON WILSON

TABLE OF CONTENTS

Unit I. Managing Income

Unit II. Banking Relations and Investments

Unit III. How Insurance Serves Us

Unit IV. The Consumer and the Marketing System

Unit V. Important Relations Between the Buyer and the Seller

Unit VI. Consumer Protection

Unit VII. General Principles of Buying

Unit VIII. Practical Studies in Buying

Unit IX. The Problems of Obtaining a Home

Unit X. Looking Intelligently at Some Consumer Problems

CHAPTER I

MANAGING INCOME: BUDGETING AND RECORD-KEEPING

Purpose of the Chapter. A *budget* in some form is a necessary control over income. A budget is a plan of spending based on estimates of income and expenditures. Even though an income may be small, it is necessary to plan spending and saving.

There are two main processes in budgeting: (a) planning or making the budget and (b) adhering to it. After an original budget has been made—usually for a year, although it may be made for a shorter period—the plan must be carried out consistently. A budget can be made from models such as the ones outlined in this chapter. Planning a budget is, however, essentially an individual or family matter; and no model budget therefore fits individual circumstances. Experience or previous records of income and expenditures are good guides in planning a budget.

The examples used in this chapter are based largely on the records of a family, but the same principles apply to the records of an individual. For some who study this course the income and the expenditures used in the examples will seem excessive, whereas for others they will seem too small. The same principles apply, however, in every case. Some people may not earn enough income to justify using an elaborate budget, but the principles discussed in this chapter will serve as helpful guides.

Section I

Planning and Budgeting

Making the Family Survey. The first step in any plan of record-keeping and budgeting is the obtaining of as much information as possible about (a) the assets, (b) the debts, and (c) what has been done in the past. Assets consist of property, such as money, furniture, and an automobile. When a system of record-keeping and budgeting is installed for the first time, it is probably difficult to obtain complete records with regard to various types of expenditures. These expenditures can be estimated, however, from checkbook stubs, canceled checks, receipted bills, and the allowances spent for various items in maintaining the family.

The following is a form that is recommended for use in making a survey of the assets and the debts of a family. This form of statement can be used for computing the net worth of a person or a family. Net worth is determined by deducting the total of all debts from the total of all assets. For instance, if a person owns assets worth $100 and owes debts amounting to $30, his net worth is $70. Notice that this summary disregards such items as clothing, which is worn out in a reasonably short time and must be replaced. Clothing, instead of being considered an asset, is charged off as an expense when it is purchased.

Statement of Assets and Debts

ASSETS OWNED BY THE FAMILY		DEBTS OWED BY THE FAMILY	
Cash in Checking Account ..	$ xxx.xx	Mortgage	$ xxx.xx
Cash in Savings Account ...	xxx.xx	Loans on Insurance	xxx.xx
Bonds	xxx.xx	Loans Owed to Bank	xxx.xx
Stocks	xxx.xx	Amount Due on an Installment Purchase	xxx.xx
Notes	xxx.xx	Amount Owed to Stores	xx.xx
Real Estate	xxx.xx	Other Debts:	
Cash Value of Life Insurance.	xxx.xx	________	xxx.xx
Social Security	xxx.xx	________	xx.xx
Household Equipment	xxx.xx	________	xxx.xx
Automobile	xxx.xx	________	xxx.xx
Other Assets:			
________	xxx.xx		
________	xxx.xx		
________	xx.xx	Total Debts	$x,xxx.xx
________	xx.xx	Net Worth (Ownership)	x,xxx.xx
Total Assets	$x,xxx.xx	Total Debts and Net Worth.	$x,xxx.xx

(Total Assets, $x,xxx.xx, — Total Debts, $x,xxx.xx, = Net Worth, $x,xxx.xx.)

Let us take as a typical example the case of Mr. J. L. Minton. Mr. Minton decides to make a family survey of assets and debts to determine what the family is worth. He uses the model above for tabulating his assets and debts. It is easy for him to determine the amount he has in his checking account and savings account, for he can refer to his

Underwood & Underwood

Illustration No. 1—Planning a Budget Is a Co-operative Problem

balances in these accounts. The cash value of his life insurance is determined by referring to the values indicated in his policies. His household equipment is evaluated by adding the cost of all the more important items and disregarding miscellaneous items that are of little value and will wear out in a short time. He sets the value of each article at less than the original cost because the equipment has been used several years and is partially worn out. He evaluates his automobile by obtaining an estimate of the trade-in value from an automobile dealer. He lists a vacant lot at the price it cost him. He knows the amount of the loan that he owes on his life insurance. He determines the amount of a debt owed to a department store by referring to his statement. The following is his summary for January 1, based on these computations:

J. L. MINTON

Statement of Assets and Debts, January 1, 194–

ASSETS OWNED BY THE FAMILY		DEBTS OWED BY THE FAMILY	
Cash in Checking Account ..	$ 84.00	Loan on Insurance	$ 100.00
Cash in Savings Account ...	400.00	Owed to Central Store	25.30
Life Insurance (Cash Value).	331.33		
Social Security	36.00		
Household Equipment	500.00	Total Debts	$ 125.30
Automobile	150.00		
Other Assets:			
Vacant Lot	150.00	Net Worth (Ownership)	1,526.03
Total Assets	$1,651.33	Total Debts and Net Worth..	$1,651.33

(Total Assets, $1,651.33, — Total Debts, $125.30, = Net Worth, $1,526.03.)

A person may possess a great many assets; but if he owes debts almost equal to these assets, his net worth is relatively small. The difference between what he owns and what he owes represents what he is actually worth. This difference was referred to above as net worth. Mr. Minton's net worth on January 1 is $1,526.03.

The statement of Mr. Minton's assets and debts, shown above, is known as a *balance sheet.* It is advisable for everyone to prepare a record of this kind at least once a year in order to determine his financial standing. Notice that the balance sheet prepared by Mr. Minton omits not only items of clothing but also such items as fire insurance on the household equipment. In preparing a balance sheet for the practical use of an individual or a family, it is not necessary to list these items. It is more simple to consider them as expenses at the time they are purchased and to disregard them as assets. An insurance policy may have been purchased in order to provide fire-insurance protection for three years. It has an asset value, but for all practical purposes it constitutes an expense at the time it is purchased.

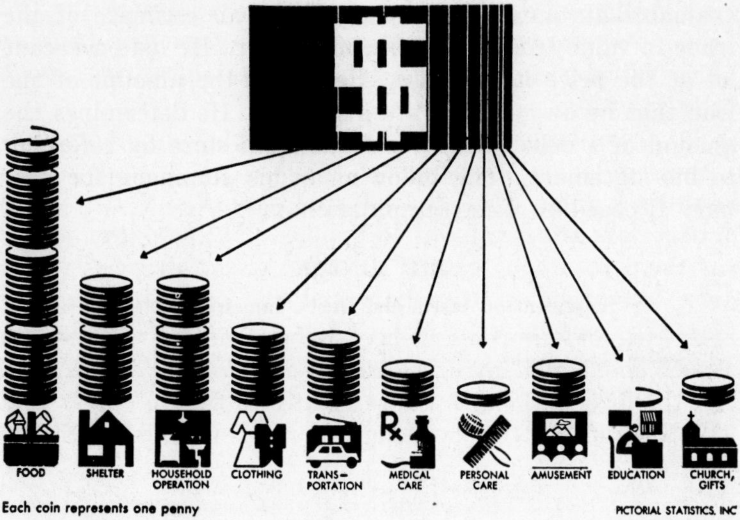

From *How We Spend Our Money,* The Public Affairs Committee, Inc., New York City

Illustration No. 2—Where a Typical Family Dollar Goes

Examples of Budgets. The next step in budgeting is to find out what experience shows others to have been doing. In considering model budgets, one must first investigate the circumstances under which these budgets were prepared. A budget that was in operation during times of prosperity might not be satisfactory during an economic depression. For instance, if prices rise and wages remain the same, an increased percentage must be allowed for food.

Model budgets should be used only for comparison. No one can prove that any particular budget is ideal. What might be good for one person or family would not be good for another person or family. The tables on the following two pages are model budgets that have been prepared after a comparison of the expenditures of individuals and families in all parts of the country. Social security deductions are included in savings.

Notice that in every model budget provision is made for savings. As the income grows larger, savings increase more rapidly than most other items. The expenditure for food increases more slowly, it being assumed, of course, that the minimum budget provides for adequate nourishment. As the income increases, it is natural to expect that the provision for recreation and mental development will increase. Expenditures for clothing, shelter, and operating should also increase.

A model budget should not be accepted as an infallible source of advice in planning a budget. It should be used only as a guide. The expenditures suggested by any model budget are affected by price changes. The amounts, as well as the percentages, change as prices rise or drop. As prices rise, the costs of essentials and the operating expenses increase, and in consequence the percentages allotted to development and savings logically decrease. If prices drop but the income remains the same, it is logical to expect that the percentages for development and for savings will in-

Suggested Budget for a Single Man

INCOME PER WEEK	$18		$20		$25		$37		$50	
	$	%	$	%	$	%	$	%	$	%
Essential:										
Food	8	$44\frac{4}{9}$	8	40	9	36	11	$29\frac{27}{37}$	12	24
Clothing	3	$16\frac{6}{9}$	4	20	5	20	6	$16\frac{8}{37}$	8	16
Housing	4	$22\frac{2}{9}$	5	25	6	24	7	$18\frac{34}{37}$	10	20
Operating	1	$5\frac{5}{9}$	1	5	1	4	4	$10\frac{30}{37}$	5	10
Development	1	$5\frac{5}{9}$	1	5	2	8	5	$13\frac{19}{37}$	9	18
Savings	1	$5\frac{5}{9}$	1	5	2	8	4	$10\frac{30}{37}$	6	12

Suggested Budget for a Single Woman

INCOME PER WEEK	$18		$21		$25		$31		$37	
	$	%	$	%	$	%	$	%	$	%
Essential:										
Food	7	$38\frac{8}{9}$	7	$33\frac{7}{21}$	8	32	8	$25\frac{25}{31}$	8	$21\frac{23}{37}$
Clothing	3	$16\frac{6}{9}$	4	$19\frac{1}{21}$	5	20	7	$22\frac{18}{31}$	9	$24\frac{12}{37}$
Housing	5	$27\frac{7}{9}$	6	$28\frac{12}{21}$	6	24	8	$25\frac{25}{31}$	8	$21\frac{23}{37}$
Operating	1	$5\frac{5}{9}$	1	$4\frac{16}{21}$	2	8	2	$6\frac{14}{31}$	3	$8\frac{4}{37}$
Development	1	$5\frac{5}{9}$	2	$9\frac{11}{21}$	3	12	4	$12\frac{28}{31}$	5	$13\frac{19}{37}$
Savings	1	$5\frac{5}{9}$	1	$4\frac{16}{21}$	1	4	2	$6\frac{14}{31}$	4	$10\frac{30}{37}$

Suggested Budget for a Man and His Wife

INCOME PER WEEK	$19		$25		$31		$38		$50	
	$	%	$	%	$	%	$	%	$	%
Essential:										
Food	8	$42\frac{2}{19}$	9	36	10	$32\frac{8}{31}$	10	$26\frac{6}{19}$	12	24
Clothing	3	$15\frac{15}{19}$	3	12	4	$12\frac{28}{31}$	5	$13\frac{3}{19}$	7	14
Housing	5	$26\frac{6}{19}$	6	24	9	$29\frac{1}{31}$	10	$26\frac{6}{19}$	12	24
Operating	1	$5\frac{5}{19}$	2	8	2	$6\frac{14}{31}$	3	$7\frac{17}{19}$	4	8
Development	1	$5\frac{5}{19}$	3	12	3	$9\frac{21}{31}$	4	$10\frac{10}{19}$	6	12
Savings	1	$5\frac{5}{19}$	2	8	3	$9\frac{21}{31}$	6	$15\frac{15}{19}$	9	18

crease, whereas the percentages for the other items on the budget will decrease.

Illustration No. 3 shows the results of an actual study made in the cities of Manchester, New Hampshire; Detroit, Michigan; Richmond, Virginia; Birmingham, Alabama; and New Orleans, Louisiana, to determine how wage-earners and lower-salaried workers spend their money.

Special Budgets. The preceding discussion has dealt with the master budget. Each major item on the budget must be broken down into minor items. When the expenditures of a family are planned, minor budgets should be set up for specific purposes. For instance, each individual should budget the expenditures for his own clothing and other necessities. If a member of the family is allowed five dol-

Suggested Budget for a Family of Three

INCOME PER WEEK	$20		$30		$40		$50		$60	
	$	%	$	%	$	%	$	%	$	%
Essential:										
Food	8	40	9	30	10	25	12	24	13	21⅔
Clothing	4	20	6	20	9	22½	9	18	9	15
Housing	5	25	9	30	10	25	12	24	15	25
Operating	1	5	2	6⅔	3	7½	4	8	6	10
Development	1	5	2	6⅔	4	10	7	14	9	15
Savings	1	5	2	6⅔	4	10	6	12	8	13⅓

Suggested Budget for a Family of Four

INCOME PER WEEK	$30		$40		$50		$60		$75	
	$	%	$	%	$	%	$	%	$	%
Essential:										
Food	11	36⅔	12	30	15	30	15	25	18	24
Clothing	6	20	9	22½	10	20	10	16⅔	13	17⅓
Housing	9	30	10	25	12	24	15	25	20	26⅔
Operating	2	6⅔	3	7½	4	8	6	10	8	10⅔
Development	1	3⅓	3	7½	5	10	7	11⅔	8	10⅔
Savings	1	3⅓	3	7½	4	8	7	11⅔	8	10⅔

Suggested Budget for a Family of Five

INCOME PER WEEK	$35		$40		$50		$60		$75	
	$	%	$	%	$	%	$	%	$	%
Essential:										
Food	14	40	15	37½	17	34	17	28⅓	19	25⅓
Clothing	8	22 6/7	9	22½	10	20	12	20	15	20
Housing	9	25 5/7	10	25	12	24	15	25	20	26⅔
Operating	2	5 5/7	2	5	4	8	6	10	9	12
Development	1	2 6/7	2	5	4	8	6	10	7	9⅓
Savings	1	2 6/7	2	5	3	6	4	6⅔	5	6⅔

lars or two dollars a week, he should plan his expenditures to take care of carfare, lunch money, and other miscellaneous items that he is expected to pay out of this allowance. If a member of the family is allowed so much a year for clothing, he should analyze his needs, apportion an amount to each need, and buy according to his budget.

Budgeting also applies to major purchases of household equipment. Young persons who establish homes usually must think in terms of utilizing funds so as to derive the maximum value. Usually when a young couple begins housekeeping, only a limited amount of money is available for buying furniture and equipment. The total amount should be budgeted according to rooms. The total expenditure for each room should be budgeted according to the furniture and equipment needed in that room.

ITEM	PERCENTAGE DISTRIBUTION				
	MANCHESTER	DETROIT	RICHMOND	BIRMINGHAM	NEW ORLEANS
Expenditures for:					
Food	34.5%	32.3%	29.4%	30.6%	35.6%
Clothing	12.3	11.8	10.9	11.3	10.6
Housing	13.5	15.1	16.4	12.5	15.9
Household Operation	13.0	10.4	12.7	13.3	10.9
Furnishings and Equipment	4.7	4.0	3.9	4.4	3.2
Transportation	6.6	10.7	8.8	9.2	7.8
Personal Care	1.9	2.0	2.0	2.4	2.4
Medical Care	3.7	4.1	5.4	5.3	4.2
Recreation	5.3	5.8	4.9	5.7	5.7
Education	.4	.6	.6	.5	.4
Vocation	.6	.2	.1	.5	.2
Community Welfare (including church)	1.9	.9	1.8	1.6	1.2
Gifts	1.0	1.6	1.8	1.9	1.4
Miscellaneous Items	.6	.5	1.3	.8	.5
Total Current Expenditures	100.0	100.0	100.0	100.0	100.0
Average Expenditures per Family	$1,399	$1,593	$1,542	$1,461	$1,299

U. S. Bureau of Labor Statistics

Illustration No. 3—Average Current Expenditures of Families of Wage-Earners and Lower-Salaried Workers

Illustration No. 4 is an example of how a budget for a dining room can be planned. This table does not include many miscellaneous items. The prices established for each item may not be in accord with particular needs and with prices in particular localities, but the table serves the purpose of showing how one should proceed to plan the ex-

	ESTIMATE A	ESTIMATE B	ESTIMATE C
Floor Covering	$ 20.00	$ 30.00	$ 40.00
Window Curtains	9.50	15.00	25.00
Furniture	80.00	150.00	190.00
Silverware	15.00	25.00	35.00
China and Glassware	8.00	15.50	20.00
Linens	18.50	25.50	40.00
Mirror	5.00	8.00	12.50
	$156.00	$269.00	$362.50

Illustration No. 4—A Budget for a Dining Room

penditure of a major amount of money when that money must be used for a certain purpose. The breaking down of the total expenditure into individual expenditures helps one to make sure that the maximum value will be derived from the amount to be spent.

Recommended Procedures. Every person affected by the budget should be consulted and should perform his part in operating the budget. The procedure for establishing a budget should be as follows:

(a) Investigation and discussion
(b) Establishing of figures that represent limits of spending and saving
(c) Careful recording of expenditures so that they can be compared with the budget

The following is a recommended procedure to ensure that the budget will be operated carefully:

STEP No. 1. Set up an amount for savings after having considered the needs for other items on the budget. Take out the savings first, and deposit the amount in a bank or in some other savings institution.

STEP No. 2. Pay the monthly bills that are due if charge accounts are used, or set aside a specific amount that will be needed to meet the current expenses of the family. Do not use any of this money for any other purpose.

STEP No. 3. Set aside a definite amount of money for education and recreation, or include this in the allowances set aside for personal expenses. Do not allow personal expenditures to overstep their bounds and to consume the amount set aside for savings or other purposes.

TEXTBOOK QUESTIONS

1. What information should be obtained as the first step in starting a plan of record-keeping and budgeting?
2. Where can information be obtained to help in establishing a basis for record-keeping and budgeting?
3. Why are expenditures for clothing considered expenses instead of assets?
4. How does Mr. Minton (page 4) compute his net worth?
5. What title is commonly used to designate a financial statement showing assets and debts?
6. Why is fire insurance considered an expense and not an asset?
7. Should one adhere strictly to a model budget in preparing a budget for himself?
8. As the income increases, what particular item of the budget should increase most rapidly in comparison with the other items?
9. What are special budgets for personal or family use?
10. What is the value of special budgets?
11. What three steps are recommended as preliminary procedure in establishing a budget?
12. What three steps are recommended in order to operate a budget successfully?

DISCUSSION QUESTIONS

1. (a) If Mr. Minton, whose balance sheet is shown on page 4, owed \$100 on his automobile, where would he list this item on his balance sheet? Why? (b) Would not the listing of the value of the automobile be sufficient?
2. (a) If a person's assets amount to \$500 and his debts are \$600, what is his net worth? (b) If a person owns assets valued at \$700 and owes debts amounting to \$500, would he necessarily have \$200 in cash if he paid all his debts?
3. Why is it not possible to follow model budgets exactly?
4. If the expenditures in specific model budgets were established in times of low prices, how would these model budgets be affected by higher prices?
5. An examination of model budgets will disclose that as salaries increase the percentage of savings increases, whereas the percentage of expenditure for food decreases. Why are these differences to be expected?
6. Why is it vitally important to make provision in a budget for the maintenance of health?
7. In budgeting why should savings be set aside first?
8. Why should the amounts in a budget be definitely established?

Section II

Making and Keeping a Budget

Preparation for the Budget. Suitable forms for keeping records may be obtained from insurance companies, department stores, banks, building and loan associations, or colleges; or they may be purchased from book and stationery stores. It is particularly important to keep some type of record, not only for controlling one's expenditures but also for income-tax purposes, because the Federal Government and many state governments now require the payment of income taxes.

If records have been kept in the past, it is simple to construct a budget for the future. Two elements are involved in preparing any budget: (a) the income and (b) the expenditures. Each must be estimated item by item. Past experience is a good basis on which to make estimates. As much information as possible should be collected from this source. If no accurate records have been kept, information can often be obtained from checkbook stubs and receipts. Many items can be estimated. Past experience may not be an accurate guide; model budgets should therefore be used for comparison and guidance.

Estimated Income. Mr. J. L. Minton, whose family survey of assets and debts was mentioned previously, decides to prepare a budget. Mr. Minton is married and works for a salary of $150 a month, payable semimonthly. He expects his salary to remain approximately the same. During July he is required to take two weeks' vacation without pay. The balance in his savings account earns interest at the rate of 4 per cent, compounded semiannually. The following table shows his budgeted income:

INCOME	JAN.	FEB.	MAR.	APR.	MAY	JUNE	JULY	AUG.	SEPT.	OCT.	NOV.	DEC.
Salary	$150	$150	$150	$150	$150	$150	$75	$150	$150	$150	$150	$150
Interest	....	....	....	....	....	8	....	....	....	....	....	10.32
Total	$150	$150	$150	$150	$150	$158	$75	$150	$150	$150	$150	$160.32

Illustration No. 5—Estimated Income

Social Security Deductions. The salaries of employees in most occupations are subject to deductions for old-age benefits, but only in a few states are deductions made for unemployment insurance. In keeping records and keeping a budget, it is therefore necessary to record the deductions from one's income. Although these deductions cannot be withdrawn as cash, they are eventually available. Therefore, they represent a specific type of savings. When Mr. Minton receives his monthly salary, the entire salary is recorded as an income, but the deduction that is withheld for old-age benefits is recorded as an asset.

Estimated Expenditures. There are many ways of classifying expenditures. Most of the methods, however, are reasonably uniform in the grouping of expenses under the various headings. The method used in this discussion adheres closely to headings recommended by the Federal Government. A satisfactory classification of the various types of expenditures for the purpose of keeping a budget is shown in Illustration No. 6.

Illustration No. 7 shows the estimated expenditures of Mr. Minton. He has based these on (a) his past experiences, (b) model budgets that he has examined, and (c) what he expects to be reasonable conditions during the coming year. The precise circumstances that may be encountered during the year cannot be predicted, although sometimes one can predict an expenditure such as school tuition, a change in taxes, expenses for a surgical operation, or some other unusual item. After including expenditures for these predictable items, the person who is making the budget may consider that the other expenditures will be somewhat in proportion to those in the past. The amount of each type of expenditure in the budget is determined after a careful consideration of each of the minor items that are included in this expenditure.

Comparison of Estimated Income and Estimated Expenditures. Illustrations Nos. 5 and 7 on pages 11 and 14 show estimates (a) of income and (b) of expenditures. According to the plan outlined in this chapter, the expenditures represent the cash outlay of funds as the result of paying

Essential

Food
- Food purchased
- Meals purchased

Clothing
- Clothes purchased
- Material used to make clothes
- Shoes
- Repairs and alterations on clothing
- Hats

Housing
- Rent
- Taxes
- Insurance
- Repairs
- Painting

Operating

Family
- Fuel
- Light
- Telephone
- Water
- Gas
- Expenses on the yard
- Cleaning clothes
- Cleaning house
- Household supplies
- Life-insurance protection
- All taxes except those on the house
- Accident insurance

Personal
- Carfare
- Toilet articles
- Jewelry and other personal items

Automobile
- Gasoline
- Oil
- Repairs
- Insurance
- License fees
- Tax
- Storage and parking fees

Development

Health
- Physician's and dentist's fees
- Nursing
- Medicine, drugs, and surgical supplies
- Optical treatment

Recreation
- Theater tickets
- Vacations
- Hunting license
- Social club dues
- Concert tickets

Education
- Tuition
- Books
- School fees
- Traveling expenses in attending school
- Magazine subscriptions
- Lecture tickets
- Newspapers

Benevolence
- Church contributions
- Donation to charity

Savings and Other Assets

Savings funds
- Savings bank
- Building and loan association

Life insurance
- Cash value of policies

Social Security
- Salary deductions

Assets (tangible)
- Furniture
- Automobile

Illustration No. 6—Classification of Expenditures

	JAN.	FEB.	MAR.	APR.	MAY	JUNE	JULY	AUG.	SEPT.	OCT.	NOV.	DEC.	TOTAL
Essential:													
Food	$ 45	$ 45	$ 45	$ 35	$ 35	$ 35	$ 30	$ 35	$ 40	$ 40	$ 40	$ 45	$ 470
Clothing	20	15	20	20	5	5	5	5	45	20	25	15	200
Housing	40	40	40	40	40	40	40	40	40	40	40	40	480
Operating:													
Family	17	4	3	5	4	13	5	3	3	4	5	3	69
Personal	3	2	3	3	2	4	3	3	3	3	2	3	34
Automobile	3	3	3	2	3	10	3	2	11	4	3	3	50
Development:													
Health	5	3	3	2	2	3	2	4	4	2	6	5	41
Education	5	3	2	4	2	3	3	4	7	4	3	5	45
Recreation	4	4	3	3	2	2	4	5	2	5	4	4	42
Benevolence	3	3	2	3	3	3	2	3	3	3	2	2	32
Savings:													
Savings Funds	15	13	23	23	23	11	10	23	23	23	10	33.32	230.32
Life Insurance (Cash Value) ...	15	......	......	......	......	12	......	......	......	......	......	......	27
Social Security	1.50	1.50	1.50	1.50	1.50	1.50	.75	1.50	1.50	1.50	1.50	1.50	17.25
Other Assets	......	10	......	......	......	......	......	......	......	......	13	......	23
	$176.50	$146.50	$148.50	$141.50	$122.50	$142.50	$107.75	$128.50	$182.50	$149.50	$154.50	$159.82	$1,760.57

Illustration No. 7—Estimated Expenditures

expenses, buying assets, or using the income for investment or savings. If a person always conducts his transactions on a cash basis, that is, pays cash for everything and does not buy on account, he will always be able to live within his budget. If purchases are made through charge accounts, the payment of the bills should be considered as a regular expenditure of cash and be included as such in the budget. The person who operates his budget carefully will compare the income and the expenditures so as to make sure that the expenditures are equal to or less than the income. Expenditures include not only the expenses of the family but also whatever part of the income is laid aside for savings and for the purchase of assets. In other words, the budgeting of expenditures represents the apportionment of the income. Part is apportioned to expenses, part to savings, and part to the purchase of various tangible assets.

The income and the expenditures should be compared to make sure that funds will be available at all times to take care of the expenditures. Mr. Minton's preliminary summary for January 1 (page 4) contained a balance of $84 in the checking account. Illustration No. 8 shows a comparison of the estimated income and the estimated expenditures. The cash is to be deposited in the checking account.

Correlating Record-Keeping and Budgeting. No budgeting system can be operated successfully without the keeping of current records. Transactions should be recorded

Comparison of Estimated Income and Estimated Expenditures

	ESTIMATED BEGINNING CASH BALANCE	ESTIMATED INCOME	CASH AVAILABLE	ESTIMATED EXPENDITURES	ESTIMATED ENDING CASH BALANCE
January	$ 84.00	$150.00	$234.00	$176.50	$ 57.50
February	57.50	150.00	207.50	146.50	61.00
March	61.00	150.00	211.00	148.50	62.50
April	62.50	150.00	212.50	141.50	71.00
May	71.00	150.00	221.00	122.50	98.50
June	98.50	158.00	256.50	142.50	114.00
July	114.00	75.00	189.00	107.75	81.25
August	81.25	150.00	231.25	128.50	102.75
September	102.75	150.00	252.75	182.50	70.25
October	70.25	150.00	220.25	149.50	70.75
November	70.75	150.00	220.75	154.50	66.25
December	66.25	160.32	226.57	159.82	66.75

Illustration No. 8

daily, weekly, or monthly in accordance with some definite plan. Records should be kept consistently and accurately, and should be as simple as possible.

Illustration No. 9 shows a record of (a) income, (b) expenditures for expenses, and (c) expenditures for savings and assets. In other words, this record shows what the income is, where it comes from, and how it is used. This type of business record is known as a *cashbook*. Items are recorded in this cashbook as they occur. In the part of the cashbook illustrated, the entries have been made for January and for part of February. At the end of a month the various amount columns are totaled.

A notebook can be used for the same purpose, if not all the information is desired on one page. If a small notebook is preferred for keeping such a record, the following procedure is recommended:

(a) List on the first page the four main classifications of expenditures used in the cashbook in Illustration No. 9 on page 17.
(b) List on the second page all the headings of the columns for the income and the expenditures recorded in the cashbook in Illustration No. 9.
(c) According to the order of the headings of the columns in the cashbook, place a title at the top of each subsequent page in the notebook. For example: Page 3, Income; Page 4, Food; Page 5, Clothing; etc.
(d) Record a transaction on the appropriate page in the same way as it was recorded in the cashbook in Illustration No. 9.

Summary of Actual Expenditures. In Illustration No. 10 is a form for use in recording the monthly totals of actual expenditures. This form is similar to that which was used in recording the estimated expenditures (Illustration No. 7, page 14). As the monthly totals of the actual expenditures are transferred from the cashbook, they should be compared with the amounts in the budget. If certain expenditures are running ahead of the estimates, they should be brought under control by reductions during the succeeding months.

CASHBOOK
For Recording Income and Expenditures

Date		Explanation	Income	Essential Expenses			Operating Expenses			Development Expenses				Savings and Assets			
				Food	Clothing	Housing	Family	Personal	Automobile	Health	Education	Recreation	Benevolence	Sav. Funds	Life Ins.	Social Sec.	Other Assets
Jan.																	
	2	Clothing			10												
	3	Automobile exp.							4								
	6	Insurance					15								20		
		Church dues											2				
		Doctor bills								4							
	15	Food		20													
		Salary	75													.75	
		Personal allow.						2									
		Rent				35											
	17	Magazine sub.									3						
		Clothing			7												
	20	Automobile exp.							2								
		Church dues											2				
	23	Theater tickets										4					
		Clothing			5												
	30	Food		23													
		Salary	75													.75	
		Savings deposits												15			
		Totals for January	150	43	22	35	15	2	6	4	3	4	4	15	20	1.50	
Feb.																	
	1	Automobile exp.							2								
		Clothing			5												
	2	Church dues											2				
	7	Theater tickets										2					
		Household sup.					5										
		Medicine								3							
	8	Living-room chair															10

Illustration No. 9

Monthly Summary of Actual Expenditures

	JAN.	FEB.	MAR.	APR.	MAY	JUNE	JULY	AUG.	SEPT.	OCT.	NOV.	DEC.	TOTAL
Essential:													
Food	$ 43.00												
Clothing	22.00												
Housing	35.00												
Operating:													
Family	15.00												
Personal	2.00												
Automobile	6.00												
Development:													
Health	4.00												
Education	3.00												
Recreation	4.00												
Benevolence	4.00												
Savings:													
Savings Funds	15.00												
Life Insurance (Cash Value)	20.00												
Social Security	1.50												
Other Assets	.....												
	$174.50												

Illustration No. 10

Summary of Actual Income. Illustration No. 11 shows a form for recording the actual income at the end of each month. As the total income is transferred from the cashbook to this summary, it should be compared with the estimated income in the budget. If the income is proving to be less than was anticipated, adjustments must be made in the expenditures to compensate for the reduced income. The purpose of this summary is to provide a total of the actual income so that it can be compared with the estimated income and with the total of the actual expenditures.

Monthly Summary of Actual Income

INCOME	JAN.	FEB.	MAR.	APR.	MAY	JUNE	JULY	AUG.	SEPT.	OCT.	NOV.	DEC.
Salary	$150											
Interest	....											
Total	$150											

Illustration No. 11

Comparison of Actual Income and Actual Expenditures. At the end of each month, after the income and the expenditures have been recorded, the total income should be compared with the total expenditures. Illustration No. 12 is an example of a form that can be used for making this comparison and for showing the cash balance. The actual income and expenditures should be compared with the original estimates to see how satisfactorily the budget is operating. Some adjustments may be necessary.

Recording from Checkbook Stubs. Some definite system must be followed in recording income and expenditures. Unless a definite plan is followed, some items of income and expenditure may be omitted through error. If a checking account is used, the following procedure is recommended:

(a) Deposit all income in the checking account, and record all deposits on the checkbook stubs. If a person's income is subject to social security taxes, the amount deducted on each payday can be recorded on the checkbook stub at the time the deposit is made.

(b) Withdraw only enough cash to take care of such items as food, clothing, and personal and automobile expenditures.
(c) When cash is withdrawn from the bank for a particular purpose, make a record in the checkbook to indicate the purpose for which the amount is withdrawn.
(d) Write checks for all major expenditures, such as rent, bills, charge accounts, insurance, and savings.
(e) At the end of the month verify the bank statement and use the check stubs as the source of information for recording all income and expenditures.

The checkbook will thus provide a record of all income and expenditures. If sufficient information is placed on the checkbook stubs, the stubs can be used as a source of information for recording the expenditures in the cashbook.

Comparison of Actual Income and Actual Expenditures

	BEGINNING CASH BALANCE	INCOME	CASH	EXPENDITURES	ENDING CASH BALANCE
January	$84.00	$150.00	$234.00	$174.50	$59.50
February	59.50				
March					
April					
May					
June					
July					
August					
September					
October					
November					
December					

Illustration No. 12

Recording Without a Checkbook. If a checking account is not used, the following procedure is recommended:

(a) When the salary payment is received, keep out only what is allotted for essential, operating, and development expenditures.
(b) Deposit the remainder in a savings account.
(c) If rent or any other major payments are not due at the time the regular income is received, the amount needed may be laid aside or may be deposited in the savings account until the payment is due.

(d) Record in the cashbook the salary and (1) the deductions for social security, and (2) the amounts that have been kept out for specific purposes.
(e) Record as expenditures all amounts that are withdrawn from the savings account for expenditures.
(f) Keep a separate savings fund in which deposits are made for the accumulation of permanent savings.

In recording an expenditure for insurance, one must consider two elements: (a) the cost of the insurance protection and (b) the accumulation of savings that results from the increase in the cash value. As will be explained in the chapter on insurance, most insurance policies have a cash or loan value. This cash or loan value increases each time a premium is paid. The increases in the cash value are shown on the insurance policy. A definite portion of each premium payment (the increase in the cash value) should therefore be recorded as savings. The remainder should be recorded as a family operating expense (the cost of protection).

J. L. MINTON

Statement of Income and Expense for Year Ending December 31, 194–

Income:			
Salary Income		$1,800.00	
Interest Income		19.47	
Total Income			$1,819.47
Expenses:			
Essential:			
Food	$490.10		
Clothing	250.00		
Housing	450.60	$1,190.70	
Operating:			
Family	$ 72.40		
Personal	35.10		
Automobile	43.90	151.40	
Development:			
Health	$ 50.00		
Education	35.50		
Recreation	45.20		
Benevolence	40.00	170.70	
Total Expenses			1,512.80
Net Income			$ 306.67

Illustration No. 13

Summary Showing Net Gain. Every businessman prepares financial statements periodically. He may do so monthly, semiannually, or annually. One of these statements, the statement of income and expense, shows the net income or net gain made during the period.

From the records that Mr. Minton has kept during the year, he can easily determine the total for each class of income and of expense. The difference between the total income and the total expenses equals the net income or net gain. The statement of income and expense in Illustration No. 13 was prepared by Mr. Minton at the end of the year. The net income represents the increase in his net worth. In other words, his cash, savings, insurance, furniture, and other assets have increased $306.67.

J. L. MINTON
Statement of Assets and Debts, December 31, 194–

ASSETS OWNED BY THE FAMILY		DEBTS OWED BY THE FAMILY	
Cash in Checking Account ..	$ 75.91	Owed to Central Store	$ 4.95
Cash in Savings Account ...	490.36	Net Worth (Ownership)	1,832.70
Life Insurance (Cash Value).	373.68		
Social Security	53.25		
Household Equipment	544.45		
Automobile	150.00		
Other Assets:			
Vacant Lot	150.00		
Total Assets	$1,837.65	Total Debts and Net Worth..	$1,837.65

(Total Assets, $1,837.65, — Total Debts, $4.95, = Net Worth, $1,832.70.)

Illustration No. 14

Summary of Assets and Debts. At the end of the year Mr. Minton also prepares a balance sheet similar to the one on page 4. This statement, which is shown in Illustration No. 14, gives Mr. Minton's financial status at the end of the year. By comparing this balance sheet with the one prepared at the beginning of the year (page 4), it is possible to compute the net gain for the year. The increase in the net worth during the year (the net worth at the end of the year minus the net worth at the beginning of the year) should equal the net gain shown on the statement of income and expense. This computation is as follows:

Net worth at the end of the year	$1,832.70
Net worth at the beginning of the year ..	1,526.03
Net gain (net income)	$ 306.67

Depreciation. The depreciation of tangible assets is usually recognized in computing the net profit of a business, and it may also be given consideration in determining the net gain from the operations of an individual or a family. Businessmen have definite methods of computing depreciation. Here is an example: If the average life of an automobile that cost $500 is four years, and the trade-in value at the end of the four years will be $100, the automobile will lose a total value of $400 during these years. This loss in value caused by use and wear is referred to as *depreciation.* In this example the depreciation will therefore be $100 a year for four years. This amount represents a yearly loss resulting from the wear and tear on the automobile. In terms of a percentage, the annual depreciation is 20 per cent of the cost of the automobile. Depreciation applies in the same way to such items as furniture.

Depreciation cannot be determined accurately but must be estimated. Ordinarily the estimated annual loss due to depreciation is charged regularly at the end of each year. The total loss during the life of an asset may, however, be recorded at the time the asset is sold. For simplicity in keeping personal records, the loss resulting from the depreciation of an asset is ordinarily not recognized until the asset is sold, discarded, or given away. If Mr. Minton had wanted, however, to recognize depreciation in computing his net gain for the year, he could have done so very easily. For instance, if he had estimated that his automobile had depreciated $20 and his household equipment $12 during the year, he could have added $20 to the automobile operating expenses and $12 to the family operating expenses. His net income or net gain would therefore have been $32 less. In preparing his balance sheet, he would have deducted $20 from the value of the automobile and $12 from the value of the household equipment. His net worth would then have been $32 less.

The advantage of computing the depreciation applicable to each year is that the net gain reported on the annual statement of income and expense is more accurate than it would be if the loss due to depreciation were not recognized until the asset had been disposed of. For example, in preparing his financial statements at the end of the year, Mr. Minton did not take into consideration any depreciation on his automobile. One year later he sells the car for $50. As he has been keeping this asset on his records at a value of $150, he must now take into account a loss of $100. If this loss is charged to the year in which the car is sold, the true amount of the net gain for that year will not be indicated.

TEXTBOOK QUESTIONS

1. Why is it becoming increasingly important to keep personal records?
2. What are some of the sources from which special forms for record-keeping and budgeting can be obtained?
3. In preparing his budget, on what did Mr. Minton base his estimates of expenditures?
4. (a) Were there any months in which Mr. Minton estimated that his expenditures would exceed his income? (b) If there were, which months were they?
5. Do expenditures mean expenses?
6. Why was part of the expenditure for life insurance recorded as a family operating expense and part entered in the Life Insurance column under the heading Savings and Assets?
7. Why is it desirable to prepare a summary of actual income and actual expenditures at the end of each month?
8. If the income proves to be less than that expected, what should be done in adjusting the budget?
9. If checkbook stubs are used as the basis for recording entries, why is it convenient to make all entries at the end of the month?
10. What is depreciation?
11. Can depreciation be calculated accurately?

DISCUSSION QUESTIONS

1. How do price changes affect a budget?
2. Why does information gathered from past experience help in establishing a budget?
3. Why do you think part of the expenditure of Mr. Minton for life insurance was recorded as a family operating expense rather than a personal expense?

4. (a) If, at the beginning of the year, Mr. Minton had planned to buy a radio for $25 in December, how would this item have been shown in his budget? (b) How would this item have affected the budget?
5. If Mr. Minton finds that, according to his budget, he is not going to have enough cash in his checking account to take care of expenses, what can he do to avoid this situation?
6. Explain in what columns of the cashbook Mr. Minton would record entries for the following items: (a) the cost of having clothes cleaned and pressed, (b) the cost of a hunting license, (c) the payment of a parking fee.
7. If Mr. Minton gets $50 as a Christmas present from his employer, how will this amount be recorded in his cashbook?
8. Why is it not desirable to compute the depreciation of clothing?

PROBLEMS

1. Mr. J. A. Smith has a wife and two children. He earns a regular income of $45 a week. On the basis of the percentages shown in the $50 model budget for a family of four (page 7), compute the estimated expenditure for each item of the budget.
2. Mr. J. O. Jones has an insurance policy that has a cash value of $135.10. The annual premium is $46.20. After the premium for the current year has been paid, the cash value will amount to $161.20. How will Mr. Jones record the premium payment in his cashbook?
3. Mr. Hansen has $92.10 in cash in his checking account when he makes his budget. He estimates that his income will be $135 a month during the year. He also estimates that the following will be his total expenditures for each month:

January	$132.10	July	$140.52
February	160.15	August	132.43
March	113.25	September	130.31
April	130.23	October	131.37
May	122.42	November	120.26
June	125.36	December	152.93

Prepare a form similar to that on page 15, showing a comparison of the estimated income and the estimated expenditures.

4. Assume that Mr. Minton's income was the same as that reported on the statement of income and expense on page 21. Prepare his statement of income and expense for the year ending on December 31, 194–, using the following expenses:

Food	$382.15	Automobile	$52.20
Clothing	214.25	Health	28.00
Housing	490.00	Education	39.50
Family	96.20	Recreation	36.25
Personal	42.10	Benevolence	52.00

5. Mr. J. O. Mason found the following information on his checkbook stubs at the end of January. Rule a cashbook similar to the one shown on page 17, and record the transactions of Mr. Mason. Total and rule the columns of the cashbook after you have recorded all the transactions.

Jan.	2.	Clothing	$10.00
		Food	18.00
	5.	Personal allowance for Mr. Mason	3.00
		Personal allowance for Mrs. Mason	3.00
		Theater tickets	4.00
	10.	Food	17.00
		Magazine subscription	2.50
	15.	Salary (Less social security tax 1%)	65.00
		Taxes on home	30.00
	20.	Telephone	3.50
		Light and gas	2.00
	22.	Gasoline	1.00
		Automobile repairs	2.00
	25.	Church dues	1.50
		Dentist bill	3.00
	31.	Salary (Less social security tax 1%)	65.00
		Savings deposit	15.00

6. Mr. Minton decides that he wants to recognize the depreciation of his automobile and his household equipment in preparing his annual statement of income and expense and his annual balance sheet. Using the statements on pages 21 and 22 as a basis, prepare a new statement of income and expense and a new balance sheet, showing allowances for $20 depreciation on the automobile and $12 depreciation on the household equipment.

COMMUNITY PROBLEMS AND PROJECTS

1. (a) List all your items of personal income and of personal expenditure. (b) Prepare a one-year budget of your income and your expenditures. (c) Rule a form for recording your actual income and expenditures, or prepare a small notebook in accordance with the suggestions given on page 16.
2. Make a study of the income and the expenditures of your family. (a) Rule a form for a cashbook, or prepare a small notebook for keeping the records of your family. Record all the items of income and expenditure for one month. (b) On the basis of this information, the appropriate model budget on page 6 or 7, and any other information you can gain from your family, prepare a budget of the income and the expenditures for twelve months.
3. Obtain a sample of a budget from some public institution such as a city, county, township, church, or hospital. If possible, get the proper official to explain how the budget is constructed. Write a report that could be understood by the average reader if it were published in the newspaper.

CHAPTER II

MANAGING INCOME: SAVING

Purpose of the Chapter. A thrifty person consciously or unconsciously budgets his income and his expenditures. Budgeting in some form or other is a prerequisite of saving. The preceding chapter discussed practical methods of budgeting and record-keeping. Saving deserves special consideration as part of a person's plan of financial management.

The amount of a person's income, of course, has something to do with the amount of his savings. Nevertheless, it is not how much he *earns* but how much he *saves* that eventually determines how much he is worth.

The purpose of this chapter is to point out some of the needs and goals for saving, as well as the means of systematic saving. The following may be considered the general principles of saving:

(a) Spend less than you earn.
(b) Invest this difference wisely.
(c) Reinvest the interest from savings.

Section I

Methods of Saving

Creation of a Reserve Fund. If economic conditions continued unchanged day after day and year after year; if everyone were assured of employment with an income sufficient to take care of his needs; if everyone were assured of an income in his old age, there would be no need to save except as a means of providing for some major purpose or luxury. Economic conditions vary, however, in all walks of life. It is therefore necessary to save as a provision for times when earnings decrease. It is also necessary to save small amounts in order to be able eventually to make an important purchase, such as a home. Therefore, a reserve fund must be created out of earnings.

The following statement shows how a business earns an income from which it may create a reserve:

Sales	$10,000.00
Cost of Merchandise Sold	8,000.00
Gross Profit	$ 2,000.00
Expenses	1,500.00
Net Profit	$ 500.00

This net profit represents the amount that is available for the expansion of the business if it is left in the business. At least a part of it should be added to the surplus of the business.

A family creates a reserve in a similar manner:

Salary	$2,000.00
Cost of Living	1.800.00
Net Income for Reserve	$ 200.00

Saving with a Purpose. A savings fund should be created with some definite objective in view. One type of savings fund can be considered as an investment that will be added to regularly and that will earn an income. Another type of savings fund is one created with the definite objective of laying aside a sufficient amount of money for some specific purpose, such as obtaining an education or buying an automobile or a home. Another type may be referred to as a temporary surplus that can be used to take advantage of buying opportunities. If a surplus has not been accumulated, a person must pass up such opportunities or, in order to take advantage of bargains, must go into debt.

The objective of a savings program may be defeated if the fund is considered available for any need, such as, for example, the buying of clothing. A reasonable surplus for use in buying clothing, making payments on a house, paying rent, taking a vacation, or the like can ordinarily be kept in a checking account. If the surplus money will not be needed, however, for several months, it may in some cases be placed in a savings account, where it will earn interest.

Going into debt is desirable in some cases, but not in others. If a special savings fund has been established, one may not need to borrow. For example, a certain amount of money may be set aside for clothing. This may be budgeted weekly out of the income. It is often possible to save 10 or 20 per cent by buying clothing, household furnishings, food, or other items at opportune times. For example, at the end of the summer season, summer clothing can be bought very cheaply. If a person is not especially interested in style, he can frequently find bargains in clothing that can be worn the next year. Some items of clothing do not change radically in style.

Merchants are anxious to sell surplus stock at the end of each season, as they do not want to leave their money invested in this stock until the next season. If purchases are made when there are sales on furniture and household equipment, considerable saving may result.

There are certain times of the year when canned goods are placed on sale. At the end of the canning season many merchants offer special sales of such items as canned peas and canned corn. If such items are purchased in large quantities and stored, a saving will result. The savings fund can then be replenished out of the amount regularly budgeted for food.

It may be possible to take advantage of special discounts or of reductions in payments on such items as insurance premiums. Insurance premiums are usually paid in advance. It is cheaper to pay a year in advance than it is to pay only one fourth of a year in advance. If the regular weekly or monthly income is not sufficient to permit a large payment, it may be necessary to pay insurance premiums quarterly. If a savings fund is accumulated, however, premiums can be paid in advance for one year at the reduced rate. This fund can then be replenished in time for the next premium payment.

Obligating Oneself. After a person has established a savings program, he should not waver in carrying it out. If ten dollars a month is to be set aside for a certain savings fund, this amount should be taken out of the income first and the remainder should be used for other purposes. In other words, a person should learn to live within the income that is allotted for living purposes. He should not penalize the savings fund by neglecting to contribute to it whenever some excuse arises. The program should be carried through to completion.

Use of the Savings Fund. The establishing of a savings plan assumes that there is some definite objective in view. The following are some of the definite purposes for which savings should be established:

Emergencies	Security Investments
Education	Major Comforts and Luxuries
Home	Financial Independence
Insurance Premiums	Future Income

When a savings fund has been established for some specific purpose, it should be used only for that purpose. If it is utilized for miscellaneous purposes, the original plan will soon collapse and the entire program will probably be jeopardized.

Saving for an Education. If some parents had been thoughtful enough years ago to establish savings for educating their children, there would be more children now obtaining college educations. As the educational requirements in all occupations are gradually increasing, it is becoming more important for capable people to obtain college educations.

If a person plans to go to college, he should start early in life to save. If it is not possible to obtain the aid of his parents, savings can probably be accumulated out of earnings from part-time jobs. The number of years before college entrance can easily be calculated, and detailed figures on the cost of a college education can be obtained from colleges or from local school officials. With a knowledge of the amount that must be saved and the time for accumulating this amount, the person should set a goal for saving that will make it possible for him to go to college.

Parents who have children that they plan to send to college should utilize a definite savings plan so as to be sure that there will be an adequate amount available at the time the children are ready for college. Various insurance policies, bank savings plans, and investment plans are designed to provide funds of this kind at the time they are needed. If a small amount is saved each year for the definite purpose of an education, the burden of financing the college education will be greatly reduced.

Illustration No. 15—A College Education Is a Worthy Goal of Saving

Comforts and Luxuries. If one's income is spent soon after each payday, the spending is probably not well planned. Such unsystematic practice will make it impossible to take advantage of opportunities to obtain the finer luxuries and comforts that can be purchased if a definite savings program has been established.

The average family that spends its income as soon as it is received finds it impossible to take a vacation trip, or to purchase an automobile or any other items of comfort or luxury, without going into debt. If the same family were to forego certain trivial pleasures, however, and to establish a definite savings program, its members could enjoy more desirable comforts and luxuries, which require a reasonably large expenditure of money.

"Keeping up with the Joneses" is a dangerous procedure. It is true that one person may deserve a luxury or comfort just as well as someone else; but if he cannot afford it, there is no justification for buying it. Many people have gone into debt just because they have wanted to pattern after someone else. Jealousy is the basis of this folly. An unwise expenditure for something that cannot be afforded will lead into further difficulties.

In making a decision with regard to buying a luxury, one should answer the question, "What will it cost me in terms of days of labor?" For example, if a stenographer earns twenty dollars a week on the basis of forty hours a week, she is earning at the rate of fifty cents an hour. Suppose she has enough to make a down payment on an automobile, but finds that it will cost her forty dollars a month to pay for it, four dollars a month for a garage, an average of two dollars a month for repairs, and an average of eight dollars a month for gasoline and oil. The monthly cost will be fifty-four dollars. This calculation does not take into consideration that the tires will wear out and will have to be replaced, nor that the automobile will wear out and that any accident will increase the maintenance costs. The minimum expenses therefore amount to fifty-four dollars a month. As this stenographer is earning only eighty dollars a month, it is obvious that the luxury of an automobile is not justified if she is required to buy her clothes and to pay for her lodging and food.

Basis of Investment. Saving is a prerequisite to investing. There can be no investing until some cash surplus has been established. Unless a person receives a gift or an inheritance of a large amount of money, there is no way for him to purchase investments or to buy a home except through savings.

It is rarely possible to start the purchase of a home without some savings that can be used as a down payment. The greater the amount of savings, the easier it is to finance the purchase of the home. The ownership of a home promotes the economic stability of the family and is a source of personal satisfaction.

Setting a Goal for Saving. The establishing of a goal for saving requires a plan. The basis of the plan is the budget. From time to time as circumstances change, it is necessary to alter the plan. There should, however, always be a definite goal that will point the way to financial success. If a person expects to make a success of his financial affairs, he must manage them as carefully as a successful businessman. The successful businessman usually sets a goal or a series of goals and intently works toward them.

END OF YEAR	2%	3%	4%
1	$ 12.13	$ 12.20	$ 12.26
2	24.51	24.76	25.02
3	37.13	37.70	38.29
4	50.01	51.04	52.10
5	63.14	64.78	66.46
6	76.54	78.93	81.41
7	90.21	93.51	96.96
8	104.26	108.54	113.14
9	118.49	124.01	129.97
10	133.00	139.96	147.49
11	147.80	156.38	165.70
12	162.90	173.30	184.66
13	178.30	190.74	204.38
14	194.02	208.70	224.90
15	210.05	227.20	246.25

Illustration No. 16—The Accumulated Value of Monthly Deposits

Anticipated needs can be calculated reasonably closely. For instance, the purchase of a home can be planned years in advance. A certain amount of money may be required as a down payment on the home. Money for this purpose can be saved under a definite plan. Illustration No. 16 shows the value of monthly deposits of one dollar at interest rates of 2, 3, and 4 per cent. This table is based on the assumption that (a) each deposit is made at the beginning of the month, (b) interest is compounded semiannually, and (c) interest is calculated according to the actual amount of time that a deposit has been in the account.

Assume that it is desirable to have accumulated a certain sum of money at a certain age without the use of insurance. The following table shows the amount of money that must be invested at the beginning of each month at any one of various rates of interest, compounded semiannually, to accumulate $1,000 in a given number of years:

The amount of money that must be deposited at the beginning of each month at any one of various rates of interest, compounded semiannually, to accumulate $1,000 in the number of years indicated.

YEARS	2%	2½%	3%	3½%	4%	4½%	5%
5	$15.82	$15.63	$15.44	$15.25	$15.05	$14.86	$14.67
10	7.51	7.33	7.15	6.97	6.79	6.61	6.44
15	4.75	4.58	4.41	4.23	4.07	3.90	3.75
20	3.37	3.21	3.05	2.89	2.73	2.58	2.44
25	2.55	2.40	2.25	2.10	1.95	1.82	1.69
30	2.00	1.86	1.72	1.58	1.43	1.33	1.21
35	1.62	1.49	1.36	1.22	1.10	.99	.89
40	1.33	1.21	1.09	.97	.86	.76	.67
45	1.10	.99	.88	.77	.67	.58	.50
50	.93	.83	.73	.62	.53	.45	.38

Illustration No. 17—The Amount to Invest to Accumulate a Certain Sum

The objection to adopting a financial program which assumes that a specific amount will be accumulated for retirement is that no one can forecast whether the amount will be adequate at the time it is needed. For instance, a young man who earns twenty-five dollars a week may consider ten thousand dollars a fortune; but as he grows older, assumes more responsibilities, earns more money, and improves his standard of living, he may frequently have to revise his estimate of how much money he should have at the time he reaches the age of sixty-five. If a person is saving for retirement, he should therefore revise his savings program each year on the basis of accumulating enough money for retirement, or of enabling his dependents to enjoy the same standard of living after he retires or in case he dies.

The value of money affects funds that have been accumulated for retirement or for dependents. For instance, Mr. Horton, a married man with a wife and two children, establishes an insurance estate of twenty thousand dollars for his family. When he buys the insurance, he is thinking in terms of what the proceeds will provide for his family in case of his death. A general rise in prices will cause each dollar to become worth less in terms of the goods and the services that it will buy. If, after Mr. Horton's death, there is a general rise in the price level to the extent of doubling prices, each dollar will buy only half as much as it would have bought at the time the estate was planned. Mr. Horton's dependents will receive only 50 per cent of the benefit that was contemplated when the insurance estate was planned.

Retirement Income. Often a person wishes to know how much his accumulated savings in the form of life insurance and other investments will pay as a retirement income. For instance, one may have his savings program arranged so that, at the age of sixty-five, he will have available five thousand dollars from insurance and five thousand dollars in the form of other investments. He will wish to know

The number of months that *each* $1,000 of a retirement fund, earning compound interest at any one of the indicated rates, will pay a monthly income of the amount shown.

RATE	$25.00	$20.00	$17.50	$15.00	$12.50	$10.00	$7.50	$5.00
3%	42	53	61	73	89	115	162	276
3½%	42	54	62	74	91	118	168	297
4%	43	54	63	75	93	121	175	325
4½%	43	55	64	76	95	125	183	360
5%	43	56	65	78	97	128	192	414
5½%	44	56	66	79	99	132	203	503
6%	44	57	67	80	101	137	215	...

Fractions of months are not included, except when they approximate a full month.

Illustration No. 18—Retirement Income

approximately how long this money will last if he retires at that age. Illustration No. 18 will answer the question. For example, if the ten thousand dollars is invested at 3 per cent, it will provide an income of twenty-five dollars a month for four hundred and twenty months (10 times 42). Similar tables can be used in connection with retirement funds of larger amounts.

As will be seen in the chapter on life insurance, the proceeds of such insurance can be left on deposit with the insurance company, with the understanding that from them monthly installments will be paid to the insured person after his retirement or to the beneficiary of the policy.

How Interest Multiplies. Interest is a very diligent and faithful worker, but it will work for one only if one has savings. This fact explains why many rich people have no difficulty in making a living. Although they cease to work, their money continues to work for them by earning interest.

If a person hoards his money, he receives no income from it in the form of interest. He also deprives other people of the use of his money. If a person lends his money or places it in some institution that uses it for making loans, the money will produce an income. Lending money is one way of sharing wealth with others. Because the lending of the money renders a service to someone who needs to borrow, the lender is entitled to compensation for his services.

Very few people realize the cumulative power of compound interest. The following table shows the rate at which money accumulates when interest is compounded semiannually. If the interest is compounded quarterly or monthly, the increase is greater.

INTEREST RATE	DOUBLED IN	QUADRUPLED IN	MULTIPLIED IN 47 YEARS (AGE 18 TO 65)
3%	23.28 YEARS	46.58 YEARS	4 1/20 TIMES
3½%	19.98 YEARS	39.96 YEARS	5 1/10 TIMES
4%	17.50 YEARS	35.00 YEARS	6 2/5 TIMES
4½%	15.58 YEARS	31.16 YEARS	8 1/10 TIMES
5%	14.04 YEARS	28.07 YEARS	10 1/5 TIMES

Illustration No. 19—The Cumulative Power of Compound Interest

For instance, if a person eighteen years of age invests one dollar at 4 per cent interest, compounded semiannually, the investment will be worth two dollars when he is thirty-five and a half years old, four dollars when he is fifty-three years old, and six dollars and forty cents when he is sixty-five years old.

Care in Buying. If a person finds that he can save more money than he had anticipated, this fact is no excuse for his spending the surplus. It is an indication that more savings should be accumulated. If money is set aside for some purpose and is not needed, the best place to put it until there is some definite need is in a savings fund. The following criteria should be observed in all spending:

(a) Refuse to buy anything that cannot be afforded.
(b) Do not buy anything that is not needed.
(c) No purchase is a bargain at any price unless there is a definite need for it.
(d) Buying the best is right if you are sure that you get the best.

Paying as One Goes. One should not go into debt for things that will have been used or consumed before they are paid for. It is frequently desirable to go into debt for a major investment, such as a home, but the same thing is not true of going into debt for current purchases. The latter practice will soon lead to the destruction of the savings program.

Mistakes in Savings. The possibilities of making mistakes in a savings program are indicated in the preceding discussion. Some of those who save make the following mistakes:

(a) They make deposits only spasmodically.
(b) They do not establish definite goals.
(c) They do not plan to take care of definite needs.
(d) They speculate with earnings.
(e) They withhold earnings and use them for whimsical luxuries.
(f) Because of unforeseen obstacles, they close their savings accounts and never open them again.

TEXTBOOK QUESTIONS

1. What are some of the major goals or needs for saving?
2. What is the first step in any savings program?
3. In what way does a man with a reserve fund have an advantage over a man without a reserve fund?
4. What are some of the ways in which you can save money as a result of having built up a reserve fund?
5. If you deposit $1 a month for five years at 3 per cent interest, compounded semiannually, how much will be in your savings account at the end of that time?
6. Why is the girl who earns $20 a week not justified in buying an automobile that would entail a monthly cost of $54?

7. Why must savings precede investments?
8. The table in Illustration No. 16 on page 33 shows that $1 deposited monthly at 4 per cent interest, compounded semiannually, will amount to $66.46 at the end of five years. If $10 is deposited monthly, how much will be in the savings account at the end of five years?
9. What are some purchases for which it is desirable to go into debt?
10. Name three common mistakes in saving.

DISCUSSION QUESTIONS

1. Some people refer to our economic system as a capitalistic system or price system. Others refer to it as a modified capitalistic system. Under our system, in what way is the laborer working for a profit in the same manner as the businessman?
2. If a person has built up a reserve cash fund, what are some of the ways in which he can utilize this fund to save money? (Do not include the ways mentioned in this chapter.)
3. Suppose that a man is able to save $20 a month. He has accumulated $100 and uses this amount as a down payment on an automobile. It will cost him $20 a month to complete paying for the automobile. Is he justified in buying it? Discuss the situation.
4. A person deposits $10 in a savings account at the beginning of each month. The interest rate is 3 per cent, compounded semiannually. How much will be in the savings account at the end of thirteen years?
5. You decide to begin a definite savings program to accumulate $10,000 by the time you are sixty years of age. By using one of the tables in this chapter, determine how much you must save monthly to accumulate the $10,000 by that time.
6. A savings fund should not be used for anything except investments and emergencies. What is an example of an emergency for which a savings fund may be used?
7. What are some luxuries that are recognized as legitimate, provided they can be afforded?
8. Mr. Wells, who owns one automobile and finds it sufficient for his own use, is offered a car at a cheap price by a friend. His friend offers to sell the car at this price because he cannot get a satisfactory price by selling it to a dealer. Mr. Wells has enough money to buy the car. Although he does not need it, he buys it because he believes that it is a good bargain at the price. Is he justified in his reasoning?

Section II

Carrying Out a Financial Plan

Where to Put Savings. The average individual has more than one opportunity to place savings where they will earn an income. The following facts should, however, be considered in opening any savings account:

(a) Will the account be safe?
(b) Will it pay a reasonable rate of interest?
(c) Will the savings be available at any time?
(d) How often is interest compounded?

Banks. There are two general types of banks in which savings may be deposited. The first is the commercial bank with a savings department, and the second is the savings bank. The commercial bank may be (a) an independent state bank, (b) a state bank that is a member of the Federal Reserve System, or (c) a national bank. All national banks are members of the Federal Reserve System.

Banks use the savings of depositors to lend to other people. These loans earn an income for the bank. Out of this income the depositors are paid interest on their deposits. The interest may be computed quarterly, semiannually, or annually.

If every depositor wanted his money at a particular time, enough cash would not be available. The bank therefore schedules its loans to assure that there will be an adequate amount of money available to pay each depositor upon demand.

Individual institutions have certain regulations. For instance, some savings banks reserve the right to ask for thirty days' notice before paying any depositor. This right may not be exercised, but the bank can utilize it as a means of protecting itself in case there should be an unusual demand on the part of a depositor. The time limit would give the bank an opportunity to obtain funds by making its borrowers pay loans, or by selling certain securities that it owned.

The rate of interest should not always be the deciding factor in selecting a place for depositing savings. Rates of interest paid on savings are, however, relatively uniform. Although the deposits in some banking institutions are insured, other banks may be just as safe. The rules and regulations of banks with regard to opening and operating a savings account may also influence the selection of a place to deposit savings.

Building and Loan Associations. In most states there are organizations known commonly as *building and loan associations.* These organizations serve essentially the same purpose as savings banks, and many of them operate in much the same way. Although such associations have relatively uniform procedures, each is regulated by the laws of the state in which it is located. There is considerable difference in the laws of the various states. In some states a person may deposit savings in a building and loan association just as he does in a bank and under practically the same regulations and restrictions. He usually receives, however, a slightly higher interest rate.

The building and loan association is organized for the purpose of lending money to people who do not have enough money to buy or build a home. The money that the association lends is accumulated from depositors. In many states, when a person makes deposits in a building and loan association, he really buys *shares* and becomes theoretically a part owner. These shares usually earn a fixed rate of income. Some building and loan associations offer four different types of shares as opportunities for savings and investments. These appeal to various classes of individuals. The only fundamental difference is that some particular types of shares can be paid for in installments, whereas the others may be bought in one cash payment.

Federal Home Loan Associations. Throughout the United States there are Federal savings and loan associations that are members of the Federal Home Loan Bank. Such institutions operate under the regulations established by the Federal Government.

The Federal Savings and Loan Insurance Corporation was organized by law to insure the accounts of all Federal savings and loan associations. It may also insure the accounts of other building and loan or savings and loan associations, of homestead associations, and of co-operative banks organized and operated according to the laws of the state, district, or territory in which they were chartered or organized. Any institution in which the accounts are insured provides an extra margin of safety for the person who places his savings in it.

Postal Savings. Some people have been timid in using banks and similar savings institutions, but have had faith in governmental institutions. By an act of Congress, approved on June 25, 1910, there was established the United States Postal Savings System. Many people who had been unwilling to use other savings institutions have utilized the postal-savings plan.

A person desiring to open a postal-savings account should apply at any post office or station. If his local post office is not authorized to accept deposits, an account may be opened at a depository office by mail. Any person ten years of age or over is eligible under this plan. No person may have more than one account, and all accounts must be of a personal nature.

Deposits are acknowledged by postal-savings certificates in denominations of $1, $2, $5, $10, $20, $50, $100, $200, or $500, which are made out in the names of the depositors. These serve as receipts and are valid until paid. The certificates are not negotiable or transferable. If a certificate is lost, stolen, or destroyed, a new certificate will be issued. No depositor may have an account in excess of $2,500, exclusive of accumulated interest.

Interest accumulates at the rate of 2 per cent for each full year that a certificate is outstanding. It accumulates for a partial year at the rate of one-half per cent for each full quarter. Interest is not compounded, but a depositor may withdraw it and use it for making a new deposit. Therefore, it is advisable to withdraw interest when it has been earned.

A depositor at any time may withdraw all or any part of his postal savings by presenting a certificate for redemption. Withdrawals may be made in person, through a representative, or by mail.

No person connected with the Post Office Department is permitted to disclose the name of a depositor or to give information about an account to any person other than the depositor.

Although deposits are required in even amounts, as indicated above by the denominations of certificates, smaller amounts can be saved by purchasing postal-savings stamps at 10 cents each and affixing them to a card until ten have been accumulated. This card can then be exchanged for a one-dollar postal-savings certificate.

United States Savings Bonds. United States savings bonds are considered by some people to be a method of saving, while they are considered by others as a method of investing. In some respects they provide an extension of the Postal Savings System, although the savings are in larger amounts. The bonds are available at the prices indicated in the following table and are payable in ten years at the prices indicated in the right-hand column:

COST		REDEMPTION VALUE
$ 18.75	increases in 10 years to	$ 25.00
$ 37.50	increases in 10 years to	$ 50.00
$ 75.00	increases in 10 years to	$ 100.00
$375.00	increases in 10 years to	$ 500.00
$750.00	increases in 10 years to	$1,000.00

Any person, corporation, or association may purchase up to, but not more than, $10,000 worth (maturity value) of bonds issued during any calendar year. In each subsequent year, however, additional bonds not exceeding the same maximum value may be purchased.

If a savings bond is lost, stolen, or destroyed, a duplicate will be issued upon satisfactory proof. The Treasury Department, through the Federal Reserve Banks, provides a means of safekeeping that is available without charge.

The individual owner of bonds may name only one beneficiary, to whom payment will be made upon the death of the owner.

While the rate of interest earned on United States savings bonds is not high, it is reasonable in comparison with the rate of earnings on some other savings. If a bond is held until maturity, it has an equivalent yield of 2.9 per cent interest, compounded semiannually. After sixty days from its date of issue, a savings bond may be redeemed at the established cash redemption value. The following table shows the redemption values.

Table of Redemption Values of United States Savings Bonds

ISSUE PRICE	$18.75	$37.50	$ 75.00	$375.00	$ 750.00
Redemption values after the issue date:					
First year	$18.75	$37.50	$ 75.00	$375.00	$ 750.00
1 to 1½ years	19.00	38.00	76.00	380.00	760.00
1½ to 2 years	19.25	38.50	77.00	385.00	770.00
2 to 2½ years	19.50	39.00	78.00	390.00	780.00
2½ to 3 years	19.75	39.50	79.00	395.00	790.00
3 to 3½ years	20.00	40.00	80.00	400.00	800.00
3½ to 4 years	20.25	40.50	81.00	405.00	810.00
4 to 4½ years	20.50	41.00	82.00	410.00	820.00
4½ to 5 years	20.75	41.50	83.00	415.00	830.00
5 to 5½ years	21.00	42.00	84.00	420.00	840.00
5½ to 6 years	21.25	42.50	85.00	425.00	850.00
6 to 6½ years	21.50	43.00	86.00	430.00	860.00
6½ to 7 years	21.75	43.50	87.00	435.00	870.00
7 to 7½ years	22.00	44.00	88.00	440.00	880.00
7½ to 8 years	22.50	45.00	90.00	450.00	900.00
8 to 8½ years	23.00	46.00	92.00	460.00	920.00
8½ to 9 years	23,50	47.00	94.00	470.00	940.00
9 to 9½ years	24.00	48.00	96.00	480.00	960.00
9½ to 10 years	24.50	49.00	98.00	490.00	980.00
Maturity value	25.00	50.00	100.00	500.00	1,000.00

Illustration No. 20—Redemption Values of U. S. Savings Bonds

Credit Unions. Credit unions are both savings and lending institutions. They are co-operative associations operating for the promotion of thrift and for the creation of funds from which members can borrow. Placing money in such institutions may therefore be considered as a savings plan, although membership in a credit union is usually not available to everyone.

In most states credit unions have operated and are authorized to operate under state laws. With the passage of the Federal Credit Union Act, approved on June 26, 1934, Federal credit unions may be organized and operated under a Federal charter issued by the Farm Credit Administration.

Credit unions are usually formed by large groups of people with common interests. For instance, they may be formed by such groups as teachers in a large school system, workers in a large factory, store employees, and church or fraternal organizations.

While the credit unions established under the laws of the various states are by no means uniform, there is uniformity in the organization of Federal credit unions. A member of a Federal credit union must agree to subscribe for at least one five-dollar share, payable in one sum of cash or in periodic installments. He may subscribe for a larger number of shares if he desires. He must also pay an entrance fee of 25 cents. Members who are in arrears in their payments are subject to a small fine unless they are excused by the directors.

When a person has become a member by being elected to membership by the board of directors and by paying the entrance fee and at least the first installment on one or more shares, he may apply for a loan. To be granted, the loan must be approved by the credit committee of the union.

When a member has paid for one share, he is eligible to his proportionate share of the annual dividends that may be declared by the members. These dividends represent interest on the savings deposited with the credit union. A credit union is a true co-operative in that its members share in the earnings. The maximum rate that may be paid, however, as a dividend is 6 per cent.

Mutual Savings Banks. In some states, mutual savings banks are permitted by law. Such banks are organized in a manner similar to credit unions. They are usually formed by responsible people, such as local storekeepers, manufacturers, lawyers, and physicians. The officers of the banks perform their duties without compensation. The regulations under which these banks operate are governed by state laws. The advantages of such banks to the individual are (a) good interest rates on savings and (b) reasonable rates on loans.

Looking Ahead Financially. The savings account plays an important role in the financial program of any individual. It is the first step and one of the most important, for upon it depend all the others. The four major steps in the financial program are as follows:

(a) Maintaining a savings account
(b) Buying life insurance
(c) Building or buying a home
(d) Investing

Although the financial program comprises these four steps, this chapter confines itself to the study of savings. Insurance, building or buying a home, investing, and banking relations are discussed in later chapters.

Saving for Retirement. After the game of life has been played, it is too late to hope to profit by looking back over the mistakes that have been made. At that time a study of one's mistakes is of no benefit except to someone else. It is advisable to study the mistakes and the successes of other people. It is essential to follow some definite plan.

In spite of the emphasis on the teaching of thrift in the United States, and the fact that Americans receive the highest real wages in the world, many people in this country become dependent when they cease to earn. This condition results largely from the fact that most people are encouraged to save merely for a "rainy day." Because of this indefinite goal the earner drifts along with little financial reserve until it is too late to save. He then becomes dependent upon charity or upon his relatives for support.

When a person's income-earning days are finished, he will still require food, clothing, and shelter. Savings funds, investments, and insurance will help to take care of him at that time. At least one company in the United States recognizes this problem and sells *installment certificates*, or *installment bonds*. An installment certificate, or installment bond, has some of the features of a savings account, an investment, and insurance. A definite program is selected with the idea of building up an investment. Payments can be made in small amounts. If the payments are accumulated according to the plan, they may be withdrawn in a lump sum, somewhat in the manner of insurance; or the investment may be withdrawn earlier by sacrificing some of the interest.

One may consider that there are four financial periods in a person's life, assuming that the person will continue to produce until he is sixty years of age. The first fifteen years may be called the *formative period*; the second fifteen years, the *stabilizing period*; the third fifteen years, the *achievement period*; and the fourth fifteen years, the *declining period.* Earning and saving are normally confined to the second, third, and fourth periods. The savings should gradually increase during the second period and should reach their peak during the third period. During the fourth period they will decline and may even cease. Unless provision is made for saving and investing during the second and third periods, there is little chance of developing a satisfactory saving and investing program in the fourth period.

Making a Will. The important reason for making a will is to arrange for a definite division and administration of an estate after the death of the owner. In the absence of a will the estate left by a deceased person will be distributed according to the laws of the state in which the person resided. The legal procedure in such a case is frequently complicated and costly. Consider these two examples:

Mr. A, who has a wife and two children, dies without having made a will. He leaves an estate of twenty thousand dollars. According to the law in his state (as in many other states), the court appoints an administrator to administer the children's share until they become of age. The court may or may not appoint the widow as the administratrix. Even if the widow is appointed administratrix, she is responsible for making a report to the court with regard to the management of the children's share.

Mr. B, who has a wife and two children, makes a will in which he stipulates that his entire estate of twenty thousand dollars is to go to his widow and that she is to administer it and to provide for the education of the children in any way that she sees fit.

In a sense, certain clauses in a life-insurance policy function somewhat as the provisions of a will, in that they serve as guides in paying the proceeds of the insurance. The insurance company is forced to use the proceeds of the insurance as the contract specifies. If the proceeds are

LAST WILL AND TESTAMENT OF C. J. HOLMAN

I, C. J. Holman, of the City of Butte and the State of Montana, do hereby declare this to be my last Will and Testament. Upon my death, I wish the following instructions carried out:

FIRST: All my just debts, funeral expenses, and the cost of administering my estate may be paid by my executrix, who will be named later in this will.

SECOND: I direct my wife, Helen Rose Holman, to sell the real property located at 126 Elm Street, Butte, Montana, and to use the proceeds for the college education of my two children, John Henry Holman and Mary Rose Holman, the education to be administered as my wife sees fit. Any surplus not needed for their education will revert to my wife.

THIRD: All the remainder of my real, personal, and mixed property I give to my wife, Helen Rose Holman.

FOURTH: I hereby appoint my wife, Helen Rose Holman, executrix of this, my last Will and Testament, and I ask that she not be required to give bond or security for the performance of her duties.

FIFTH: I hereby revoke any or all former wills made by me.

IN WITNESS WHEREOF, I have set my hand and signature this sixteenth day of November, in the year nineteen hundred and forty.

C J Holman

Signed, published, and declared by C. J. Holman, named above, as and for his last Will and Testament in the presence of us and each of us, who, in his presence, and at his request, and in the presence of one another, have subscribed our names as witnesses on the day and in the year indicated above.

Frank R. Walls — 417 Silver Street, Butte, Mont.
Robert M Craig — 5712 Cedar Street, Butte, Mont.
H. J. Beck — 216 Vine Street, Butte, Mont.

Illustration No. 21—A Simple Form of a Will

made payable, however, to the estate of the deceased person, they are administered in the manner provided by the will, or, if there is no will, according to the laws of the state.

The safest procedure for any person is to have a will drawn by a lawyer. A new will may be written later if the original needs changing. The writing of a will is one means of looking into the future and making plans for dependents.

TEXTBOOK QUESTIONS

1. What facts should be considered in opening a savings account?
2. What are the two general types of banks in which savings may be deposited?
3. Under what regulations may a bank operate?
4. Is a building and loan association a bank?
5. For what purpose is a building and loan association organized?
6. What is the Federal Savings and Loan Insurance Corporation?
7. How may deposits be withdrawn from the Federal Postal Savings System?
8. What is the interest rate on postal savings?
9. (a) What is the maximum amount that one may deposit in the Federal Postal Savings System? (b) What is the maximum amount that one may invest in United States savings bonds in any calendar year?
10. What is the rate of interest (yield) on United States savings bonds if the bonds are held until maturity?
11. Give examples of groups of persons who may organize credit unions.
12. May persons other than members of a credit union borrow from the union?
13. Give the distinguishing features of a mutual savings bank.
14. What should be the four major steps in a person's financial program?
15. Why do some banks and other savings institutions reserve the right to wait thirty days or some other stipulated length of time before paying money to depositors?

DISCUSSION QUESTIONS

1. Should a depositor use a bank that is convenient or one that is small and therefore has officers who are acquainted with him and are friendly?

2. A particular loan company is liberal in lending on mortgages and offers a high rate of interest to depositors. If you were seeking a place to accumulate savings, would you select this loan company or one that is conservative in making loans and offers a rate of interest that is ½ per cent less?
3. If you had savings of $500, would you place them in (a) an institution that pays 3 per cent interest and insures deposits or (b) an institution that pays 5 per cent interest but does not insure deposits? Assume that the institution that pays 5 per cent interest has a good reputation and is conservative.
4. Do you think you would get better service on your personal account at a commercial bank than at a savings bank?
5. Some people borrow money and also buy on account and on the installment plan in order to have furniture and luxuries comparable to those of people with larger incomes. They follow this plan because they feel that they deserve these things. What advice would you give to a person of this kind?
6. Why is it necessary to correlate budgeting, saving, and buying a home?
7. A man says, "What is the use of saving? I always have to spend my savings in case of an emergency." Discuss this statement.
8. If there is no bank or building and loan association or any other private banking institution in your community, where may you place your savings so that they will be safe and earn a little interest?
9. Bonds are ordinarily thought of as investments. Why do some people consider United States savings bonds as a means of saving?
10. In what respect is a member of a credit union a stockholder?

PROBLEMS

1. If $2 a month is deposited in a savings account on which 3 per cent interest is compounded semiannually, how much will be available (a) in five years? (b) in ten years?
2. If the interest rate is 3½ per cent, compounded semiannually, how much will one have to deposit at the beginning of each month to accumulate (a) $5,000 in twenty years? (b) $3,000 in fifteen years?
3. If a person has $5,000 on deposit at 3 per cent interest, (a) for how many months can he withdraw $15 a month? (b) for how many months can he withdraw $25 a month?
4. Calculate how much should be saved in ten years at 4 per cent interest by (a) a family of three with an income of $30

a week, (b) a family of four with an income of $40 a week, and (c) a single man with an income of $37 a week. Consider four weekly deposits as one monthly deposit, and use the model budgets on pages 6 and 7 and the table on page 33.

5. A man has an average balance of $400 in his checking account. The minimum amount that he may keep in the account without having to pay a service fee is $100. He draws no interest on the balance in his checking account. Assume that he places the surplus $300 in a savings account. Calculate the amount of interest that he will earn in ten years if interest is paid at the rate of 3 per cent and is compounded semiannually.
6. If a man who is thirty-five years old wants $5,000 besides his insurance at the time he is sixty years of age, how much must he save monthly at 4 per cent interest, compounded semiannually?

COMMUNITY PROBLEMS AND PROJECTS

1. Make a list of all the local places where savings can be deposited. List the rate of interest paid by each one, and indicate whether the interest is computed monthly, quarterly, semiannually, or annually.
2. Make a study of the savings institutions in your community with regard to the rules governing (a) deposits, (b) withdrawals, (c) the payment of interest on balances that have not been in accounts for the full length of the interest period, and (d) the payment of interest when withdrawals have been made during the interest period.
3. Make a study of the cost of attending some particular college or several colleges. From the college or colleges obtain information with regard to tuition, laboratory fees, room rents, and cost of meals and laundry. Add to these amounts the cost of clothing, amusement, transportation, and any other items that you believe should be included in the cost of a college education. Make an estimate of the total cost for each of the four years of a college education. Prepare a report showing how you believe it will be possible to finance this education through (a) income from parents or relatives, (b) loans, (c) scholarships, (d) personal savings, (e) earnings made while you are in school.
4. (a) Calculate your yearly requirements for clothes. (b) Compute the amount of regular weekly savings that must be accumulated to provide for buying the clothes as they are needed. Assume that the amount you will need for clothes will be provided through weekly allowances.

CHAPTER III

OUR BANKING RELATIONS

Purpose of the Chapter. Everyone, sometime in his life, has dealings with a bank. Banks are an indispensable part of our financial system; without them our system of money and credit would not function. To many individuals the work of a bank is something of a mystery; therefore banking is regarded by them with awe. Banks are business institutions in the same sense that your grocery or drugstore is a business institution. The major difference is that a bank is a buyer or a seller of credit. Because money and credit are so vital to the common welfare, banks are closely regulated by the governments, both state and Federal. As everyone is affected by banks, this chapter is concerned primarily with the information that all individuals should have about them.

Section I

Using Bank Services

The Citizen's Function in Banking. For the safety of our economic system the individual should understand the importance of his function in the banking system. In the first place, banks depend upon individuals and business concerns for deposits. On the basis of these deposits loans can be made. By making loans, banks earn a profit for themselves.

If all the money deposited in a bank were paid out as loans, there would not be any money left to pay to depositors. Such a situation does not, however, occur. When a loan is made, the borrower usually accepts a credit to an account. He can then write a check on this account. The borrower therefore becomes a depositor and also a debtor of the bank.

Our banking system works smoothly because not all depositors want their money at the same time. As some withdrawals are made, new deposits are also made. The withdrawals and the deposits therefore tend to balance one another. If all depositors wanted their money at the same time, there would not be enough money available. Through our system of credit there is not enough ready cash in the United States to pay in cash the amount that is represented by bank deposits.

If a bank is operated conservatively and makes loans that can be collected when they become due, each depositor is assured that he can obtain his money when he wants it. The experiences of the past prove, however, that thoroughly sound banks are sometimes unable to pay when depositors become hysterical and demand all their money at the same time.

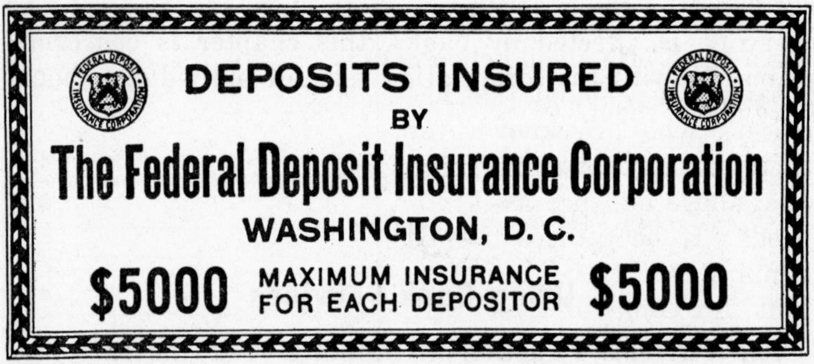

Illustration No. 22—A Sign Announcing That a Bank's Deposits Are Insured

Deposit Insurance. In periods of normal business, people have little or no uncertainty about the safety of money deposited in banks. The possibility of loss to depositors during periods of business recession has largely been removed through the insurance of bank deposits. This insurance is administered by The Federal Deposit Insurance Corporation, which all national banks are compelled to join and other banks may join voluntarily. Each individual account in a bank having this insurance is insured up to five thousand dollars.

Safety and Convenience. Convenience in banking facilities is important, although safety should not be sacrificed to convenience. When deposits are guaranteed, one bank is essentially as safe as another. There are, however, ways of determining the safety and conservativeness of a bank. The most common means is through an analysis of the bank's financial statements. The ratio of cash and Government bonds to the deposits in one bank may be compared with the same ratio for another bank. The bank that has the higher ratio is essentially the safer and more conservative bank.

Even though the deposits of a bank may be insured in some way, a person should not be relieved from the responsibility of selecting a bank that meets his requirements. He should not trust to luck or depend entirely on convenience of location. Integrity is the important factor in choosing a bank. He should choose a bank that is sound, that has officers who are known for their honesty and integrity, and, above all, that meets his needs. If he utilizes normal banking facilities, it is important for him to deal with bankers whom he can consult confidentially and who will give honest advice.

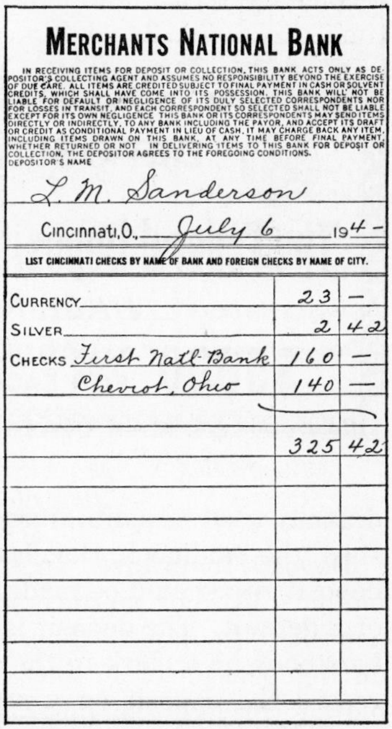
MERCHANTS NATIONAL BANK

IN RECEIVING ITEMS FOR DEPOSIT OR COLLECTION, THIS BANK ACTS ONLY AS DEPOSITOR'S COLLECTING AGENT AND ASSUMES NO RESPONSIBILITY BEYOND THE EXERCISE OF DUE CARE. ALL ITEMS ARE CREDITED SUBJECT TO FINAL PAYMENT IN CASH OR SOLVENT CREDITS, WHICH SHALL HAVE COME INTO ITS POSSESSION. THIS BANK WILL NOT BE LIABLE FOR DEFAULT OR NEGLIGENCE OF ITS DULY SELECTED CORRESPONDENTS NOR FOR LOSSES IN TRANSIT, AND EACH CORRESPONDENT SO SELECTED SHALL NOT BE LIABLE EXCEPT FOR ITS OWN NEGLIGENCE. THIS BANK OR ITS CORRESPONDENTS MAY SEND ITEMS DIRECTLY OR INDIRECTLY, TO ANY BANK INCLUDING THE PAYOR, AND ACCEPT ITS DRAFT OR CREDIT AS CONDITIONAL PAYMENT IN LIEU OF CASH. IT MAY CHARGE BACK ANY ITEM, INCLUDING ITEMS DRAWN ON THIS BANK, AT ANY TIME BEFORE FINAL PAYMENT, WHETHER RETURNED OR NOT. IN DELIVERING ITEMS TO THIS BANK FOR DEPOSIT OR COLLECTION, THE DEPOSITOR AGREES TO THE FOREGOING CONDITIONS.

DEPOSITOR'S NAME L. M. Sanderson

Cincinnati, O., July 6 194-

LIST CINCINNATI CHECKS BY NAME OF BANK AND FOREIGN CHECKS BY NAME OF CITY.

CURRENCY	23	—
SILVER	2	42
CHECKS First Natl Bank	160	—
Cheviot, Ohio	140	—
	325	42

Illustration No. 23—A Deposit Slip

Size and Type of Bank. In some communities there is an advantage in placing a personal account in a small bank because the officers and personnel of such a bank learn to know each customer and appreciate his business. They are also probably more willing to accommodate a customer who may need a loan. The advantages of a small bank, however, are sometimes offset by those of a larger bank. Dealings with a large bank may sometimes be impersonal, but such a bank frequently can offer facilities that are not otherwise available. These facilities comprise a number of miscellaneous services. It is also frequently true that a large bank is in a position to make a loan, whereas a small bank is not.

Another consideration has to do with the type of bank. Some banks prefer to have commercial accounts rather than personal accounts. Obviously, an individual who is making a personal deposit will get better consideration from a bank that prefers personal accounts than he would from a bank that prefers commercial accounts.

The rate of interest paid on deposits does not demand special consideration in most communities, because interest rates on deposits are becoming more or less standardized. Charges for banking services also are much the same.

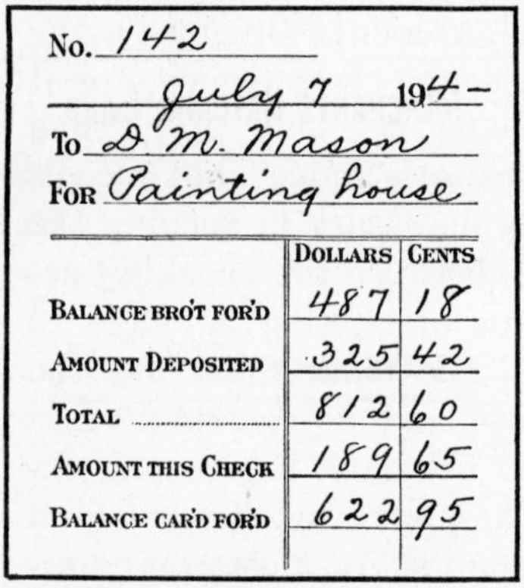
No. 142
July 7 194-
To D. M. Mason
For Painting house

	DOLLARS	CENTS
BALANCE BRO'T FOR'D	487	18
AMOUNT DEPOSITED	325	42
TOTAL	812	60
AMOUNT THIS CHECK	189	65
BALANCE CAR'D FOR'D	622	95

Illustration No. 24—A Checkbook Stub

Checking Account. Although there is some slight variation in the operation of checking accounts in different communities, the procedure is essentially the same everywhere. The instruments ordinarily used in maintaining a checking account are deposit slips, the bankbook, the checkbook, and counter checks. The deposit slip should be made out by the depositor as evidence of a deposit. The deposit is then recorded in the depositor's bankbook by a clerk in the bank. The depositor should also record the deposit on a stub of his checkbook. Disbursements by check should be recorded on the checkbook stubs. If a counter check is used to withdraw cash from the account, this withdrawal should likewise be recorded on a check stub. It is important to keep checkbook stubs up to date so that they will show the correct balance.

Using a bank for deposits is advantageous not only to the bank and its borrowers but also to the depositor. Although a checking account usually does not earn interest, the facilities provided by it are valuable. The following are some of the advantages:

(a) The money is in a safe place and can be transferred conveniently and safely simply by writing checks.
(b) The check stubs provide a convenient record of deposits, expenditures, and bank balances.
(c) The canceled bank check is valuable as a receipt and is evidence of the date, the manner, and the amount of payment.
(d) A checking account helps to enhance one's personal and business standing.

Cost of Maintaining a Checking Account. Obviously, the service provided by a checking account costs money, for it must be remembered that the bank not only provides a place of safekeeping for the depositor's money but also is responsible for all the bookkeeping necessary in keeping the records up to date. Furthermore, because the checking account provides a convenient means of making payment to other persons and to businesses, the bank must use the services of the local clearinghouse and of clearinghouses in other parts of the country. As the bank has to pay expenses incurred in rendering all these services, it must earn something from the checking accounts. In most communities there is consequently a charge for small accounts. Since the size of these accounts varies, the tendency is to base the charge upon the actual cost of operating the account. In states in which there is a tax on deposits and on checks, the bank may or may not pay the tax. If it pays the tax, it must realize enough profit from the accounts to compensate for the tax as well as for other expenses involved.

The wisest use of a checking account in paying personal and family expenses is to pay by check only the larger amounts and particularly those that require remittances by mail. Smaller amounts should be paid from a cash fund. The habit of paying all small amounts by check places a burden on the bank and is one cause for the bank's making a charge for checking service.

FIRST NATIONAL BANK
CINCINNATI, OHIO

VOUCHERS RETURNED 9

L. H. Masters
131 Dayton Street

DATE April 30-39

DATE	CHECKS	DATE	DEPOSITS
	BALANCE BROUGHT FORWARD ☞	April 1-39	1,076.31
April 3-39	71.52	April 3-39	150.00
April 7-39	20.25		
		April 10-39	35.50
April 8-39	8.06		
April 14-39	102.58	April 14-39	74.09
April 19-39	15.71		
		April 18-39	129.45
April 23-39	90.00		
April 24-39	134.92	April 23-39	250.60
April 27-39	45.53		
		April 27-39	42.50
April 29-39	62.18		
PLEASE EXAMINE AT ONCE	BALANCE ☞	April 30-39	1,207.70

IF NO ERROR IS REPORTED IN TEN DAYS THE ACCOUNT WILL BE CONSIDERED CORRECT

Illustration No. 25—A Bank Statement

Reconciliation of the Bank Statement. Illustration No. 25 shows a bank statement. The accuracy of this bank statement can be proved by the following procedure:

(a) Verify the checks recorded on the bank statement by comparing them with the canceled checks accompanying the statement.

(b) Determine from the checkbook stubs which checks were outstanding on the date of the bank statement.

(c) Verify all deposits by checking those listed on the bank statement with those recorded in the bankbook and on the check stubs.

(d) Use the following method in reconciling the balance on the bank statement with the balance shown by the checkbook:

(1)	Cash balance indicated by the bank statement	$1,207.70
(2)	Total of checks still outstanding	215.60
(3)	Cash balance that should agree with the balance in the checkbook	$ 992.10

The last amount shown on the bank reconciliation ($992.10) should agree with the checkbook balance for the date on which the reconciliation is made. Suppose, however, that in the preceding example a bank service charge of $1.50 was made for the month and one deposit of $74.09, shown on the statement, was not recorded on a checkbook stub. In this case the balance indicated by the bank statement would be $1,206.20 ($1,207.70 minus $1.50), and the balance in the checkbook would be $918.01 ($992.10 minus $74.09). The following would be the procedure for making the adjustments required by the service charge and the deposit:

CHECKBOOK ADJUSTMENTS

Checkbook balance	$918.01
Deduct:	
Service charge made by bank	1.50
	$916.51
Add:	
Deposit made but not recorded in the checkbook	74.09
Adjusted checkbook balance	$990.60

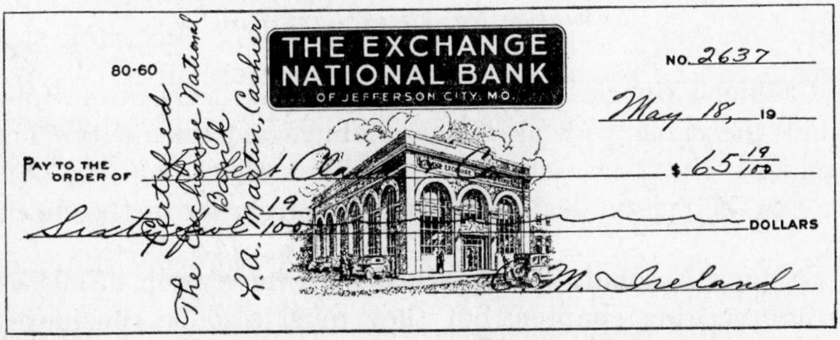

Illustration No. 26—A Certified Check

Certified Check. It is sometimes desirable to transfer money by using a certified check. A certified check is useful when the person receiving it must be assured that the drawer of the check has the proper amount of money in the bank. Such a check certifies that it will be paid upon presentation. As soon as the cashier of the bank certifies the check, he charges the amount to the depositor's account. The amount will not then be utilized for any other purpose unless the certified check is canceled.

Bank Draft. A bank draft is a check of a bank upon funds deposited to its credit with some other bank. A bank draft is a convenient means of transferring money when the individual who is making payment is not known in the part of the country to which the money is to be sent. He may obtain the draft by purchasing it from a bank. People will usually accept a bank draft provided the bank that has drawn it is known. A certified check has practically the same status as a bank draft, provided the bank is known and has a good reputation.

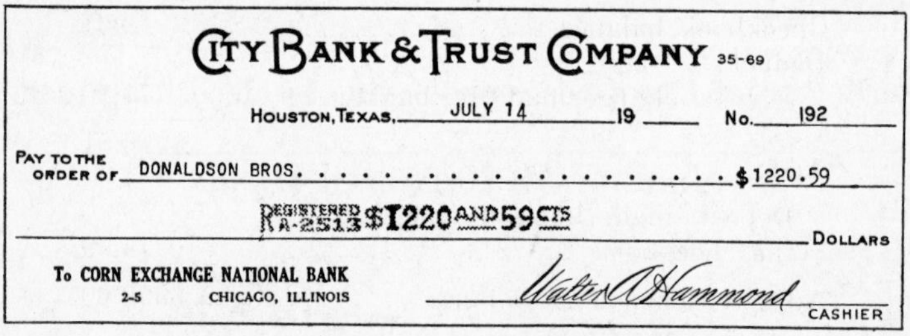
CITY BANK & TRUST COMPANY 35-69
HOUSTON, TEXAS, JULY 14 19 No. 192
PAY TO THE ORDER OF DONALDSON BROS. $1220.59
REGISTERED RA-2513 $1220 AND 59 CTS
DOLLARS
To CORN EXCHANGE NATIONAL BANK
2-5 CHICAGO, ILLINOIS
Walter A Hammond
CASHIER

Illustration No. 27—A Bank Draft

Cashier's Check. One may buy a cashier's check in somewhat the same way as a person buys a bank draft. The cashier's check is a check on the bank that issues it, payable to the person designated by the purchaser of the check.

Savings Account. Savings accounts have been discussed in a preceding chapter, but they must also be considered here because of their function as one of the services of banks. Savings accounts may be maintained in what are commonly known as savings banks or in the savings departments of other banks. The bankbook is the most im-

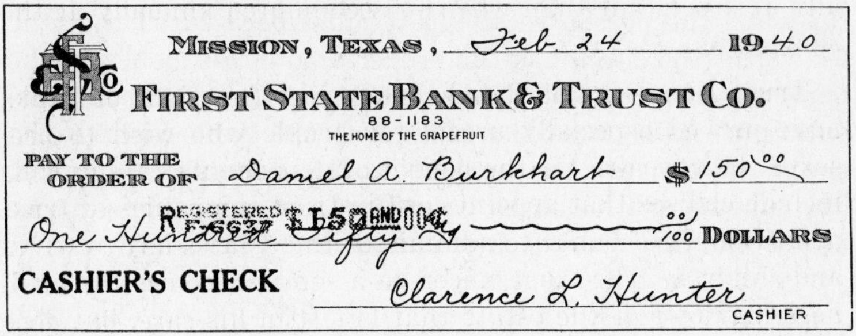
MISSION, TEXAS, Feb. 24 1940

FIRST STATE BANK & TRUST CO.

88-1183

THE HOME OF THE GRAPEFRUIT

PAY TO THE ORDER OF Daniel A. Burkhart $150.00

One Hundred Fifty 00/100 DOLLARS

CASHIER'S CHECK

Clarence L. Hunter

CASHIER

Illustration No. 28—A Cashier's Check

portant instrument in operating a savings account. In it are recorded all deposits and all withdrawals. Deposit slips are used as a record of deposits, and receipts as a record of withdrawals; but the bankbook must be presented each time money is deposited or withdrawn. Checks cannot be written on savings deposits, and many banks also reserve the right to require preliminary notice of the withdrawal of savings.

Savings accounts in banks usually pay interest, the rates varying from 1 to 4 per cent. Saving by depositing money

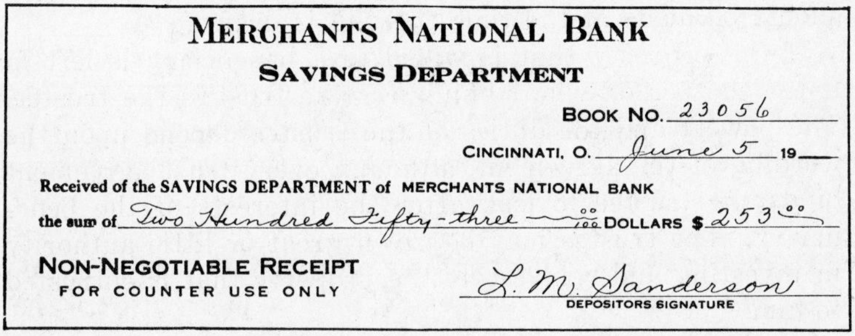
MERCHANTS NATIONAL BANK

SAVINGS DEPARTMENT

BOOK NO. 23056

CINCINNATI, O. June 5 19

Received of the SAVINGS DEPARTMENT of MERCHANTS NATIONAL BANK

the sum of Two Hundred Fifty-three 00/100 DOLLARS $253.00

NON-NEGOTIABLE RECEIPT

FOR COUNTER USE ONLY

L. M. Sanderson

DEPOSITORS SIGNATURE

Illustration No. 29—A Withdrawal Slip for a Savings Account

in a bank is a conservative means of investing, but it is usually a safe means as compared with investments in many types of securities. There is some difference in the yield of interest, depending upon the number of times a year the interest is calculated. Obviously, the income from a savings account is greater when interest is compounded semiannually at 4 per cent than when it is computed annually at the same rate.

Trust Functions of Banks. The trust functions of banks have proved especially useful for people who wish to preserve their wealth for the benefit of dependents. Many wills include clauses that appoint certain trust companies or trust departments of banks to administer the estates left to wives and children. The trust officer, in a sense, becomes the business manager of the estate that is left in his care, but does not guarantee a fixed rate of income from the estate.

The desirability of making a will was mentioned in a preceding chapter. Because of the close relation between wills and trusts, it is appropriate to consider wills again. Some people believe that, if the necessity arises, they will make a will. They keep putting off the task, however, until it is too late. Laws in most states definitely prescribe the way in which property will be divided if there is no will.

As a matter of policy, a will should not be "homemade." It should be written with the aid of a competent lawyer and according to the legal requirements. In some states the law requires two witnesses to the signature of a will. If a will is made and property is left in trust, the trust agreement should be made at the time the will is drawn.

If the property that is willed to a beneficiary is left in trust, the person who administers the trust is the trustee. The powers and the duties of the trustee depend upon the wording of the agreement, although every trust agreement binds the trustee to look after the interests of the beneficiary. The trustee may be given great or little authority in investing and reinvesting the property that is entrusted to him.

Safe-Deposit Boxes. Safe-deposit boxes in the vaults of banks are provided on a rental basis. Such a box provides protection against burglary and fire, and should be used for valuables that are not safe in the home or in the business office.

A bank cannot open a private safe-deposit box except upon the order of a court. In most states, if a safe-deposit box is registered in the names of a man and his wife, the

Irving Trust Company

Illustration No. 30—A Safe-Deposit Vault

bank is legally required to seal the box upon notice of the death of either person. The box may not then be opened except on the order of a court. It is therefore frequently advisable to have the safe-deposit box registered in the name of the wife alone. Then, in case of the death of the husband, the wife has access to the box. Under this arrangement the husband may also have regular access to the box, authority being granted to him by his wife. In case the wife dies without having transferred the title to the husband, the latter cannot gain access to the box except upon the order of a court.

Other Bank Services. Miscellaneous services, such as those pertaining to travel, real estate, and foreign trade, are provided by banks in order to encourage business activity as well as to produce additional income for themselves.

Certain banks operate travel departments and collect a commission on the charges for steamer passage and on other costs in connection with tours of foreign countries. They usually provide plans and complete information in connection with tours of various types. They may also sell foreign exchange and various credit instruments that can be used in foreign countries.

Real-estate departments are sometimes operated by banks in connection with trust departments. These function also as service departments for depositors by maintaining or disposing of property that has been taken as security on loans.

Foreign-trade departments provide means of contact with foreign agencies and serve to stimulate foreign trade by establishing credit, finding outlets, studying markets and trade conditions, and handling financial transactions between buyer and seller. Such a department therefore serves in an advisory capacity as well as in the functional capacity of establishing relations between buyer and seller.

A bank will act as custodian of bonds and other securities that need attention from time to time. In return for a moderate fee, it will take charge of stocks, bonds, mortgages, and other negotiable papers and will collect the dividends, the interest, and the principal when they become due. The bank, for example, will clip the coupons on bonds, collect the interest represented by the coupons, and credit it to the account of the client. The bank will also assume responsibility for handling interest payments and principal payments on the amounts borrowed by a client. In other words, the bank will act as an agent.

The Bank's Income. If a bank could not lend money, it could not earn a satisfactory income. With the exception of the amount of cash originally invested in the bank by the stockholders, the bank has practically no money to lend except what is deposited by individuals, business concerns, and other institutions. When a depositor takes his money to a bank, he expects a safe place of deposit and either a service in checking or an income from the deposit. He certainly expects to get his money when he wants it. The problem of the bank is, therefore, to utilize its capital and all the deposits either by lending to others or by investing in securities and other assets that will produce an income.

Laws regulate the way the money may be used. A bank must maintain a sufficient reserve of cash to pay out deposits when they are demanded. If every depositor should withdraw his money at the same time, no bank in the United States would be able to pay all its depositors in cash because the depositors' cash, except for a reasonable reserve that is kept on hand to take care of ordinary demands from depositors, has been lent to other people and business enterprises.

In lending money, the bank must be assured of two things: (a) the honesty of the borrower and (b) the ability of the borrower to pay at the time agreed upon. Obviously, the first involves character; the second, capacity to pay. A person who intends to borrow from a bank should therefore become acquainted with the banking officials in order to provide a first-hand basis for being judged. A loan is made to a business when the bank feels satisfied that the borrower will be able to purchase or manufacture goods and sell them at a profit, thus making it possible to repay the loan. The banker obtains information with regard to the past experiences of the business by studying the financial statements of the business. Illustration No. 31 on page 65 shows the first page of a typical four-page form that a business must submit to a bank in applying for a loan.

Financial Advice. Most bankers have the problem of advising those who apply for credit. This advice must be given to individuals as well as to business owners. A wise banker will not make a loan to an individual if he believes that the loan cannot be repaid or that to repay the loan would place an undesirable hardship upon the borrower. Regardless of the character of the borrower or the security that would be pledged to the bank, the making of a loan in such a case might result in financial disaster.

Protection of the Borrower and the Depositor. Many banks have a trained personnel to do nothing but decide upon the desirability of making loans to individuals and to business concerns. These persons analyze the assets, the liabilities, the financial condition, the business methods, and the future possibilities of the individual or the business requesting a loan. This analysis often enables the bank to be of service to the borrower by suggesting improvements in financial organization or changes in purchasing and production plans.

Obviously, the bank wants to protect its borrowers as well as its depositors. Its borrowers provide the source of its income, while its depositors provide the means of its income. Hence it is to the advantage of the bank to conduct its affairs so as to ensure the prosperity of the depositor, the borrower, and the bank.

Regulations on Loans. State and Federal laws limit banks, according to their classification, in the types of loans that they can make. State banks are governed by the laws of their respective states. Members of the Federal Reserve System are governed by the following restrictions:

(a) The Federal Reserve Board has power to fix the percentage of loans that the banks in any Federal reserve district can make with bonds and stocks as collateral. No member of a Federal Reserve System may, however, lend to any person an amount in excess of 10 per cent of its capital and surplus.

(b) Member banks may make loans secured by staple agricultural products, goods, wares, or merchandise.

(c) Loans secured by direct obligations of the United States, such as Government notes or bonds, may be made to individuals, partnerships, or corporations.

(d) No member bank is permitted to lend money to an affiliated organization or to individuals in an affiliated organization. It may not accept securities of an affiliated organization as collateral for a loan if the loan exceeds 10 per cent of its capital and surplus.

(e) Loans can be made on improved real estate, including improved farm land. Such a loan must not, however, exceed 50 per cent of the actual value of the real estate offered for security and must not extend for a period greater than five years. Only a limited amount of the funds of a member bank may be used for loans on real estate.

Types of Loans. A loan may be classified according to the basis on which it is made. It may be based (a) on confidence, (b) on security, or collateral, or (c) on the indorsement of another person. If the conditions for a loan seem unusually favorable, the banker may not require security, but will rely upon the borrower's character and capacity to pay. Conservative commercial banks, however, usually require security in some form of property. This property can be taken over and sold by the bank to protect

Financial Statement

To THE FIFTH THIRD UNION TRUST CO.

INDIVIDUAL
Manufacturing or Mercantile Lines

Name B. D. Phillips

Business Manufacturing - Machine Tools

Location Baltimore, Maryland Branches None

For the purpose of procuring credit, or extension of existing credit, or any other accommodations or benefits, which may be requested, direct or otherwise, from you from time to time, I furnish the following as being a true and correct statement of my financial condition on date named below, and of all facts herein set forth, and hereby agree to notify you immediately, either verbally or in writing, of any materially unfavorable change in my financial condition; in the absence of such notice, this to be considered as a continuing statement.

Fill all blanks, writing "NO" or "NONE" where necessary to complete information.

CONDITION AT CLOSE OF BUSINESS December 30, 1940

ASSETS	DOLLARS		CENTS
Cash:			
On Hand		100	00
In bank	8	900	00
Due from Customers:			
Open Accounts—good	12	550	00
Notes Receivable—good	10	500	00
Trade Acceptances—good	6	950	00
Merchandise:			
Finished (Cost or Market—whichever is lower)	34	000	00
Unfinished	20	000	00
Raw (Cost or Market—whichever is lower)	36	850	00
Merchandise paid for in advance			
U. S. Government Securities: (itemize—Page 3)			
Other Active Assets (itemize—Page 3)			
TOTAL QUICK ASSETS	129	850	00
Due from Controlled or Allied Concerns:			
For Merchandise			
For Advances			
Other Stocks, Bonds & Investments (itemize—Page 3)			
Real Estate used in operations (itemize—Page 3)			
Land (how valued—Cost or ~~Appraised~~)	40	000	00
Buildings (how valued—Cost or ~~Appraised~~) (list mortgages, if any, in liabilities)	80	000	00
Land & Buildings not used in operations (itemize Page 3)			
Machinery & Equipment	120	000	00
Furniture & Fixtures	16	000	00
Horses, Wagons & Automobiles	12	000	00
Miscellaneous Materials, Supplies, etc.	5	680	00
Notes & Accounts past due or extended			
Prepaid Expenses—Interest, Insurance, Rent, etc.	1	200	00
Cash Surrender Value Life Insurance			
Goodwill, Patents, Trade Marks, etc.	16	000	00
Other Assets (itemize)			
TOTAL	420	730	00

LIABILITIES	DOLLARS		CENTS
Notes Payable			
To Bank—secured			
—unsecured			
For Merchandise—not due	12	000	00
—past due			
Open Accounts Payable:			
For Merchandise—not due	33	000	00
—past due			
Due Controlled or Allied Concerns			
Due Others			
Deposits of Money or other Trust Funds			
Provision for Federal Taxes	2	900	00
Accrued Expenses—Interest, Taxes, etc.	3	030	00
Provision for estimated loss on Receivables			
Mortgages maturing within 12 months			
Any other Quick Liabilities (itemize)			
TOTAL QUICK LIABILITIES	50	930	00
Mortgages or Liens on Real Estate (when due)	80	000	00
Long Term Notes (when due)			
Chattel Mortgages			
Any other Liabilities (itemize)			
TOTAL LIABILITIES	130	930	00
Reserves (itemize)			
Bad Debts	1	840	00
Buildings	16	000	00
Machinery & Equipment	46	000	00
Furniture & Fixtures	6	100	00
Automobiles	4	400	00
NET WORTH (see Page 2)	215	460	00
TOTAL	420	730	00

Illustration No. 31—The First Page of an Application for a Loan

itself in case the borrower cannot pay the loan when it is due. In a sense, an indorsement is a form of security. If a person indorses a note in order to aid a borrower to obtain money, the indorser is held responsible for the payment of the note in case the borrower is unable to pay.

Warehouse receipts and mortgages on real property are forms of securities. For instance, a person who wishes to borrow from a bank may have placed one thousand bushels of wheat in a grain elevator. If he has receipts for this wheat, he may turn these receipts over to a bank, thus transferring to the bank the right of ownership of the wheat in case he does not pay his loan when it becomes due. Likewise, a person may borrow money on real estate and grant a mortgage that gives the lender the right to take possession of the real estate if the loan is not paid.

Personal Loans. Many banks, including those which are members of the Federal Reserve System, have installed so-called personal loan departments. These departments operate in some respects like other small-loan lending agencies.

15-1

$ 150.00 PERSONAL LOAN DEPARTMENT No. ______

The FIFTH THIRD UNION TRUST Co.
CINCINNATI, OHIO

CINCINNATI, OHIO January 5, 1940.

FOR VALUE RECEIVED, WE, THE UNDERSIGNED, JOINTLY AND SEVERALLY, PROMISE TO PAY TO THE ORDER OF THE FIFTH THIRD UNION TRUST COMPANY OF CINCINNATI, OHIO, THE SUM OF

One Hundred and Fifty DOLLARS

AT ITS OFFICE IN CINCINNATI, OHIO, WITH INTEREST AT THE RATE OF EIGHT PER CENT PER ANNUM AFTER MATURITY UNTIL PAID, WAIVING PRESENTMENT, DEMAND FOR PAYMENT, PROTEST, NOTICE OF PROTEST AND NOTICE OF NON-PAYMENT OF THIS NOTE, THE FIRST OF THE UNDERSIGNED (NAMELY, THE BORROWER) HEREBY AGREEING TO PAY PROMPTLY $ 12.50 ON March 6, 19 40 AND AT REGULAR monthly (SEMI-MONTHLY OR MONTHLY) INTERVALS THEREAFTER FOR 11 INSTALLMENTS AND $ 14.50 AS THE LAST INSTALLMENT, AND THE OTHERS OF THE UNDERSIGNED JOINTLY AND SEVERALLY AGREEING TO MAKE EACH OF THE SAID PAYMENTS PROMPTLY IF THE SAID BORROWER SHOULD DEFAULT IN MAKING THE SAME. AS OFTEN AS THE MAKING OF ANY SUCH PAYMENT MAY BE DELAYED BEYOND THE DAY AS HEREIN AGREED TO BE MADE, THE UNDERSIGNED JOINTLY AND SEVERALLY PROMISE TO PAY TO THE HOLDER HEREOF AT OR BEFORE THE MATURITY OF THIS NOTE, A SUM CALCULATED AT THE RATE OF FIVE CENTS FOR EACH ONE DOLLAR OF SUCH DELAYED PAYMENT, BUT IN NO EVENT SHALL THE TOTAL CHARGE IN CONNECTION WITH ANY ONE DELAYED PAYMENT BE IN EXCESS OF FIVE DOLLARS ($5.00), AND TO MAKE SUCH PAYMENTS AS COMPENSATION FOR THE DAMAGE OCCASIONED BY SUCH DELAY.

UPON FAILURE TO MAKE ANY PAYMENT AS HEREIN AGREED, OR IN THE EVENT OF THE DEATH OF THE SAID BORROWER, OR IN CASE OF INSOLVENCY, BANKRUPTCY, OR FAILURE IN BUSINESS OF ANY OF THE UNDERSIGNED, THIS NOTE SHALL, AT THE OPTION OF ITS HOLDER, BECOME IMMEDIATELY DUE AND PAYABLE, WITHOUT DEMAND OR NOTICE. UPON THIS NOTE MATURING UNDER ANY OF ITS TERMS AND PROVISIONS, AND NOT BEING FULLY PAID AND SATISFIED ON THE DAY OF ITS MATURITY, THE TOTAL SUM THEN DUE HEREUNDER MAY FORTHWITH BE DEBITED TO ANY ACCOUNT OR ACCOUNTS MAINTAINED BY ANY OF THE UNDERSIGNED WITH THE HOLDER HEREOF, WITHOUT NOTICE TO OR FURTHER CONSENT FROM ANY OF THE UNDERSIGNED, THEY HEREBY AGREEING TO BE AND REMAIN JOINTLY AND SEVERALLY LIABLE FOR ALL INDEBTEDNESS REPRESENTED BY THIS NOTE IN EXCESS OF THE AMOUNT THEN TO THE CREDIT OF SUCH ACCOUNT OR ACCOUNTS.

EACH OF THE UNDERSIGNED HEREBY AUTHORIZES SAID TRUST COMPANY TO (1) PAY THE PROCEEDS OF THIS NOTE TO Mr. J. C. Murphy, (2) DATE THIS NOTE AS OF THE DAY WHEN THE LOAN EVIDENCED HEREBY IS MADE, (3) COMPLETE ANY BLANK SPACES IN THIS NOTE ACCORDING TO THE TERMS UPON WHICH IT GRANTS SAID LOAN, AND (4) CAUSE THE SIGNATURE OF ONE OR MORE CO-MAKERS IN ADDITION TO THE ORIGINAL NUMBER, TO BE ADDED AT ANY TIME OR TIMES HERETO, AND TO DO SO WITH OR WITHOUT NOTICE TO ANY OF THE UNDERSIGNED, WHO HEREBY CONSENT THERETO AND ACKNOWLEDGE THAT SUCH MAY BE DONE WITH OUT AFFECTING THE JOINT AND SEVERAL OBLIGATION OF EACH OF THE UNDERSIGNED, AS HEREINBEFORE SET FORTH.

UNDERSIGNED, JOINTLY AND SEVERALLY, HEREBY IRREVOCABLY AUTHORIZE ANY ATTORNEY AT LAW, CLERK OF COURT OR PROTHONOTARY TO APPEAR FOR UNDERSIGNED, JOINTLY OR SEVERALLY, BEFORE ANY JUSTICE OF THE PEACE, OR IN ANY COURT OF RECORD, STATE OR FEDERAL, IN THE UNITED STATES OF AMERICA, IN TERM TIME OR VACATION, AND TO WAIVE ISSUE AND SERVICE OF PROCESS AND CONFESS JUDGMENT AGAINST THE UNDERSIGNED, JOINTLY OR SEVERALLY, IN FAVOR OF THE HOLDER HEREOF, FOR SUCH AMOUNT AS MAY APPEAR TO BE UNPAID HEREON, AFTER MATURITY, TOGETHER WITH INTEREST, AND TO RELEASE ALL ERRORS AND WAIVE ALL RIGHT OF APPEAL.

ADDRESSES (GIVE COMPLETE ADDRESS)	SIGNATURES (WRITE IN FULL AND IN INK)
528 Wakefield Drive, Cincinnati, Ohio	1. J. C. Murphy — BORROWER
528 Wakefield Drive, Cincinnati, Ohio	2. Catherine Murphy — CO-MAKER—WIFE OR HUSBAND OF BORROWER
2564 Williams Street, Norwood, Ohio	3. Carl A. Frederick — CO-MAKER
3151 Reading Road, Cincinnati, Ohio	4. Clifford Edwards — CO-MAKER

Illustration No. 32—A Personal Loan Agreement

For example, loans are made to individuals for the purchase of automobiles and household equipment. The bank requires the borrower to sign a chattel mortgage on the property. The chattel mortgage is held as security until the loan is repaid.

Interest Rates. Interest rates vary according to the states and the types of lending institutions. Statutes in most states govern the interest rates of such institutions as pawnshops and loan associations. The state banking laws and the rules of the Federal Reserve System govern largely the interest rates of banks, although the demand for and the supply of money have important influences on interest rates on bank loans.

In nearly every state there is a *legal rate* and a *contract rate* of interest. In the absence of any agreement with regard to the interest rate, a bank may charge the legal

STATES AND TERRITORIES	LEGAL RATE (PER CENT)	CONTRACT RATE (PER CENT)	STATES AND TERRITORIES	LEGAL RATE (PER CENT)	CONTRACT RATE (PER CENT)
Alabama	6	8	Montana	6	10
Alaska	6	10	Nebraska	6	9
Arizona	6	8	Nevada	7	12
Arkansas	6	10	New Hampshire	6	Any rate
California	7	10	New Jersey	6	6
Colorado	6	Any rate[1]	New Mexico	6	10[2]
Connecticut	6	12	New York	6	6
Delaware	6	6	North Carolina	6	6
District of Columbia	6	8	North Dakota	4	7
Florida	8	10	Ohio	6	8
Georgia	7	8	Oklahoma	6	10
Hawaii	6	12	Oregon	6	10
Idaho	6	8	Pennsylvania	6	6
Illinois	5	7	Puerto Rico	6	9[3]
Indiana	6	8	Rhode Island	6	30
Iowa	5	7	South Carolina	6	7
Kansas	6	10	South Dakota	6	8
Kentucky	6	6	Tennessee	6	6
Louisiana	5	8	Texas	6	10
Maine	6	Any rate	Utah	6	10
Maryland	6	6	Vermont	6	6
Massachusetts	6	Any rate	Virginia	6	6
Michigan	5	7	Washington	6	12
Minnesota	6	8	West Virginia	6	6
Mississippi	6	8	Wisconsin	6	10
Missouri	6	8	Wyoming	7	10

[1] When any rate is permitted for contracts, there usually is a limit for a small loan of approximately $300 or less, although this limit may be as high as 3 per cent a month.

[2] When a loan is unsecured by collateral, the contract rate may be 12 per cent.

[3] When the amount is more than $3,000, the maximum contract rate is 8 per cent.

Illustration No. 33—Legal and Contract Rates of Interest

rate. A special agreement may be made to permit a bank to charge the contract rate, which is limited in most states.

The table in Illustration No. 33 shows the maximum interest rates of the various states and territories. These rates are determined by law and are changed from time to time. If an individual wants to know the maximum rates in his state, he should consult the latest law.

Paying Interest. When a short-term loan is obtained from a banking institution, the interest is usually deducted in advance. The amount that is credited to the borrower's account is therefore the amount of the loan less the interest charged. For example, on a loan of $5,000 for ninety days at 6 per cent interest, there would be a deduction of $75. The borrower would therefore have $4,925 credited to his account, or would receive that amount in the form of a check.

Paying a Loan. Bankers have found that borrowers will pay long-time obligations with less difficulty if some provision is made for paying off the loan at intervals instead of in one amount at the expiration of the loan period. If the average borrower is given the privilege of waiting until a specified date to pay the entire amount, he may carelessly or intentionally utilize his income for other purposes and not have available the proper amount of money when the loan becomes due. The property that has been given as security may by that time have decreased in value so much that the bank will not have adequate protection on its loan. The bank may insist upon additional security.

There is a tendency during periods of inflation to borrow money without any definite intention of repaying it, the idea being to renew the loan constantly and to pay merely interest without making payments on the principal. Borrowing without a definite intention and a specific plan of paying off the principal is a dangerous practice for both the borrower and the lender. It will eventually result in catastrophe for those involved. The borrower will be forced into bankruptcy; the bank will be unable to collect the debt and may consequently be unable to pay depositors.

When to Borrow. Dealings with a competent bank should be frank. The intention of the borrower should be to reveal his status and limitations so that a definite agreement can be reached as to what can be done and what will be done. The only way for a bank to determine the desirability of making a loan is for the intended borrower to answer all questions fully and to provide all the financial information that is requested. The best advice to the borrower is (a) to borrow only when a loan is needed for definite advancement that can be foreseen, (b) not to overborrow, and (c) to borrow only when there can be a definite plan of repayment.

Borrowing and lending are business transactions in the same way as buying and selling. A request for a loan is not asking a favor; it is a request to make a legitimate business transaction. Of course, it is not wise to borrow in order to obtain goods that depreciate readily or are to be consumed before the loan will be paid; but it is good business to borrow money with which to buy or build a home, to buy substantial household furniture and equipment, to repair or improve property, to educate members of the family, or to go into business, provided there exists some definite and plausible means of repaying the loan.

Paying Off Old Debts. As the result of a study made by it, the Public Affairs Committee has laid down certain recommendations with regard to borrowing money and to paying off old debts. The clearing up of overdue debts is a difficult task. The sooner it is faced, however, the better. The following plan [1] is recommended as a sensible solution of this problem:

(a) Leave out all bills, if any, that are not just claims, and refuse to pay illegal lenders. If any creditor who is thus ignored makes trouble, consult your lawyer. If you cannot afford to pay a lawyer, consult a legal aid society.

(b) Make a list of the remaining bills that are due and those that are soon to become due.

(c) Pare your expenses to the bone. If taking that action means moving to a cheaper residence or giving

[1] From LeBaron R. Foster, *Credit for Consumers,* The Public Affairs Committee, Inc., New York City.

up your car, better do it now, deliberately, than be forced to do it later. Now compare your income with your expenses. Have you enough left to pay your debts in a few months? If you have, make out an exact dollars-and-cents plan for paying each creditor a share on each payday. Show the plan to all creditors who are demanding immediate payment. If the plan is practicable, usually all creditors will co-operate.

(d) You may find that, because an important creditor refuses to wait or because your debts are too large, your self-made plan does not work. In that case a loan may help. Although the loan charges will add to your burden, you can reduce the size of the payments by spreading them over ten months, twelve months, or, in the case of some lenders, as much as twenty months. Often lenders will suggest ways to cut expenses and will assist borrowers in budgeting. In your clean-up plan be sure to take all debts into account.

(e) If there is no reasonable prospect of getting out of debt through borrowing, do not borrow even though you can find a willing lender. Use the new machinery that the Federal Bankruptcy Act of 1938 (discussed in Chapter IX) provides for wage-earners with incomes of not more than thirty-six hundred dollars. Without going through bankruptcy and without hiring a lawyer, you may submit a repayment plan to a Federal court, for approval by the court and a majority of your creditors. If it is found necessary, your debts may be scaled down. While you are making payments under the plan, the court will protect your property and your wages against attachment.

(f) Bankruptcy is the last resort. It may happen, although very rarely, that important creditors will refuse to co-operate, or that the court finds it impossible to arrange a plan of payment because the debts are so large. If such is the case, bankruptcy may be necessary to free your wages and your job from the persecution of creditors. Beware, however, of shyster lawyers who seek clients in the field of bankruptcy.

Obligations of Depositors. When a bank assumes obligations and performs services for depositors, it also has a right to impose some obligations on the depositors. It has a right to ask that the checkbook and the bankbook be kept in balance; that an accurate record of each check be entered on a check stub; and that a sufficient balance be kept in the bank account to prevent overdrawing and to compensate the bank for the service it gives. If a sufficient balance is not kept in the account, the bank has a right to charge for the service of the checking account.

As a matter of good business, all canceled checks should be kept for at least a year in an accessible place or on file with bills that have been paid. Important checks should be kept indefinitely.

A bank statement should be obtained monthly. It should any misunderstanding and to be sure that the bank account be reconciled immediately with the checkbook to prevent does not become overdrawn.

A bank is a service agent for not only many individuals and businesses but also the entire community. It should not be imposed upon or be expected to violate rules and show preference. The bank must follow the same policy with everyone for the protection of all depositors and all members of the community.

TEXTBOOK QUESTIONS

1. Is there enough cash in the United States to pay in cash the amount represented by bank deposits?
2. Why is it possible for banks to lend more money than they have cash on hand?
3. Even though deposits are insured, why is it important to investigate the honesty and integrity of bankers with whom one deals?
4. What determines whether a bank is in a good position to pay depositors on demand?
5. In the selection of a bank why is it important to distinguish between the various types of banks?
6. What are some of the services that banks offer in addition to checking accounts and savings accounts?
7. Name four advantages of a checking account.

8. Why is it sometimes necessary for a bank to charge for the facilities of a checking account?
9. What is a certified check?
10. What is a bank draft?
11. What is the distinction between a savings account and a checking account?
12. When money is left with a bank under a trust agreement, does the bank guarantee a definite income from the trust fund?
13. Why is it not desirable for a man and his wife to have their safe-deposit box registered in both names?
14. From what source does a bank obtain most of its income?
15. Why is a banker justified in refusing to make a loan to a person who cannot repay the loan under some definite plan?
16. In what way can banking experts be of assistance to people who apply for loans?
17. (a) What is meant by security for a loan? (b) Are loans ever made without security?
18. What are some types of security for loans?
19. When money is borrowed from a bank, is interest usually paid when the loan is repaid or at the time the money is borrowed?
20. Why do bankers find it desirable to have a long-term loan paid in installments instead of in one amount at the expiration of the loan period?
21. If you use the services of a bank as a depositor, what are some of your obligations to the bank?

DISCUSSION QUESTIONS

1. When business conditions are apparently bad, why is it absurd for people to become afraid and rush to their banks in order to withdraw their funds?
2. Some people who oppose the insurance of bank deposits assert that such a practice will tend to make depositors and bankers careless. (a) In what way do you think this assertion may be true? (b) If you believe that it is true, how can such a tendency be avoided?
3. Do you believe that deposit insurance justifies "shutting your eyes" in choosing a bank?
4. Why do some large companies in remote parts of the United States borrow from banks in New York?
5. Some people assert that we have been following the wrong policy with regard to banking. They believe that we should pay for the services of checking accounts and that the payment for such services should include the cost of 100 per cent insurance on deposits. Do you agree? State your views.

6. What are the essential differences between a certified check and a bank draft?
7. If the interest rate on savings deposits in banks drops from 3 per cent to 2 per cent, what do you think such a decrease indicates as to the condition of banks?
8. Why are funds frequently left in trust with a bank instead of in the care of the widow or the children?
9. Would you recommend putting cash in a safe-deposit box? Why, or why not? Discuss.
10. "A bank makes money because of the service it renders." Do you agree? Discuss this statement.
11. During financial depressions, prospective borrowers who are refused loans by banks criticize the latter because they believe the banks do not want to lend money. What do you think may cause banks to refuse to lend in such times? Is the reason justifiable?
12. A man who is known to be successful and thoroughly honorable feels highly insulted when he applies for a loan at a bank and is asked for considerable information on his assets, debts, and income. He believes that the bank has no right to this confidential information. What is your opinion? Discuss the situation.
13. Some people, because of mistakes and carelessness in keeping the records of the balances in their checking accounts, overdraw their accounts. In many states there are laws for the punishment of people who overdraw their accounts. Do you believe that these laws are justified?
14. Why is it a matter of good business to keep all canceled checks for at least a year?

Section II

Obtaining Small Loans; Negotiable Instruments

Financial Advice. The best place to seek financial advice and to obtain loans is always the banking institution with which contacts have already been established. If credit relations have been established with a bank, a loan should be solicited from this source. Large commercial banks that make a practice of lending money to businesses are, however, sometimes not interested in making small loans to individuals. In obtaining a loan, a person should consider the obligation assumed as well as the fact that he wants the loan. No loan should be sought unless it can be repaid under a definite plan.

The better business bureaus and state authorities in all parts of the country have been co-operating to eliminate "loan sharks." A loan shark is a person or an institution that, by charging an exorbitant rate of interest, usually on small loans, takes advantage of inexperienced, hard-pressed people of low incomes who ordinarily do not have security or any other means of borrowing from a bank. The best protection against loan sharks is to obtain as much information as possible before seeking a loan. If a person has already let himself get into the clutches of a loan shark, however, he should communicate with a better business bureau, the district attorney, the attorney general of the state in which he lives, the secretary of state, the superintendent of banks, or the supervisor of loan agencies, if there is one in the state.

Borrowing on Insurance Policies. Most insurance policies have a cash value and a loan value. These values are usually the same. An insurance policy can be used as the basis of obtaining a loan, usually at from 4 to 6 per cent interest. The policy must be given to the insurance company as security, and the loan can be repaid when it is convenient. If death occurs before the loan is repaid, the amount of it is deducted from the payment due the beneficiary.

The amount that can be borrowed on an insurance policy will depend entirely on the face of the policy and the length of time the policy has been in force. A bank will occasionally lend on an insurance policy in the same way as an insurance company.

Borrowing on Bonds and Stocks. Bonds and stocks are used frequently as collateral security for loans. Loans of this type can usually be obtained from banks except some of the large commercial banks that are interested mainly in making loans for business purposes.

Any stock or any bond that is traded on recognized exchanges will serve as collateral, provided there is evidence to indicate that the stock or the bond is good. A bank will ordinarily lend about 50 per cent of the value of a good stock or a good bond. Suppose, for example, that a loan of $200 is required for three months and that the bank charges 6 per cent interest. Good bonds or stocks with a market value of approximately $400 may be used as security. In making the loan, the bank will deduct the interest in advance as follows:

Amount given to borrower	$197.00
6 per cent interest in advance for three months	3.00
Amount to be paid bank in three months	$200.00

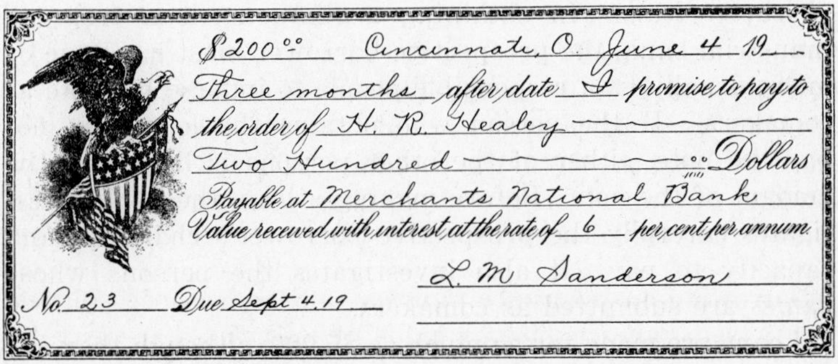
$200.00 Cincinnati, O. June 4 19
Three months after date I promise to pay to
the order of H. R. Healey
Two Hundred 00/100 Dollars
Payable at Merchants National Bank
Value received with interest at the rate of 6 per cent per annum.
L. M. Sanderson
No. 23 Due Sept 4, 19

Illustration No. 34—An Ordinary Note

In this example the interest charge is actually more than 6 per cent, for $3 is being charged for using $197 for three months. If the loan is not repaid in three months, the bank has the privilege of selling the securities to obtain the $200. Suppose that, at the end of three months, this loan has not been repaid. It may be possible for the borrower to have the loan renewed by paying $3 interest in advance and by signing a new note to take the place of the old one. Or he may pay $100 and sign a new note for $100 after paying $1.50 interest in advance on the new loan.

If the securities are sold to protect the bank, more or less than the amount of the loan may be obtained, depending upon the fluctuation of the market rate of the securities. Suppose that in the preceding example nothing is paid on the loan and the bank sells the securities at the end of the three months for $300. The additional $100 will go to the person who obtained the loan. If the securities were sold for only $175, however, the person who obtained the loan would still owe the bank $25.

Industrial Banks. In more than half of the states, banks commonly referred to as *industrial banks* have been organized. In many states they are better known under the name of *Morris Plan banks.* Such banks are regulated by the laws of the states in which they are located. The methods of operating such banks and the laws governing their operations are similar in the various states.

Industrial banks operate largely on the basis of making *character loans.* In obtaining a character loan from an industrial bank, the prospective borrower must have one or more, usually two, responsible people to indorse his note as comakers. If the person who obtains the loan does not pay the note, either of the other persons is liable for the amount of the note. Before making a loan, the bank investigates carefully the prospective borrower's character and capacity to pay. It also investigates the persons whose names are submitted as comakers.

Loans are made for as much as $5,000, although they are usually smaller. They ordinarily extend for one year, but they may cover a shorter or a longer period of time. Some banks accept mortgages on homes and on other property as a guarantee of the payment of loans.

The bank deducts interest in advance and usually charges a service fee. The following table shows the proceeds of a typical loan:

Amount of cash received by borrower	$185.00
6 per cent interest for one year	12.00
Service charge	3.00
Amount of loan	$200.00

Repayment of a loan must be made weekly or monthly. The interest is charged in advance on the total amount of the loan. The actual rate of interest on the loan mentioned

APPLICATION FOR LOAN

January 15, 1940

To Perpetual Building and Loan Association

I/~~we~~ hereby apply for a Loan for which purpose I/~~we~~ submit the following information:

Name Carol Ann Quinn Res. Phone Cherry 1780

Residence 1620 Sidney Lane, Cincinnati, Ohio

Employed by Gem Electric Company Bus. Phone Main 8834
(If in business for yourself, so state)

I refer you to Arthur Kees in the above concern. His Position Manager

Type of Business Electric Supplies

Position Held Saleslady No. of Years 5

Amount Desired $ 150.00 Date Required February 1

Purpose of Loan To meet personal obligations

Plan for Payment $3.00 per week

Security Offered

Endorsers (Names and Addresses) Miss Louise Teaney, 315 Wabash Avenue, Cincinnati, Ohio
Miss Rose Mary Patcher, 2937 Glenway, Cincinnati, Ohio

Income,—Salary $ 21.00 Per week Other Income None

Rent Paid per Month $ 20.00 Obligated for Monthly Installments on Real Estate $

Obligated for Monthly Installments on other than Real Estate $

Overdue Debts other than on Real Estate $ Kind

Married or Single Single Number of Dependents One Full Name of Husband or Wife

Life Insurance and Annuities One life insurance policy.

Loans on Policies $ Beneficiary Mother

Securities Owned

REAL ESTATE

Description

Location

Deed in Name of

Occupied by me By Tenants Total Rent Received per Month $

Mortgaged: First $ Second $ Assessed Value $

Payments Overdue: Principal $ Interest $ Taxes $ for years

Other Debts or Obligations on Real Estate $ Kind

Illustration No. 35—An Application for a Personal Loan

above is, however, more than 6 per cent, because the borrower obtains only $185 and must repay $200 in weekly or monthly installments. As the borrower must repay the loan in periodic installments, he will not have the use of $185 for a year.

Uniform Small-Loan Law. Individuals and businesses that have been accustomed to lending to the ordinary wage-earner agree that the average person of moderate means who is honestly earning a living will always pay his debts if he can and that he is thoroughly honest in his intentions. The Russell Sage Foundation, in conducting an investigation, found that there are many people who need to borrow amounts of $300 or less, but who do not have any securities that can be used as collateral to obtain such loans. Many people cannot find other persons to sign notes so that they will be able to borrow from industrial banks. Others do not care to have their friends obligated in this manner; they prefer to go to a place where money can be borrowed on a different basis.

As a result of findings of the Russell Sage Foundation, the Uniform Small-Loan Law was sponsored. It has been adopted in many states. On the basis of this law many *personal finance companies* have been organized. Several thousand are now in operation. No borrower should deal with any personal finance company that is not licensed by the state and is not under state supervision. If there is any question about a personal finance company, information can be obtained from such organizations as the better business bureau, the chamber of commerce, and the local welfare organization.

The costs of obtaining small loans of this kind are very high. The average rate allowed in most states is 3½ per cent a month on the unpaid balance of the principal, although the rate is lower in some states. The loans usually run from ten to twenty months. A loan can be obtained by giving a *chattel mortgage* on home furnishings. This type of mortgage gives the loan company permission, through legal proceedings, to obtain possession of the furnishings in case of default in payment of the loan, and to sell them

CO-MAKER'S STATEMENT

BORROWER'S LIFE WILL BE INSURED FOR BALANCE DUE ON NOTE

Please answer ALL the questions

Full name Mary Alice Gehring

Home address 2122 Rose Place Tel. East 1780

Former address 1620 Hewitt Avenue

Age 32 Married

Relation to Applicant Aunt

Living with wife or husband Ages of children

Business address 215 Race Street

Name of employer and business Mr. G. W. Arnold
Singer Company

Your position Stenographer

How long with present firm 5 years

Salary $ 25.00 per week ~~month~~

Have you any other income Amount $ per week month

From what source?

Do you own an automobile? Make

Year Value $ Mortgaged $

Location real estate owned

Title in name of

Estimated value $ Tax value $

Mortgages $ 1st $ 2nd

Held by whom?

Have you a loan now or are you a co-maker on any other loan at this bank? ✓

For whom? Amount $

Is the applicant a co-maker on a loan in your favor at any bank or loan ✓
company? No Where? Amount $

Monthly Payment Amount $

Bank references Merchants National Bank ~~Checking~~ Savings

Business references. (Give at least two):

The H. & S. Pogue Co.

The Fair Store

I have read the applicant's completed statement and am agreeable to becoming a co-maker with the applicant in signing the note. I am aware of the responsibility I will assume in signing the note, and I am also aware that you will rely on the truth of the above statement in considering the credit risk of this loan. ✓

Mary Alice Gehring

19428 BAKER SYSTEM —NEW ALBANY, IND. 15-6B **Co-maker's Signature.** ✓

Illustration No. 36—An Indorser's or Comaker's Statement

to recover the amount of the loan. Actual practice discloses, however, that licensed loan companies do not foreclose on property unless there is definite evidence of fraud or a lack of desire to pay.

Although the rate of interest on the unpaid principal of the loan is usually 3½ per cent a month, the net interest charged on the original loan amounts to less than this because of the monthly payments. The table above shows how a loan of $100 at 3½ per cent a month is repaid in one year.

MONTH	AMOUNT PAID ON LOAN	INTEREST CHARGES	TOTAL PAYMENT
1	$ 8.33	$ 3.50	$ 11.83
2	8.33	3.21	11.54
3	8.34	2.92	11.26
4	8.33	2.62	10.95
5	8.33	2.33	10.66
6	8.34	2.04	10.38
7	8.33	1.75	10.08
8	8.33	1.46	9.79
9	8.34	1.17	9.51
10	8.33	.88	9.21
11	8.33	.58	8.91
12	8.34	.29	8.63
Totals	$100.00	$22.75	$122.75

Illustration No. 37—Repaying a Small Loan

Credit Unions. Credit unions arise out of a co-operative effort of people with common interests. No one can obtain a loan from a credit union unless he is a shareholder. To become a shareholder, he must buy shares in the credit union. He usually must also pay a membership fee. The earnings of the credit union are paid as dividends to the shareholders. Some credit unions accept deposits at a specified interest rate just as savings banks do.

The shareholder of a credit union can obtain a loan in the same way that a loan is obtained from an industrial bank. Some unions permit the granting of loans on chattel mortgages and on second mortgages on real estate. The interest rate is usually about 1 per cent a month on the unpaid principal of the loan. It varies, however, in different states and is usually regulated by state laws.

Federal Credit Unions. The Federal Credit Union Act, administered by the Farm Credit Administration, provides for the establishment of co-operative thrift associations in much the same way as credit unions are organized under state laws. Membership in a Federal credit union is limited to persons having a common occupation or association, or to groups within a well-defined neighborhood, community, or rural district. Loans made by a Federal credit union must not exceed two years in length. The interest rate must not exceed 1 per cent a month on the unpaid balance, including all charges incidental to making the loan.

Pawnbrokers. In most states, pawnbrokers are licensed by the cities in which they are located. The rate of interest charged on loans obtained from pawnbrokers varies widely, but it is usually extremely high.

To obtain a loan from a pawnbroker, one must turn over personal property, such as jewelry or tools, as security. The maximum amount of the loan is usually extremely low in proportion to the value of the property; it is seldom more than 50 per cent of the appraised value. Such a loan is seldom repaid in installments. It must be repaid in full before the pledged property will be returned.

Investigate Before Borrowing. Almost everyone has occasion to borrow at some time in his life. It is desirable, however, to borrow from some organized and reputable source. The following precautions are suggested in obtaining small loans:

(a) Be sure you borrow from a company that is under state supervision. If you are in doubt, investigate.
(b) Borrow no more than is necessary.
(c) Borrow no more than you can repay according to your agreement.
(d) Be sure that you understand your obligations and the obligations of the lender.
(e) Be sure that you understand the amount of the loan, the cost of the loan, and the specific details with regard to repayment.
(f) Read the contract carefully before you sign it.
(g) Be sure that you get credit for every payment and receive a canceled contract when you have completed the payments.

Legal Aspects of Negotiable Instruments. The legal relations of borrowing and lending center largely around a *negotiable instrument.* A negotiable instrument is a written evidence of some contractual obligation and is ordinarily transferable from one person to another by indorsement. It is frequently referred to as *negotiable paper* or *commercial paper.*

The most common forms of negotiable instruments are (a) promissory notes and (b) checks. A promissory note is an unconditional written promise to pay a sum certain in money at a certain time or on demand to the bearer or the order of one who has obtained the note through legal means. The one who executes a promissory note, that is, the one who promises to pay the amount specified in the note under the terms indicated, is the *maker.* The person to whom the note is payable is known as the *payee.* A check is a written order on a bank to pay previously deposited money to a third party on demand. The person who writes the check is the *drawer.* The person to whom the check is payable is the *payee.* The bank on which the check is drawn in the *drawee.*

The maker of a note or the drawer of a check is unconditionally required to pay the amount specified. This obligation assumes, of course, that the transaction relating to the use of the instrument has been proper and legal. The drawer of a check is required to pay the amount of the check if the drawee (the bank) does not pay it, but there are certain limitations on this rule in many states.

The person who indorses a negotiable instrument and transfers it to someone else is known as the *indorser.* The person to whom he transfers the negotiable instrument is referred to as the *indorsee.*

Transfer of Negotiable Instruments. Much of our money consists in notes that circulate as money without indorsement. The promissory notes issued by individuals and businesses may also circulate without indorsement, although the person receiving such a note usually demands an indorsement.

A person who signs a negotiable instrument as an indorser is liable under varying conditions. For instance, if he indorses a note to help a friend obtain a loan from a bank, he must pay the amount of the note to the bank or to a subsequent indorser if his friend fails to pay it when it is due. The obligation of the indorser depends upon the type of indorsement used. There are five kinds of indorsements used in transferring negotiable instruments. These are as follows:

(a) *Indorsement in full.* An indorsement in full is frequently referred to as a *special indorsement.* It mentions the name of the indorsee. The indorser is liable only to the indorsee or to any person who subsequently takes title to the instrument through the indorsee.

(b) *Blank indorsement.* An indorsement in blank consists in merely the name of the indorser. A subsequent holder may add any stipulations to the indorsement that are consistent with the transfer.

(c) *Qualified indorsement.* A qualified indorsement is, as its name implies, one that limits the obligation of the indorser. Assume, for instance, that a person has a check that he wishes to transfer to another. He does not wish to assume responsibility for the payment of the check by the person who originally wrote it. He may therefore use a qualified indorsement with words such as "without recourse."

Although a person may make a qualified indorsement, he is not relieved from complete responsibility for the payment of the instrument. When a person signs a qualified indorsement, he implies or warrants (1) that the instrument is genuine and the facts stated in it are as they are represented to be, (2) that he has a good title to the instrument, (3) that all persons who have previously indorsed the instrument have been legally capable of making the indorsements, and (4) that he is not aware of any circumstances that impair the validity of the instrument.

(d) *Conditional indorsement.* A conditional indorsement is, as its name implies, one that entails an obligation only under certain specified conditions. Those conditions must be stated in the indorsement. For instance, one might indorse a note as follows: "Pay to G. O. Thomas upon delivery of a Model C mower."

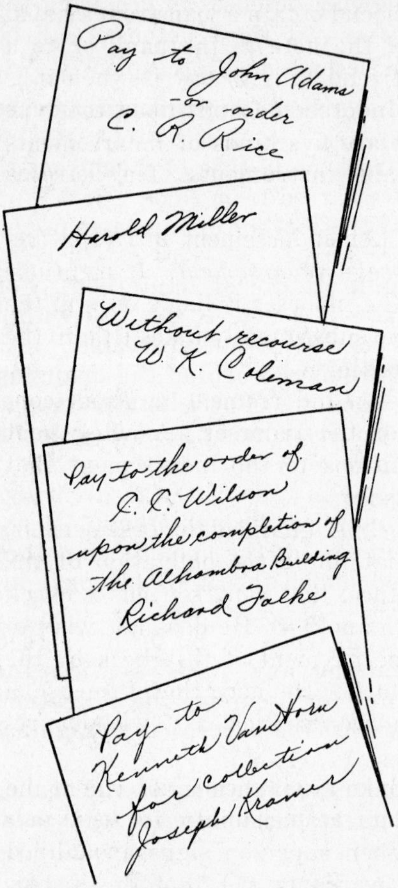

Indorsement in Full

Indorsement in Blank

Qualified Indorsement

Conditional Indorsement

Restrictive Indorsement

Illustration No. 38—Forms of Indorsement

(e) *Restrictive indorsement.* The restrictive indorsement is very common. It is one which specifies that the person to whom it is indorsed (the indorsee) may dispose of the instrument only in the manner indicated by the indorser. Checks, for instance, are frequently indorsed restrictively and mailed to a bank for deposit.

Illustration No. 38 shows examples of the various forms of indorsement.

Defenses of the Maker. If the holder of a note wishes the maker to be responsible for payment, the maker may be able to offer one of the following defenses in declaring the instrument invalid. If any one of these defenses can be proved, the instrument will become unenforceable.

(a) Lack of capacity of the maker to contract, as in case of infancy or insanity.
(b) Illegality of the contract, as in case of a contract to pay for goods that are barred from sale.
(c) Forgery, as in case of the forgery of the name of the maker.
(d) Lapse of time under a statute of limitations. For instance, in most states if a note is not paid within a certain number of years, it is unenforceable.
(e) Alteration of the instrument, such as the changing of the date or the amount. (But a holder in due course may enforce the instrument according to its original tenor.)
(f) False representation, as in case of the maker's signature having been obtained through fraud.
(g) Force or threat, as in case of the maker's signature having been obtained under threat of personal injury.
(h) Lack of consideration, as when the maker has signed a note without obtaining any goods, services, or other benefits in return for assuming the obligation. (This is a defense against the payee, but not against a holder in due course.)
(i) Previous payment of the obligation. If the maker can prove that the obligation has already been paid, he need not pay it again.

The first five defenses are real defenses against all holders of negotiable instruments, but the last four do not apply to all holders.

TEXTBOOK QUESTIONS

1. What is a credit union?
2. Distinguish a Federal credit union from other credit unions.
3. Which type of lending institution do you think is most likely to make a character loan: a commercial bank, a savings bank, an industrial bank, a pawnbroker?
4. Which loan is more economical to the borrower: a loan from a regular bank with stocks or bonds as security, or a loan from an industrial bank?

5. What is a Morris Plan bank?
6. If an insured person borrows money on an insurance policy but dies before the loan is repaid, how do these circumstances affect the proceeds of the insurance?
7. Who is the comaker of a note used in borrowing from a Morris Plan bank?
8. If a person has no collateral security or insurance that could be used in obtaining a loan, and cannot find anyone to sign a note as a comaker, what are some of his other choices in obtaining a loan?
9. (a) What is the average interest rate charged on loans under the Uniform Small-Loan Law? (b) How does this rate compare with the rates charged by regular banks?
10. In the selection of a personal finance company from which you want to obtain a loan, what factors should you investigate first?
11. What is a negotiable instrument?
12. Who is the maker of a negotiable instrument?
13. In general, what is the legal obligation of a person who indorses a negotiable instrument?
14. What are the five kinds of indorsements used in transferring negotiable instruments? Explain each.

DISCUSSION QUESTIONS

1. Why should one be careful in signing a note as a comaker?
2. Why is the interest rate on a small bank loan of $100 to an individual higher than the rate on a bank loan of $50,000 to a businessman?
3. Do small loans for less than $100, extended by industrial banks and pawnshops, bear higher interest rates than larger loans extended by ordinary commercial banks?
4. What is one of the disadvantages of borrowing money on insurance?
5. What are some of the good features of borrowing on insurance?
6. Is a service charge in obtaining a loan the same as interest? Explain your answer.
7. If $1,000 is borrowed for a period of three years, which is the most advantageous plan of repayment (that is, the most economical): weekly installments, monthly installments, or payment in one amount at the end of the three years?
8. Why do you believe that it is necessary to have special small-loan laws?
9. In what way do you think borrowing is related to budgeting?
10. If you indorse a note and transfer it to someone else, why is the note your potential liability until it is paid?

PROBLEMS

1. On the basis of the following information prepare a reconciliation of his bank statement for Mr. H. L. Jones: (a) Cash balance indicated by the statement, $236.10. (b) Checks outstanding: No. 103, $10.20; No. 104, $14; No. 105, $23.10.
2. Assume that a service charge of 50 cents was made for the month. Show the reconciliation of the bank statement mentioned in Problem No. 1.
3. Assume that you obtain a loan for $300 on your insurance policy at 6 per cent interest for one year. Compute the actual rate of interest that you pay, assuming that the interest is paid in advance and that the full amount of the loan must be repaid at the end of the year.
4. On the basis of the $200 Morris Plan loan mentioned on page 77 as an example, compute the actual rate of interest that was charged (a) if the loan was repaid in one amount at the end of the year; (b) if the loan was repaid in twelve installments of $16.67 at the end of each month.
5. Mr. D. H. Collins borrowed from the Merchants' National Bank $500 on a 90-day note. The bank gave him cash for the face of the note less interest at 6 per cent for 90 days. (a) How much cash did he receive? (b) How much cash did he pay at maturity?

COMMUNITY PROBLEMS AND PROJECTS

1. From your telephone directory or from some other source of information, make a list of all the sources of small loans in your community (not including regular banks). Classify them according to the types of lending institutions discussed in this chapter.
2. Find out whether there are small-loan laws in your state or your local community, and make a study of the nominal and the actual interest rates charged by small-loan agencies. Write a report.
3. Investigate the various types of services offered by the banks in your community. Summarize these services in the form of a table, indicating what services are available in each particular institution.
4. Go to your own bank or to a bank with which you believe you would like to deal and obtain the following: (a) All forms necessary for opening a checking account. (b) A list of the regulations governing a checking account. (c) Samples of all the forms used by depositors, such as a bank statement, a bankbook, a regular check, a counter check, and a deposit slip. Make a report on the method of opening a checking account and on the regulations governing such an account.

CHAPTER IV

INVESTING YOUR MONEY

Purpose of the Chapter. A planned system of investment is the logical outcome of systematic saving. All investments should be made with, first, safety of the principal and, secondly, certainty of the income in mind. As a general principle, the safety of an investment depends upon the certainty, not the size, of the income as indicated by past and present records and future possibilities. The problem of investment is complicated because of the desire of individual investors to obtain large returns, and because of the amount of inexpert and biased information that the amateur investor usually receives. The purpose of this chapter is to state the more important principles that an individual should follow in investing his funds.

Section I

A Program for Safe Investing

Investing, Speculating, Gambling. Securities that are bought as an investment are purchased primarily with the expectation of receiving a certain, though small, income. Securities that are purchased from a speculative point of view are bought largely in the hope that the capital value will be increased. Investment usually means a long-run program, whereas speculation means a purchase in the hope of selling at an increased capital value within a short time. In both cases there are risks, to be sure, but these risks are inherent in the business process.

Gambling means taking an artificial and unnecessary risk in the hope of gain. We may, for instance, buy a lottery ticket, if and when lotteries are legal. This act is pure gambling because lotteries perform no useful economic function. Investment and speculation both serve functions in the business and economic world. Gambling may be, though socially and morally questionable, a form of amusement for some people.

Who Should Invest? There is a definite distinction between saving and investing. Saving refers to the accumulation of earnings. It should therefore be distinguished from investing in some type of security, real estate, or other income-producing property. Saving must precede investing. The average person must deposit small amounts in a savings account regularly in order to accumulate enough to make an investment in a security or other type of property.

No one with only a few hundred dollars in a savings account should withdraw the sum for investment. Furthermore, a person who is inadequately insured or who is paying rent instead of owning a home takes an unnecessary risk when he uses his money for an investment. Even buying a perfectly safe bond is an unwise investment for him under the circumstances. If the money is needed suddenly, he may be forced to sell the bond at a discount and will also have to pay a broker's commission.

Many successful businessmen and bankers will agree that the first one thousand dollars that is accumulated should be invested conservatively so that the money will be readily available, even though it may earn only a modest income. Many financial advisers recommend that it be placed in a savings bank or invested in government bonds. The effect of economic conditions on the soundness of savings institutions and on the stability of governments will, however, have an important bearing upon the selection of a sound means of saving. The next one thousand dollars should go toward providing a home. From then on investing in securities can begin.

Simple Investment Program. The Public Education Commission of the American Bankers Association recommends the following financial program for persons of small means:

First. Deposit money regularly in some amount in a savings account. This account will make it possible to meet emergencies and to accumulate funds for later investment.

Second. Buy life insurance. This form of investment offers protection to dependents—protection that the person of moderate means usually cannot provide in any other manner.

Third. Buy a home as soon as possible. Home ownership has a stabilizing influence that leads to greater contentment and to a larger measure of financial independence.

Fourth. Buy good bonds and sound stocks in established companies with a proved record of earnings and good management.

Types of Securities for Investment. Assume that a man has accumulated a reasonably adequate savings fund that will be immediately accessible in case of emergency, has obtained adequate insurance protection, and has provided a home for his family. He now wishes to make an investment. The types of securities suitable for this purpose are listed below in the order of their preference.

(a) High-class bonds of the United States Government, of states, and of municipalities
(b) Preferred stocks of the highest class
(c) Common stocks of the highest class

Some financial advisers with good reputations do not recommend the purchasing of preferred stocks. They contend that, if a person wishes to take the risk of buying a stock, he should buy a common stock with greater potential earning power. The argument of these financial advisers is that, if a common stock becomes worthless, the preferred stock of the same company will probably also become worthless.

Any bonds, preferred stock, or common stock should be bought upon the basis of the past record, the present conditions and earning power, and the future prospects of the issuing corporation. Regardless of the past experience of the business or other institution that issues the security, the investment will not be sound if the prospects for the future are unfavorable.

The problem of deciding what is a good security is a difficult one. This will be discussed subsequently. When se-

Better Homes and Gardens

Illustration No. 39—Buying a Home Is the Third Step in an Investment Program

curities are bought, however, they should be bought with the avowed intention of keeping them as investments.

Four Important Points. Speculations are often disguised as sound investments. Because of this fact, it is desirable for the prospective investor to rely on someone who is capable of giving sound advice. The banker in a small town may or may not be able to do so, although any banker is usually more capable than the average investor. Large banks have an expert personnel qualified to analyze securities and to give advice. Brokerage businesses have similar experts. The opinions of bankers and brokers are, however, sometimes biased by personal interest. Taking these facts into consideration, the prospective investor should investigate the following points with regard to a security:

(a) Suitability of the investment
(b) Safety of the principal
(c) Satisfactory and certain income from the investment
(d) Marketability of the security

Suitability of the Investment. A bond, a stock, a note, or a mortgage may prove to be safe as an investment, but it may not fit into the investment program of a particular person. The suitability of a certain investment is therefore important. The following are important considerations in determining the suitability:

(a) *Acceptable amount.* Bonds are usually available in denominations of one hundred, five hundred, or one thousand dollars, although the market value may vary. Sometimes a thousand-dollar bond can be purchased for five hundred dollars or less. When a bond sells far below its stated value, there is a cause for the loss in value.

Stocks may have par values from one dollar to one hundred dollars, although the market value may be widely different from the par value. No-par-value stock also has a wide price range.

The number of units of a bond or a stock to be purchased will be regulated by the amount of money that can be invested.

(b) *Diversification of the investment.* There is an old saying, "Don't put all your eggs in one basket." There is also a contradictory saying, "Put all your eggs in one basket and watch the basket."

The first rule is probably the better one for the average investor. It means that he should diversify his investment. By diversifying his investment, he diversifies his risks. If a person puts all his money into one type of security and that security decreases in value or becomes totally worthless, the loss will probably be severe. On the other hand, if a person invests his money in ten different securities and only one of them decreases in value or becomes worthless, the loss is not so severe.

Each security should be selected carefully. It is better to confine the investment to a few good securities than to purchase several questionable securities.

(c) *Period of the investment.* An investment in a bond, a mortgage, or a note continues a definite period of time before the obligation matures. For instance, a bond may mature in six months or in forty to one hundred years. If a person wants to make an investment for a long period of time without the trouble of reinvesting, he should consider the date of maturity.

(d) *Value of the security as collateral.* Frequently an investor may want to use a security as collateral in obtaining a loan. If the need for obtaining a loan is a possibility, he should buy a security that will be acceptable to a bank as collateral. Securities that do not have a ready market are not desirable as collateral.

(e) *Income periods.* Bonds have definite dates on which interest is payable. The interest may be calculated quarterly, semiannually, or annually, and the specific dates of payment are set. Stocks may have quarterly, semiannual, or annual dividend dates. The person who has a diversified investment program may want to buy securities that have interest and dividend dates that fit into the complete investment program and assure a relatively steady income.

Bonds in some cases are callable before maturity. In such a case the corporation or other institution that issued the bonds may call them in and pay the owners at a specified rate. If a person wishes to invest his money in bonds for a definite length of time without the bother of reinvesting, he will want to determine whether the bonds are callable. A good income-producing bond may soon be called in unexpectedly.

Safety of the Principal. Any good investment involves the protection of the principal. If there is any question about the safety of the principal, the investment should not be made. The following are some tests of the safety of the principal:

(a) *Ability of the management of the corporation issuing the security.* Competent management is indispensable to the success of any business. Before purchasing a stock or a bond, the investor should make certain that those who manage the business have ability. Ability should have been demonstrated through successful previous operations, through the standing of the enterprise, and through the personal records of the managers.

(b) *Reliability of the managers of the corporation and of the investment promoters.* The integrity of the managers of the business and the promoters of the sale of the security should be investigated thoroughly. No one should buy a security issued by an unknown company. The statement of an unknown person should not be accepted without investigating through a person of known integrity and ability.

(c) *Past performance of the corporation.* The past performance of the business should be measured by the assets and the earning record. The outstanding bonds and the outstanding stock should have a very conservative relation to the assets. Any well-established company with securities listed on the open market can be investigated through the stock exchanges and banks, or through such listings of securities as Poor's *Manual* and Moody's *Manual.* From these same sources information can be obtained with regard to the earning performance of the corporation.

(d) *The future earning position of the corporation.* Some investments in once well-established companies have been lost because of technical developments, changes in consumer buying habits, or loss of markets. Although there is no way of judging the future earnings of a given company except by the past performance of the company, consideration must be given to whatever will likely affect the future of the company.

Comparisons should be made between different companies. If a company has found it difficult to pay operating costs and interest on indebtedness and still have a comfortable margin for dividends, it is not advisable to purchase a bond or a stock of this company. At least there is no reason to believe that the purchase will result in a conservative investment.

Satisfactory Income from the Investment. The safety of the principal is more important than a satisfactory income. If the principal is lost, there will be no income. The following are, however, considerations with regard to the income:

(a) *Rate of return.* It should be remembered that a sound investment does not have a yield that is higher than the average rate of interest used to attract investors. A conservative rate of interest on a good bond will be determined by the conditions that exist at the time the bond is offered for sale. A high-grade bond sometimes pays no more than 2 or 3 per cent interest on the face value. If the bond sells below its face value, it may, however, pay a higher rate on the basis of its actual selling price. When the rate of return offered on a bond is ½ per cent to 2 per cent above the rate of interest on high-grade government bonds, special care should be taken in investigating the quality of the security. If some of the tests of quality cannot be met, the reason for this failure should be determined.

(b) *Guaranteed rate of return.* A bond assures a definite rate of interest. If the company fails to pay the interest, the bondholder has a legal right of action to obtain the property (or income, in the case of debenture bonds) that has been pledged by the issuer of the bonds. Preferred stock also carries a stipulated rate of dividend and has preference in the distribution of earnings to stockholders. The earnings on common stock are regulated in many ways. A corporation is not obligated to pay any established rate of dividend on such stock. There may be two or three grades of common stock, one of which has preference with regard to sharing in the profits of the company. Before buying common stock of any kind, a person should investigate the stipulations regarding dividends. As owners of stock are part owners of the company that has issued the stock, they are paid out of the earnings of the company after the bondholders and other creditors have been paid.

(c) *Regularity of the income.* Most investors are interested in having a steady and reliable income. The continuous payment of interest or dividends is therefore one of the first considerations in evaluating a security. The prospects of future income from the security can be judged on the basis of the records of past earnings of the company. In most cases it is very simple to determine whether a company has paid its interest and dividends regularly in the past. Unless the prospects of future income can be judged, the purchase of the security on the basis of the return is largely a speculation.

(d) *Margin of safety.* The margin of earnings regulates the safety of not only the income that is paid to the investor but also the principal. If past records show that the company has had difficulty in earning enough to pay interest and dividends, it is questionable whether it could pay interest and dividends under any unusual circumstances. The safety of the income is therefore questionable.

Marketability of the Security. Although an investor, in the true sense of the word, is not interested in buying a security with the thought of selling it immediately, he must give consideration to this possibility. No one can foresee every emergency that may arise.

With regard to the marketability of an investment, one may ask the question, "Is there a market?" Unless a security can be disposed of by some satisfactory means, it may have to be sold at a sacrifice in an emergency, or perhaps it cannot be sold at any price. A security that is listed on an organized exchange is usually salable. If there are no buyers who want it, however, it may prove to be an undesirable investment for a person who wants to be able to convert his investment quickly into cash. A security that is not listed on an exchange may be handled by certain exchanges and brokers without being listed. If there is no ready market for such a security, however, it is questionable whether this security should be considered as an investment. A security may meet all the regular tests of quality, but unless it is well known there may be no demand for it.

Getting Information About Investments. The main sources of information for the inexperienced investor are:

Bank	Investment services
Investment brokers	Local better business bureau
Newspapers and financial journals	Local chamber of commerce

One's banker should be the first source of information. If he is not competent to give advice, he can at least recommend someone who can give advice. He can make available certain sources of information that might not otherwise be available. For instance, he can obtain bulletins and records with regard to the earnings and the past history of a particular corporation, and can uncover additional sources of information. Experiences of the past have shown, however, that bankers who have securities for sale are no better sources of information than stockbrokers because their interest is inclined to be partial. Impartiality is important in judging the value of the information to be used as a guide in buying a security.

Long-established and reputable investment brokers are in a position to give expert advice. The prospective investor should deal only with a reputable investment broker. The reputation of the broker can be investigated through the chamber of commerce or the better business bureau.

Many newspapers and financial journals publish information with regard to investments. As this information is, however, given as an opinion, it should not be accepted as the sole means of proof.

There are several other sources of investment data. Investment services are available in the form of monthly or weekly bulletins and magazines. Some of the services are expensive; others are not. Only long-established and reputable investment services should be used. These can be investigated through the local chamber of commerce, the local better business bureau, or the investor's bank.

Personal Investigation. A prospective investor should always remember the slogan of the National Better Business Bureau: "Before you invest, investigate." This organization recommends the use of organized means of obtaining information with regard to investments. It also recommends that a prospective investor ask the following questions of the person who is attempting to sell him a security:

(a) What are the names and the addresses of your employers, and how long has your company been in business?

(b) With what bank does your company do business, and what are its other references?
(c) What was the net worth of your company on the date of organization, and what is the net worth now?
(d) What are the liabilities of the company?
(e) What are its earnings?
(f) How many times has the interest [or the dividend] on this security been earned in the past five years?
(g) Who are the officers of the company, and what is their record of business activity?
(h) What experience have these officers had in the business in which the company is engaged?
(i) Is this security accepted as collateral for loans at banks?
(j) What is the market for this security?

TEXTBOOK QUESTIONS

1. If a person has saved only a few hundred dollars, why is it unwise for him to withdraw this money from the savings institution and invest it?
2. What are the four steps in the financial program recommended by the American Bankers Association?
3. What is the general order of preference with regard to investments in a simple investing program?
4. What is the essential distinction between investing, speculating, and gambling?
5. Should the average investor rely upon his own knowledge and resources of information in selecting investments? Why?
6. What are the five points that determine whether a security is suitable for a particular investment program?
7. What are the three criteria that govern the safety of the principal of an investment?
8. What are the four factors that help to determine whether an investment will pay a satisfactory income?
9. What factor determines the marketability of a security?
10. Who has preference with regard to earnings, a common stockholder or a preferred stockholder?
11. What are some of the sources from which the inexperienced investor can obtain information on investments?
12. Through whom could you investigate the reputation of a journal that provides information about securities?
13. What are some of the questions that you have a right to ask of anyone who attempts to sell you a security?

DISCUSSION QUESTIONS

1. If a person is reasonably sure of remaining permanently in the town where he is working, do you think that the purchase of a home should come before investing? Why, or why not?
2. If a friend of yours tells you about a stock that is not paying dividends but that he has heard will soon begin to pay dividends, would the buying of this stock be a speculation, an investment, or a gamble?
3. "A bond is an investment; a stock is a speculation." Discuss this statement. Is it true or false?
4. A person wants to invest one thousand dollars for an indefinite period of time. He prefers purchasing a bond, and finally selects a good first-mortgage bond of an outstanding utilities corporation. The bond is marked "callable." Do you think this bond will be satisfactory as an investment?
5. Would you reject a stock because it is not sold actively on a market?
6. (a) If the earning records of a corporation show that the corporation earns just enough income to pay a 4 per cent dividend on the basis of the present selling price of the common stock, would you consider the purchase of such common stock as an investment or a speculation? (b) How would you consider the purchase of preferred stock of this corporation?
7. Which do you think would pay the higher rate of interest: (a) a good bond with poor marketability or (b) a good bond with good marketability? Why?
8. Do you think that the investment advice obtained from a private subscription service would be more or less valuable than the information that you could obtain from a newspaper? Explain your answer.
9. How do you think you could test the collateral value of a security?
10. A person who is earning 2 per cent interest on a savings account considers buying bonds that pay interest at a net rate of 4 per cent. Discuss the merits and the demerits of this plan.

Section II

Selecting Investments

Real Estate. No one should buy real estate unless he is prepared to spend the time and the energy required in taking care of it. In order for real estate to produce a steady income as an investment, it must be managed and preserved carefully. On the basis of its management real estate can be either a very profitable investment or a serious loss.

When real estate is purchased as an investment, the following points should be considered conservatively after the desirability of the location and the quality of the property have been determined:

(a) Can the property be rented?
(b) At what price can the property be rented?
(c) What will be the annual cost of repairs?
(d) What will be the taxes and assessments?
(e) What will be the yearly loss from depreciation?
(f) During what percentage of time will the property be vacant?
(g) What will be the approximate net earnings from the investment?

Real estate is subject to fluctuations in price. The cost of a piece of property is therefore no indication of the value. The community may change rapidly with a resulting decrease or increase in the value of the property. Because of a change in business conditions the value of the property may be raised or lowered. Because the values that arise out of changes in business conditions are temporary, they cannot be used as a permanent basis for determining the rate of income to be expected from a piece of property.

Business Enterprise. People with money are frequently tempted to buy an interest in a partnership, stock in a small corporation in which a friend is interested, or in a small closed corporation, or to lend money to a friend or a relative in business. Such investments should be made with the utmost care.

Investing in a partnership involves complicated legal responsibilities in most states. Even though one of the partners may not be actively engaged in the business, under the laws of many states, he is equally responsible with the other partners. For instance, suppose that you become a part owner of a business and allow your partner to operate it. The business fails to make a profit, and the creditors demand payment. As your partner cannot pay, the creditors demand payment from you. Under the laws of many states the creditors can attach your personal property to satisfy the debt.

Many people with experience will advocate not investing in the enterprise of a friend. The friend usually feels that he has the right to operate the business as he sees fit. He may legally have the right, but sooner or later trouble may arise.

A closed corporation is one in which the stock is owned usually by a small group of people, and sometimes by only one or two families. Those who own the greater share of the stock are generally the managers. Those who own the minority share of the stock have practically nothing to say with regard to the management, but take what dividends are allotted to them on the basis of their holdings. Those who operate the business may pay themselves large salaries and thus leave very little for distribution as dividends.

Mortgage Notes and Mortgage Bonds. Illustration No. 40 shows a mortgage note. To understand the use of a mortgage note, one must first understand a mortgage. A mortgage is a claim on real estate, personal property, or

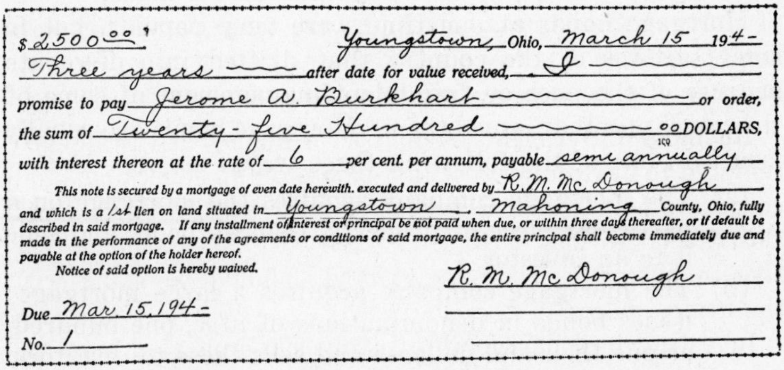
$2500.00 Youngstown, Ohio, March 15 194-
Three years after date for value received, I
promise to pay Jerome A. Burkhart or order,
the sum of Twenty-five Hundred 00/100 DOLLARS,
with interest thereon at the rate of 6 per cent. per annum, payable semi annually

This note is secured by a mortgage of even date herewith, executed and delivered by R. M. McDonough and which is a 1st lien on land situated in Youngstown, Mahoning County, Ohio, fully described in said mortgage. If any installment of interest or principal be not paid when due, or within three days thereafter, or if default be made in the performance of any of the agreements or conditions of said mortgage, the entire principal shall become immediately due and payable at the option of the holder hereof.

Notice of said option is hereby waived.

R. M. McDonough

Due Mar. 15, 194-

No. 1

Illustration No. 40—A Mortgage Note

income. The most common type of mortgage, the one issued on real estate, will be used in this discussion.

When a person borrows money on real estate, he usually signs (a) a mortgage and (b) a note or series of notes.[1] He gives both the mortgage and the note or notes to the one from whom he is borrowing the money. The mortgage is a written contract giving the lender permission to dispose of the property to satisfy the debt in case the debt is not paid. If the note or notes are not paid in accordance with the terms specified, and in accordance with local laws, the holder of the mortgage can, through legal proceedings, take possession of the property. A mortgage note usually extends for a specified length of time at a certain rate of interest.

Without some advice and assistance the ordinary individual cannot safely decide the merits of a mortgage note. Advice should be obtained from a banker, a lawyer, and a competent real-estate broker. The banker can pass upon the desirability of the investment; the lawyer, upon the legality of the transaction; and the real-estate broker, upon the merits of the property.

There are first-mortgage notes, second-mortgage notes, and third-mortgage notes. The first-mortgage note is the most common. The loan that it represents should not exceed 50 or 60 per cent of the appraised value of the property. The second-mortgage and the third-mortgage note are not so desirable as the first-mortgage note and usually pay a higher rate of interest. Mortgage notes are explained in a later chapter dealing with the purchase of a home.

Mortgage bonds at one time were very popular, but in some sections of the country they drifted into disrepute because of the poor or fraudulent management of some of the companies that issued them. Mortgage bonds are usually issued in one of the following three ways:

(a) The mortgage company acquires the mortgage on a particular piece of property, issues a bond, and sells it to an investor.

(b) The mortgage company acquires a large mortgage; issues bonds in denominations of fifty, one hundred, or one thousand dollars; and sells these to investors.

---

[1] In some states mortgage bonds are used instead of mortgage notes.

(c) The mortgages on several pieces of property are pooled. One large bond or a number of bonds in smaller denominations are issued against these mortgages and sold to investors.

The value of mortgage bonds is measured by the value of the property behind them and the ability of this property to provide funds for the payment of the interest and the principal on the due dates.

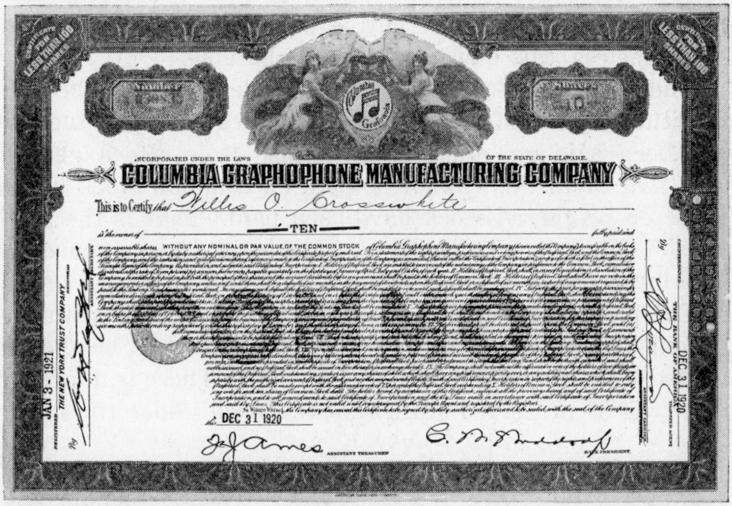

Illustration No. 41—A Common-Stock Certificate

Stocks. There are two general types of stocks, common stocks and preferred stocks. Illustration No. 41 shows a common-stock certificate, while Illustration No. 42 shows a preferred-stock certificate. There is, however, such a great variety in each class that it is difficult to distinguish between the different grades. The provisions governing a stock should be read carefully to determine one's rights and obligations. For instance, the purchase of a stock may carry with it the right to purchase at a certain price additional stock of a new issue that may be made. This right may or may not be valuable. The holders of one grade of common stock may have voting power, whereas the holders of another grade may not. The dividends on one grade of common stock may be regulated by certain conditions, whereas those on another may be regulated in a different manner. When there are various grades of a common stock, the public is usually urged to buy the least desirable class. The better classes are reserved for those who are promoting the sale of the stock.

Although, on the basis of past experience and earnings, some types of common stock are considered as good as preferred stock, the general opinion is that preferred stock represents a more conservative investment than common. Nevertheless, this question is still debatable.

Under the laws of most states, dividends cannot be paid on either preferred stock or common stock unless all interest has been paid on outstanding bonds. It is also a general rule that dividends cannot be paid on common stock unless those on preferred stock have been paid. That is the main reason that preferred stock is considered a more conservative investment.

The preferred stock of most companies carries with it a specified dividend rate, but the dividends may be discontinued if the corporate earnings dwindle. There is, however, one type of preferred stock that is issued under the agree-

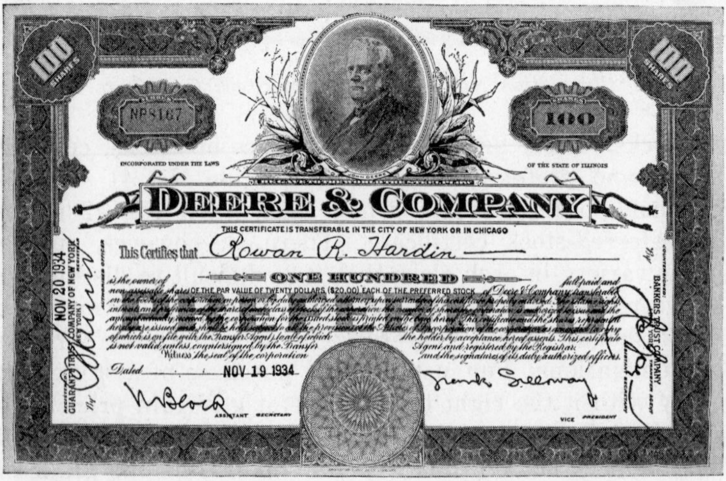

Illustration No. 42—A Preferred-Stock Certificate

ment that back dividends will be paid to the holders of the stock at the regular rate if the dividends are ever discontinued temporarily. This type of preferred stock is called *cumulative.* For example, if the dividends on a preferred stock are discontinued for one year, the preferred stockholders will receive those dividends as soon as the company earns enough profits to pay them. These back dividends must be paid before any other dividends are declared.

Some preferred stocks are classified as *participating.* In the case of such stock, if there are excess earnings after the regular dividend on preferred stock and a specified dividend on common stock have been distributed, the preferred stockholders will participate with the common stockholders in the surplus earnings. For example, the regular dividend rate on a preferred stock may be 6 per cent. If the earnings of the company, however, become large enough to pay a dividend at a specified rate on the common stock, in addition to the 6 per cent dividend on the preferred stock, the preferred stockholders will share with the common stockholders in the surplus earnings.

Stockholders are part owners of the business in which they have stock. In case the company ceases operations, the creditors have first claim on the assets. The bondholders have a right to claim the assets that are security for the bonds. The preferred stockholders have next preference, and the common stockholders have last preference.

Stocks are also designated as *par-value stocks* or *no-par-value stocks.* Par value means very little to the average investor or even to the expert, for the par value of a stock has no specific relation to the actual value. A stock may bear a par value of one hundred dollars, but may be sold for only sixty-five or seventy-five dollars. The use of a definite par value for a stock was probably intended originally to indicate the worth of the stock, but the practice of assigning par values to stocks has resulted in many abuses. For instance, there have been cases in which promoters have sold stock to unsuspecting investors on the assumption of the latter that the stock was worth approximately the par value assigned to it. Inasmuch as shares of stock represent ownership in a corporation, the stock of one person represents that part of the ownership equal to the percentage that his shares bear to the total number of shares issued. The use of no-par-value stock is intended as a means of avoiding the inference that the stock is worth a certain amount. A no-par-value stock bears no designated value. Its value, just as the value of par-value stock, is regulated by what the investing public believes the stock is worth.

Bonds. Bonds do not represent a share in the ownership of an enterprise; they are evidence of a debt owed by the enterprise. When a business or a government issues bonds, it acknowledges that it owes the holders a certain sum of money and agrees to repay the sum on a certain date and under certain conditions. It also agrees to pay interest at a specified rate and at specified intervals.

A *short-term bond* is frequently referred to as a note and serves the same purpose as a note. A *mortgage bond* usually extends for a relatively long period of time and is essentially the same as a mortgage note. The bond shown in Illustration No. 43 is a *coupon bond*. Anyone who owns a coupon bond can tear off the coupons and present them to his bank for the collection of interest. A *registered bond* is a bond that is recorded by the issuer in the name of the person to whom it has been sold. The interest on the bond will be paid only to the registered owner. From the point of view of theft a registered bond is therefore safer than a coupon bond.

When a bond is issued, the issuing corporation usually pledges some security such as specific property, mortgages on property, or the right to certain earnings. A *debenture bond* is one for which no security is pledged to guarantee the safety of the principal. A railroad may pledge some of its equipment or real estate. A municipality or a county may pledge its water system or light system.

Although certain property or rights are pledged to insure the safety of the principal of a mortgage investment, various difficulties are encountered if the bondholders are forced to take over the property or the rights in case the interest is not paid. It is therefore desirable to investigate bonds from the following points of view:

(a) Record of past earnings and likelihood of future earnings
(b) Record of past market prices of the bonds
(c) Competitive and general business conditions
(d) Marketability of the bonds

The same general investigation should be carried on in connection with bonds of a governmental unit. The taxes of a governmental unit are comparable to the earnings of

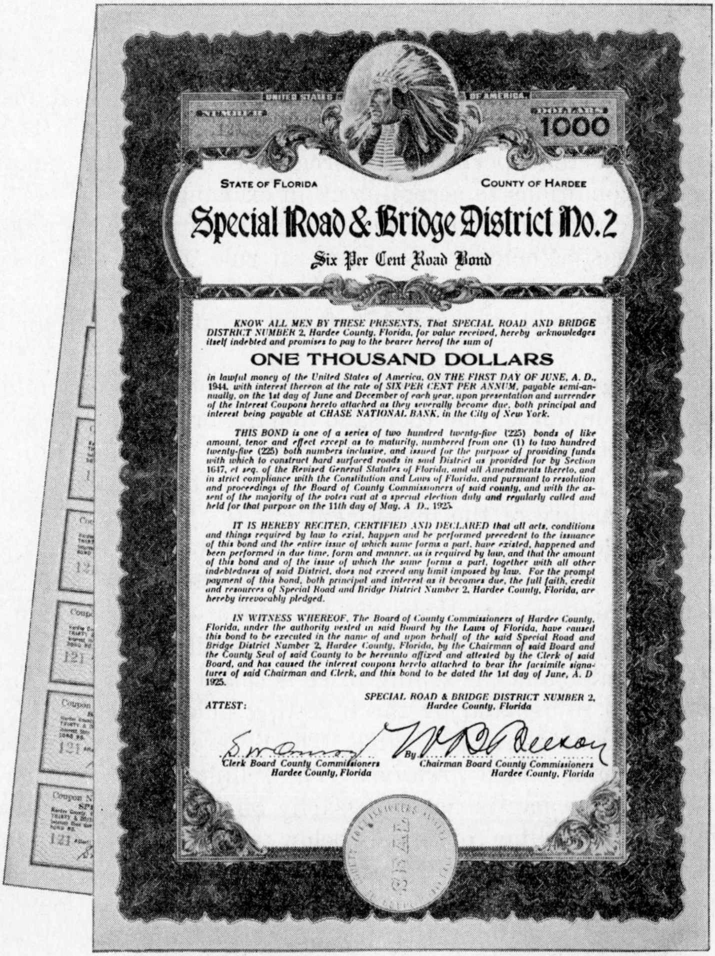
UNITED STATES OF AMERICA

1000

STATE OF FLORIDA COUNTY OF HARDEE

Special Road & Bridge District No. 2

Six Per Cent Road Bond

KNOW ALL MEN BY THESE PRESENTS, That SPECIAL ROAD AND BRIDGE DISTRICT NUMBER 2, Hardee County, Florida, for value received, hereby acknowledges itself indebted and promises to pay to the bearer hereof the sum of

ONE THOUSAND DOLLARS

in lawful money of the United States of America, ON THE FIRST DAY OF JUNE, A. D., 1944, with interest thereon at the rate of SIX PER CENT PER ANNUM, payable semi-annually, on the 1st day of June and December of each year, upon presentation and surrender of the Interest Coupons hereto attached as they severally become due, both principal and interest being payable at CHASE NATIONAL BANK, in the City of New York.

THIS BOND is one of a series of two hundred twenty-five (225) bonds of like amount, tenor and effect except as to maturity, numbered from one (1) to two hundred twenty-five (225) both numbers inclusive, and issued for the purpose of providing funds with which to construct hard surfaced roads in said District as provided for by Section 1647, et seq. of the Revised General Statutes of Florida, and all Amendments thereto, and in strict compliance with the Constitution and Laws of Florida, and pursuant to resolution and proceedings of the Board of County Commissioners of said county, and with the assent of the majority of the votes cast at a special election duly and regularly called and held for that purpose on the 11th day of May, A. D., 1925.

IT IS HEREBY RECITED, CERTIFIED AND DECLARED that all acts, conditions and things required by law to exist, happen and be performed precedent to the issuance of this bond and the entire issue of which same forms a part, have existed, happened and been performed in due time, form and manner, as is required by law, and that the amount of this bond and of the issue of which the same forms a part, together with all other indebtedness of said District, does not exceed any limit imposed by law. For the prompt payment of this bond, both principal and interest as it becomes due, the full faith, credit and resources of Special Road and Bridge District Number 2, Hardee County, Florida, are hereby irrevocably pledged.

IN WITNESS WHEREOF, The Board of County Commissioners of Hardee County, Florida, under the authority vested in said Board by the Laws of Florida, have caused this bond to be executed in the name of and upon behalf of the said Special Road and Bridge District Number 2, Hardee County, Florida, by the Chairman of said Board and the County Seal of said County to be hereunto affixed and attested by the Clerk of said Board, and has caused the interest coupons hereto attached to bear the facsimile signatures of said Chairman and Clerk, and this bond to be dated the 1st day of June, A. D 1925.

SPECIAL ROAD & BRIDGE DISTRICT NUMBER 2,
Hardee County, Florida

ATTEST:

Clerk Board County Commissioners
Hardee County, Florida

By
Chairman Board County Commissioners
Hardee County, Florida

SEAL

Illustration No. 43—A Coupon Bond

a business. The economic conditions within such a unit are comparable to the competitive conditions within an industry. Such factors have a definite effect upon the ability of the issuer of the bonds to pay interest and to repay the principal on the maturity date. State and national legislation also has a definite bearing upon the value of governmental bonds. For instance, state legislation allowing a governmental unit to postpone interest payments on bonds would have the effect of reducing the value of the bonds.

Some bonds are designated as *convertible*. There are so many possible stipulations in relation to convertible bonds that any particular bond should be investigated and studied carefully. A convertible bond is one in which there is a stipulation that permits or forces the bondholder under certain conditions to accept stock in exchange for his bond. The bondholder may therefore change in status from a creditor to a stockholder. As a general rule, bonds are more stable in price than stocks, but under certain conditions a convertible bond may not be of any greater value than a stock.

Bonds are usually sold in denominations of fifty, one hundred, five hundred, one thousand dollars, or more. Different issues bear varying rates of interest, the rates depending upon the prevailing investment rates, the time of sale, and the desirability of the investment.

The amount appearing on the face of a bond is called the *par value*. The interest is based on the par value. If, for various reasons, bonds cannot be sold at their par value, they are sold at less than par value. The difference between the par value and the selling price is called *discount*. If the bonds are in demand by the investing public, they will be sold at a rate above par value. The difference between the two values is called *premium*. The selling of bonds below par or above par is not necessarily an indication of their value. The selling of bonds below par may result from (a) unsatisfactory security that has been pledged by the issuer of the bonds, (b) an interest rate that is low in comparison with interest rates on other similar securities, or (c) unfavorable economic conditions that result in a lack of demand for bonds.

Certificates of Deposit. The certificate of deposit (Illustration No. 44) is a very simple device for investing money for a specified length of time. It may usually be obtained from a commercial bank, a savings bank, or a building and loan association. A deposit of one hundred, five hundred, or more dollars is made for six months, a year, or longer at a specified rate of interest. The institution that issues the certificate of deposit pays a good rate of interest under the assumption that it will have the use of the money for a specified length of time. The depositor gets this good

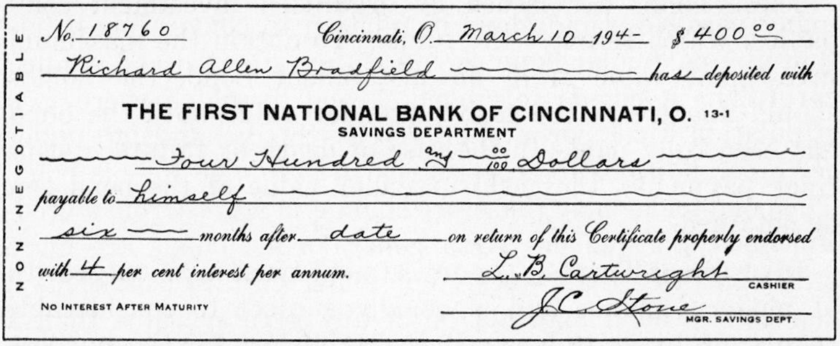
NON-NEGOTIABLE

No. 18760 Cincinnati, O. March 10 194- $400.00

Richard Allen Bradfield has deposited with

THE FIRST NATIONAL BANK OF CINCINNATI, O. 13-1

SAVINGS DEPARTMENT

Four Hundred and no/100 Dollars

payable to himself

six months after date on return of this Certificate properly endorsed

with 4 per cent interest per annum.

L. B. Cartwright CASHIER

No Interest After Maturity

J. C. Stone MGR. SAVINGS DEPT.

Illustration No. 44—A Certificate of Deposit

rate of interest by agreeing not to withdraw his money until the end of the specified time. In some cases the money may be withdrawn sooner, but in that case the depositor does not receive any interest on his money.

Some people regard a certificate of deposit as a means of saving; others regard it as an investment. It is really not a permanent means of investing, but it is frequently a means of obtaining a greater income than that which would be derived from ordinary savings. As an investment it therefore ranks between a regular savings account and a permanent investment. It is as safe as a savings account, and it will usually earn a greater rate of interest.

Installment Bonds. To the average person the problem of investing money seems to be a simple one. The difficulty arises, however, in accumulating enough money to make an investment. A program of saving must be formulated and put to work so that it will provide a consistent substantial return. The incentive to save, however, is not always sufficient. Many people need to assume some definite obligation in a saving and investing program. The installment bond has therefore become popular with many people. An installment bond is, in a sense, a savings certificate or a certificate of deposit. It is a legal obligation on the part of the issuing company to pay the holder a fixed sum of money in cash at a definite maturity date. The purchaser of the bond assumes no legal liability, but is required to make installment payments, or deposits, of a certain sum at regular stated intervals for a definite period of years.

These bonds are issued by organized investment companies, which reinvest the funds. To obtain the maximum investment value from an installment bond, the holder should not accept the cash-surrender value until the bond has been fully paid. In the case of death or failure to continue payments, the cash-surrender value of the bond can be obtained.

Investment Trusts. The investment trust is an outgrowth of modern finance and is usually subject to considerable regulation by state laws. It is established for the purpose of accepting funds and reinvesting them in a variety of securities. Thus small sums are combined and used to purchase business and governmental securities of a wide diversification.

The investment trust, if operated honestly and efficiently, has two great advantages for the small investor. These are:

(a) Wide diversification of the investment
(b) Expert analysis in the purchase of securities

The person with a small sum of money to invest cannot buy securities in any great number of companies and usually cannot obtain satisfactory expert advice. An investment in a good investment trust is therefore usually more desirable for him than an attempt to invest money on the basis of his personal opinion.

It is especially important to investigate the investment trust in which one is interested. Although investment trusts are fundamentally excellent outlets for the small investor's funds, there have been many badly managed investment trusts. It is therefore important to get unbiased information on the character, the history, and the management of the trust in which one is considering an investment.

First-Class Investments. A study of the preceding part of this chapter should lead to the reasonable conclusion that the following represent the most conservative investments:

(a) United States Government bonds
(g) Bonds of Federal organizations, such as farm-loan banks
(c) Municipal bonds of the highest grade
(d) Conservative industrial bonds
(e) First mortgages of the highest grade, covering not more than 60 per cent of the actual value of the property
(f) Preferred stocks of the highest grade

No one should invest in even the highest grade of security until a reasonable reserve for emergencies has been set aside in some form of savings account. No investment should be considered to be in the highest class if it yields more than a normal rate of interest. An investment also should be salable at a price that is approximately the same as the original purchase price. The average investor is not in a position to judge the worth of most industrial securities. It is therefore wise for him to consult an established bank or a reputable investment company.

Second-Class Investments. Second-class investments should be made only with surplus funds after a substantial amount has been invested in first-class securities. Securities of this type are essentially the same as those in the first class except that some of them pay a slightly higher rate of return. They are considered by bankers and investment authorities to be safe so far as the principal and the rate of return are concerned.

Second-class investments include a slightly wider variety of municipal bonds as well as carefully selected foreign bonds and some common stocks. Improved real estate is also included in this class if the amount of the investment is considered to be only the amount of cash that could be obtained for the real estate at a forced sale.

Third-Class Investments. Third-class investments are justified only when a partial loss of such investments will not jeopardize savings and future financial security. Such investments are somewhat speculative, although no investment should be considered as belonging in this class if there is any apparent danger of loss of principal or of earnings. A third-class investment is made when there is some hope of an increase in the asset value of the security.

The investments in this group consist usually of stocks and bonds and occasionally of real estate, investment-trust securities, and interests in small business enterprises. The yield of earnings is large as compared with that of first- and second-class investments. The amount of money ordinarily available for an investment in third-class securities is not sufficient to permit diversification in the buying of common stocks. A better choice is therefore to put one's money into an investment trust.

Fourth-Class Investments. Investing in this class of securities could be classified more properly as speculating or gambling. No investment in fourth-class securities should be made until there is definite assurance that the reserve fund and other investments will protect the investor and his dependents. In other words, a fourth-class investment should be made only by one who can afford to lose.

Fourth-class investments include securities of reputable business enterprises with honest managers, although these concerns may not have paid dividends or earned a surplus for several years. The investment is made on the basis of predictions for the future. There is, however, no justification whatsoever for an investment without some kind of security.

TEXTBOOK QUESTIONS

1. Why should a person not buy real estate as an investment unless he has the time and the energy to take care of it?
2. When real estate is to be purchased as an investment, what are some of the factors that should be investigated in determining its desirability?
3. Why do some people advise against investing in an enterprise managed by a friend?

4. What is a closed corporation?
5. Why is it sometimes inadvisable to buy stock in a closed corporation?
6. If the person who has a mortgage outstanding on his property does not pay the mortgage-holder according to his contract, what may the mortgage-holder do to protect his investment?
7. Who should be consulted before buying a real-estate mortgage note?
8. (a) What is the most common type of mortgage? (b) What is the maximum percentage of the appraised value of property that is normally covered by this type of mortgage?
9. What are the two general types of stocks?
10. Do all stocks have the same voting power?
11. Distinguish between cumulative stock and noncumulative stock.
12. What is meant by participating stock? To what general type of stock does the term apply?
13. Does the par value of a stock indicate the true value?
14. In what way does a bond differ from a stock?
15. What are commonly used as security for bonds?
16. Before a bond is purchased, what factors should be investigated in relation to the bond?
17. As a general rule, which is more stable in price: a bond or a stock? Explain.
18. (a) If a one-hundred-dollar bond is selling for ninety dollars, is it selling at a premium or a discount? (b) What are some of the reasons why bonds sell below their par value?
19. Does a certificate of deposit represent a permanent or a temporary investment?
20. What are some of the advantages of an investment trust that is operated efficiently and honestly?
21. What would you include in first-class investments?

DISCUSSION QUESTIONS

1. Discuss the merits of real estate as an investment for an old woman.
2. You have an opportunity to invest some money with two other men in a partnership in a neighboring town. You expect to continue your work and to allow the other two persons to operate the business. Discuss the disadvantages of this plan.
3. Which do you think would be easier to investigate: (a) residential property pledged as security for a mortgage note or (b) property of a corporation pledged as security for bonds?

4. In some states it has been difficult, if not impossible, during financial depressions, for mortgage-holders to foreclose on the property pledged as security for the payment of the interest and of the principal due them. How do you think such a condition affects (a) the mortgage-holders, the persons who own the mortgages; (b) the future market for mortgages; and (c) interest rates?
5. If a stock is issued by a reliable corporation, is there any need for reading the provisions that are printed on the stock certificate?
6. Assume that you are contemplating buying some common stock in either of two outstanding corporations of approximately equal size. Both corporations have good reputations and good records of past earnings. They have issued approximately the same number of shares of stock. One has cumulative preferred stock and one grade of common stock; the other has noncumulative preferred stock and one grade of common stock. From your point of view which common stock would be more desirable? Why?
7. Some people believe that, if a person is going to buy stock, he should buy common stock instead of preferred stock. Why do you think that they are of this opinion?
8. What kind of preferred stock combines some of the features of a preferred stock and a common stock?
9. A broker once said, "A bond is only as good as the earning ability of the corporation that issues it." Explain this statement.
10. How well do you think an investor is protected if he buys a municipal bond on which the security is the sewage system of the city?
11. Compare a certificate of deposit with (a) a bond and (b) a savings account.
12. Why do you think that a good investment trust provides the small investor with a better investing program than he could carry out himself?
13. In this chapter you have studied some classifications of investments according to their relative conservativeness. Can you point out any reasons why these classifications might change in such a way that some of the first-class investments might become third-class or fourth-class investments?

Section III

Fraudulent Investment Schemes

Methods of Deception Used by Investment Promoters. In spite of the fact that most of our financial transactions are conducted in an ethical and honorable manner, everyone must recognize the fact that some people try to make their living by defrauding others. Most of the fraudulent promoters prey upon people who desire to "get rich quick." The National Better Business Bureau has issued a bulletin entitled *What an Investor Should Know*. The following paragraphs are quoted from that bulletin:

"The swindler relies for success upon the universal human desire to make money—as much money as possible, as quickly as possible. The average salesman in order to make a sale has to convince his prospects of two things: first, that they want something and, second, that what he has to offer will satisfy that want. For the swindler, the task is simplified. Everyone wants to make money. The swindler needs only to convince his prospects that his particular proposition will enable them to do so. To accomplish this end, he appeals to their greed, prejudices, and self-esteem. He takes advantage of their lack of investment knowledge. Above all, he tries to prevent them from making an investigation or, when this is impossible, to discredit what he knows in advance will be the outcome of that investigation.

"Thus, if a hesitant investor suggests that he would like to consult his banker, the swindler will seek to discourage him. 'Don't ask your banker for advice,' the glib-tongued salesman will argue. 'Don't tell him why you're drawing out your money. He'll be sure to tell you not to do it. And why not? He's paying you 2 per cent on your money and investing it to bring him in five times that much. Be smart and put your money in that kind of proposition yourself—the kind I'm offering you.'

"Sometimes the argument works. And suppose the investor does consult the banker and the latter disapproves of the 'investment.' Wasn't that what the salesman predicted? And isn't the banker acting from selfish motives?

"Another favorite trick is to attempt to discredit the banker, better business bureau, or other source of disinterested information by trying to tie it up with the 'interests.' 'The Better Business Bureau is the tool of Wall Street,' the swindler rants. 'The monopolies don't want us to go into production because they know we'll cut into their profits. The big shots tried to buy us out and failed and now they're trying to throw suspicion on us. They want to keep the gravy for themselves. We believe in giving the little fellow a chance.'

"The prospect, being a little fellow himself, is likely to lend a sympathetic ear to this fantastic tale of persecution. He may not know that 'little fellows' or small stockholders own a majority of the stock of most large corporations.

"Under different circumstances, however, the dishonest promoter is far from reticent in claiming endorsement of his proposition by 'big names.' This financier owns 5,000 shares in the company, that prominent industrialist has bought 10,000, he assures his listener. (An examination of the list of corporation stockholders would tell a different story.) Or he will exhibit an imposing list of directors. Frequently such names may have been used without consent. Sometimes prominent men do lend their names thoughtlessly to promotions of dubious merit, generally, however, without making any substantial investment themselves.

"Unfounded comparisons with successful companies are also part of the sharper's stock in trade. 'Look at Homestake!' he urges. 'A few hundred dollars put in that company orginally would be worth millions now. Our mine has even better prospects today.' He fails to state that, for every successful mining company, there have been thousands of failures—all with marvelous 'prospects.'

"Flattery is often an effective weapon in dulling the suspicions of the investor. 'We're limiting this offer to a few important people like you.' 'You're one of the first to have a chance to take advantage of this opportunity. You're right in on the ground floor.' 'This is strictly inside information. I wouldn't take a chance of passing the tip along to everyone.' These timeworn arguments are calculated to make the investor feel important and put him in an amiable frame of mind to part with his money.

"Promises are cheap but effective—promises that a stock will be listed on a stock exchange; promises that a dividend will be declared at an early date; promises to redeem the stock whenever the investor wants to surrender it; promises that are beguiling but fail to materialize. Sometimes the promise is made in the form of a guarantee. But a guarantee is only as strong as the company behind it. Guarantees may be worthless and often are.

"Claims of Government approval are also made with marked success. 'If our offering were not strictly on the level,' the swindler argues, 'the Government would put us out of business. We couldn't use the United States mails unless we were all right.' If this argument were true, there would be no such thing as fraud.

"One point in common to all these arguments which swindlers have used so successfully is that the arguments have practically no bearing on the intrinsic value of the investment offered. The value can be determined only on a basis of facts."

Types of Investment Swindles. The National Better Business Bureau has issued a bulletin entitled *Safeguarding Your Savings.* In this booklet a great deal of information is given on the practices of swindling, deceiving, and defrauding. The following comments are based upon the warnings issued by the National Better Business Bureau:

Prominent names. Promoters know that the names and the endorsements of successful men carry weight. The promoter therefore often obtains the endorsement of some prominent person; or, if the prominent person has purchased the particular security, the promoter may truthfully tell all his prospects, "Mr. Johnson has purchased ten shares of this stock. If it is a good investment for him, it must be a good one for you." Some prominent men are careless in lending their names without due investigation. Sometimes such names are used without authorization. The prudent man will ascertain whether the persons whose names are used actually have a voice in the management

Illustration No. 45—A Warning of Cincinnati Better Business Bureau

of the enterprise involved. The sensible man will look beyond names and endorsements and investigate the merits of a stock or other security before he buys.

The "ground floor." An opportunity to "get in on the ground floor" often turns out to be the sort of invitation that the proverbial spider extends to the fly. The so-called "ground floor" is oftentimes merely a grave for hopes that soon die. A high percentage of all new enterprises eventually fail. An invitation to invest in a new enterprise may be an invitation to lose one's money.

Every year a great many legitimate, as well as fraudulent, promotional schemes are started on the basis of new ideas and new developments. The railroad, the automobile, the radio, the airplane, and television have all brought their prolific supply of promotional schemes. New businesses are started, and new inventions are promoted each year. The prospective investor is encouraged to get in on the "ground floor." If he would stop to think, however, he would soon realize that the chances are against him even though he may be investing in an honest and legitimate enterprise, for only a small percentage of these new ventures will be successful. Investing in any one of these enterprises is therefore usually a speculation.

Economic changes and legislation cause additional promotional schemes. Changes in our monetary system cause new promotion in gold mining or silver mining. Old mines are revived, and new ones are promoted. The repealing of the Eighteenth Amendment of the Federal Constitution caused a great variety of new ventures and revived many old ones. After a moment's thought anyone could have predicted, as proved to be true, that many of these ventures would be unsuccessful.

Inside information. "Inside tips" are usually expensive pieces of misinformation. "Confidential information" may have a basis in fact and be disseminated through reliable friends, or it may be merely manufactured and therefore spurious in character. Be careful, for even a trusted friend from whom "confidential information" is received may himself be deceived. Secrecy is a much-used instrument of irresponsible manipulators. Oftentimes obscure publications with confidence-begetting titles serve no purpose except to exploit their readers.

The tipster sheet is a dangerous device in selling securities, but it can be detected easily. The prospect receives through the mail a publication that appears to give advice on investments. He then receives a telegram urging the purchase of a certain security. The next step is a telephone call urging the purchasing of that security. The use of the telegram and the telephone is usually for the purpose of avoiding Federal prosecution for defrauding through the mails. The safest precaution against this type of fraud is: "Do not deal with strangers." Obviously, it is unwise to deal with persons whom one knows nothing about. They certainly have no interest in one's welfare, although they indicate their desire to help one make money.

Comparative figures. The stock vendor or the real-estate promoter who endeavors to impress the prospective investor by tabulating the fabulous returns supposed to have been realized from an investment of small sums in some other enterprise during the early stage of development, unwittingly admits that his offering cannot stand on its own feet. Such figures fire the imagination, but generally they are deceptive. They are not a true index to the profits likely to be realized from the new venture into which the investor is urged to put his money. For instance, if a promoter is offering to sell a stock that, according to his statistics, will produce an income of from 10 to 20 per cent a year, it is obvious that something is wrong with his figures because, if the returns were so high, the securities would not be available for the average investor.

The fictitious advance. By artificial transactions, professional promoters sometimes cause an arbitrary advance in the market price of a security that they intend to and do unload upon the public when their selling campaign has gained headway. These tactics have been used in connection with both listed and over-the-counter securities. Recent National legislation has set up new difficulties for such tactics; but even with these safeguards it is well for the investor to be alert and to analyze calmly the underlying causes for such an advance in the market price of a security. The object of such operations is usually to create buying excitement and to provide the *appearance* of an increased value so that those who have already bought will be kept satisfied while new buyers are being induced to "get in before the next rise."

Solicitations by telephone. In recent years the telephone —that indispensable instrument of communication—has been used extensively by stock swindlers to plunder individuals. This use is deplored by telephone companies, which are watchful to help combat abuses of the telephone; but usually they cannot deny their facilities to users any more than a railroad company can discriminate in choosing the kind of passengers that may ride on its trains.

Investment houses with an established reputation, however, do not solicit new clients by telephone. Rarely can the individual selling securities through the use of the telephone be identified when he was previously unknown to the prospect; and moreover there is no tangible record of his representations. Thousands of persons who have lost hundreds of millions of dollars have learned to their sorrow that it is unsafe to buy securities from strangers who solicit business through the use of the telephone.

The "sell and switch." Through this practice individuals are persuaded, by telephone solicitation, to purchase shares of stock in well-known corporations on a 50 per cent margin. After the money put up as margin is received by the seller, the victim is induced to "switch" his purchase into the stock of some obscure promotional corporation. These latter shares are practically always the property of the vendor and are sold to the victim at an unconscionable profit. This practice is inherently deceptive, and misrepresentations are almost always a part of it.

The "reload." Persons having once made purchases of securities that turned out badly are often hopeful of the ultimate vindication of their original judgment. Stock swindlers, cognizant of this human trait, obtain shares of these usually worthless stocks and, through adroit misrepresentation, induce these stockholders to purchase more of the same shares. This practice is known as "reloading."

Future price guaranties. It often occurs that, in eagerness to promote sales of a security, the vendors verbally guarantee that the present price of the security will be maintained or that the price at some specified future date will be in excess of the price at which the security is sold. On rare occasions the guaranty is in writing.

Reputable investment dealers do not make such promises or guaranties. Under certain conditions a corporation taking over the assets of another corporation does guarantee a fixed return to the shareholders of the latter corporation. Dealers or brokers of established financial standing, however, do not assume such a risk. Established standards in the investment banking business prohibit such guaranties.

The partial-payment plan. This legitimate method of enabling persons of limited means to acquire sound securities has been much abused. Irresponsible dealers, lacking capital to acquire and keep in their custody, or under their control, the securities they have contracted to deliver to their customers when the specified payments have been made, have often taken a chance. Either they do not acquire the securities; or, having acquired them and confirmed the purchases to the customers, they immediately resell the securities to replenish their capital.

Thereafter, if the market price of these securities rises, they fail to make delivery. In that event they are obliged to close their doors, and the customers consequently lose. Subsequent litigation, either civil or penal, rarely is of value in recovering the customers' funds.

Frequently dealers of this kind, facing ruin, endeavor to induce their clients to put up more money or to use their established equities for additional purchases. Partial-payment contracts should not, however, be "pyramided." Each contract should be completed before another is entered into.

Oil and other mineral ventures. Honorable and capable men are constantly endeavoring to extract our rich oil and other mineral resources from the earth and to seek the financial assistance of investors. When such enterprises are promoted by men of this type, public participation is invited by honest representations. It is, however, so easy to deceive individuals as to the physical conditions of distant properties, by falsehoods, by half truths, or by withholding material facts, that extreme care should be exercised to gather all available information before purchasing an interest in such an enterprise.

Concerns that drill for oil negotiate leases with the landowners. Such a lease, in addition to requiring the payment of a fixed annual amount to the lessor (the landowner), provides that the lessee give to the lessor one eighth (sometimes one sixth) of the oil recovered from the property. The landowner may sell this oil at the well and receive the prevailing price for it, or he may dispose of it as he chooses. A common plan is to accept the proper percentage of the total sales of the oil that is produced and sold.

It often happens that the landowner disposes of all or a fractional part of his interest in the oil on his property by selling it to a dealer in such interests. The dealers who acquire such interests, or oil royalties as they are called, dispose of them to members of the investing public. The ownership of a royalty interest is evidenced by a negotiable, recordable document styled a mineral deed.

The methods of many of these dealers have been fraudulent, and extravagant prices have been charged for royalty interests. Misrepresentations regarding the property itself have been frequent; and, because of the technical nature of these interests, inexperienced purchasers find it difficult to detect deceit. Before purchasing such an interest, one should get full details in writing from the vendor and should check this information with that available from established sources, such as a better business bureau. The price that the royalty dealer himself paid for the interest is an important item of information.

One practice of oil-well promoters is to place with an independent trustee the royalty interests they have acquired, receiving in return therefor participation certificates. The promoters then sell these certificates to the public. All material facts regarding each royalty in the trust, especially the price paid for it by the depositor or sponsor of the trust, and the price at which it was taken into the trust, should be obtained by a prospective investor before he makes any commitment. The standing, the impartiality, and the financial strength of the trustee are of vital importance.

Investments in mining schemes have formed the basis of some of the most romantic adventures of the past. Probably because of this fact many people who invest in mining ventures have a romantic picture of fulfilling a dream by becoming fabulously wealthy through a stroke of luck. Many families have poured their life's savings into fraudulent mining ventures merely on the promise of becoming rich. They failed to "investigate before investing."

Anyone who invests in a mining venture should be prepared to take his loss "without pain." Many mining promotions are speculations. Even many of the legitimate mining ventures are not successful. Stocks in mining ventures are often sold under pressure by brokers who have an interest in the commissions that result from the sales. In some cases the broker may get more than the company that is being promoted. Even though an individual is financially capable of taking the risk of buying mining stock, he should not make an investment without thoroughly investigating the security.

Many conservative bankers and investment counselors advise against buying any mining or oil security because of the difficulty of investigating and estimating the potential value of the security. The purchase of a security of this type is therefore largely a speculation rather than an investment. Before oil stock or an oil royalty right is purchased, the following points should be investigated:

(a) What are the percentages of producing areas and nonproducing areas?
(b) How much property is owned? What is the location of it? How much was paid for it?
(c) What is the authority for the estimated producing life of the oil field?
(d) How was the property acquired?
(e) How have the values been established?

TEXTBOOK QUESTIONS

1. What weakness of people makes it possible for swindlers and fraudulent promoters to continue their practices every year?
2. What devices does a swindler use to convince his victims?
3. What does the swindler often tell the victim when the latter desires to obtain advice from his banker?
4. What argument do fraudulent promoters sometimes use against the better business bureau as a source of investment information?
5. If a promoter states that a certain important individual or several important businessmen are holders of the stock he is selling, how should this part of his story be investigated?
6. What is the fallacy of comparing a new venture with a profitable existing venture of a similar type?
7. What is meant by "being let in on the ground floor"? Why should an investor be cautious when such an assurance is made?
8. What is the fallacy of the promoter's argument, "This investment is all right or the Government would put us out of business"?
9. Why should an investor not consider solicitations made by telephone?
10. What is the "sell and switch" plan?
11. Why should an investor look with suspicion upon a guarantee of future prices or income?

DISCUSSION QUESTIONS

1. On what basis of reasoning can you condemn an investment tipster sheet that comes to you unsolicited?
2. (a) What is your opinon of the securities of mining corporations? (b) Is the average person justified in buying such securities? (c) Who should buy these securities?
3. Why is the inducement "to get in on the ground floor" always dangerous to an amateur investor?
4. Why would it be absurd for you to believe a stranger who, in trying to sell you a certain stock, stated that you were one of the few invited to participate in the investment?
5. If a promoter tells you something over the telephone or in a personal interview, why would it be advisable to have him verify his statements in writing by mail?
6. Oil and mining ventures are particularly hazardous for amateur investors. Why are they?
7. Just because stock in a seemingly legitimate oil venture is offered for sale in the producing region, is there assurance that the oil property is valuable?

PROBLEMS

1. A stenographer who had saved $1,000 asked her banker what investment he would recommend. He recommended a United States Government bond. She purchased it for $1,045, including the commission. She obtained $40 a year as interest. (a) What was the rate of yield? (b) Was there any relation between the yield and the chance of loss?
2. A man considers buying a house for $3,000 and paying cash. An investigation discloses the following additional information: (a) The house is now occupied by a family that is paying $28 a month rent. This amount is considered reasonable compared with the rent on other similar homes. (b) The statistics of real-estate agents show that, on the average, rented houses are vacant one month out of every year. (c) The house will require immediate repairs costing $100 and annual repairs of about $40. The taxes on the property amount to $36 a year; there are no assessments. (d) Real-estate men estimate that the maximum life of a house of this kind is twenty years. At the end of that time the house and the lot will probably not be worth more than $2,000. (e) The commission of the real-estate agent in buying the house, and the cost of transferring and recording the title, will amount to $100. (1) Calculate the total cost of the house, including the cost of immediate repairs and the cost of buying the property as well as having the title transferred and recorded. (2) Calculate the total operating costs, the net income, and the percentage of income based on the original investment. (3) Do you think the purchase of the house would be a good investment?
3. From a newspaper, your local banker, or from some financial journal, obtain the latest prices on some particular issue of Government bonds. (a) Figure the gross cost of buying $1,000 worth of the Government bonds, including the commission. (b) Compute the rate of net interest on the basis of the cost price.
4. From a local newspaper, your local banker, or a financial journal, obtain the price quoted (at the close of the previous day) on some stock specified by your teacher. (a) Determine the rate of the latest dividend. (b) Calculate the cost of buying one hundred shares. (c) Using the rate of the latest dividend, compute the rate of net income on the basis of the cost.
5. Mr. Stinson has ten shares of each of ten different preferred stocks. The total value amounts to $6,323. He also has ten different bonds valued at a total of $1,116. Ten shares of stock valued at $46 a share become worthless. Mr. Brown has fifty shares of stock in three different corporations, the

total value of which are $5,200, and ten bonds, the total value of which are $1,046. Fifty shares of Mr. Brown's stock are the same as the ten shares of Mr. Stinson's stock that became worthless. (a) Figure Mr. Stinson's percentage of loss on his total investment. (b) Figure Mr. Brown's percentage of loss on his total investment. (c) Can you draw any conclusions?

COMMUNITY PROBLEMS AND PROJECTS

1. (a) Make a list of the ways in which it is possible to invest money in your local community. (b) For each type of investment indicate whether it is suitable for the small investor or the large investor, and whether it is conservative or not conservative.
2. Select as an investment some local piece of residential real estate that is offered for sale. (a) Make a study of the total cost of the property, including the costs of purchasing it and the expenses of upkeep and depreciation. (b) Compute the amount of income that can be expected from the property and the percentage of income based on the cost.
3. Obtain financial statements of a bank, a building and loan association, and an insurance company. (a) Compare the types of securities owned by the various institutions. (b) Draw some conclusions as to the conservativeness of the investments.
4. Investigate the investment services of a local bank. Write a report describing how this bank can serve you as an investor.
5. From a daily newspaper select ten stocks and ten bonds, or follow the instructions of your teacher in selecting the securities. Determine the current market prices and dividend and interest rates. (a) Compute the market price quoted daily on each stock and on each bond for a period of two months. (b) Average the prices of the stocks and those of the bonds for each day of the period. (c) Draw a graph that shows a comparison of the fluctuation in the average prices of the stocks and of that in the average prices of the bonds. (d) Draw some conclusions with regard to these price fluctuations.

CHAPTER V

PROTECTION AGAINST ECONOMIC RISKS

Purpose of the Chapter. Risk is the possibility of loss, cost, or damage. Some individual or business risks are unavoidable, but others can be avoided by various means. Many risks are uncertain not only as to the amount of the possible loss, but also as to the time of the loss. When a risk is transferred to an insurance company, it ceases to be a risk on the part of the insured person but it becomes a definite cost. In some cases the person may choose to build up a reserve in anticipation of a loss in order that he will be able to take care of the loss when and if it happens. In such a case the risk really becomes a cost.

The purpose of this chapter is to analyze various types of risks and to discuss the methods of protection against them.

Section I

Risks and Methods of Protection Against Them

Types of Risks. Risks of nature, which arise from the physical environment, are occasionally referred to as *natural risks.* These include the possibilities of loss caused by rainstorms, earthquakes, cyclones, floods, droughts, and fires. The uncertainty of all except the last depends upon nature. It is possible to obtain protection against storms and earthquakes by constructing stronger buildings. It is difficult to obtain protection against floods without building dams, reservoirs, dikes, or levees; without changing the channels of streams; or without reforestation. Irrigation and the storage of water furnish protection against droughts. The exercise of care will help to overcome the risk from fire. Protection against cyclones is difficult, if not impossible, to obtain.

There are two general types of *social risks:* (a) risks that arise from such acts as robbery, strikes, riots, racketeering, and forgery; and (b) risks that are attributable to taxes, tariffs, price fluctuations, panics, and laws. Those of the first type are results of the lack of moral character on the part of members of society. It is easier to obtain protection against such risks than it is against those of the second type.

Personal risks include those that arise from unemployment, accident, ill health, old age, and death. Workers are interested in unemployment protection. Various industrial enterprises, cities, states, and Federal agencies have established means of protecting workers from loss due to unemployment and to old age. Most of the other types of personal risks are covered by various kinds of insurance.

Various means have been devised to obtain protection against almost all types of risks. The discussion in this chapter and in Chapter VI will show how businessmen and individuals protect themselves against the most common types of risks. Insurance is one of the most important means of providing protection.

Methods of Meeting Risks. Individuals or businesses can meet the problem of risk in various ways. Some risks must be borne without any means of protection, but for many types of risks there are risk-bearing agencies. For instance, the risks of loss of life, fire, and theft can be covered by insurance. Farmers may insure their crops; but some farmers may choose to plant side by side a dry-weather crop and a wet-weather crop so that, regardless of the weather, a marketable crop will be obtained. Sometimes a risk can be reduced or eliminated by research. As a result of research it is possible sometimes through better management to find out the causes for risks and to eliminate them. Obviously, risks can be reduced by direct methods, such as the installation of safety devices.

Changes in Demand. Everyone who has operated a business has discovered for himself that people change in respect to their needs, desires, and wants. These changes give rise to serious business risks. In our system of large-scale production, quantities of food, clothing, and other goods are produced and offered for sale in the anticipation that buyers will want them. Frequently the time consumed from the point of original production to the point of sale is six to twelve months. During this period the buyers may change their wants and desires. Their needs may even change.

When fashions change suddenly, many manufacturers and merchants find themselves stocked with more cloth and clothing than they can sell at a profit. Since the kind of clothing worn is regulated largely by style, the production of this commodity involves great risk. That risk is one of the reasons why the prices of women's clothing are high. The risk is so great that producers of women's clothing must charge high prices in order to protect themselves against loss. For instance, a manufacturer who produces one thousand women's garments may sell the first five hundred at twenty dollars each, the next two hundred at fifteen dollars each, the next two hundred at ten dollars each, and the next one hundred at five dollars each. If he could sell all of them at a predetermined price, he could afford to make this price lower than the original.

Changes in methods of transportation, heating, and lighting present serious business risks, but also offer new opportunities. When the automobile displaced the horse, many carriage and wagon manufacturers went out of business. A few foresaw the change and went into the production of automobiles. The possibility of using steel in place of other building materials is a risk of many manufacturers. The development of airplanes is a possible threat against other forms of transportation.

Specialization. From the point of view of economics, *specialization* means that each person does the thing that he is most capable of doing. He specializes in doing one job or a limited number of jobs and therefore becomes proficient in a restricted field. Specialization therefore makes everyone in society dependent upon others. It is also the source of the risk of unemployment. If a worker, for example, has been accustomed to doing nothing but nickel-plating parts of stoves, he will find himself without a trade if all stoves are henceforth to be enameled. He is faced with unemployment unless he can adapt himself to some other form of specialization in production. Many people suffer in this manner.

The members of society are so interdependent that many risks arise from this interdependence. For instance, all of us are dependent upon the banking system. If banks collapse, business collapses. If business concerns cannot obtain loans, they decrease their production and discharge workers. When workers are thrown out of employment, they buy less. Consequently the grocer, the wholesaler, and the farmer all sell less. The cause of these unfavorable conditions is specialization with its resulting interdependence.

Speculation and Investment. Everyone who invests assumes some risk. Speculation, however, is recognized as the more decided form of risk. One who speculates realizes fully the extent of the risk, but takes the risk in anticipation of a profit. For instance, the person who speculates in stocks tries to buy during a period of low prices and sell during a period of high prices. In other words, when he buys stock, he is taking the risk that the price will fall. If the market goes down and he has to sell at a price lower than that which he paid, he will suffer a loss.

The rates of income that are promised on investments are some indication of the risks involved. Some large loans pay only 2 or 3 per cent a year; others pay 4 to 8 per cent; and a few pay even more. Take, for instance, the three common types of opportunity for investment in corporations. These are bonds, preferred stock, and common stock. If the bonds of a corporation pay interest at 5 per cent, the preferred stock will probably carry a dividend of 6 or 7 per cent. The common stockholders frequently get a dividend higher than 6 or 7 per cent.

Cyclical, Seasonal, and Long-Time Risks. Certain risks, including some of those previously discussed, can be designated as cyclical risks. A cyclical risk is one that is repeated in a fairly regular or predictable sequence. The recurrence of periods of depression and prosperity over many years has been cyclical. Fluctuations in business conditions from one season to another are cyclical. From one year to another, cyclonic storms in some parts of the country present cyclical risks.

Seasonal risks and risks of weather are fairly easy to understand. Merchants sometimes suffer losses because of abnormal weather conditions. Workingmen lose employment time because of extremely cold or wet weather. Shipments of perishables are sometimes damaged or delayed because of weather. Because of the uncertainties of weather, seasonal risks are a common source of loss.

Long-time risks are numerous. Most of them represent shifts and changes in customs. The shift from the wagon to the automobile was a long-time shift. The change in a community from a good residential section to a business section is a long-time shift that creates a risk for property owners. Property may become more valuable if it is in a location that can be used for business purposes; but if it merely adjoins suitable business property, it will probably decrease in value. If the trend toward installing municipal power plants is continued, the shift from privately owned power plants to publicly owned plants will represent a risk to the owners of securities in the corporations.

How Governments Reduce Risks. The Federal Government, state governments, and local governments act in many ways to reduce various types of business risks. Governments act indirectly and directly. The Federal Government established the Federal Reserve Banking System to stabilize our financial system and to protect the nation from violent fluctuations in the business cycle. Governments, through their laws, create agencies to reduce various kinds of risks. Laws themselves, which are as much for the protection as for the assistance of business, represent a means of reducing risks.

Some of the direct means of reducing business risks are the services provided by such agencies as the Weather Bureau; the health service of the Federal Government; Federal, state, and local secret service and police; the United States Department of Commerce; the United States Department of Agriculture; and many other agencies established by the Federal Government. Some of these have been described in later chapters. As an example of the services performed, the Weather Bureau distributes weather reports for the aid of aviators, operators of transportation lines, and others who are interested. Through the Weather Bureau fruit growers and farmers are able to get forecasts of frosts in time to protect their crops from damage.

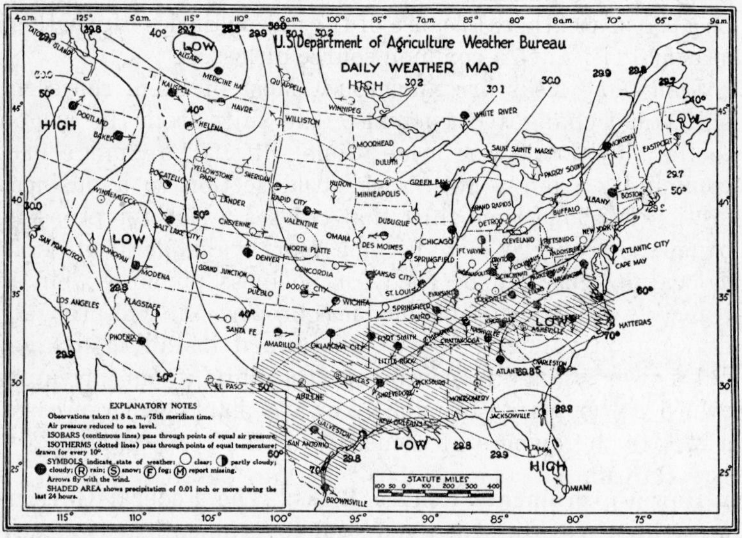

Illustration No. 46—A Daily Weather Map

Private Agencies That Reduce Risks. There are numerous agencies that make a profit by furnishing risk-reducing services to clients. Some of these duplicate the services furnished by the Federal Government. Others supplement these services, and still others are entirely original in the scope of their services. The furnishing of credit information is, for example, one of the most important private services for the reduction of risks. Through Dun and Bradstreet, Incorporated, the names of businesses in all parts of the United States are listed with information on the size, characteristics, and credit rating of each business. If a businessman contemplates selling on credit to a concern to which he never sold before but which is listed in

United States Weather Bureau

Illustration No. 47—An Airport Weather Bureau

the Dun and Bradstreet book, he can obtain information that will help to reduce the risk of granting credit. Several agencies publish and distribute reports on credit and business conditions.

Newspapers and financial magazines publish interest rates, stock prices, bond prices, commodity prices, information on the general trend of business conditions, and forecasts.

Many other private agencies and co-operative groups attempt to overcome or to reduce various types of risks. For instance, the socialized medicine plan under which families can buy medical service at a fixed rate is one means of protection against the risk of high medical expenses. In certain large cities there are hospitalization plans similar to the medical-service plans. Illustration No. 48 shows the first page of a typical hospital service plan. Under this plan a yearly fee entitles members of the family to certain prescribed hospital services.

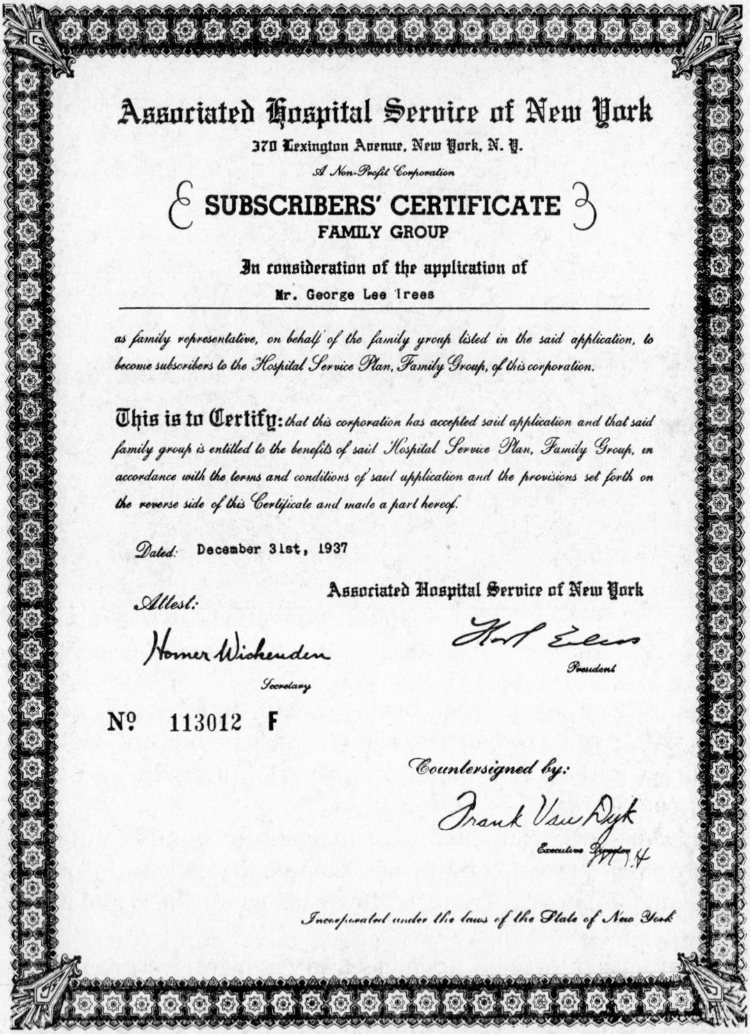

Associated Hospital Service of New York

370 Lexington Avenue, New York, N. Y.

A Non-Profit Corporation

SUBSCRIBERS' CERTIFICATE

FAMILY GROUP

In consideration of the application of

Mr. George Lee Irees

as family representative, on behalf of the family group listed in the said application, to become subscribers to the Hospital Service Plan, Family Group, of this corporation.

This is to Certify: that this corporation has accepted said application and that said family group is entitled to the benefits of said Hospital Service Plan, Family Group, in accordance with the terms and conditions of said application and the provisions set forth on the reverse side of this Certificate and made a part hereof.

Dated: December 31st, 1937

Associated Hospital Service of New York

Attest:

Homer Wickenden
Secretary

President

No. 113012 F

Countersigned by:

Frank Van Dyk
Executive Director

Incorporated under the laws of the State of New York

Illustration No. 48—A Hospital Service Plan

Scientific Management Reduces Risks. In the early days businessmen depended upon their own wits and good memories in managing their businesses. Their success in many cases was due, not to their particular ability, but to the rapid economic expansion that made their businesses profitable in spite of much mismanagement. Of course, not all of these older businessmen were inefficient. Today, however, business conditions and methods change so rapidly that businessmen must keep up to date in order to be able to compete.

Research is therefore a prime requisite of success. The chemical laboratories of businesses, colleges, state governments, and the Federal Government are working constantly on new chemical processes and on improvements in the methods of production and in the quality of products. In earlier years many chemical products were made somewhat crudely; but as science has progressed, processes have been refined. There was a time when producers of steel could not be sure of turning out a uniform grade of steel. Sometimes large batches of steel were spoiled. Scientific control now ensures a uniform quality and reduces the risk of spoilage.

Scientific accounting is one of the most important means of reducing risks in the management of modern business. A great number of the business enterprises in the United States are so large that no single person could remember all the details of management and be sure of correlating everything properly. Modern accounting makes it possible to know (a) the detailed costs of production, (b) the changes in the costs of production, (c) the actual present profit and the estimated future profit, (d) the kinds and the values of the assets available at any particular time. In addition, accounting makes it possible to control expenditures and to correlate production and sales. Through their accounting systems many business managers have figures on sales and production placed on their desks daily for the purpose of analysis. Other figures are analyzed weekly, monthly, and yearly. With this detailed information available, the managers of business concerns can reduce risks by eliminating the need for guessing.

Speculation and Future Contracts. Although speculation is usually condemned as being unjustifiable, it nevertheless serves an important function in the commodity markets. Speculators make it possible for legitimate manufacturers to reduce their risks. The professional speculator is a person who spends all his time and thought in forecasting price changes. The businessman who takes advantage of the opportunity to hedge a loss is doing the opposite of gambling: he is protecting his business.

Here is the way a manufacturer can hedge a loss through a speculative contract: A miller gets a contract to deliver flour in four months at a specified price. He wants to begin producing the flour in two months. If he wishes to protect himself from the risk of rising prices of wheat, he must enter into a future contract. In other words, he must immediately order wheat to be delivered to him in two months at a specified price. The speculator who takes his order and agrees to deliver the wheat is hoping that the price at which he can buy in the future will assure him a profit. The producer is assured that he will have the wheat when he wants it, and he knows the exact price that he must pay. He can therefore figure his profit accurately. If he could not order wheat immediately for future delivery at a specific price, he would either have to wait until the end of the two months and then buy it at whatever the price might be, or he would have to buy the wheat and hold it until he was ready to use it. If he waited to buy it, he would run the risk of paying a high price. If he bought it immediately and had it delivered, he would have a lot of money invested in wheat. By buying under a future contract, he passes the risk on to the expert speculator.

Other Means of Protection Against Risks. There is a constant battle of individuals, business concerns, societies, associations, and governments to reduce risks. Sea walls and levees are built to prevent floods. Lightning rods are used to prevent damage from lightning. Safety devices on machinery and vehicles reduce danger from fire and accidents. Clean-up campaigns in cities prevent disease and fire. The inspection of buildings prevents fire and damage from collapse. Safety education programs reduce accidents. These and many other activities are being carried on constantly to reduce the possibilities of physical injury and economic loss.

By advertising, many business enterprises reduce the hazards of marketing. If a product is offered for sale without an advertising effort, it cannot compete satisfactorily with other products. The chance of its being marketed successfully is very small. Advertising therefore serves to reduce business risks.

Protection Through Insurance. The buying of insurance is the opposite of gambling. Gambling is wagering on something that is an uncertainty. If a person who owns a home does not buy insurance, he is gambling on the uncertainty that his house will not be burned. Unless he is very wealthy, the burning of the house will be a severe financial setback. The average owner cannot afford to lose his home. Many people who own homes could never rebuild or buy new ones if their homes were to burn. The same facts are true of many businesses. A business may be operating successfully; but if its plant were to be destroyed by fire or a windstorm, it might not be able to rebuild because its own funds would be insufficient or because not enough money could be borrowed by it. The following section presents a discussion of several types of insurance; Chapter VI gives a detailed study of life insurance.

TEXTBOOK QUESTIONS

1. Name the three general types of risks.
2. What are some means of protection against (a) storms and earthquakes? (b) floods?
3. What are the two general classes of social risks?
4. Give an example of how a change in demand for goods or services creates a serious business risk.
5. Show in what way specialization creates a risk from the point of view of the individual worker.
6. Show how all of us are affected by specialization because of the interdependence in our economic system.
7. In what way does every investor assume some risk and to some extent become a speculator?
8. In what way do rates of interest compensate for risks?
9. (a) What is a cyclical risk? (b) What is a long-time risk? (c) Give some examples of each.
10. Give some examples of how governmental units help to reduce risks.

11. Give some examples of how private agencies, other than insurance companies, help to reduce risks.
12. Give some examples of how research and scientific management reduce risks in business.
13. Explain briefly how a flour miller can take advantage of speculation to protect himself against loss.
14. Explain how insurance is the opposite of gambling.

DISCUSSION QUESTIONS

1. Why do you think some orders and invoices bear the statement, "Not responsible for the delivery of goods in case of strikes, riots, floods, etc."?
2. Mr. Cooper drives his automobile only occasionally. The insurance rates for fire, theft, and casualty are very high in his community. In view of these circumstances he does not feel justified in buying insurance on his automobile. What is your opinion of his decision? Give your reasons.
3. In every generation, and during various stages of the business cycle, people make comments on the change in the value of the dollar. In what way does the change in the value of the dollar constitute a risk?
4. Can you describe some cases in which scientific research has helped to reduce risks?
5. Mr. Brown, who owns a house, does not buy fire insurance because he thinks it costs too much. Mr. Brandon, who also owns a home, does not buy fire insurance because he believes there is little chance of fire and because he considers that he can afford to take the risk in view of his saving the cost of insurance. Do you agree with the reasoning of these two men?
6. Explain how advertising helps to reduce the risks of marketing.
7. Show how specialization in an occupation is advantageous to an individual and how it is also a risk.
8. How do personnel services, such as recreational facilities, medical care, and insurance, help large corporations to reduce certain risks?

Section II

Insurance and Risks

Risk-Bearing Agencies. There are many agencies that serve as institutions for the bearing of business and individual risks. The speculative exchanges, such as grain, cotton, and other commodity markets, aid manufacturers in avoiding the risk of falling prices or of rapidly rising prices. The major risk-bearing agency in modern society is, however, insurance. Insurance organizations can bear the risks that individuals or businesses cannot afford to bear, for the simple reason that insurance companies can combine a large number of similar risks and apply the law of averages.

Development of Insurance. Insurance as a device for meeting risks originated many years ago. It goes back to the time of Old World commerce, when merchants and shipowners were interested mainly in the commerce of the sea. The owners of ships frequently had to borrow money to finance each voyage, and they often pledged the ships as security for the loans. The owner of a ship who did not carry insurance was in a doubly precarious situation. If his ship was destroyed at sea, he not only suffered the loss of it but also had to repay the loan. A practice therefore developed whereby the shipowners could transfer their risks to the merchants and the bankers from whom they borrowed money. The cost of borrowing the money included interest and a charge for the risk. If a ship failed to make a safe voyage, the loan was not repaid.

Lloyd's insurance company in London is probably the world's largest and best-known insurance company. Lloyd's at one time was no more than a coffeehouse. Merchants met there daily and insured one another. These men were the forerunners of Lloyd's, of London. This institution will now insure almost any risk.

Many American insurance companies also will insure practically any type of risk. For instance, a football team can obtain insurance against rain. The football teams of large colleges must guarantee a certain payment to visiting teams. If rain prevents a game, there is no income that can be used in paying the visiting team. If the game is insured against rain, however, the insurance company guarantees payment of the stipulated sum. Likewise, dancers insure their feet; pianists, their fingers; and businessmen, the payment of their accounts receivable.

Organization of Insurance Companies. Insurance companies collect from policyholders amounts that are called *premiums*. A premium is a payment for protection against some risk such as fire, sickness, accident, or death. Premiums are paid weekly, monthly, quarterly, semiannually, or yearly, the time of payment depending upon the kind of insurance, the type of policy, and the nature of the company. The funds collected from policyholders are used by the companies in somewhat the same manner as cash deposits are used by banks. In other words, insurance companies use the funds paid by policyholders in making investments that will earn an income. The insurance companies must, of course, keep a reasonable amount of cash available to pay the claims of policyholders in case of fire, accident, death, ill health, or other similar happenings.

There are two general types of insurance companies. One is known as the *stock company*; and the other, as the *mutual company*. The stock company is a corporation that is formed according to the laws of the particular state. The stockholders own the company and elect directors, who in turn hire executives to run the business. The stockholders are, however, not necessarily policyholders. An insurance company of this type obtains money from the purchase of stock by stockholders, as well as from the collection of premiums from policyholders. The profits of the company are paid to the stockholders, who are the owners of the business. In some companies the policyholders also share in the earnings after the stockholders have been paid a stipulated amount.

A mutual company must also be organized under the laws of the particular state. The policyholders in such a company are, however, the owners. Each person or business concern that is insured in a mutual company becomes a member of the company and is entitled to a share in the ownership, the control, and the earnings. There are no stockholders as in a stock company. Although the officers do not have stock to assure them of continuous control, in many cases they find a means of perpetuating their control over the management of the company.

Policyholders in mutual companies usually pay premiums at a predetermined fixed rate, comparable to the rate established by stock companies. The policyholders in mutual companies, however, may receive dividends or have to pay assessments. If the company makes a profit, each policyholder shares in proportion to the amount of his policy. If the company fails to make a profit, each policyholder (except those in most life insurance companies) is assessed an amount to make sure that the income of the company will be equal to its expenditures. Usually the maximum amount of an assessment cannot exceed the original premium.

The operation of mutual fire insurance companies usually increases fire-prevention activities. If the buildings insured in a mutual company are seldom visited by fires, the rates are correspondingly low. If there are many fires, the rates are high. Some mutual companies are organized to insure against only a selected group of high-grade risks. Some companies confine their insurance to restricted localities, to particular types of industries, or to selected groups of individuals.

Theory of Probability. Strange as it may seem, a great many uncertainties may be combined to form certainties that can be predicted with reasonable accuracy. The mortality experience of individuals is a good example. For many years insurance companies have tabulated very carefully statistics in relation to the deaths of individuals. From a study of these figures it is possible to determine very nearly the exact number of people in a given group who will die each year. The insurance companies, of course, cannot predict who will die, but they can estimate with reasonable accuracy how many will die. It is on the basis of these figures that insurance rates are calculated.

The figures used in calculating the probability of death comprise what is known as the *American Experience Table of Mortality*. This table is shown in Illustration No. 49

AGE	NUMBER OF PERSONS LIVING	NUMBER OF DEATHS EACH YEAR	DEATH RATE PER THOUSAND	EXPECTATION OF LIFE
10	100,000	749	7.49	48.72
11	99,251	746	7.52	48.08
12	98,505	743	7.54	47.45
13	97,762	740	7.57	46.80
14	97,022	737	7.60	46.16
15	96,285	735	7.63	45.50
16	95,550	732	7.66	44.85
17	94,818	729	7.69	44.19
18	94,089	727	7.73	43.53
19	93,362	725	7.76	42.87
20	92,637	723	7.80	42.20
21	91,914	722	7.85	41.53
22	91,192	721	7.91	40.85
23	90,471	720	7.96	40.17
24	89,751	719	8.01	39.49
25	89,032	718	8.06	38.81
26	88,314	718	8.13	38.12
27	87,596	718	8.20	37.43
28	86,878	718	8.26	36.73
29	86,160	719	8.34	36.03
30	85,441	720	8.43	35.33
31	84,721	721	8.51	34.63
32	84,000	723	8.61	33.92
33	83,277	726	8.72	33.21
34	82,551	729	8.83	32.50
35	81,822	732	8.95	31.78
36	81,090	737	9.09	31.07
37	80,353	742	9.23	30.35
38	79,611	749	9.41	29.62
39	78,862	756	9.59	28.90
40	78,106	765	9.79	28.18
41	77,341	774	10.01	27.45
42	76,567	785	10.25	26.72
43	75,782	797	10.52	26.00
44	74,985	812	10.83	25.27
45	74,173	828	11.16	24.54
46	73,345	848	11.56	23.81
47	72,497	870	12.00	23.08
48	71,627	896	12.51	22.36
49	70,731	927	13.11	21.63
50	69,804	962	13.78	20.91
51	68,842	1,001	14.54	20.20
52	67,841	1,044	15.39	19.49
53	66,797	1,091	16.33	18.79
54	65,706	1,143	17.40	18.09
55	64,563	1,199	18.57	17.40
56	63,364	1,260	19.88	16.72
57	62,104	1,325	21.33	16.05
58	60,779	1,394	22.94	15.39
59	59,385	1,468	24.72	14.74
60	57,917	1,546	26.69	14.10
61	56,371	1,628	28.88	13.47
62	54,743	1,713	31.29	12.86
63	53,030	1,800	33.94	12.26
64	51,230	1,889	36.87	11.67
65	49,341	1,980	40.13	11.10
66	47,361	2,070	43.71	10.54
67	45,291	2,158	47.65	10.00
68	43,133	2,243	52.00	9.47
69	40,890	2,321	56.76	8.97
70	38,569	2,391	61.99	8.48
71	36,178	2,448	67.66	8.00
72	33,730	2,487	73.73	7.55
73	31,243	2,505	80.18	7.11
74	28,738	2,501	87.03	6.68
75	26,237	2,476	94.37	6.27
76	23,761	2,431	102.31	5.88
77	21,330	2,369	111.06	5.49
78	18,961	2,291	120.83	5.11
79	16,670	2,196	131.73	4.74
80	14,474	2,091	144.47	4.39
81	12,383	1,964	158.60	4.05
82	10,419	1,816	174.30	3.71
83	8,603	1,648	191.56	3.39
84	6,955	1,470	211.36	3.08
85	5,485	1,292	235.55	2.77
86	4,193	1,114	265.68	2.47
87	3,079	933	303.02	2.18
88	2,146	744	346.69	1.91
89	1,402	555	395.86	1.66
90	847	385	454.54	1.42
91	462	246	532.47	1.19
92	216	137	634.26	.98
93	79	58	734.18	.80
94	21	18	857.14	.64
95	3	3	1,000.00	.50

Illustration No. 49—The American Experience Table of Mortality

The table may be interpreted by means of the following example: In an average group of 100,000 people at the age of ten, there will be 749 deaths in the first year. This is a rate of 7.49 a thousand. The members of this group are expected to live an average of 48.72 additional years. At the age of twenty there will be 92,637 still living. The rate of mortality will then be 723 deaths a year or 7.8 a thousand. Those who are living at the age of twenty should expect to live 42.2 additional years.

It may seem strange at first that a fire insurance company, for instance, can assume the risk of paying all losses and yet charge each policyholder only a small fee. Frequently the total yearly fee is as low as one tenth of 1 per cent of the possible loss. The reason why insurance companies can follow this practice is that they know from the *theory of probability* what losses can be expected. They can therefore keep in a reserve fund a sufficient amount to pay each loss as it occurs. It is true that unusual circumstances, such as an exceptionally large fire, may cause unforeseen losses; but, over a long period of time, the losses are predictable. The surplus fund that an insurance company keeps is used as a protection against any unusual losses.

The theory of probability is based upon a study of experiences in the past. For instance, a fire insurance company finds that three out of every one thousand houses in a certain city have burned each year. The company can therefore reasonably assume that this average will continue; that three houses in every thousand will burn during the succeeding year. There may be various factors, however, that change this condition. One large fire may cause an unusual loss of ten or twelve houses; or, on the other hand, the use of new fire equipment may reduce the loss from fires.

The law of probability cannot be based upon a study of a comparatively small number of houses—one thousand, for example—because such a group of houses might be subject to many unusual conditions. Furthermore, the loss in one city may decrease in one year, whereas that in another city may increase in the same year. When the number is increased to a million or more houses in several communities, the average chance of unusual disasters is decreased. In other words, the chance of loss per house is less. Insurance companies therefore try to spread their risks over a wide area to protect themselves.

How Insurance Rates Are Computed. The person who buys insurance is interested in what it costs. In other words, he wants to know the *premium rate.* In determining rates, insurance companies must provide for (a) losses that are to be paid, (b) expenses of operation, (c) commissions, and (d) profits. In determining future rates, the insurance company bases its calculations on past experience. In the case of a stock company the earnings go to stockholders; whereas in the case of a mutual company they are applied to reducing the premium rates.

Each state is usually taken as a unit when fire insurance rates are to be established on the basis of losses. Some states are divided into sections. Cities are rated by classes, ranging from one to ten. A first-class city has the lowest rate, for it has the best fire protection. A tenth-class city has the highest rate because it has no fire protection. The following factors are considered in classifying cities:

(a) Water supply
(b) Fire department
(c) Fire-alarm system
(d) Police system
(e) Building laws
(f) Hazards
(g) Structural conditions
(h) Climatic conditions
(i) Correlation between the water supply and the fire department
(j) Fire-sprinkler system

Insurance rates for fire and other purposes are calculated in somewhat the same manner as life insurance rates. For example, statistics on fires show that a certain number of homes will be burned each year in a certain city. No one can predict which particular homes will burn, but approximately the same number will be destroyed by fire each year unless conditions change. One favorable year would not be sufficient to justify a reduction in the insurance rates for any community. Likewise, one unfavorable year would not justify raising the rates. The average conditions are taken into consideration.

As no one can determine whether his home will be burned, most people carry insurance against fire. People who own homes have found that it is safer to pay a small definite sum each year for insurance than to run the risk of losing their homes through fire. Each person, in other words, pays a *certain definite loss* each year in place of an *uncertain large loss.*

Regulation of Insurance. Insurance is such an important factor in the stability of modern business that all states have found it necessary to place some regulation upon insurance companies. All insurance policies are contracts that call for the fulfillment of conditions at some future time. The insured person is usually dead when the proceeds are paid. The states therefore believe it their duty to protect the interests of those who buy insurance.

Each state has a special insurance law and usually designates some official whose duty it is to administer and enforce the law. The most important function of state regulation is to make sure that all insurance companies are able to pay all obligations as they become due. The payment of all obligations is the paramount duty of an insurance company, for it involves the fundamental purpose of insurance.

State regulation also protects insurance buyers from fraud. Most states require reports from insurance companies, as well as inspection of the securities, accounting records, and business methods of the companies. In most states, insurance companies are regulated as to the ways in which they can invest the money collected from policyholders. These investments are usually confined to high-grade bonds of the Federal Government, of states, utilities, and cities, and high-grade real-estate mortgages and mortgage bonds. If an individual followed the example of a good insurance company in investing funds, he would be following an investment policy that is far above the average.

Although special bureaus provide information for establishing insurance rates, the state governments retain the right to regulate these rates. Court rulings have established the principle that fire insurance is subject to regulation because it is a matter of public interest.

Fields of Insurance. In the United States there are four principal divisions of insurance: *life, fire, marine,* and *casualty.* Among these four types of insurance there are variations and overlappings.

Life insurance and its uses will be discussed completely in Chapter VI. There are various uses of life insurance. For instance, a person may have his life insured so that when he dies his debts can be paid. The partners in a business may insure each other so that, upon the death of either partner, the surviving partner will have funds with which to continue the business. Many business executives are insured because of the possible loss that may result from their death. Suppose, for example, that the success of the Central Manufacturing Company is due largely to the peculiar ability and popularity of its president, Mr. J. W. Cook. The directors of the corporation decide that it is wise to insure Mr. Cook's life for $500,000. They are reasonably certain that, if Mr. Cook should die suddenly, it would be difficult to make adjustments in the business to replace him. It is reasonable to expect that the profits of the business would be less for a considerable time until someone would be able to take his place. The $500,000 payable upon Mr. Cook's death can therefore be used to protect the company against any unfavorable circumstances following his death. The proceeds of this insurance will reduce the risk of failure of the business after the death of Mr. Cook. In other words, the money can be used to keep the business running until necessary adjustments are made.

Fire insurance provides funds to replace buildings or materials destroyed by fire. Many business concerns carry fire insurance on buildings, furniture and equipment, machinery, raw materials, and finished goods. Insurance on a building usually does not cover the machinery, stock, and equipment. Ordinarily separate policies are required to give full protection from fire loss. The owner of a building should be interested in fire insurance to protect his investment. The occupant of a rented building should be interested in such insurance to protect his business. In buying fire insurance, one should know just what is covered by the policy.

The actual loss in property destroyed by fire is not the only loss to a business concern. The interruption to business until a new place can be obtained and operations can be resumed will result in a loss of profits and considerable incidental expense. Special types of insurance can be obtained to cover the costs caused by the inconvenience of the fire.

Marine insurance is often called *transportation insurance*. This type of insurance has many uses. If a shipment is sent by water, the person who owns the goods will want protection against damage, theft, and loss. The person who owns the goods may obtain this insurance, or the company that transports them may provide it as a part of the cost of transportation. The transportation company may carry its own insurance and pay its own losses, or it may insure all its shipments through some separate company.

Shipments hauled by express companies are usually insured, and the cost of the insurance is included in the transportation charges. Railway freight shipments may be sent insured or uninsured. Parcel-post packages may also be sent in either way.

Insurance may be obtained to cover loss due to theft or embezzlement. Theft insurance may cover specified items such as money, or it may cover all the merchandise and equipment of a company. Insurance of this type is frequently referred to as *burglary insurance*, although the theft may be performed by an employee of the company. Banks and companies that handle large amounts of money carry insurance against robbery. Many businesses carry insurance that protects them from loss in case of theft or embezzlement by dishonest employees. Some employees who handle large sums of money are covered by surety bonds. If such an employee proves dishonest, the company can recover from the surety company the loss to the extent of the bond. A surety bond is one form of insurance.

Automobile insurance is one of the most common types of casualty insurance. It may cover potential loss caused by fire, theft, collision, property damage, bodily injury, a tornado, a windstorm, rain, flood, or the like involving the insured automobile.

Underwood & Underwood

Illustration No. 50—Two Types of Losses

Almost every owner of an automobile agrees that *fire and theft insurance* is desirable. There are relatively few automobile owners who do not carry this protection. The insurance rates are therefore low because the risks are spread among a great number of automobile owners. It formerly was the custom for companies to issue policies in which they agreed to pay a fixed amount in case of the loss of the automobile by fire or theft. The most common practice now is to issue policies that state that the market value of the automobile at the time of loss will be paid. Most policies are worded in such a manner that the insurance company may replace the car with a similar one or pay the market value at the time of loss, regardless of the amount of insurance carried on the car. When there is only a partial loss, the insurance company repairs the damage or pays the amount of cash equivalent to the cost of the repairs. Most policies include protection against loss due to fire and theft while an automobile is being transported on a boat or a railroad.

Collision insurance is usually meant to be protection against loss arising from damage to one's own car. This type of insurance is becoming somewhat unpopular because it is costly and because some unscrupulous people damage their own cars to collect the insurance.

Although fire and theft insurance are the most widely used forms of automobile insurance, property-damage and bodily-injury insurance are probably the most important. Some states have passed legislation that makes it necessary for automobile owners to take out these types of insurance before they can obtain licenses for their cars.

Property-damage insurance provides protection against loss resulting from damage to an automobile or some other property of another person, while *bodily-injury insurance* provides protection against loss arising from the injury of any living person. These two forms of insurance are often sold jointly in the same policy, although they can be bought separately. They are important because the hazards of not carrying them are unknown and potentially great. On the other hand, the hazards from fire and theft are definitely known and are not particularly great.

Ordinarily bodily-injury insurance should be carried for not less than ten thousand dollars in case of the injury of a single person, or not less than twenty thousand dollars in case of the injury of more than one person. Most claims can be settled within the limits of these amounts. If ten thousand dollars' worth of bodily-injury insurance is carried as protection against loss due to a single injury, the person who is injured can collect from the insurance company an amount not exceeding ten thousand dollars. The extent of the injury must be determined by a court or established by an agreement between the injured person and the insurance company. A good insurance company will take care of all legal details. If the amount of damages exceeds the amount of insurance, the insured person will have to pay the difference.

Ordinarily it is considered wise not to carry less than five thousand dollars' worth of property-damage insurance. If an automobile driver who carries five thousand dollars' worth of property-damage insurance damages the automobile of another person or the front of a store, for instance, the person whose property has been damaged may collect damages from the insurance company to the extent of five thousand dollars.

Insurance against such hazards as tornado, windstorm, and rain is used less frequently, although the rates for such protection are low. The rates are low because the chance of loss from these hazards is relatively small.

Analysis of Insurance Needs. Nearly everyone is interested in some kind of insurance. He is therefore confronted with the problem of choosing what insurance to buy, how much to buy, and from whom to buy. In some cases the person does not have any choice as to whether he will carry insurance or not. If he has purchased a home, and a bank or a loan association holds a mortgage on the home, he will be required to insure the home. In an increasingly large number of states, a person cannot obtain an automobile license without buying bodily-injury and property-damage insurance.

The mere fact that a person has never suffered a loss is no reason to believe that he will continue to be so fortunate. One cannot assume the attitude, "It has not happened to me thus far. What reason is there to expect it to happen?" One must look upon the buying of insurance from the point of view of (a) the cost of carrying insurance, (b) the results of not carrying insurance, and (c) the benefits of carrying insurance. It is just as foolish to carry too much insurance as it is not to carry any. For instance, a person would be foolish to use all his surplus income for buying life insurance. He would not have any money left for emergencies, for investment, for acquiring a home, or for personal advancement.

A person who has a million dollars and who owns a large estate might not find it desirable to insure a small building on that estate or a motor boat that he owns, for the loss of either of these would not cause him any special handicap. On the other hand, a person who owns his own home and has only a small amount of additional savings should, by all means, insure the home. If he did not carry insurance and the home were destroyed, he would have difficulty in replacing it.

If a person owns a small cottage that he uses during his summer vacation, he may debate whether to insure it. The loss of the cottage would be inconvenient, but it would not impose upon him a great financial loss. If the insurance rate on a cottage of this type is high, the insurance will not be justified. On the other hand, if the same man owns a small building that he uses for a workshop in making a living, he will want to insure it even though its value may not be equal to that of the summer cottage. The destruction of the workshop would result in a severe handicap.

The use of insurance should be looked upon as a means of enabling one to carry out fixed plans through life without the hazards of uncertainty. Insurance makes plans certain, whereas the lack of it makes plans uncertain. A sudden large loss might disrupt an otherwise good plan.

Insurable Interest. Everyone has an insurable interest in his own life. Whether a person has an insurable interest in the life of another depends upon whether he will be deprived of some benefit by the death of the other. One need not be a relative of a person in order to insure that person's life. A creditor, under some circumstances, may insure the life of a debtor. Close kinship is often, but not necessarily, sufficient to constitute an insurable interest.

When property is insured against loss due to fire or other causes, the purpose of the insurance is considered to be the protection of the interest of the person who buys the insurance. The policyholder must have an insurable interest in the property. A person is considered to have an insurable interest in property if there is a reasonable expectation that he will derive a financial benefit from the existence of the property or will suffer a loss from the damage or the destruction of the property. For instance, both the owner of a home and the person who holds a mortgage on the home have an insurable interest. If the property is not insured and is later destroyed, the owner will lose the money he has invested in it, and the person who owns the mortgage may lose the money that is due him on the mortgage.

Most mortgages contain a clause that requires the owner of the property to carry enough insurance to protect the mortgagee. If this insurance is carried in accordance with the agreement, the mortgagee is entitled, in case of loss resulting from fire or some other cause, to enough money from the proceeds to equal the unpaid balance on the mortgage. The remainder of the proceeds goes to the owner. If there is no such agreement between the mortgagor and the mortgagee, the mortgagee may protect his interest by purchasing enough insurance to cover the unpaid balance on the mortgage. There are many variations with regard to the rights and the liabilities of the mortgagee, the mortgagor, and the insurance company in cases of insurance on property that is mortgaged. The laws of the particular state, the clauses in the mortgage, and the clauses in the insurance policy should therefore be studied carefully.

Change in the Insurable Interest. If there is any change in the title to insured property or in the possession of such property, the protection under the policy usually becomes void. For instance, if a house is insured by Mr. Smith and is sold to Mr. Howard, the insurance policy taken out by Mr. Smith becomes void, for it was written to protect the latter's interest and cannot be transferred to Mr. Howard without the consent of the insurance company. An exception to this rule arises in case of the death of the person who has purchased the insurance. If a person dies after he has insured his home, his heirs are protected under the insurance.

Automobile insurance is essentially the same as fire insurance with regard to a change in the insurable interest. If an automobile is sold, the insurance company should be requested to transfer the policy immediately in order to assure protection to the new owner. As insurance policies differ in many respects, their clauses should be read carefully to determine one's rights and the nature of the protection.

Proof of Loss. A person who carries any kind of insurance should protect his policy carefully, for it is the first evidence of claim in case of loss. If possible, life insurance policies should be kept in safe-deposit boxes. If they are stolen, destroyed, or lost, they can be replaced only through a tedious process. Even if a policy cannot be presented, however, as evidence of claim in case of loss, the claim will usually be paid after sufficient identification has been made.

When property is insured against fire, it is extremely important to keep a record of the property that is insured. In case of loss the insurance company will require some kind of evidence to serve as the basis for paying the loss. The insurance company will frequently accept a sworn statement as to the loss. The safest practice, however, is to keep some type of record. Illustration No. 51 shows a sample record for household furniture that has been insured.

A record of insured property should be kept in a place where it will not be destroyed in case the property that is insured is destroyed. A safe-deposit box is a good place. A policy may contain a clause that makes it mandatory for the insured person to maintain an inventory record and to keep this record in a place where it cannot be destroyed.

Living Room				
No.	Article	Date of Purchase	Cost	Description
	Carpets,			
	Chairs,			
	Clock,			
	Couch,			
	Curtains,			
	Cushions,			
	Jardinieres,			
	Lamps,			
	Mirrors,			
	Piano,			
	Stool and Cover,			
	Rugs,			
	Shades,			
	Window Fixtures,			
	Tables,			
	Tapestry,			
	Pictures,*			
	Vases,			
	Smoking Stand,			
	Draperies,			
	Radio,			
	* See Special List			

Illustration No. 51—A Sample Record for Household Furniture That Is Insured

How Fire Insurance Operates. A person usually insures his property for a specified amount. For example, Mr. Thompson's house and lot may be valued at five thousand dollars. If there is a garage on the property, the insurance company will require a separate valuation for the house and the garage. Suppose the lot is valued at one thousand dollars; the house, at thirty-eight hundred dollars; and the garage, at two hundred dollars. Mr. Thompson decides to insure his house for thirty-eight hundred dollars and his garage for two hundred dollars. If the house is burned completely, he can collect the maximum amount of his policy, which is thirty-eight hundred dollars. If it is not burned completely, the insurance company has the privilege of replacing it as nearly as possible in its original condition. Suppose, however, he insures his house for only two thousand dollars. If it is completely destroyed, he can collect only two thousand dollars. If it is only partially destroyed, he can collect up to the amount of two thousand dollars.

How Coinsurance Operates. Coinsurance is a type of insurance commonly used in business, but it does not apply to insurance on a home, household furnishings, or any personal possessions in any building. A home is considered to be a one- or a two-family house. Coinsurance may be used, however, on an apartment building housing three or more families, but not on the household furnishings or the personal property contained in such a building. Through the use of coinsurance it is possible to take advantage of low premium rates. Coinsurance means that property is insured jointly by the insurance company and the owner. Each bears a part of the risk. Under coinsurance the reduction in premium rates on dwellings averages from 10 to 15 per cent. Coinsurance clauses are referred to by percentages, as 50 per cent coinsurance, 60 per cent coinsurance, or 100 per cent coinsurance. The most common clauses provide for 80 or 90 per cent coinsurance. Suppose, for example, that Mr. Thompson has a ten-thousand-dollar apartment building that is insured under a 100 per cent coinsurance clause. Under the contract Mr. Thompson has agreed to insure his property for 100 per cent of its value. If he carries ten thousand dollars' worth of insurance and his apartment building is damaged to the extent of two thousand dollars, he will collect the full amount of the loss.

Suppose, however, that instead of carrying ten thousand dollars' worth of insurance, Mr. Thompson carries only five thousand dollars' worth. If his apartment building is damaged by fire to the extent of two thousand dollars, he will not be entitled to recover the full amount of the loss because he has not been carrying insurance at 100 per cent of the value of the property. He has actually been carrying insurance that amounts to only one half of the value of his building. He must therefore share the loss with the insurance company. He will be entitled to collect one half of the loss, or one thousand dollars.

If Mr. Thompson's apartment building is insured under an 80 per cent coinsurance clause, he is expected to carry insurance equal to 80 per cent of the value of the property, or eight thousand dollars. Any loss not exceeding this amount will be paid, provided Mr. Thompson has kept his property insured for this amount. If the damage amounts to two thousand dollars, he will collect that amount. If, on the other hand, he carries only five thousand dollars' worth of insurance, he must share in the loss. The percentage of the loss that will be paid by the insurance company is computed by dividing eight thousand dollars into five thousand (the amount of insurance actually carried). Mr. Thompson is entitled to only five eighths of the amount of the loss. The insurance company will pay five eighths of two thousand dollars, or twelve hundred and fifty dollars.

In no case will the insurance company pay an amount greater than the amount of the policy.

TEXTBOOK QUESTIONS

1. For what purposes do insurance companies use the funds that are collected from policyholders as premiums?
2. (a) What is a stock company? (b) Compare a stock company with a mutual company.
3. (a) What kind of insurance company makes assessments against policyholders? (b) Under what circumstances are assessments made?
4. In what way do fire-prevention activities affect the insurance rates of a mutual company or of a stock company?
5. How does the selection of policyholders affect the premium rates and the dividends of mutual companies?
6. Explain briefly how losses such as those due to fires, deaths, accidents, or the like are predictable.
7. What various elements are included in computing the premium rates for fire insurance?

8. (a) How many classes of cities are recognized for the purpose of establishing basic fire insurance rates? (b) In what respect does the highest rate differ from the lowest rate?
9. If an automobile on which you have a fire insurance policy is damaged by fire while it is being shipped, are you protected from the loss?
10. Under the agreements in most automobile insurance policies, what options does the insurance company have if the automobile is destroyed by fire?
11. (a) What is bodily-injury insurance on an automobile? (b) What is property-damage insurance?
12. On what basis is a person considered to have an insurable interest in the life or the property that is insured?
13. Under what circumstances does insurance become void because of a change in the insurable interest in property?
14. What precaution should be used in order that proof of loss can be provided in case insured property is stolen, destroyed, or lost?
15. (a) Explain briefly the difference between ordinary fire insurance on an apartment building and coinsurance on the same property. (b) Give an example of how an 80 per cent coinsurance clause operates.

DISCUSSION QUESTIONS

1. (a) How could an insurance company determine rates for insurance against loss due to rain? (b) Do you think such rates would be high or low as compared with the rates for automobile insurance? Why?
2. (a) What type of resident in Florida would be interested particularly in weather reports? (b) Why would people in other parts of the country be interested in weather reports?
3. Two companies of equal size and financial standing insure farmers against the risk of crop losses. Company A operates nationally, and Company B operates in a section that comprises ten states. (a) From your consideration of these facts only, draw some conclusion as to the relative merits of these companies. (b) In which one would you take out insurance?
4. If you were buying automobile insurance, what consideration would you give to the type of policy and the general attitude of the company in paying claims?
5. Mr. Nelson travels by automobile in several states. Point out some of the important facts that he should consider in buying insurance on his automobile.
6. What, in your opinion, represents the more serious risk of an automobile owner: (a) the risk of property damage or (b) the risk of injury to a person? Why?

Section III

Social Security

Functions of Social Security. For many years some foreign countries have had various kinds of unemployment insurance and certain forms of old-age pension systems. Arizona was the first state in the United States to enact an old-age pension law. That law was declared unconstitutional, but in more recent years other states have individually enacted old-age pension laws. The theory of unemployment insurance is that certain funds should be laid aside during times of employment to take care of dependent workers during periods of unemployment. The theory of an old-age pension plan is that it is easier to lay aside small sums representing a certain percentage of the wages of workers, so that the government can systematically render assistance to people when they have become too old for employment, than it is to wait and let individual communities or relatives take care of aged persons who need assistance. In other words, the old-age pension plan is regarded not only from the practical point of view of taking care of risks that are involved, but also from the social point of view of looking after the welfare of dependent people.

Federal Social Security Act. The Federal social security program provides for insurance against industrial unemployment, old-age pensions, aid to dependent children, aid to dependent mothers, and aid to the blind. The Social Security Act provides a plan under which each state has adopted its own unemployment insurance system. All the other aspects of the law are administered by the Federal Government.

Unemployment Insurance. Under the Social Security Act every state has enacted its own law providing for an unemployment insurance system. The Federal Government levies on each enterprise employing at least eight persons a 3 per cent pay-roll tax, but allows the employer a credit for a certain amount of the unemployment insurance tax

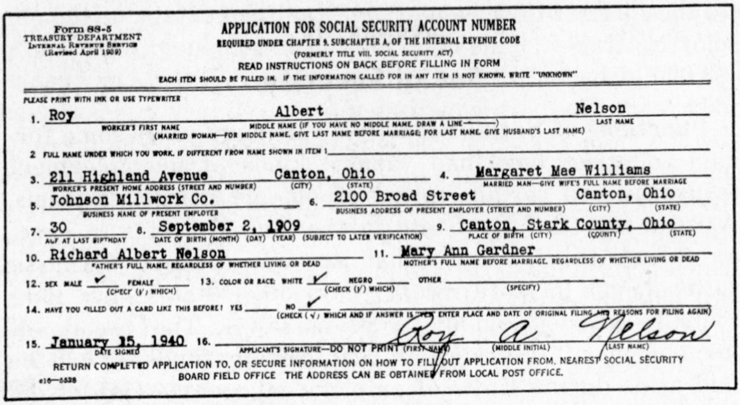

Form SS-5
TREASURY DEPARTMENT
Internal Revenue Service
(Revised April 1939)

APPLICATION FOR SOCIAL SECURITY ACCOUNT NUMBER
REQUIRED UNDER CHAPTER 9, SUBCHAPTER A, OF THE INTERNAL REVENUE CODE
(FORMERLY TITLE VIII, SOCIAL SECURITY ACT)
READ INSTRUCTIONS ON BACK BEFORE FILLING IN FORM
EACH ITEM SHOULD BE FILLED IN. IF THE INFORMATION CALLED FOR IN ANY ITEM IS NOT KNOWN, WRITE "UNKNOWN"

PLEASE PRINT WITH INK OR USE TYPEWRITER

1. Roy — WORKER'S FIRST NAME; Albert — MIDDLE NAME (IF YOU HAVE NO MIDDLE NAME, DRAW A LINE———) (MARRIED WOMAN—FOR MIDDLE NAME, GIVE LAST NAME BEFORE MARRIAGE; FOR LAST NAME, GIVE HUSBAND'S LAST NAME); Nelson — LAST NAME

2 FULL NAME UNDER WHICH YOU WORK, IF DIFFERENT FROM NAME SHOWN IN ITEM 1 ______

3. 211 Highland Avenue — WORKER'S PRESENT HOME ADDRESS (STREET AND NUMBER); Canton, Ohio — (CITY) (STATE)

4. Margaret Mae Williams — MARRIED MAN—GIVE WIFE'S FULL NAME BEFORE MARRIAGE

5. Johnson Millwork Co. — BUSINESS NAME OF PRESENT EMPLOYER

6. 2100 Broad Street — BUSINESS ADDRESS OF PRESENT EMPLOYER (STREET AND NUMBER); Canton, Ohio — (CITY) (STATE)

7. 30 — AGE AT LAST BIRTHDAY

8. September 2, 1909 — DATE OF BIRTH (MONTH) (DAY) (YEAR) (SUBJECT TO LATER VERIFICATION)

9. Canton, Stark County, Ohio — PLACE OF BIRTH (CITY) (COUNTY) (STATE)

10. Richard Albert Nelson — FATHER'S FULL NAME, REGARDLESS OF WHETHER LIVING OR DEAD

11. Mary Ann Gardner — MOTHER'S FULL NAME BEFORE MARRIAGE, REGARDLESS OF WHETHER LIVING OR DEAD

12. SEX MALE ✓ FEMALE ____ (CHECK (✓) WHICH)

13. COLOR OR RACE WHITE ✓ NEGRO ____ OTHER ______ (CHECK (✓) WHICH) (SPECIFY)

14. HAVE YOU FILLED OUT A CARD LIKE THIS BEFORE? YES ____ NO ✓ (CHECK (✓) WHICH AND IF ANSWER IS "YES" ENTER PLACE AND DATE OF ORIGINAL FILING AND REASONS FOR FILING AGAIN)

15. January 15, 1940 — DATE SIGNED

16. Roy A Nelson — APPLICANT'S SIGNATURE—DO NOT PRINT (FIRST NAME) (MIDDLE INITIAL) (LAST NAME)

RETURN COMPLETED APPLICATION TO, OR SECURE INFORMATION ON HOW TO FILL OUT APPLICATION FROM, NEAREST SOCIAL SECURITY BOARD FIELD OFFICE. THE ADDRESS CAN BE OBTAINED FROM LOCAL POST OFFICE.

16—5538

Illustration No. 52—Application for Social Security Number

paid to the state. In most states the tax is borne entirely by the employer; whereas in a few states both the employer and the employees share the contribution that is paid to the state for unemployment insurance. The total tax on wages for unemployment insurance in most cases amounts to about 3 per cent and is based on the first $3,000 of the worker's wages for a year.

As the unemployment compensation laws are not uniform in all states, it is impossible to give an example that will apply to every state. Nevertheless, the benefits that are paid to workers are usually of two kinds: (a) one for total unemployment and (b) one for partial unemployment. The benefits for total unemployment are usually about one half of the worker's average weekly wage, but the maximum payment for unemployment compensation is ordinarily limited to about $15 a week and is paid for a limited number of weeks during any particular year. The benefits for partial unemployment depend upon the amount of time during which the worker is idle and the rate that is paid in the particular state. To receive unemployment benefits, the worker must register with the proper state agency and file a claim for unemployment compensation.

Old-Age Insurance. Under the Social Security Act a reserve fund is accumulated as in the case of life insurance. The employer and the employee must contribute regularly to the Federal Government a certain percentage of the employee's wages. This contribution is computed on the first $3,000 of income earned by the employee during any calendar year. The part contributed by the employee is deducted by the employer from the employee's wages. The percentage is subject to change by law; but, regardless of the rate in effect in any particular year, the employer pays a certain percentage as a pay-roll tax and the employee pays the same percentage as a portion of his wages that is laid aside for old-age assistance. As the Federal Government keeps a separate account for each individual, each must have a social security number. This number and other information are shown on the social security card of the individual. Such a card is shown in Illustration No. 53.

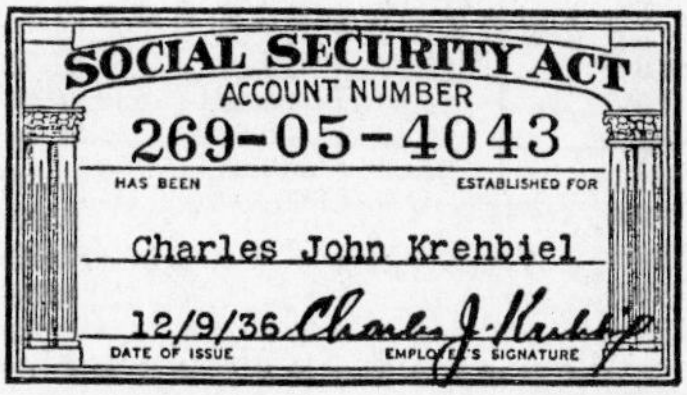

Illustration No. 53—A Social Security Card

Social Security Records. Every individual who is subject to social security taxes should keep a record of his wages and the amount of taxes paid. The employer is required by law to furnish regularly to each employee a written statement or statements showing the wages paid to the employee during the year. Each statement must be suitable for permanent retention. It may cover one, two, three, or four quarters of the year.

Whenever an employee changes employment, he should see that his new employer has his correct social security number so that he will receive credit for any wages that are earned.

Old-Age Benefits. Because the Social Security Act is subject to change by new legislation, it is impossible to predict exactly what benefits a person may expect when he attains the age of sixty-five. Nevertheless, Illustration No. 54 shows old-age benefits that have been computed on the basis of existing rates and the present plan of figuring such benefits. For example, if a single person has earned an average wage of $100 a month for five years previous to his retirement, he will get a retirement income of $26.25 a month. If a married person earned that wage, he and his wife will receive a combined income of $39.38.

ILLUSTRATIVE MONTHLY OLD-AGE BENEFITS
Benefits Begin on January 1, 1940

YEARS OF COVERAGE	AVERAGE MONTHLY WAGE OF $50		AVERAGE MONTHLY WAGE OF $100		AVERAGE MONTHLY WAGE OF $150		AVERAGE MONTHLY WAGE OF $250	
	SINGLE	MARRIED	SINGLE	MARRIED	SINGLE	MARRIED	SINGLE	MARRIED
3.......	$20.60	$30.90	$25.75	$38.63	$30.90	$46.35	$41.20	$61.80
5.......	21.00	31.50	26.25	39.38	31.50	47.25	42.00	63.00
10.......	22.00	33.00	27.50	41.25	33.00	49.50	44.00	66.00
20.......	24.00	36.00	30.00	45.00	36.00	54.00	48.00	72.00
30.......	26.00	39.00	32.50	48.75	39.00	58.50	52.00	78.00
40.......	28.00	40.00	35.00	52.50	42.00	63.00	56.00	84.00

Illustration No. 54—A Table Showing Old-Age Benefits

The chart in Illustration No. 55 is interpreted as follows: Assume that a person with no dependents has earned an average monthly wage of $100 for twenty years. Follow the line across to the twenty-year coverage line. From this point drop vertically down to the scale for monthly benefits. The monthly benefits will be almost $30.

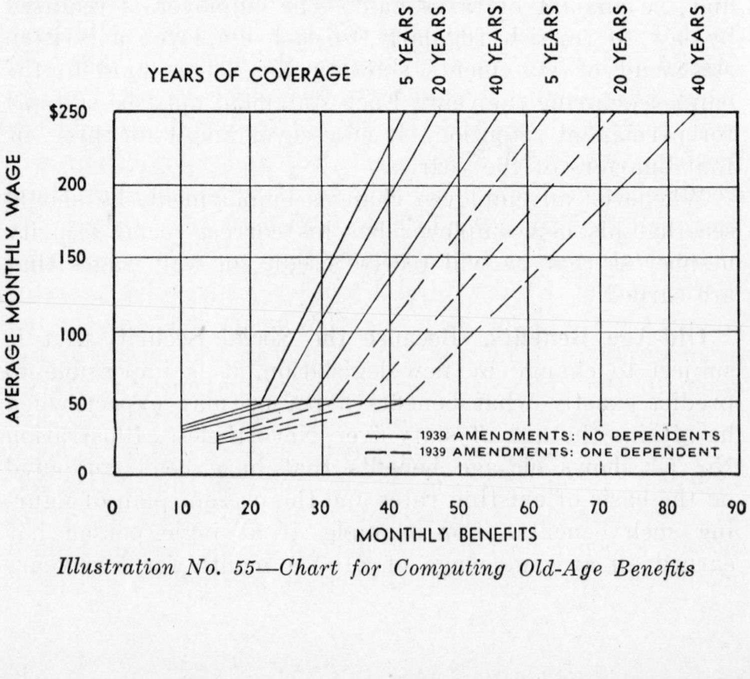

Illustration No. 55—Chart for Computing Old-Age Benefits

Need for Other Insurance. Some persons have gained the impression that the Social Security Act makes it unnecessary for a person to carry other insurance. An examination of the table in Illustration No. 54 indicates the limitations. If a person wants to have more income when he retires at the age of sixty-five, he must provide that income through other insurance, an investment, or savings. Furthermore, he may want insurance to provide a certain fixed sum for his dependents upon his death. He will have to use regular insurance to provide for this type of protection.

Exemptions. The Social Security Act does not cover all forms of employment. For instance, it exempts farmers, domestic help, Federal employees, teachers, and several other classifications. Some of these classifications may change from time to time in accordance with amendments to the Law.

Assistance to Widows and Orphans. Under the Federal Social Security Act, if an employee dies before reaching the age of sixty-five, his widow and other dependents are provided for. A widow of sixty-five years or more whose husband was insured under the Social Security Act is entitled to half the benefits that she and her husband would have shared if he had lived. A widow, regardless of her age, who has one or more children under eighteen years of age will receive half the monthly benefits to which she and her husband would have been entitled, and in addition will receive for each child benefits equal to one half of those to which the father would have been entitled.

Illustration No. 56 shows how survivor benefits are paid. For example, if the wife of a worker is sixty-five years of age or more and the wages earned by her husband for ten years previous to his death amounted to an average of $50 a month, the widow will receive a monthly benefit of $16.50.

If there are no children and the widow is under sixty-five years of age, a lump-sum payment is made to defray funeral expenses. Lump-sum benefits are shown in Illustration No. 57. For example, if the widow is less than sixty-five years of age and her husband has earned an average of $100 a month for five years, she will receive $157.50.

ILLUSTRATIVE MONTHLY SURVIVOR BENEFITS
Benefits Begin on January 1, 1940

	One Child or Parent 65 or Over	Widow 65 or Over	Widow and One Child	One Child or Parent 65 or Over	Widow 65 or Over	Widow and One Child
Years of Coverage	Average Monthly Wage of Deceased, $50			Average Monthly Wage of Deceased, $100		
3	$10.30	$15.45	$25.75	$12.88	$19.31	$32.19
5	10.50	15.75	26.25	13.13	19.69	32.81
10	11.00	16.50	27.50	13.75	20.63	34.38
20	12.00	18.00	30.00	15.00	22.50	37.50
30	13.00	19.50	32.50	16.25	24.38	40.63
40	14.00	21.00	35.00	17.50	26.25	43.75
Years of Coverage	Average Monthly Wage of Deceased, $150			Average Monthly Wage of Deceased, $250		
3	$15.45	$23.18	$38.63	$20.60	$30.90	$51.50
5	15.75	23.63	39.38	21.00	31.50	52.50
10	16.50	24.75	41.25	22.00	33.00	55.00
20	18.00	27.00	45.00	24.00	36.00	60.00
30	19.50	29.25	48.75	26.00	39.00	65.00
40	21.00	31.50	52.50	28.00	42.00	70.00

Illustration No. 56—A Table Showing Survivor Benefits

ILLUSTRATIVE LUMP-SUM DEATH PAYMENTS
Benefits Begin on January 1, 1940

	Average Monthly Wages			
	$50	$100	$150	$250
Years of Coverage				
3	$123.60	$154.50	$185.40	$247.20
5	126.00	157.50	189.00	252.00
10	132.00	165.00	198.00	264.00
20	144.00	180.00	216.00	288.00
30	156.00	195.00	234.00	312.00
40	168.00	210.00	252.00	336.00

Illustration No. 57—A Table Showing Lump-Sum Benefits

Other Assistance. The preceding discussion on social security has dealt with the benefits that are paid as a result of deductions from wages and on the basis of previous earnings. Under the Social Security Act, however, the Federal Government has made provisions for assistance to other needy groups. In general, the plan provides for funds to be furnished for (a) needy aged, (b) needy dependent children, (c) needy blind, (d) maternal welfare of infants

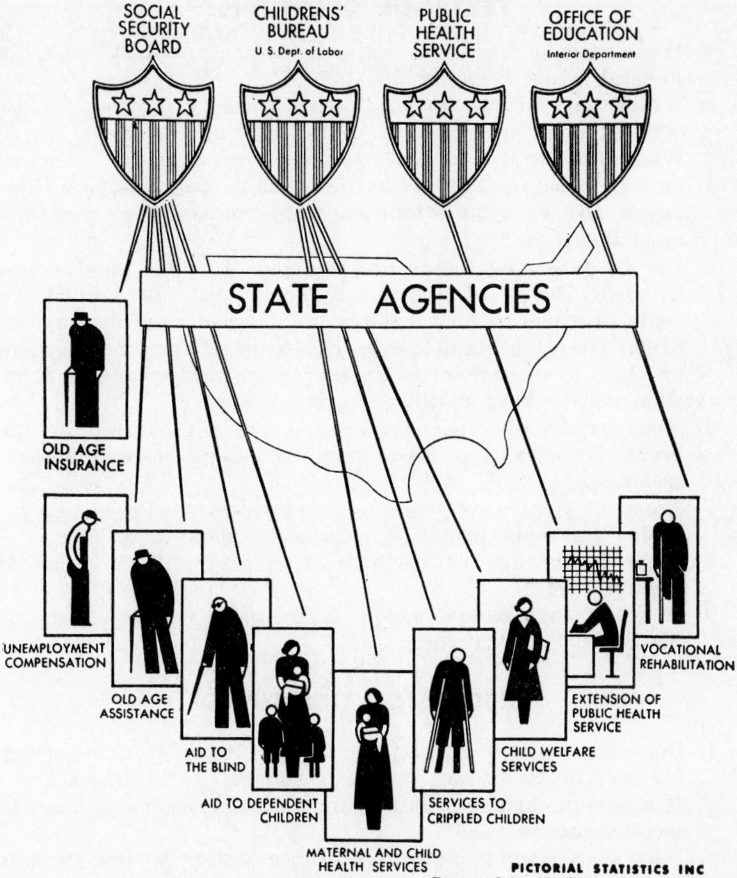

PICTORIAL STATISTICS INC
Prepared for the Social Security Board

Illustration No. 58—How the Social Security Program Is Administered

and mothers, (e) crippled children, (f) child welfare, (g) vocational rehabilitation, and (h) public health. If a state has a plan satisfactory to the Federal Government, that state may obtain from the Federal Government a contribution up to 50 per cent of the state expenditures, provided those expenditures do not exceed a certain amount. For example, if a state that has an old-age assistance plan acceptable to the Federal Government pays $40 a month or more as a pension to the needy aged, the Federal Government will contribute as much as $20 a month.

TEXTBOOK QUESTIONS

1. What types of insurance and benefits are provided under the Federal Social Security Act?
2. Which part of the Federal social security program is dependent upon laws enacted by the individual states?
3. Who pays the tax for unemployment insurance?
4. (a) To what extent are wages taxable for old-age assistance? (b) To what extent are wages taxable for unemployment insurance?
5. (a) By referring to the proper table, state the monthly retirement income of a married person who has worked ten years previous to retirement at an average monthly wage of $100. (b) If a single person has worked for twenty years previous to retirement at an average monthly wage of $150, what will be his monthly old-age benefits?
6. Some aged and dependent persons are not covered by the Social Security Act. How may these persons receive some assistance?
7. Name at least two types of employment that are not included under the provisions of the Social Security Act.
8. What is the age of retirement under the Federal Social Security Act?
9. In what ways may a widow share under the provisions of the Social Security Act?

DISCUSSION QUESTIONS

1. Does the Federal Social Security Act make it unnecessary for individuals to buy various forms of life insurance?
2. If a person earns $3,600 a year, is all this income subject to social security taxes?
3. Why does unemployment insurance differ in the various states, although it is a part of the Federal social security program?
4. Can one withdraw the amount accumulated for him in an old-age pension fund?
5. Can you think of any reasons why farmers are not included under the Federal Social Security Act?
6. Employees of railroads are not included under the Social Security Act. Can you think of any reasons why?
7. Explain how the provisions for old-age benefits under the Federal Social Security Act are a device to eliminate economic risks.
8. Most of the state unemployment insurance laws place a penalty on employers in proportion to the number of employees that are employed. What do you think may be some of the effects of this plan?

PROBLEMS

1. If the annual insurance rate on merchandise is $2.30 for every $100 of merchandise, what will be the annual premium on merchandise valued at $8,500?
2. Property is often insured in more than one company in order to distribute the risk. In case of loss each insurance company pays its share of the loss in proportion to the amount of insurance that it carries on the property. The Mercantile Store carries fire insurance of $3,000 with Company A; $2,000 with Company B; and $5,000 with Company C. The total value of the insured property is $12,000. A loss by fire is established at $4,000. How much will each insurance company pay?
3. Mr. Anderson's apartment building is appraised at a value of $5,000. He buys an 80 per cent coinsurance policy amounting to $4,000. (a) If a fire loss amounts to $1,500, how much will Mr. Anderson receive from his insurance? (b) If he had carried insurance amounting to $3,000, how much would he receive from the insurance?
4. Under the Federal Social Security Act what will be the monthly benefits of a widow with two children under eighteen years of age (a) if her husband worked ten years previous to his death at an average monthly wage of $100? (b) if he worked twenty years at an average monthly wage of $150?

COMMUNITY PROBLEMS AND PROJECTS

1. Obtain a policy for fire insurance on a home. Study its clauses and regulations. Write a report on it.
2. Obtain a sample of some kind of fire insurance policy for a business. Study its clauses and regulations. Write a report on it.
3. Make an investigation of the local rates for theft, property-damage, bodily-injury, and fire insurance on automobiles. Compare these rates with those in other communities. Write a report summarizing your findings.
4. Obtain an automobile insurance policy of some kind. Study its clauses, and make a report on its features. Point out some of the ways in which the automobile owner may not be protected adequately by the policy.
5. Obtain a copy of your state law pertaining to unemployment insurance. Make a report on it, and figure out specifically how an unemployed person is compensated.

CHAPTER VI

PROBLEMS OF BUYING LIFE INSURANCE

Purpose of the Chapter. Practically everyone needs some form of life insurance. As there are many forms suited to persons in various circumstances, a policy must be bought with much care. It is possible to own too much insurance as well as to own the wrong kind. Furthermore, it is difficult to get unbiased advice on insurance unless one can afford to hire an insurance broker or adviser. There are differences in types of companies and variations in the purposes and the provisions of policies.

The purpose of this chapter is to provide an understanding of the various types of life insurance policies and companies. A study of this chapter will disclose methods of evaluating such policies and companies.

Section I

Purposes and Kinds of Life Insurance

How Sure Is Life? None of us can forecast the length of his life. We are certain about the inevitability of death, but the time when each of us must die is very uncertain. Although death is not predictable for individuals, it is for large groups of people. The fact that it is predictable for large groups makes it possible for the individual to protect himself, and forms the basis for one of our largest businesses—life insurance.

The death of an individual may cause dependents the loss of happiness and security. The death of a wage-earner or of a man or a woman who holds an important position in a business frequently means severe economic losses to the family or to the business enterprise. Life insurance is a form of security against such losses.

Many tables have been constructed to show the financial condition of persons at the time of their death. These studies are based upon the figures collected by insurance companies. The tables vary considerably because they are based to some extent on estimates. The following table shows the estimated financial history of one hundred average Americans, beginning at the age of twenty-five and extending to the age of seventy-five:

	AT AGE 25	AT AGE 35	AT AGE 45	AT AGE 55	AT AGE 65	AT AGE 75
Living	100	95	84	80	64	37
Dead	....	5	16	20	36	63
Wealthy	....	10	1	1	1	1
Well-to-do	....	10	3	3	4	2
Living on their earnings	....	70	65	46	5	2
Not self-supporting	....	5	15	30	54	32

Illustration No. 59—The Financial Status of People

Statistics further indicate that the following are the estates of any average group of one hundred men at death: one leaves wealth, two leave a comfortable income for dependents, fifteen leave from two to ten thousand dollars, eighty-two leave nothing.

The Value of a Life. Very few men appreciate the economic value of their lives. In many respects lives are not evaluated so carefully as a building or a piece of machinery. If a businessman owns a piece of machinery that produces a profit of two hundred dollars a month for him, he certainly will want to protect that machinery from sudden loss. If his business has only a small surplus, and if he should lose the machinery through fire or accident, the loss might be too great for him to sustain.

The same facts are true when one considers a life. In this case also, the economic value is the value of the productiveness of the life. The table in Illustration No. 60 shows the value of a person's life in terms of his earnings.

If a young man twenty-one years of age is earning $100 a month and will probably continue to earn that amount until he is sixty, his earning power is $46,800. A person thirty years of age who will earn $100 a month until he is sixty has a total earning power of $36,000. The value of a human life is therefore great when the life is considered

PRESENT AGE	$100 MONTHLY	$125 MONTHLY	$150 MONTHLY	$175 MONTHLY
21	$46,800	$58,500	$70,200	$81,900
22	45,600	57,000	68,400	79,800
23	44,400	55,500	66,600	77,700
24	43,200	54,000	64,800	75,600
25	42,000	52,500	63,000	73,500
26	40,800	51,000	61,200	71,400
27	39,600	49,500	59,400	69,300
28	38,400	48,000	57,600	67,200
29	37,200	46,500	55,800	65,100
30	36,000	45,000	54,000	63,000

Illustration No. 60—The Value of a Life in Terms of Earnings

as an investment that will produce an income. If one were to invest money at 3 per cent in order to obtain an income of $1,200 a year, the investment would have to amount to $40,000.

The preceding illustration shows how the value of a life can be computed from the point of view of earning power. Another way to estimate the value of a life is to compute the amount of an investment that is needed at a certain time to produce an income during the normally expected life of the person. The following table shows how one insurance company has computed the present value of a man's life in terms of an investment. These figures are based on the assumption that money can be invested at 3 per cent interest, compounded annually.

PRESENT MONTHLY EARNINGS	PRESENT AGE			
	25	30	35	40
$100	$27,738	$25,785	$23,521	$20,896
150	41,607	38,677	35,281	31,344
200	55,475	51,569	47,041	41,792
250	69,344	64,462	58,801	52,239

Illustration No. 61—The Present Value of a Life in Terms of an Investment

In other words, if a person who is twenty-five years of age is earning $100 a month and will earn that much throughout his normally expected life, the present value of his life is $27,738. If he were to invest that sum at 3 per cent interest, he would be assured of an income of $100 a month for his entire life. A person who is thirty-five years of age may invest $47,041 and expect a monthly income of $200 a month during the remainder of his life. The present value of his life is therefore $47,041, provided he will continue to earn $200 a month until he dies.

Is Insurance Gambling? Some people assert that insurance is gambling, for it involves the paying of a small sum regularly with the possibility that a larger sum may be received. Obviously, however, the one who has no insurance against premature death is the one who is gambling against the uncertainties of life. If a wealthy person, in return for a small annual payment, were to agree to compensate another person for the loss of a single life, the procedure would be nothing more than a gamble of doubtful merit. This method, however, is not that of assuming risks in insurance.

However uncertain may be the length of the life of any particular individual, it is surprising how accurately the rate of death among a large group over a long period of time can be computed. By studies of a large number of lives, it is possible to determine approximately how many persons will die in each year and how many will die at each age. In other words, the *average* length of life of a person can be computed rather definitely. Insurance is thus based on a scientific application of the law of averages.

The Travelers Standard

Illustration No. 62—Life, Not Insurance, Is a Gamble

If an individual dies without insurance, the loss to his family may be severe. When each of a large number of people, however, contributes a small amount annually, each is, in a sense, substituting a small annual loss for a possible great loss. The small annual payment is certain, whereas the potential loss without insurance is uncertain. Life insurance therefore is not a wager. It makes it possible for an individual to avoid the risk of a great loss.

Types of Life Insurance. There are several general types of life insurance, all of which are intended to distribute the loss among many people. Each type has, however, distinct provisions. These general types are fraternal, assessment, group, industrial, and legal-reserve insurance. Legal-reserve insurance is frequently referred to as "old-line" or "ordinary" life insurance.

Fraternal Insurance. In fraternal life insurance a group of individuals, usually belonging to a club or lodge, makes provision that, when a member dies, his dependents or his estate shall receive a sum of money as a death benefit. This sum is usually definitely stated in advance or is easily calculated. The various types of life insurance should not be confused with life insurance contracts. Life insurance contracts are discussed in Section 2 of this chapter.

Underwood and Underwood

Illustration No. 63—If the Young Man Knew What the Old Man Knows, He Would Buy Insurance

In the older types of fraternal insurance, money needed to finance the insurance was usually provided by assessments on the surviving members. These members paid little in the years when there were few deaths, but paid a great deal when deaths occurred through epidemics or through the increase in the average age of the group. Sometimes the dues included the estimated assessments, but usually provision for additional assessments was made if the deaths were more frequent than anticipated. Some of this fraternal insurance is still in force; but much of it is now operated largely on the same basis as legal-reserve insurance, which is discussed later in this section.

While the old forms of fraternal insurance had many commendable features, most of them have proved unsatisfactory because little or no selection of risks was possible. The group frequently did not provide in youth for the greater risk of death as old age approached. Many of the groups did not become large enough to benefit by the law of averages, which requires large numbers and the passage of many years. Although some of the fraternal groups operate on a basis that provides an adequate reserve for the future, the insured members do not have the advantage of low premiums during youth.

The comments on fraternal insurance as a specific type should not be confused with the more or less stationary forms of legal-reserve insurance that are sometimes sponsored by fraternal institutions. The laws in many states, however, require all insurance to be sold on a legal-reserve basis.

Assessment Insurance. Assessment insurance follows pretty closely the general principles of the old forms of fraternal insurance, except that there is usually an attempt to make use of scientific data concerning the chances of death at average age levels. These data are used in determining the amounts of regular assessments. As the individual becomes older and the liability of death increases, he is expected to pay a larger annual sum.

This plan of insurance has been found impractical for permanent insurance, that is, insurance throughout a lifetime. As men get older, the rates increase to huge amounts. The insured person usually finds himself unable to continue paying the assessments. He therefore drops the insurance in his old age, when death is not far away.

Group Insurance. Group insurance is best used to protect the workers of a common employer. Under this plan many employees can be insured through one policy and without medical examination. The cost is determined by an analysis of the group and is based on the losses indicated by the ages, environment, occupation, and general health of the members. The rates may be increased or decreased annually, but they are usually very low.

This plan of insurance has been quite helpful in providing moderate death protection to people who might otherwise be unable or unwilling to provide it as individuals. There are many objections, however, to too great reliance on group insurance as permanent protection. For example, as the employer usually pays at least part of the premium, he may terminate the insurance at any time.

When an employee leaves the employment in which he has been insured, his policy is canceled unless he chooses some permanent plan of insurance at a higher rate. Under most policies he may become reinsured at a rate covering his existing age, and need not undergo a physical examination. The likelihood of cancellation of the cheap group insurance at a time of unemployment and the need for conversion to higher-cost permanent insurance represent a real objection to this plan. Conversion is probably an advantage, however, in the case of a person who would be unable to obtain insurance in any other way.

Industrial Insurance. Group insurance protects workers under a common employer, whereas industrial insurance is written on the basis of individual policies without regard to employment. Industrial insurance is the type that requires small weekly, or sometimes monthly, payments from the members of the industrial or wage-earning group. The payment required each week is usually five cents or some multiple of five cents. This type of insurance furnishes varying amounts of protection, according to the age of the insured person and the plan selected. A fairly large proportion of industrial insurance is on the lives of children and women. The medical examinations are usually not stringent. In fact, this type of insurance is sometimes issued without a medical examination.

The rates reflect the high cost of collecting the small premiums and the high rates of mortality resulting from the lack of rigid standards in medical examinations. The high percentage of policies that are allowed to lapse because of failure to pay the weekly or monthly premium causes a serious loss to the policyholders. Industrial insurance may therefore incur a great economic loss among the classes who cannot afford to take such a loss.

This type of insurance serves essentially the following useful purposes: it reaches many people who would otherwise not buy any insurance; it teaches these people to save and to guard against unfavorable possibilities; it enables many people who are not insurable under most of the other plans to obtain insurance.

Savings-Bank Insurance. For many years the state of Massachusetts has had in operation a so-called savings-bank plan of selling insurance. Under that plan savings banks accepted payments for insurance policies in the same way as they accept deposits in savings accounts. Premiums are not collected by solicitors. Savings-bank insurance applies to the so-called industrial insurance sold largely to wage-earners. It is contended that the savings-bank insurance plan saves 20 to 50 per cent because commissions, as well as much of the other overhead, are eliminated.

A few other states also permit the sale of savings-bank insurance. In all cases there are certain restrictions on the amount that a person can buy. For instance, in the state of New York no person can buy more than $1,000 from a single bank or more than a total of $3,000.

Legal-Reserve Insurance. Legal-reserve, or level-premium, life insurance constitutes the chief type in force today. Approximately 90 per cent of the life insurance is of this kind. The weaknesses of the fraternal and assessment plans indicate the need for some plan of life insurance that is individual in its application and that has a premium that does not increase with advancing years. Legal-reserve insurance is designed to meet this need.

The probability of death increases at a rapid rate as the age of the individual increases. If this increased risk were reflected in the annual premium, the cost would increase steadily, becoming more and more burdensome and finally impossible to pay. The practice therefore is to determine a level premium that, because it is more than enough in the early years, will provide a reserve for the later years when the cost of protection exceeds the level premium. The reserve really may be called a savings fund, or investment element. It accumulates with interest at a guaranteed rate until the insurance policy matures under its own terms or is paid at the death of the insured person. It is the practice of legal-reserve life insurance companies to regard this investment element as the property of the insured person and to make it available for his use with certain restrictions.

TEXTBOOK QUESTIONS

1. Why does a death frequently represent a severe economic loss?
2. According to a study that has been made by insurance companies, how many people need some support at the age of sixty-five?
3. Out of an average group of one hundred men at the age of twenty-five, how many leave nothing when they die?
4. According to the table on page 168 what is the present value of his life, in terms of an investment, if a person thirty years of age earns $100 monthly and will continue to earn this amount during his normally expected life?
5. What are the general types of life insurance?
6. To whom is fraternal insurance available?
7. What are some of the disadvantages of fraternal insurance?
8. What is an advantage of fraternal insurance?
9. Why is assessment insurance usually unsatisfactory as a permanent form of life insurance?
10. Who are eligible for group insurance?
11. Are people who are insured under group policies selected through medical examinations?

12. If a person who is insured under a group policy quits working for his employer, what choices has he with regard to his insurance?
13. Why are the rates on industrial insurance high?
14. What is an advantage of industrial insurance?
15. What is savings-bank insurance?
16. What is the asserted advantage of savings-bank insurance?
17. Why is legal-reserve insurance sometimes referred to as "level-premium insurance"?
18. Why does not the premium on a legal-reserve insurance policy increase as one grows older and the risk of death becomes greater?

DISCUSSION QUESTIONS

1. Why is the death of a person usually considered to be an economic loss?
2. From the point of view of good business practice, why is insuring a life very much the same as insuring a machine?
3. In what respects is a life like an investment?
4. "Insurance is the opposite of gambling." Explain this statement.
5. A young man who spends his money freely says, "I don't need insurance; I have no dependents." Discuss this statement.
6. A young unmarried man has become thoroughly convinced of the value of life insurance. He therefore puts all his savings into such insurance. Discuss the merits or the demerits of this plan.
7. If the expenditures for assessment insurance are based on a budget, how may they disrupt a savings program?
8. Who get the greatest bargain in group insurance?
9. Is fraternal insurance fair to all who are insured under this plan?
10. What useful purposes are served by group, fraternal, and industrial insurance but are not served by legal-reserve insurance?
11. What is the best type of permanent life insurance?
12. Savings-bank insurance has definite advantages from the point of view of economy, but what are some of its disadvantages?

Section II

Types of Life Insurance Contracts

Insurance Contracts. There are many types of life insurance contracts, usually referred to as policies. Some of them are simple; others involve a combination of elements that cannot be explained without considerable detail. The following are the more or less basic types of policies: term, ordinary life, limited-payment life, single-premium life, endowment, combination, and annuity.

Term Insurance. Term insurance, as the name implies, is insurance that covers a specified period of time and is usually obtained to cover a specific need. For example, if a man has a debt that he expects to pay off in ten years, provided he lives, he can buy a ten-year term policy for the amount of the indebtedness. This insurance will protect his family from the debt in case he dies.

Term insurance is often referred to as "pure insurance" because it provides protection only. It does not have (a) a cash-surrender value, (b) a loan value, and (c) an investment or savings value. One of the major advantages of term insurance is the low cost. Although this type of insurance is considered primarily as temporary insurance, some individuals prefer to obtain insurance protection entirely through it and to establish a savings plan independently of the insurance program. Term insurance therefore has some advantage for those who can successfully save or invest.

The most common periods covered by term insurance are five years and ten years. Such policies are usually convertible into other types of contracts that provide protection over longer periods of years and involve the accumulation of reserves. For instance, a man may wish a large amount of protection at a low cost while he is educating his children. After they have been educated, he may convert the term insurance into some other type of insurance at a higher cost and thereby create an investment value in the insurance.

Ordinary Life Insurance. The ordinary life plan may be called the basic life insurance policy for protection over a long period of years. This type of insurance policy is sometimes called "whole-term life." If one has dependents and is anxious to provide primarily for their protection in the event of death, the ordinary life plan is ideal. The premium rate is lower than that for any other type of permanent insurance. When the premium is calculated, a reserve is created so that the costs of protection for the maximum estimated period of the life of the insured person are "leveled off." The long period of years involved makes it necessary to create a substantial reserve. This reserve is usually made available to the policyholder as a loan or as a cash-surrender value. While it is customary for the insured person to continue paying premiums for the entire length of his life, the reserve is available for emergencies and for use particularly at the age of retirement.

The practice of leaving dividends with the company to accumulate to the credit of the policy is frequently advocated as a means of increasing the amount available for old age. A dividend represents that part of the earnings of the company that is distributed among the policyholders in proportion to the insurance owned by each policyholder. Companies have a variety of plans under which the dividends can be left to accumulate. The following are advantages that usually result from not drawing the dividends: (a) the loan value of the policy increases; (b) the cash-surrender value increases; and (c) the policy becomes paid up eventually.

Limited-Payment Life Insurance. The purpose of a contract purchased under the limited-payment life plan is primarily to protect against death for the whole length of life. The premiums are limited, however, to ten, fifteen, twenty years, or to some other definite period of years. When these premiums have been paid, the insurance policy is said to be fully paid. If the face value of the policy is, for example, ten thousand dollars, the insurance company will pay this amount whenever death occurs. When premiums accumulate as in (c) above, an ordinary policy may become paid up.

Such a contract is desirable when the earning years are limited. If a person is reasonably sure that his earning days will cease when he is fifty-five years of age, he certainly will not want to continue to pay premiums after that age. This type of policy is therefore based on the idea that the payment of premiums should cease when the person's earnings dwindle. As it is assumed, in calculating the premium rate for a limited-payment policy, that there will be fewer annual payments than in the case of the ordinary life policy, each annual payment must be larger than it would be for the ordinary life policy.

Single-Premium Life Insurance. Single-premium insurance is not common, for it involves the payment of a large sum of money at one particular time. This type of insurance is excellent for the person who has a large sum of money to invest, such as an inheritance or the proceeds from the sale of property or a business. If a person suddenly receives five or ten thousand dollars from an inheritance or the sale of property, this type of insurance will permit him to invest the entire amount immediately in one policy. The payment of the single amount will make a larger sum available in the event of death. Furthermore, within only a few years the available cash-surrender or loan value will exceed the initial payment.

Endowment Insurance. The company that issues an endowment policy agrees to pay a definite sum of money at a specified time to the insured person or, in the event of death, to the beneficiaries of this person. An endowment policy costs more than a limited-payment policy for an equivalent number of years. It is available, however, as cash at the end of the period; whereas, in the case of the limited-payment policy, the face amount of the policy is available only in the event of death.

An endowment policy is an excellent means of accumulating a definite amount for a future need. Short-term endowments for periods of from five to twenty years are ideal to create sums of money that will be needed to educate children, to start a child in some particular profession or business, to purchase a home, or to pay off a debt.

Frequently, and particularly in the case of young people, the short-term endowment policy should not be used. In such a case the amount of insurance that can be purchased may be limited by the comparatively high premium rates made necessary for the accumulation of sums. The money becomes available too early in life and the protection against death ceases, although the insured person will have a great need for the protection in later life. When the policy matures, he may even find himself physically impaired and thus uninsurable.

It is usually most desirable to obtain a long-term endowment policy so that the money will become available at about the age of sixty or later. At this stage in life the insured person may have little or no earning power. If the policy matures at that time, its face value will be available to provide comfort during the later years of life. Many estimates and surveys that have been made indicate the need for old-age income. As emphasized by Illustration No. 59 on page 167, the number of aged people who have no source of income is surprisingly high.

Combination Insurance. Many contracts in force today involve combinations of various types of life insurance.

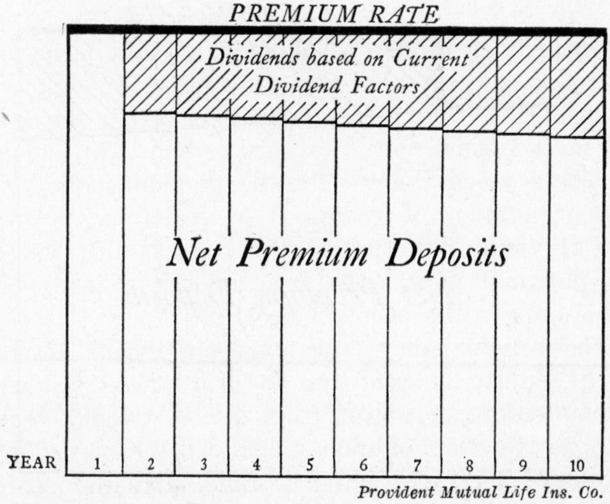

Illustration No. 64—The Usual Type of Premium Payment

For example, one particular type of combination policy provides a low rate for the first four or five years and a higher rate in later years. The same insurance plan would be carried out if an individual purchased a term insurance policy and then, at the end of four or five years, converted it into an ordinary life, a limited-payment life, or an endowment policy.

Combination policies usually provide immediate protection against death in return for a minimum cash outlay. The real question is, as in the case of any other policy, What do I want this policy to do for me?

Annuity Insurance. Many people purchase an *annuity* by turning over to an insurance company a specified sum of money. In return for this sum of money the insurance company agrees to pay a specified monthly or yearly income over a definite period of years or until the death of the insured. Some insurance contracts that are paid up can be converted into annuity contracts. In this way a specified income is assured to the person who is insured or to his beneficiaries after his death.

Annuities are not limited to wealthy people. They can be purchased for as low as one thousand dollars. An

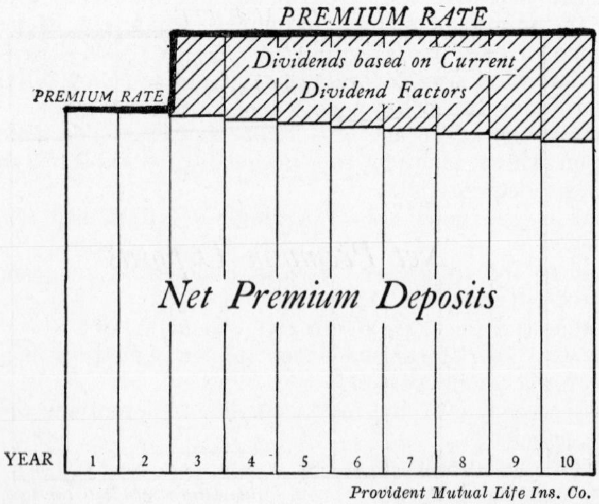

Illustration No. 65—Premium Rates Under a Combination Policy

annuity fund in a life insurance company can be accumulated through annual savings of as little as twenty-five dollars. Under the terms of the contract the insurance company distributes this fund in regular payments to the one who accumulated it, or to his beneficiaries.

TEXTBOOK QUESTIONS

1. When a person enters into an agreement to buy insurance, he makes a contract with the insurance company. What is an insurance contract usually called?
2. What are the recognized basic types of life insurance policies?
3. What does the name *term insurance* imply?
4. What is the most important merit of term insurance?
5. Would you recommend term insurance for temporary or permanent insurance?
6. What is ordinary life insurance sometimes called?
7. Is ordinary life insurance recommended for permanent or temporary insurance?
8. As compared with a limited-payment life, a single-premium life, and an endowment policy, does an ordinary life policy have a lower or a higher premium rate?
9. If an insurance company shares profits with policyholders by declaring dividends, what are some of the advantages of leaving the dividends to accumulate?
10. If a person has dependents and wants to buy permanent insurance that will provide the maximum amount of protection for the minimum amount of money, what type of policy is recommended?
11. In what ways does a limited-payment life policy differ from an ordinary life policy?
12. What is the advantage of a limited-payment life policy to a person whose earnings can reasonably be expected to cease at some definite time?
13. What is one good use of a single-premium life insurance policy?
14. What is the difference between endowment insurance and limited-payment life insurance?
15. What is one good use of an endowment policy?
16. Why is a short-term endowment policy sometimes not desirable for a young person?
17. What are some of the most common combinations of insurance policies?
18. Describe an annuity in a few words.
19. How can the proceeds of an insurance policy be converted into an annuity?

DISCUSSION QUESTIONS

1. If you borrow some money to buy a home and want to obtain an insurance policy at the lowest possible cost as a protection until the loan is paid, what kind of insurance will you buy?
2. While he is in school, a student obtains some assistance from his widowed mother. Most of her savings are needed for financing his education, but he earns some of his own money. He hopes to finish school and then to support his mother. He believes that he should carry some insurance to protect his mother. What kind of insurance do you recommend? Why?
3. Mr. Mason, a young man twenty-five years of age, discovers that term insurance is the cheapest that he can buy. He tells a friend that he is going to buy as much term insurance as he can afford, for he needs a maximum amount of protection. He plans to buy additional term insurance as each policy expires. What do you think of Mr. Mason's plan? Discuss it.
4. Mr. Brown has no dependents, but he wants to buy some insurance so that he can accumulate the maximum amount of savings with reasonable protection and at the same time save some money that can be used to buy a home in ten years. What kind of policy will best suit his needs?
5. Under certain circumstances is a limited-payment policy similar to an ordinary life policy?
6. If you want to obtain an insurance policy that will provide permanent protection, become paid up eventually, and have a cash-surrender or a loan value, what kind of policy will you obtain?
7. Why do some insurance agents encourage spendthrifts to purchase endowment policies?
8. Which type of policy provides the greatest element of saving but the least element of protection in proportion to the premiums?
9. What will be the result of overinvestment in endowment insurance?
10. Some policies combine term insurance with some other form of insurance, such as ordinary life. (a) What is the advantage of a policy of this type as compared with a separate term policy and a separate ordinary life policy? (b) What is the disadvantage?
11. What would you think of an insurance agent who tried to sell you all the insurance that you would buy or could buy?
12. In what way is an annuity largely an investment?

Section III

How Life Insurance Companies Operate

Mutual Companies and Stock Companies. Some life insurance companies, including most of the large ones, are *mutual companies.* Theoretically a mutual company is owned and managed by its policyholders; practically it is in most cases controlled and managed by a small group of individuals. The policyholders in a mutual company participate in the earnings of the company. A *stock company* is one that is owned and operated by its stockholders. Policyholders in some stock companies participate in earnings.

A fair judgment of the premium rates on equivalent policies of different companies can be made only when dividends are taken into consideration. Dividends are paid to each policyholder from the earnings of the company in proportion to the value of his policy. When the annual earnings of a company are determined, the dividend for the year is computed and apportioned. The policyholder has the options of accepting the dividend in cash, leaving it with the company for the purpose of paying up the policy earlier, applying it on the premium payment, or using it in some other way.

After a surplus reserve is built up by a mutual company, as much as possible of the earnings are usually distributed to the policyholders as dividends. A portion of the earnings is usually retained as a surplus to provide greater safety for all policyholders. Since, as nearly as is practicable, dividends are paid to the policyholders according to the values of their contracts, they are truly a refund of an overcharge. In other words, the company charges the policyholders what is considered a fair rate and then distributes to them the earnings in excess of the surplus that is retained to provide greater safety for all policyholders.

The contracts of mutual life insurance companies are not subject to assessments, for the maximum annual premium rates are fixed. No higher premium rate than that specified in the contract can be charged. Furthermore, there is a likelihood that the dividends will increase year by year and reduce the net premium payable as the policyholder becomes older. The following factors contribute to the increase of the dividend rate of a mutual company: savings effected through good management, increased income from investments, decreased death rate. The dividends of a mutual company cannot, however, be predicted definitely over a period of years. By varying the amounts of the dividends and by building up a surplus, the company can provide for unusual conditions, such as epidemics or depressions.

How Funds Are Obtained. An insurance company obtains funds by insuring large numbers of selected people. On the basis of statistics governing the lives and the deaths of average groups, and in accord with the laws of the state in which the company operates, the premiums and the reserves are calculated. The premiums include allowances for operating expenses, such as salaries, commissions, rent, and taxes. As the company grows older and develops a good reputation, money comes in faster in payment of premiums than it goes out in payment of claims and expenses. Every company, however, is legally required to keep a sufficient reserve to be able to pay all claims and expenses.

How the Money from Premiums Is Invested. Today the investments owned by life insurance companies on behalf of their policyholders exceed twenty billion dollars. Anything that would jeopardize the investments of insurance companies would seriously affect a great many individuals. Insurance companies are the wealthiest business organizations in the world. The income from the investments is a huge sum from which are built up reserves to pay the claims.

The investment of the funds of a company calls for a high degree of skill and integrity. Fortunately, a company can determine when various sums of money are most likely to be needed. Sometimes the amount of the premiums that are being collected will provide an adequate amount of cash to pay all claims and expenses when they become due. This condition does not, however, always exist. The insurance company therefore has to plan its investments so that a sufficient amount of cash can be obtained at the proper times to pay claims and expenses.

Practically all investments of life insurance companies are in securities that have tangible property as collateral. For instance, the insurance company may buy a mortgage bond. If the interest and the principal of the bond are not paid, the company has the right to take over the property that serves as security for the payment of the mortgage bond. As the property is usually worth more than the amount of the debt, the insurance company does not ordinarily run the chance of loss. Of course, an insurance company's investment policy may be unwise. For example, a company may concentrate too much of its investments in one particular area or in a certain field of business. By spreading out its investments, a company decreases the risk of a loss on its investments. In order to protect the public, the insurance commissions in some states maintain strict regulations concerning the investment practices of insurance companies. These regulations, however, vary from state to state.

Types of Investments. Life insurance investments are widely scattered among a variety of securities, such as first mortgages on urban and rural real estate; bonds of municipalities, states, and the Federal Government; bonds of railroads and other utilities; and bonds of other high-grade types of businesses. Loans to policyholders, in a sense, constitute securities. When a policyholder borrows money from an insurance company, he is usually required to sign an interest-bearing note. Such notes in the possession of an insurance company constitute securities. A very small part of the investment of insurance companies is in common stock. Common stock, as was explained previously, is normally not considered to be so conservative an investment as government bonds, railroad bonds, high-grade preferred stock, or the like.

The investments usually cover a wide geographic area in order to decrease the chance of loss resulting from the economic conditions in any particular part of the country. Illustration No. 66 shows how insurance companies have diversified their investments over a period of years. Such great diversification is intended as a means of lessening

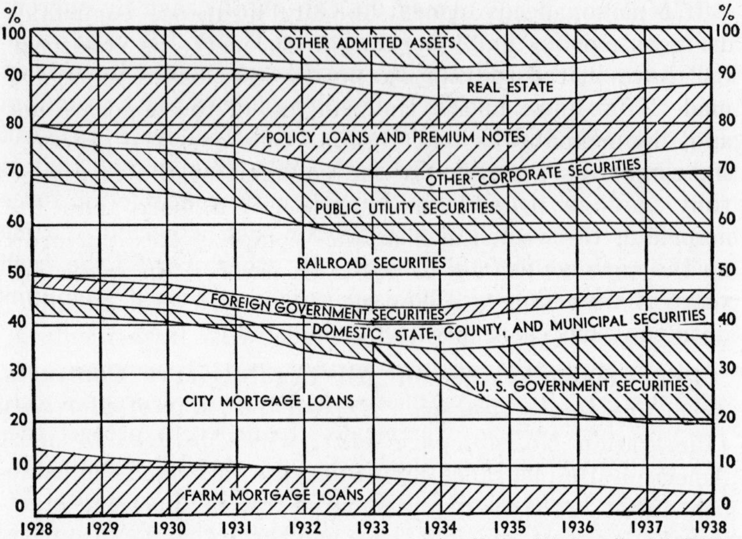

National Underwriter Life Edition

Illustration No. 66—The Diversification of Life Insurance Investments

the risk of loss and of stabilizing the income from the investments.

All investments are subject to constant supervision by authorities in each state in which the companies do business. In addition, statistics and facts regarding each company are available to the public and are open to the criticism of competitors and of policyholders. A more important safeguard is the recognition by life insurance executives that they are, in effect, trustees of the funds and the happiness of their policyholders, and guardians of the dependents of insured people and, in turn, of the prosperity of the United States. This recognition of responsibility has helped to guide insurance executives away from the pitfalls of speculation.

Nonforfeiture Values. There are certain cash, loan, paid-up, or extended term-insurance values available to policyholders. These are technically called *nonforfeiture values*. Because of these values, legal-reserve life insurance is now recognized as a "live-to-win" rather than a "die-to-win" contract.

If a person needs money, he can obtain cash by surrendering his policy or by borrowing on it, for the cash value will have increased year by year as payments have been made. If one does not have enough money to pay a premium as it becomes due, he has two options as follows: (a) Ask the company to change the policy to a smaller one that is fully paid, or (b) allow the policy to continue in force according to the original terms for such a period of time as the cash value will permit. In other words, the cash value of the policy will be used in paying future premiums until the cash value has been exhausted.

Endowment Feature of All Legal-Reserve Contracts. According to the *American Experience Table of Mortality* (Illustration No. 49, page 142), which is used by most American life insurance companies, the fact has been established that out of every one hundred thousand persons starting at the age of ten, only three will reach the age of ninety-five and they will die before the age of ninety-six. The last age is therefore considered as the extreme of life. If, for instance, any person who has an ordinary life policy reaches that age, he will be paid the proceeds of his policy just as if he had originally purchased an endowment policy to mature at the age of ninety-six. Basically, therefore, any life insurance policy in legal-reserve companies, except a term contract, is an endowment contract that will pay to the insured person the previously determined amount if he lives to reach a designated age. If he dies before that time, the company will pay the amount to his beneficiary.

Insurance as a Form of Saving. In considering insurance as a form of saving, one must compare it with at least two other forms of saving utilized by individuals: (a) the deposit of savings in a bank and (b) the purchase of government bonds. There are advantages to each of the three forms. Certain types of insurance policies, such as the endowment policy, are in reality insurance plus the savings element. Of course, insurance savings may not accumulate so rapidly as bank savings because, in the case of insurance, payment must be made for the protection involved. A comparison of the difference between saving by making deposits in a bank and saving by means of insurance may be made by computing the amount that must be deposited annually in a bank account in order to accumulate a given sum, for example, one thousand dollars, and the insurance premiums that must be paid on a thousand-dollar policy over the same period of time. A similar comparison may be made in the case of government bonds.

Bank savings offer no financial protection beyond the amount of the deposits and the accumulated interest. These savings can, however, be readily withdrawn and therefore form a more liquid reserve. As bank deposits are "owned" by the individual, withdrawals from them do not involve an interest charge; whereas funds borrowed on insurance do. Government bonds in small denominations offer an excellent medium of savings because they can be bought in small denominations, and they pay a fair rate of interest.

Incontestable Clause. The purchaser of life insurance should understand the meaning of the *incontestable clause* in his policy. The essence of such a clause is that, if the insurance company and its agents have not discovered within a specified time (indicated in the clause) that the insured person intentionally or unintentionally made misstatements of fact with regard to age, diseases, or other information required in the application, the insurance company cannot contest the validity of the policy. In other words, if any error has been made or if there has been any fraud in obtaining the insurance policy by giving false information, it is the responsibility of the insurance company to discover such a fact within the time limit specified in the incontestable clause.

All standard policies permit the insured person to ride in an airplane, but if one has ridden in an airplane or expects to ride in an airplane, he should give these facts in his insurance application. If he fails to give this information and rides in an airplane before the expiration of the time limit set in the incontestable clause, the insurance company may choose to cancel the policy. Some of the policies written during the early days of the airplane forbid the policyholder to ride in an airplane under any circumstances. Insurance companies will, however, without charge, grant such policyholders, upon application, a supplementary clause that can be attached to their insurance policies. This clause permits those policyholders to ride in airplanes without jeopardizing the validity of their policies.

Other Important Clauses. The purchaser of an insurance policy should read the policy carefully to see what agreements and what options are being made and to be sure that he understands the contract. For instance, if a dividend is payable to a policyholder, the dividend may usually be withdrawn in cash, applied to the payment of premiums, or left with the company to accumulate at compound interest. There are also various other dividend options. The settlement options in every insurance policy are important. The amount of the insurance may be paid to the beneficiary in a lump sum; or it may, under the provisions of the policy, be paid to him in installments, retained by the company at interest, or paid as a fixed guaranteed income to the beneficiary. Each company sets its own standard practices. However, the clauses in policies of the same type issued by one company in different states may not always be alike, for the various clauses must conform to the laws of the states in which the company operates and the policies are issued.

TEXTBOOK QUESTIONS

1. Explain what is meant by a mutual life insurance company.
2. Explain what is meant by a stock company.
3. What are dividends on insurance policies?
4. Does a mutual company have variable premium rates?
5. Are the insurance contracts of a mutual company subject to assessments?
6. Is it possible for a stock company to have lower premium rates than a mutual company?
7. What are some of the factors that contribute to an increase in the dividend rate of a mutual company?
8. What are some of the operating expenses that are paid out of the funds accumulated from premiums on insurance policies?
9. In what kind of securities do most life insurance companies invest their money? Give examples.

10. Do insurance companies invest much money in common stock?
11. What is the purpose of investing in a wide variety of securities?
12. Can you obtain information with regard to the financial status of your insurance company?
13. What are some of the nonforfeiture values of legal-reserve insurance?
14. Why are legal-reserve contracts said to have an endowment feature?
15. Compare saving through insurance and saving through a bank savings account.
16. What is the responsibility of an insurance company as indicated by the incontestable clause in policies?
17. Do life insurance policies provide protection while the insured person is riding in an airplane?

DISCUSSION QUESTIONS

1. Assuming that the management of a stock company and that of a mutual company are equally capable and that the conditions surrounding each company are the same, which company would you expect to have cheaper net rates on insurance? Why?
2. Why might it be better to take out insurance with a stock company rather than with a mutual company?
3. If the income from the investments of an insurance company decreases, can the insurance company use money collected from premiums in order to maintain high rates of dividends?
4. Why is it extremely important for an insurance company to invest in conservative securities?
5. (a) What is meant by the diversification of investments? (b) Why is the policy of diversification good or bad?
6. Why is it normally possible for a person to accumulate more in a savings account than through insurance?
7. What may be the advantage of buying a combination policy instead of two or more separate insurance policies?
8. Why are policies of the same type that are issued by the same insurance company not alike in all the states in which the company operates?

Section IV

How to Buy Life Insurance

Selecting a Company. One of the first principles to be observed in buying life insurance is to select a reliable company. The points that can be used to determine a reliable company are (a) its age and reputation, (b) the conservativeness of its investments, (c) its rate of earnings on investments, (d) its attitude toward policyholders, (e) the mortality rate of its policyholders, (f) its overhead costs, including the costs of its selling and advertising, and (g) the character of the state laws that supervise the investment practice of the company.

To sell life insurance, a company must be licensed in each state in which it operates. From the point of view of the buyer of insurance, the best insurance laws and the strictest supervision are in the states of New York, Massachusetts, and Ohio. If you are planning to buy insurance from a company that is licensed to do business in any of those states, you therefore have assurance that the company has passed a rigorous inspection.

In evaluating the cost of a policy, a person should determine the basic rates on the equivalent type of policy in other companies. He should then investigate past earnings and dividends. If a company does not grant dividends, the basic rate is the premium that must be paid. If the company does grant dividends, the average dividend that has been granted may be used as a reasonable rate in computing the deduction to be made from the premium in order to determine the actual net cost. The following tables show the rates on various policies of two typical companies. Assume that both Companies A and B are reliable. After deducting the average dividends of Company B, the rates of that company may be lower than those of Company A. On the other hand, Company A may be cheaper than Company B.

Some participating companies set their original rates higher than do other participating companies. The extent to which policyholders may participate in earnings is not the same in all companies. There are, however, tables published each year that show the rates of each company and the prevailing dividends. Every insurance salesman should be prepared to give such information to a prospective purchaser of an insurance policy.

AGE OF INSURED AT ISSUANCE OF POLICY	ORDINARY LIFE ($1,000)	20-PAYMENT LIFE ($1,000)	20-YEAR ENDOWMENT ($1,000)	5-YEAR TERM CONVERTIBLE ($1,000)
20	$14.44	$22.35	$40.93	$ 8.40
25	16.16	24.21	41.31	8.71
30	18.38	26.49	41.64	9.15
35	21.38	29.41	42.44	9.82
40	25.38	33.08	43.76	11.40
45	30.94	38.17	46.23	13.94
50	38.63	44.94	50.33	18.60
55	49.33	54.20	57.30	26.78

Illustration No. 67—Company A, Nonparticipating

AGE OF INSURED AT ISSUANCE OF POLICY	ORDINARY LIFE ($1,000)	20-PAYMENT LIFE ($1,000)	20-YEAR ENDOWMENT ($1,000)	5-YEAR TERM CONVERTIBLE ($1,000)
20	$18.00	$27.76	$48.92	$10.23
25	20.14	29.98	49.21	10.61
30	22.85	32.62	49.64	11.15
35	26.35	35.82	50.36	11.96
40	30.94	39.77	51.62	13.28
45	37.08	44.82	53.88	15.57
50	45.45	51.54	57.89	19.95
55	56.93	60.79	64.71	27.61

Illustration No. 68—Company B, Participating

Let us assume, for example, that the average dividend on each $1,000 of ordinary life insurance in Company B is $3.50 on a policy issued at the age of twenty. The net rate after the dividend has been deducted is $14.50. This rate is still slightly higher than that of Company A, but it is essentially the same.

Selecting a Policy. In buying insurance and in comparing one policy with another, one must consider: (a) the uses for which the insurance is intended, (b) one's present and expected income, (c) the cost of the insurance, and (d) one's willingness and capacity to save.

In examining any policy, one should compare the cash-surrender value, the paid-up insurance, and the extended insurance with those of other policies. The next problem is to choose the best policy for one's individual needs. After a study of the various types of policies, the soundness of the following conclusions should be evident:

(a) Term policies should be used when it is essential to obtain immediate protection for an amount as large as possible, or to cover a special need for a short period.

(b) Ordinary life or limited-payment life policies should be used when future obligations will probably be as important or more important than present ones.

(c) Ordinary life policies, rather than limited-payment life policies, should be used if it is more important to get protection for a large amount than to avoid the payment of premiums in old age.

(d) Endowment insurance should be used when the accumulation of funds is the main objective. Caution should be taken, however, not to buy an excessive amount of endowment insurance in early life.

(e) The best solution should be determined; it should then be followed, changes in the plan being made only as circumstances require them.

Comparative analyses of the four most important types of insurance policies are shown on pages 194 and 195. These analyses are convenient for judging the advantages and the disadvantages of the various types.

Some Guiding Principles. No one can decide how much insurance to carry on a particular life without knowing all the circumstances surrounding the person and his family.

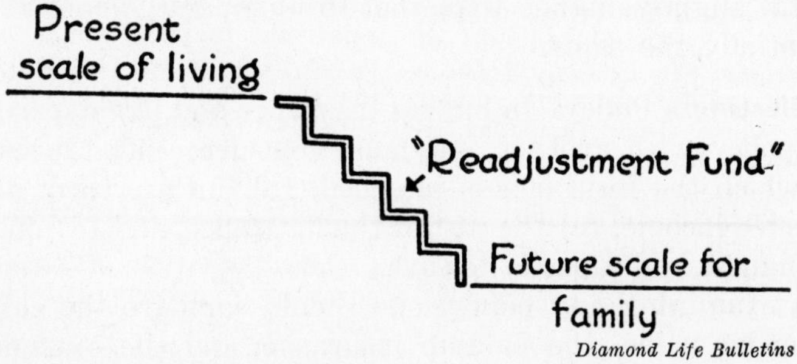

Diamond Life Bulletins

Illustration No. 69—Insurance Protects the Family During the Readjustment Period

Comparison of Types of Policies

1. Term Insurance

Description. The insured pays annual premiums for a certain period, for example, five or ten years. If he dies at any time during that period, the company will pay the face value of the policy to the beneficiary. If the insured lives to the end of the period, he will get no return from the company. The premiums are smaller for shorter terms.

Most companies that issue term insurance allow the policyholder to convert it into any one of the other three types without having to take another medical examination. This provision is valuable because, at the end of the term, the insured may no longer be able to pass a physical examination, and he would otherwise be left without any insurance or any way of getting it.

Advantages and disadvantages. Of all the forms of life insurance now regularly offered, term insurance involves least of the investment element. It has the distinct advantage of low cost. More insurance can be bought under this policy for a certain amount of money than under any other type; or, vice versa, a particular amount of insurance can be bought for a much smaller premium under this policy. Term insurance is, however, unattractive to most people because there is nothing left when the term ends. It is, in general, suitable when maximum protection is desired for a short time at the smallest expense.

2. Ordinary Life Insurance

Description. The insured continues to pay the same premium each year until his death. The company pays the beneficiary the face value of the policy upon the death of the insured. In a mutual company an ordinary life policy can become paid up if the insured does not accept dividends in cash or as a reduction in premiums, but allows them to accumulate.

Advantages and disadvantages. Ordinary life insurance is the next lowest in cost to term insurance. There is no time limit as in term insurance; the policy remains in force as long as the premiums are paid. For this reason it may become burdensome as the insured approaches old age and perhaps retires. To keep up the full insurance, even after he has ceased earning money, he will have to continue paying premiums. A good alternative in such a case is to cease paying premiums and to accept the paid-up value of the policy, which is less than the face value. Another is to take the cash value and invest it in order to increase income.

Ordinary life insurance is relatively inexpensive as compared with limited-payment life insurance and endowment insurance. Ordinary life insurance is frequently desirable when a high rate of protection is desired at a reasonably low cost. Although the cost is greater than that of term insurance, an ordinary life policy does not need to be converted into another policy at the end of a specified time.

Comparison of Types of Policies (Concluded)

3. LIMITED-PAYMENT LIFE INSURANCE

Description. The insured pays the same premium each year for a limited period, for example, twenty or thirty years. At the end of this period the policy becomes paid up; that is, the insurance continues in force as long as the insured lives, but no further payment of premiums need be made. Upon the insured's death the company pays the beneficiary the face value of the policy. Policies for the periods mentioned are called twenty-payment life and thirty-payment life.

Premiums for long periods are lower than those for shorter periods. For example, the premium on a thirty-payment life policy is less than that on a twenty-payment life policy; but the payments in the former case must, of course, be made for ten years longer.

Advantages and disadvantages. Limited-payment life insurance costs more than either term or ordinary life insurance. This type of insurance, however, avoids the difficulty of having to pay premiums throughout the entire life and possibly after earning power has ceased.

From the psychological point of view, such insurance is more gratifying for many people and consequently enlists their wholehearted support in their insurance program. It gives them satisfaction as they see themselves making progress toward the day when the insurance will be paid up and will remain in force for the rest of their lives without further payment.

4. ENDOWMENT INSURANCE

Description. The insured pays a fixed premium each year for a limited period, for example, twenty or thirty years. If he dies during that time, the company will pay the face value of the policy to the beneficiary. If he is alive at the end of the period, the company will pay him the face value of the policy.

Advantages and disadvantages. Endowment policies cost more than other types of policies when the term of protection is the same. An endowment policy is desirable for one who wishes a lump sum of money for some specific purpose if he lives. For instance, an endowment policy will provide an income in old age or a sum of money for starting in business or buying a home.

Endowment policies contain more of the investment element than any of the other types described. They are, however, sometimes less advantageous than combining a cheaper form of insurance, such as term or ordinary life insurance, with an investment of the difference between the annual premiums in a savings bank at 2 or 3 per cent interest, and then, as the amount in the bank becomes large enough, purchasing a good bond or stock.

For people who do not feel that they will be resolute enough to deposit a small sum in the bank for investment, the endowment policy provides a good method for building up a cash fund. Long-term endowments scientifically combine protection and investment.

Adapted from *Selecting a Life Insurance Policy,* Western Electric Company.

The amount of an expenditure for insurance should be governed by the budget. Three important considerations are:

(a) Adequate savings through insurance
(b) Adequate protection for specific needs
(c) Expenditures at the time of life when income is available

In the case of most insurance policies a part of the expenditure constitutes a saving, while the remaining part of it constitutes an expense for the protection obtained. The saving is a result of the gradual increase in the cash value or the loan value of the policy. Expenditures for insurance should therefore be considered from the point of view of savings and expenses.

As a general rule, insurance salesmen are honorable and consider seriously the needs of clients. A buyer of insurance should, however, bear in mind that even an honorable insurance salesman may be so eager to sell that he will intentionally or unintentionally make recommendations that are not worthy of consideration. The buyer of insurance must therefore learn the first principles of insurance. Even though he cannot be expected to be an expert, he should know enough to be able to judge the merits of the recommendations of an insurance salesman.

A reliable agent who is working for a reliable company will give good advice to prospective purchasers of insurance. In making application for an insurance policy, the individual is usually required to indicate the amount of insurance he already owns. This information gives the insurance company an opportunity to determine whether the applicant is justified in purchasing additional insurance. In the insurance field there are many agents who have been approved as *chartered life underwriters*. These men have made a study of life insurance and are qualified to give advice to applicants.

From the point of view of the person who is buying insurance, the amount that should be bought will be governed largely by the additional factors discussed in this section.

Amount of Insurance Based on Income. When a married person's income is small, he needs insurance because he must have some protection for his dependents. The amount that is set aside for insurance should be budgeted in the same manner as his other expenditures of income. As a person's salary increases, the amount spent for insurance should also increase. People with large incomes, such as those, for example, with incomes of ten thousand dollars, do not need much insurance for the protection of their dependents. They can accumulate through other means of saving and investment.

The amount of insurance that should be bought is a special problem in the case of each individual. It must be determined by considering the income, the necessary expenditures, the provision of a home, the accumulation of a cash savings fund, and the care of dependents. There are, however, reasonable percentages that have proved to be satisfactory. The following table shows the percentages of insurance expenditures recommended for individuals with incomes ranging from one thousand to five thousand dollars:

ANNUAL INCOME	PERCENTAGE	ANNUAL OUTLAY
$1,000	2–3½	$ 20 to $ 35
1,200	3–4½	36 to 54
1,500	3½–5	52 to 75
1,800	4–5½	72 to 99
2,000	4½–6	90 to 120
2,500	5–6½	125 to 162.50
3,000	5½–7	165 to 210
3,500	6–8½	210 to 297.50
4,000	6½–9	260 to 360
4,500	7–9½	315 to 427.50
5,000	7½–10	375 to 500

Illustration No. 70—The Amount of Income to Spend for Life Insurance

An analysis of this table discloses that a person earning three thousand dollars a year should expect to spend from 5½ to 7 per cent of his income for insurance. Obviously, the percentage expended in any particular case will depend upon (a) one's standard of living, (b) one's sense of responsibility, (c) the cost of living, (d) the number of dependents, and (e) the type of insurance that is bought.

Amount of Insurance Required for a Future Income. Another way to determine the amount of insurance that should be purchased is to determine the amount that one wants to accumulate to provide a future income. An income from insurance can be provided in any one of three ways:

(a) By creating a cash estate, which will be reinvested to provide an income.
(b) By buying sufficient insurance to yield a fixed amount of income for life after a certain age.
(c) By arranging with the insurance company to use the proceeds of the insurance policy for paying a fixed income to dependents after the death of the insured.

Under the first plan the person can consider his insurance and his other savings in computing the amount of income that will be available. Suppose, for example, that a person has planned his insurance program so that the cash proceeds available at his contemplated retirement age of sixty will amount to $25,000. If this amount is invested at 3½ per cent, it will pay an annual income of $875. This income, plus the income from other savings and investments, will represent the sum that the person may expect for use after he retires, provided he does not use part of the original principal.

Under the second plan it is possible for a person to make a contract with an insurance company whereby the proceeds of insurance are to provide (a) a guaranteed income for life or (b) a guaranteed income for life with a cash settlement if death occurs within a certain period. The following table shows the monthly retirement income guaranteed by one insurance company for each $1,000 of the proceeds from insurance. The payments given in this table are guaranteed for life. Tables such as this vary, of course, according to the companies with which the contracts have been made.

BEGINNING AT AGE	GUARANTEED MONTHLY INCOME FOR LIFE FOR EACH $1,000 IN INSURANCE FUND
50	$4.79
55	5.28
60	5.88
65	6.57
70	7.32

Illustration No. 71—Monthly Retirement Income for Life

For example, if a person has, under this plan, a $10,000 paid-up life insurance pòlicy at the age of fifty, he will receive from the insurance company $47.90 a month for the rest of his life. Some settlement options guarantee such payments for a certain number of years, such as fifteen or twenty years, and for life thereafter if the person lives longer. If he does not live beyond the fixed number of years, his beneficiary will get a specified cash settlement.

Under the third plan the person who is insured can provide for the proceeds of his insurance to be left with the insurance company after his death so that his dependents can be paid a fixed income for a specified number of years. The following table shows the proceeds that must be left with the company in order to provide fixed monthly payments of from $50 to $150 for a period of from five to fifteen years:

NUMBER OF MONTHLY PAYMENTS	MONTHLY PAYMENTS FROM CASH VALUES INDICATED BELOW							NUMBER OF YEARS PAYABLE
	$50	$70	$75	$90	$100	$125	$150	
60	$2,792	$ 3,909	$ 4,188	$ 5,026	$ 5,585	$ 6,981	$ 8,377	5
72	3,303	4,624	4,954	5,945	6,606	8,277	9,909	6
84	3,799	5,318	5,698	6,838	7,598	9,497	11,396	7
96	4,280	5,992	6,420	7,704	8,560	10,700	12,840	8
108	4,748	6,646	7,121	8,546	9,495	11,869	14,242	9
120	5,201	7,281	7,801	9,362	10,402	13,002	15,603	10
132	5.642	7,898	8,462	10,155	11,283	14,104	16,924	11
144	6,069	8,497	9,104	10,924	12,138	15,173	18,207	12
156	6,484	9,078	9,727	11,672	12,969	16,211	19,454	13
168	6,888	9,642	10,331	12,398	13,775	17,219	20,662	14
180	7,279	10.190	10,918	13,102	14,557	18.197	21,836	15

Illustration No. 72—The Cash Value Needed to Provide a Fixed Monthly Income for Dependents for a Certain Number of Years

From this table it is apparent that, when a person dies, the proceeds from his insurance policy must amount to $5,201 to guarantee a payment of $50 a month to his dependents for a period of ten years. The cash values vary, of course, according to the companies with which the contracts have been made.

The buying of insurance should be just one part of the plan of building up savings and providing for the protection of dependents. In deciding how much insurance to buy, a person should consider his entire financial program.

Example of How to Save Through Insurance. Suppose a young man aged twenty begins to save his money systematically. He wants safety and expects his money to earn a nominal rate of interest so that he will have five thousand dollars by the time he is sixty-five years of age. It is a simple task to calculate how much he must save each year to have the amount desired at that time. However, the loss of any part of the principal, the failure to lay aside the required amount, a decrease in the interest rate, or any withdrawal of the principal will upset his plan. If he should die, his estate will receive only the amount he has actually saved plus the interest up to the time of his death. The transfer of that amount to someone in whom he was interested will also be subject to delay and expense through the legal procedure of carrying out the provisions of his will.

He may, however, purchase an endowment life insurance policy for five thousand dollars that will mature in forty-five years, that is, when he has reached the age of sixty-five. This policy will provide a safe depository for payments that will be invested at a guaranteed rate of 2 or 3 per cent, and it may even participate in the excess earnings of the insurance company. He will know definitely the maximum amount to be paid each year, and he will receive a reminder in the form of a premium notice when each payment should be made. If he should die before the completion of the plan, his estate will receive not only the entire amount of his savings, but also enough from the collective funds of the life insurance company to bring the total payment up to the original goal of five thousand dollars. This money will be paid directly to the person or persons who have been specified as beneficiaries in the policy. In order to dispose of the proceeds of the insurance policy, it will not be necessary to go through the legal procedure of carrying out the provisions of a will.

Pitfalls in Buying Life Insurance. Almost everyone needs some form of life insurance. Life insurance is not, however, the solution to every problem. The following precautions should be observed in handling one's life insurance program:

1. Remember that there is no single form of insurance that is best for everyone. After an insurance plan is started, it should be studied carefully each time a new policy is purchased.

2. Read the policy carefully before any insurance is purchased. After the policy has been purchased, study it so that it is understood thoroughly.

3. Do not buy more insurance than can safely be kept in force. One always suffers a financial sacrifice when insurance is canceled.

4. Do not buy insurance that is too high in price for you. For instance, a young man who buys, at an early age, an endowment policy may be making a mistake for the probability is that he will marry and require lower-priced protection in a larger amount for his family, or that his parents as they grow older will need protection. Endowment policies may subsequently be changed to lower-priced policies for larger amounts, but evidence of insurability is required.

5. Do not surrender old insurance or change to a cheaper policy in order to obtain new insurance unless you are sure that the change will be to your advantage.

6. If you are approached by an insurance consultant, be sure that he represents a bona fide and honest organization. Be cautious if he tries to frighten you into believing that endowment policies steal money from the insured or that term insurance is the only good type of insurance.

7. Have no dealings with an unintelligent agent who is not conscious of his relationship with his client and his company. If the agent is a stranger, it is advisable to determine whether he is an authorized agent of the company being represented. Advance no money to an agent unless a receipt authorized by the company is obtained.

8. If you cannot pay the first premium in cash, avoid, if possible, paying it by premium note. Signing a premium note is the same as signing any other kind of note. The signer becomes indebted to the insurance company for the amount of the premium. Do not purchase new insurance if the first premium on such insurance will be paid by borrowing on the old policy.

9. Remember that an agent has no authority to make, alter, or discharge any contract in the name of the company, or to bind the company by any promise or statement, except upon the company's previous written consent.

10. A beneficiary must be named in each insurance policy. From time to time the insured person should consider the advisability of changing the beneficiary because of marriage, deaths in the family, or the birth of children. When a new policy is purchased, there should always be a recheck of the beneficiaries on previous policies. All previous policies and the new policy should be studied to see what changes may be desirable in disposing of the proceeds of the insurance in case of death.

11. Premiums should be paid when due. Companies ordinarily permit a period of thirty days of grace before the policy goes out of force, but companies are not required to grant this period of grace. Unless premiums are paid when due, the insured person may not be covered by the necessary protection and may be required to reinstate the policy by proving insurability.

12. If money is borrowed on an insurance policy, it should be repaid as soon as possible. If it is not repaid, the beneficiary does not have the protection that was originally planned.

13. Buy insurance only from a legal-reserve company.

TEXTBOOK QUESTIONS

1. On what points should an insurance company be judged?
2. When the listed premium rates of companies are compared, what should be considered in computing the net rates?
3. What four factors should be considered in selecting an insurance policy after a good company has been chosen?
4. What types of policies would you use for the following purposes: (a) when a special need must be covered for a short period, (b) when future obligations will be more important than present obligations, (c) when it is more important to get protection for a large amount than to avoid the payment of premiums in old age, (d) when the accumulation of a savings fund is the main objective?
5. What should be the guiding principles in establishing a satisfactory life insurance program?

6. Some people consider insurance entirely as an expense. Are they correct?
7. (a) When a person applies for an insurance policy, why does the insurance agent ask how much insurance the person already owns? (b) Why is it desirable for the person to tell how much he owns?
8. Can the amount of insurance that any person should buy be determined specifically on the basis of his income?
9. What are some of the factors that determine the upper and lower limits of one's expenditures for insurance?
10. What are the three ways in which income can be provided through the proceeds of insurance?
11. From the table on page 198 determine the guaranteed monthly income of a person who retires at the age of sixty if he has $12,000 in an insurance fund.
12. From the table on page 199 determine how much the cash value of insurance must be to pay the dependents of the insured a monthly income of $90 a month for 108 months.

DISCUSSION QUESTIONS

1. (a) Why do insurance companies spend considerable money each year in publishing health advertisements and in conducting health campaigns? (b) Why does an insurance company go to the expense of offering free medical examinations to policyholders?
2. Suppose Company B, the rates of which are listed on page 192, has been paying an average dividend of $6.42 a thousand on an ordinary life policy. Is the net rate lower or higher than the rate on the equivalent policy of Company A? (Base your figures on the rates for a person who is thirty years of age.)
3. A man plans to go into business. He knows that he needs insurance protection, but he wants to buy insurance that will provide the maximum loan value. What kind of insurance would you recommend?
4. A man wants the most protection that he can obtain, but he wants the policy to become paid up eventually. What kind of insurance should he buy?
5. A man forty years of age knows that in the position in which he works he must retire at the age of sixty. He would like to buy an ordinary life policy, but he wants all premium payments to cease by the time he retires. What options are open to him?
6. Why do insurance companies consider it unwise to issue a great amount of insurance on one person?
7. (a) Why is it undesirable for a person to carry too much insurance? (b) What is too much insurance?

PROBLEMS

1. A man thirty-five years of age buys a $5,000 twenty-year endowment policy from Company A, the rates of which are shown in the table on page 192. He dies after making nine annual payments. (a) How much less would have been his total payments if he had bought an ordinary life policy? (b) Can you draw any conclusions with regard to the desirability of buying an endowment policy at the age of thirty-five?
2. A man thirty-five years of age has two children, aged four and eight. He has a good position and has almost paid for his home. He has $500 in a savings account, an endowment policy of $2,000, and an ordinary life policy of $5,000. His budget provides for a yearly saving of approximately $200. He decides that he wants to spend $100 of this amount for insurance that will provide the maximum amount of protection, but will become paid up before he is sixty years of age. What kind of policy and how much insurance can he buy from Company A, the rates of which are listed in the table on page 192?
3. A man aged twenty who is planning to marry has $200 a year available for insurance. He wants to be assured of having $2,000 to use as a payment on a home by the time he is forty years of age. He also wants the maximum amount of protection from his insurance. Outline a plan of insurance for him based on the rates of Company A (page 192).

COMMUNITY PROBLEMS AND PROJECTS

1. Obtain samples of insurance policies from your parents, from friends, or from some insurance agent. Make a comparison of them with regard to (a) net cost, (b) premium rates, (c) dividends, and (d) paid-up and cash values.
2. (a) Make a list of the insurance companies that operate in your community. (b) Find out whether they are stock companies or mutual companies, and whether any of the stock companies allow policyholders to participate in earnings.
3. If your parents are paying insurance premiums monthly, quarterly, or semiannually, calculate the amount of savings that would be accumulated if the money were deposited in a savings account and used to pay the premiums annually.
4. Select some particular insurance company, and obtain its financial statement. If possible, get a detailed statement showing the diversification of the investments. Write a report on the types of investments and the diversification.
5. Obtain a copy of a form used in applying for an insurance policy, and fill out the form for yourself.

CHAPTER VII

HOW THE MARKETING SYSTEM SERVES THE CONSUMER

Purpose of the Chapter. The big problem of producers and distributors is to find people to buy their goods. The problem of consumers is to obtain what they want at the time they want it and at a reasonable price. Ordinarily, sellers are experts and specialists, whereas the average consumer is an inexperienced buyer. If a person expects to buy intelligently, he must learn to know what he wants and how he can be served most effectively through the marketing system. The object of this chapter is to describe the organization, the functions, and the methods of those agencies that distribute goods from producers to consumers. It will have the twofold purpose of (a) creating a better understanding of the economic system and (b) providing a background of information and understanding that will be helpful in buying.

Section I

Functions Performed in Marketing

Place of the Middleman. The so-called *middleman* has been the subject of criticism for many years. A middleman is one who performs a service between the producer and the consumer. Criticism of the middleman may be attributed largely to a lack of understanding of the functions he performs. Many buyers fail to realize that after goods are produced many additional services are required before consumers can enjoy these goods. These services are performed by the middlemen. Some of the most common types of middlemen are wholesalers, jobbers, commission merchants, and retailers. The term *jobber* arose out of the custom of certain dealers to buy from producers in quantities called "job lots." Jobbers and wholesalers are now almost indistinguishable because they serve essentially the same purpose. If middlemen perform useful services at reasonable cost, their existence is justified.

Whenever the services of a legitimate middleman are discontinued, his function must be taken over by someone else. The services may be consolidated, but nevertheless they are still performed. A wholesale grocery company, for example, collects a wide variety of food products and other grocery items from all parts of the United States and even from various foreign countries. These goods may be obtained in large lots from canneries, jobbers, commission merchants, manufacturers, and importers. Buying in these large quantities is economical. The goods are transported to the warehouses of the wholesaler, are stored, and are then sold in smaller lots to retailers. During all this time the wholesaler has his money invested in the goods going in and out of his warehouses. Without the assistance of a middleman, such as this wholesaler, the small retailer would not have access to this wide variety of products, or he would have to assume the function of collecting a large variety of goods.

In chain stores the wholesaling and retailing functions are combined, but the essential services are not eliminated. Any savings that are evident are obtained largely through efficiency of management and operation.

The functions performed by all types of wholesalers are relatively the same. Every wholesaler must go through the procedure of buying, storing, selling, transporting, financing, and risk-bearing; but not all wholesalers perform these functions in the same manner. Illustration No. 73 shows the relative importance of the various types of distributive channels for a typical year. The percentages indicate the amounts of goods that the various types of wholesalers distributed during the year.

There are various attempts at times to make the distributive system more economical or at least more advantageous to some persons who are interested in the marketing system. For instance, farmers have organized numerous co-operative marketing associations, which perform some of the functions of buying, assembling, storing, transporting, financing, risk-bearing, and selling. None of the processes is eliminated, but some of the benefits go to the farmers. Co-operative organizations are explained in detail in Chapter XXI.

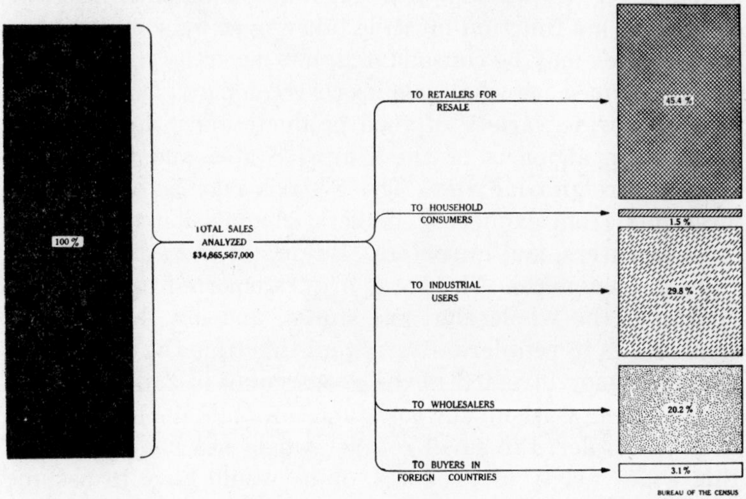

Illustration No. 73—Percentages of Sales in Various Distributive Channels for a Typical Year

Assembling Goods. The assembling of goods is one of the first steps in marketing. Through this service, goods are placed where they are wanted at the time they are wanted. Assembling is performed in part by the retailer, the wholesaler, and the manufacturer. It is a particularly important function in agricultural marketing. Creamery stations, grain elevators, and stockyards are important agencies in the assembling of products for consumers.

Storing Goods. Storing and assembling are closely related. Storing is a function that is performed during many stages of the process of delivering goods from producers to consumers. Those who assemble goods in large quantities hold them for the demand of those to whom they sell. We ordinarily think of cold-storage plants, commercial warehouses, and grain elevators as places of storage. Nevertheless, the function of storage is performed at other points along the line of distribution. The wholesaler stores goods in large quantities and then sells them in smaller quantities

Chamber of Commerce, Hutchinson, Kansas

Illustration No. 74—A Grain Elevator Where Wheat is Collected and Stored

to retailers. The retailer stores goods on his shelves and in his warehouse for the convenience of his customers, who buy in very small lots for immediate consumption.

Many people fail to realize the extremely important function of storage. Without storage many products could not be enjoyed. This fact is especially true of such products as meat, eggs, and fresh vegetables. Fresh meat is available in practically every community at all times of the year. Eggs are stored during seasons of high production for use in seasons of low production. Fresh vegetables are available during the twelve months of the year in most cities and towns. These foods are available as the result of cold storage. The introduction of quick-freezing methods of storage brings to our tables fresh fruits and vegetables in all seasons, preserved with their original flavors.

Grading and Standardizing Goods. Grading is rapidly becoming one of the most important functions of distribution. Tobacco, wheat, corn, and other agricultural products are carefully graded before they are marketed. They are sold in large lots on the basis of grade. Meat especially is

Frosted Foods Sales Corporation

Illustration No. 75—Quick Freezing Brings Fresh Foods to the Consumer

marketed on the basis of inspection and grading. Grading determines the differentials in value.

The Federal Government and many associations organized to promote standards are performing an important function for the consumer. Many products can now be bought to meet standard specifications. Canned food products—as will be discussed in more detail later—are now being graded for the protection of the buyer. Grading and standardizing save time and money in buying.

Creating a Demand for Goods. The preceding functions deal with the accumulation and the preparation of goods for dispersion through the various channels of trade. Those who have collected goods, graded them, and stored them cannot always rest assured that people who want these goods will seek them. Advertising and salesmanship are therefore used in stimulating a demand for the goods. These functions are closely correlated.

The creation of demand has one or the other of the following objectives:

(a) Creating a demand for a particular product
(b) Creating a demand for one class of product as opposed to another class

Advertising performs the function of telling prospective buyers about a product in the hope that they will want to buy it. Advertising is carried on through newspapers, magazines, radio programs, billboards, and a variety of other means. Salesmanship is a personal means of obtaining orders for a product, either with or without the assistance of advertising. The person who sells is called a salesman, and the technique of selling is referred to as salesmanship.

There are two general methods of creating demand. The first method is to pass on to each member in the distributive system—the broker, the jobber, and the retailer—the responsibility of selling the product at a particular stage in distribution. Under this method the manufacturer sells to the broker, the broker sells to the jobber, the jobber sells to the retailer, and the retailer sells to the consumer. The retailer has the final responsibility of selling the product to the consumer. The second method is to create consumer demand. Under this method the function of selling is partially reversed. The consumer demands the product from the retailer, the retailer buys it from the jobber, the jobber buys it from the broker, and the broker buys it from the manufacturer.

Boston Chamber of Commerce

Illustration No. 76—Grading Wool

Although one or the other of these plans may be used for some particular product, neither plan should be considered as representative of all types of distribution. In practice both methods are intermingled to some extent, although most manufacturers try to follow the second; that is, they try to create consumer demand. Creating consumer demand gives the manufacturer a better control over his distributive system, provided he is successful in his advertising efforts. Great sums of money are expended annually for advertising.

Merchandising Function. After demand has been created, it must be satisfied. Merchandising is therefore the next step in distribution. It involves the actual process of filling demands for products. It is particularly important in retail stores, and in such cases includes the following:

(a) Systematic credit policy
(b) Delivery service
(c) Attractive window displays
(d) Careful arrangement of counters and other store facilities
(e) Careful display of goods
(f) Procedure and personnel for showing and demonstrating goods to prospective customers
(g) Installation and repair service

Not every retailer performs all these functions, but he must perform some of them. For instance, a retailer may have no delivery service, and he may not require installation and repair service; but he probably does have to perform the other functions.

A very important function in the merchandising of household equipment is installation and repair service. For instance, if a person buys an electric refrigerator, he wants to be assured that it will be installed properly, will operate properly, and can be repaired if there is need.

Transportation and Communication. Although transportation and communication represent indispensable services in the distributive system, they need no particular comment. Every civilized person is familiar to some extent with such means of transportation and communication as railroads, boats, airplanes, trucks, telephones, and telegraph and postal service. These are self-evident services that help each person to obtain the goods that he needs.

The map in Illustration No. 77 indicates the main sources of 85 per cent of the fresh fruits and vegetables consumed in the metropolitan area of New York during the months of February, March, and April of a typical year. The transportation costs take an average of 18 cents from each dollar that the consumer spends for these foods.

Financing Distribution. Whenever goods are assembled, stored, or graded, or any of the other functions of distribution is performed, money or credit is needed. Suppose, for example, that a farmer stores his wheat in a grain elevator until he can sell it. He will have to pay for the storage and will probably need to borrow some money until he can sell his wheat. On the other hand, if the operator of the grain elevator buys the wheat to hold for future sale, he must have the cash with which to pay the farmer, or he must borrow the money. It is usually possible to borrow money for this purpose.

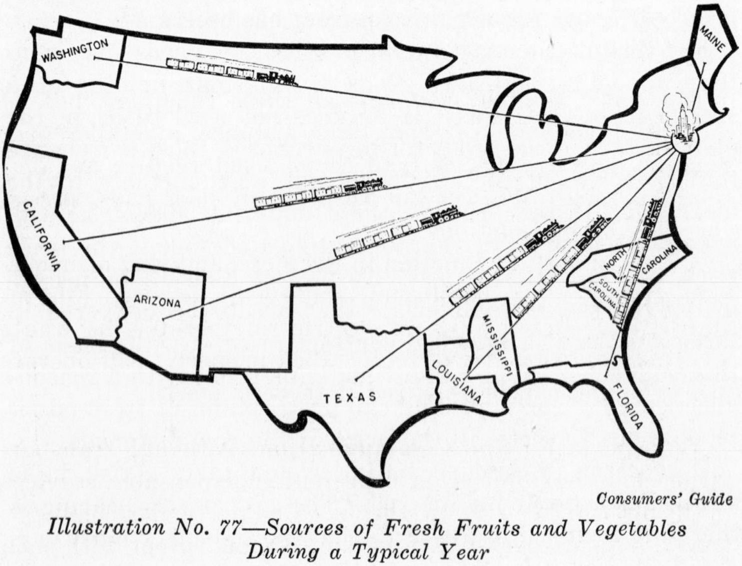

Consumers' Guide

Illustration No. 77—Sources of Fresh Fruits and Vegetables During a Typical Year

When a product such as wheat is stored, a receipt is given to the person who has stored the product. This receipt can be left with a banker or an individual as security for a loan. If the loan is not paid, the product that is stored becomes the property of the person who has lent the money.

There are a great many costs of distribution. Interest on money borrowed, advertising, selling, office expense, storage, packing, delivery, losses from spoilage and damage, and loss from bad debts are some of them.

Risk-Bearing. Constant risks occur all along the line of distribution. These include theft, fire, breakage, spoilage, shrinkage, and a drop or a rise in prices. Taking a risk means bearing the chance of a loss. Insurance can be obtained to provide protection against most risks. Some other type of protection must, however, be obtained to prevent loss resulting from price changes.

Businessmen often protect themselves from loss due to price changes through a process that is commonly referred to as *hedging.* Hedging involves (a) making a contract to deliver goods at a certain price at a specified future time, and (b) contracting to buy materials or goods at a future time at a price that will make it possible to deliver at a profit the goods for which a contract has been made.

For instance, a manufacturer of cotton goods may contract to deliver finished goods within four months at a specified contract price. If he does not need to begin the manufacture of the goods for three months, there is a chance that the price of the raw materials may fluctuate in the meantime. If the price of these materials drops, he will make a greater profit than he anticipated; but if the price rises, he may suffer a loss. To protect himself, he hedges by purchasing raw materials that are to be delivered in three months at a specified contract price. On the basis of this contract price he can estimate his profit with a reasonable degree of certainty and can protect himself from possible loss due to a rise in the price of the raw materials.

If a person in the distributing system takes a risk, he is entitled to a profit for his risk. The cost of risk-bearing is therefore included in the price that the consumer must pay.

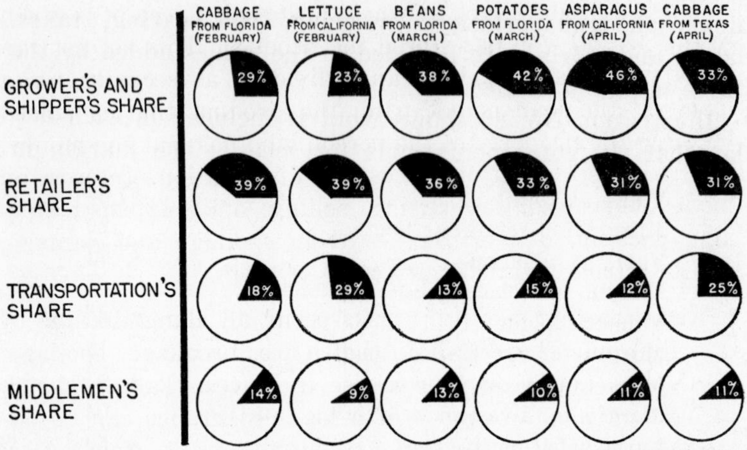

Consumers' Guide

Illustration No. 78—Where the Consumer's Vegetable Dollar Goes

Costs of Distribution. Some consumers have the idea that all costs of merchandise except those representing labor and materials are economic wastes. Such persons overlook the fact that goods would be valueless unless they were transported, stored, and made available to them in convenient quantities, in convenient places, at convenient times. It is therefore appropriate to study a few typical cases in order to see where the consumer's dollar goes. The table in Illustration No. 79 was prepared by the Marketing Research Division of the United States Bureau of For-

PRODUCTS	CONSUMER PRICE	VALUE ADDED			MANUFACTURER'S MATERIAL COST
		RETAIL MARGIN	WHOLESALE MARGIN	BY MANUFACTURE	
Canned fruit	100.0%	20.0%	8.0%	27.5%	44.5%
Toilet item	100.0	35.0	9.8	38.1	17.1
Man's suit	100.0	33.0	3.5	33.7	29.8
Loaf of bread	100.0	15.0	...	43.0	42.0
Pair of man's shoes	100.0	35.0	10.0	25.6	29.4
Cigarettes	100.0	15.0	7.0	51.0	27.0

Illustration No. 79—The Distribution of the Consumer's Dollar

eign and Domestic Commerce. It shows the distribution of the consumer's dollar for specified articles. Such other items as transportation, financing, risk-bearing, taxes, labor, and storing are included in the values added by the three main middlemen.

Illustration No. 80 shows what is included in each dollar that the consumer spends for meat.[1] The margin in

Value at retail	$1.00
Margin for retailing function	.26
Value at wholesale	$ .74
Margin for wholesaling function	.05
Value at plant	$ .69
Margin for processing function	.15
Market value of livestock	$ .54
Margin for livestock marketing function	.04
Farm value of livestock	$ .50

Illustration No. 80—The Distribution of the Consumer's Meat Dollar

each case covers all the expenses and the profit of the particular middleman. Illustration No. 81 shows the various items included in the margin for retailing.[2] These two tables combined illustrate the fact that there are various functions performed and various costs added at each stage in the distributive system.

Margin for retailing:	PERCENTAGE OF THE CONSUMER'S MEAT DOLLAR
Wages and salaries	14.0
Store rent	2.7
Other store expense	5.7
Profit	3.6
Total	26.0

Illustration No. 81—Costs That Are Included in Margins

TEXTBOOK QUESTIONS

1. What is a middleman?
2. What are some of the most common types of middlemen?
3. What are some of the distributive functions performed by a wholesale grocery?

1 From Tobin, Bernard F., and Greer, Howard C., *What Becomes of the Consumer's Meat Dollar?* University of Chicago Press, Chicago, Illinois, 1936.
2 *Loc. cit.*

4. What is meant (a) by assembling goods? (b) by storing goods?
5. How does the function of grading and standardizing goods aid in the distributive system?
6. What are two means of creating a demand for goods?
7. What function is performed by advertising?
8. What activities are included in the merchandising function of retail stores?
9. In what respect does the function of transportation and communication help in the distributive system?
10. Why are banks necessary in the distributive system?
11. What are some of the risks that are involved in the distributive system?
12. (a) In the tables on pages 214 and 215, which product has the greatest amount of cost added from the time the raw material goes into production until the product is sold to the consumer? (b) Which has the least amount of cost added?

DISCUSSION QUESTIONS

1. (a) Are there any advantages to the consumer in allowing farmers to peddle products without restriction in cities? (b) Are there any disadvantages?
2. Do you think we could get along without the services of the wholesaler? Explain your answer.
3. "The commission market helps the farmer to make more money." Is this statement true? Explain your answer.
4. Does the retailer in any way serve as an assembler and a storer of goods?
5. Explain in what way storage may have aided in distributing the food that you consumed in your morning meal.
6. What happens to the distributive system if farmers become bankrupt in great numbers?
7. If manufacturers cease to be able to make profits, what happens to the distributive system?
8. (a) In what way is advertising wasteful? (b) In what way is it economical and advantageous to the consumer?
9. Under which type of distribution would the producer be likely to have the greater amount of control over his market: (a) when a demand is built up through advertising; (b) when the responsibility of creating a demand is passed on to the various distributors, such as the wholesaler and the retailer? Why?
10. "Advertising reduces the cost of distribution." Discuss this statement. Is it true or false?
11. How does hedging make it possible for us to obtain flour at a lower price than we would have to pay if hedging were not carried on?

Section II

How the Marketing System Operates

What Is a Market? The word *market* is used in a variety of ways. When a businessman says that he has a good market for his goods, he means that there is a good demand for them. If he says that he has a large market for his goods, he means that these goods are distributed over a wide geographical area.

The word *market* is also used to refer to a place used for buying and selling. In many cities there are public market squares where produce merchants and farmers gather to sell to people who are seeking their products. Exchanges are markets. The New York Stock Exchange, for instance, is a security market. The Chicago Board of Trade is a grain market.

The word *market* is used in still another way. For instance, if a person says, "How is the stock market today?" he has reference to the trend of prices and conditions in the entire United States, although most transactions are centralized in New York City.

Wholesale Markets. A wholesale market is distinguished by its practice of trading only in large lots. A large lot may be one hundred cases, a carload, or an entire shipload of goods. Wholesale markets are classified as (a) general wholesale markets, (b) commission markets, and (c) auction markets. Dealers and brokers operate in all types of markets. A dealer buys with the hope of selling goods at a profit. The broker acts as an agent in buying for someone else. He does not take the title to the goods, but assists in the transaction between the buyer, whom he represents, and a seller.

Dealers are ordinarily the principal operators in general wholesale markets. A dealer takes the title to goods and sells the goods in smaller lots to other wholesalers, to retailers, or directly to consumers. For instance, dealers may buy hogs and cattle that have been brought to a central marketing place and sell them to packing houses.

Commission markets are ordinarily operated by merchants who take possession of goods but do not take the title. In some commission markets, however, the merchants, for all practical purposes, take possession of the goods and

Chicago Merchandise Mart

Illustration No. 82—A Modern Centralized Market

also take the title. The commission markets in such cities as New York, Cincinnati, and Chicago are highly organized. Fresh vegetables and poultry are common commodities sold in such markets. The commission merchant acts merely as an agent in handling products. He usually sells the products entrusted to him at the highest price he can obtain, although he is sometimes subject to special instructions from his client with regard to the price to be obtained. For his service he obtains a commission.

Suppose, for example, a farmer brings to a commission merchant in Cincinnati fifty sacks of potatoes. In the absence of specific instructions with regard to the price at which the potatoes must be sold, the commission merchant will sell them at the highest price that he can obtain for them on the basis of bids offered by buyers. For his services he will charge either a percentage of the sale or a fixed amount.

An auction market is one in which buyers congregate and bid for products that are offered for sale. Fruits, tobacco, and furs are frequently sold in this manner. Important tobacco auction markets are located in Lexington and Louisville, Kentucky. An important fur market is in St. Louis.

The wholesale markets of the United States are concentrated in sections where they can serve most effectively the concentrated areas of population. The map on this page shows the principal wholesale centers in the United States.

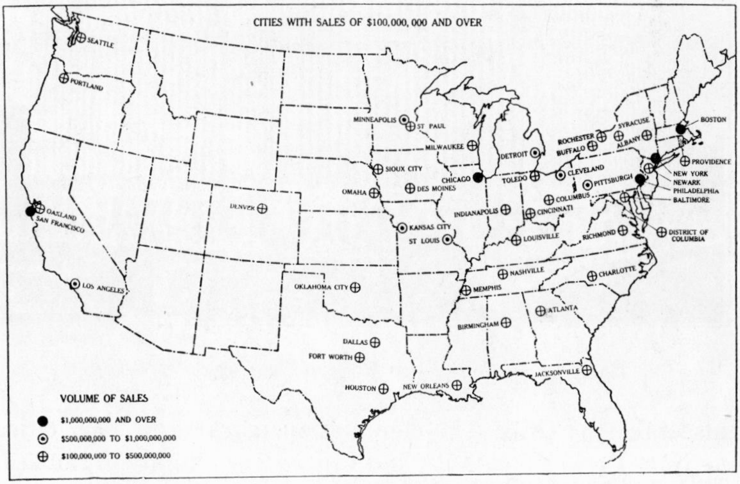

Illustration No. 83—The Principal Wholesale Centers

Retail Markets. A retail market is the final outlet in the distributing system—the final link in the chain between the producer and the consumer. There are more retailers than there are business proprietors of any other type. Grocery stores, department stores, filling stations, meat markets, shoe stores, and clothing stores are some representative types of retail markets. These are places to which individual buyers may go in order to obtain the goods they want.

Organized Markets. An organized market is a place where buyers and sellers can congregate for the purpose of trading in securities or products. Such a market is commonly referred to as an *exchange.* For instance, the Chicago Board of Trade operates a commodity market.

Organized commodity markets are located in many parts of the country and have increased in number rather rapidly during the last ten years. Commodity markets and security exchanges are so numerous that one would have difficulty in preparing a complete list. Some of the smaller exchanges maintain close contact with the larger exchanges. Canned food, cottonseed, grains, feed, eggs, hides, lard, lead, pota-

Underwood & Underwood

Illustration No. 84—Trading on an Organized Market

toes, rubber, silk, minerals, sugar, tobacco, wool, and many other products are sold on organized exchanges in various parts of the country. Products are sold on the basis of grades and frequently by samples.

Although the transactions completed on exchanges may lead to speculation, the activities of the exchanges are fairly well controlled. These markets serve a useful purpose in our economic system. They provide an organized means of buying and selling. As a general rule, they benefit the seller by providing an assured market of a wide scope, whereas without the exchange he would have to depend upon selling his products locally. Exchanges benefit the buyer by providing a relatively sure and constant supply of goods. As it is possible on almost all organized markets to buy goods for future delivery, manufacturers can hedge against possible losses. Hedging is explained on page 213. The exchanges also serve another useful purpose by establishing the prices of commodities. For instance, one can determine very quickly the price of a commodity by looking at the latest market quotations. These quotations are often broadcast over the radio.

Scope of Markets. In general, markets are considered to be (a) *local,* (b) *national,* or (c) *international.* International markets are frequently referred to as *world markets.*

The large geographical area of the United States has enabled many businesses to develop large national markets. There is an interesting contrast between a manufacturer's potential market in the United States and a manufacturer's potential market in one of the small European countries. The manufacturer in a small European country must face a barrier of tariff between his country and other countries. A large national market encourages production in large quantities. As this type of production is usually economical, the consumer benefits. For instance, if an automobile manufacturer were limited to a market the size of Michigan, the company could not produce automobiles in large numbers. Both the cost of production and the price to the consumer would therefore be high. Many automobile manufacturers have national markets, and some have international markets. A few of the latter make their products in foreign countries in order to avoid the tariff barrier.

Not all products or services can reach out into the national market. The nature of the product or the service and various other influences tend to restrict the market. Laundries, for instance, are usually confined to local communities. Without establishing branches, a laundry seldom finds it profitable to solicit business at greater distances than twenty or thirty miles. The nature of the service rendered by a laundry does not permit reaching out into distant regions. A single retail meat market is necessarily confined to its own neighborhood. It sometimes enlarges its territory by delivery service.

The marketing of vegetables at one time was confined to areas close to the points of production. The marketing areas for these products have, however, been extended to almost every point of the United States through the use of transportation and storage facilities. Nevertheless, the market for seasonal fresh vegetables is usually confined to relatively small areas around producing regions. For instance, during the producing season, it would be foolish for a person who raises beans in Missouri to attempt to sell fresh beans in New York City if beans are produced economically within a few miles of New York City. Certain regions, such as the South and the West Coast, have national markets for fresh fruits and vegetables during the seasons when other regions cannot produce these foods.

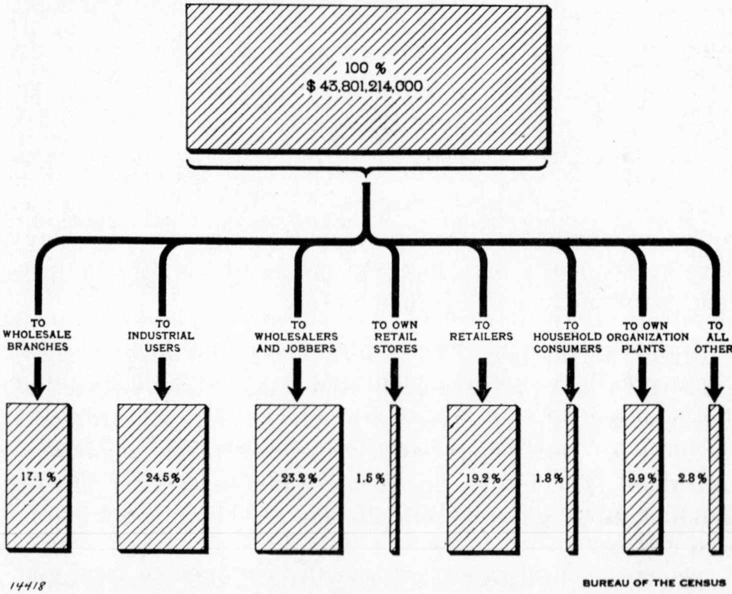

Illustration No. 85—The Distribution of All Manufactured Products

Route from Producer to Consumer. Illustration No. 85 is a summary of the methods of distribution in all manufacturing industries in the United States. There are wide variations in the distributive channels used by various industries. Some industries use several middlemen, but others use only a few.

Indirect Marketing. Distribution through the wholesaler and the retailer is frequently referred to as *indirect marketing*. Indirect marketing has acquired its designation because products pass through several hands in going from the producer to the consumer.

There is usually a very good justification for indirect distribution. For instance, a farmer may produce vegetables that he plans to sell to people in the city. He has either of two choices in marketing them. If he decides to market them directly, he must cease his productive efforts, transport his vegetables to a market, and attempt to sell them there. Suppose, for example, he decides to sell the vegetables to housewives. He hauls a truckload of vegetables to the city and spends the day in marketing them. This time is lost from production. His other choice is to sell his vegetables to someone who specializes in distribution. If he does so, he can spend all his time in producing, while the person to whom he sells his vegetables can spend all his time in distributing them. This method encourages specialization and efficiency. In this respect indirect marketing is economical. Sometimes, however, indirect marketing becomes so complicated that it is slow and expensive. There have consequently been many attempts to simplify the procedure for the benefit of consumers.

Direct Marketing. *Direct marketing* and *direct selling* are terms that mean essentially the same. Strictly speaking, direct selling is the process by which the manufacturer sells, through his own representatives, directly to the ultimate consumer. The Fuller Brush Company has been following this process of distribution. Some of the clothing companies also use it.

The theory of direct marketing is that this process eliminates some of the costs of distribution. When a company eliminates the usual channels of distribution, however, by engaging in direct marketing, it must set up its own elaborate plan of selling. No fundamental functions of distribution are eliminated. The success of a direct marketing plan depends entirely upon the efficiency and the economy with which the plan is carried out.

Combined Wholesaling and Retailing. Frequently it is said that the mail-order house, the department store, and the chain store use direct marketing. In only a few characteristics can their methods of distribution be compared with the definite type of direct marketing. Mail-order houses, department stores, and chain stores combine the services of the wholesaler and the retailer. They do not eliminate any of the essential functions of distribution; they merely combine these functions. Some of these organizations are able to buy in larger quantities than many wholesalers. All of them buy in large quantities and sell in as small quantities as does the typical retailer.

Mail-order distribution is characterized by large central warehouses and offices from which all merchandise and all advertising are distributed by mail. Department-store distribution is characterized by large stores located in thickly populated communities. Each store has a variety of departments with a wide selection of products. A department store is essentially a combination of many specialty stores. The chain store is characterized by a central organization with a number of retail outlets.

Department stores sometimes consist of a collection of leased departments. In other words, a company operating a department store may lease the shoe department, the clothing department, the radio department, and others to companies that wish to sell their products in the department store. Sometimes only a few of the departments are leased to outside companies. Studies show that almost half of the millinery departments in department stores are leased. All the various leased departments are operated under the name of the store and are not identified as separate businesses.

Efficiency and economy are frequently effected in large organizations by the consolidation of services, the reduction of the equipment and the personnel required to handle the business, and the employment of a greater proportion of skilled help.

Supermarkets. So-called supermarkets are a relatively new development, particularly in the field of food merchandising. The supermarket does not eliminate any fundamental economic functions of marketing. In some cases the supermarket combines the functions of wholesaling and retailing. The supermarket, as is true of many chain retail stores, does eliminate some services and features that are available in other retail outlets. These include credit, delivery, and convenience of location. The success of a supermarket depends upon a good location in a large shopping area, where customers can be attracted to make purchases of food in rather large quantities at infrequent intervals. Such supermarkets draw away from the small neighborhood retailer most of the profitable purchases and leave to him the many small unprofitable purchases.

Governmental Control. There are numerous state and Federal laws now affecting the marketing system. Most of these laws are known as fair-trade acts. For instance, the Federal law known as the Robinson-Patman Act is designed to prevent any manufacturer or distributor from discriminating against one customer in favor of another. The Federal law known as the Tydings-Miller Act provides re-enforcement of state laws that permit the price-fixing of branded merchandise. For instance, when this law is supported by appropriate state legislation, a manufacturer can set a retail price upon branded merchandise. The purpose of the Act is to prevent price-cutting. It is therefore a protection to the manufacturer and to some retailers, but it penalizes efficient retailers and also the consumer.

All other marketing activities that extend from one state to another come under the jurisdiction of the Federal Trade Commission and other Federal agencies, which have control over branding, labeling, advertising, and trade practices.

TEXTBOOK QUESTIONS

1. If a person says, "What is the condition of the security market today?" what does he mean?
2. If a person says, "There is a good market for this product," what does he mean?
3. What distinguishes a wholesale market from a retail market?
4. On the basis of their principle of operation, what three general classes of wholesale markets are there?

5. What is the distinction between a broker and a dealer?
6. Name some products that can be bought in organized markets.
7. On the basis of their scope, how are markets classified?
8. How does a large local market help American enterprises to expand their business?
9. What factors of distribution enable people in most parts of the United States to enjoy fresh foods of practically all kinds during the twelve months of the year?
10. Does a mail-order house eliminate any essential function of distribution?
11. What is the distinction between direct marketing and indirect marketing?
12. Give some examples of organizations that combine wholesaling and retailing.
13. What is the basis of success of the supermarket?
14. Name at least three functions that are performed by Federal laws in controlling interstate commerce.

DISCUSSION QUESTIONS

1. What kinds of markets would you expect to find in a city with a population of ten thousand?
2. A canner of fruits, instead of selling at the future price, holds his canned goods for the winter market. What functions is this canner performing in addition to his regular functions as a producer?
3. Exchanges that provide for the buying and the selling of coffee, sugar, and many other products are located in New York and other large cities. These products are not produced, however, near the cities. (a) How do you account for the location of the exchanges in these cities? (b) How do you account for the location of tobacco markets in such places as Louisville and Lexington, Kentucky?
4. How, in your opinion, does a commodity exchange, such as a wheat exchange, aid the farmer? Assume that the exchange is allowed to conduct the usual types of transactions, such as future buying and future selling.
5. How does the consumer's demand for prompt service increase the costs of distribution?
6. Fresh yeast was formerly distributed only in large cities near producing plants. Now it is available in most cities. How has this change in distribution been made possible?
7. "Transportation competes with storage." Explain this statement.
8. How do transportation and storage reduce the profits of producers in some regions?

9. A manufacturer of clothing sends an agent to your door to attempt to sell clothes to you. Does the manufacturer perform distributive functions in addition to the functions of manufacturing and selling?
10. If a method of distribution has survived through many years of use, is this fact a true indication that it is the best method of distribution?
11. In some states there are sales taxes. Because of the Federal Constitution and state constitutions, however, it is frequently not possible to tax the sales of mail-order houses if these organizations are located outside the state and sell their products within the state. How do you think that this condition affects local businesses?
12. (a) In what way is a supermarket advantageous to the consumer? (b) In what way is it disadvantageous?

PROBLEMS

1. (a) On the basis of the table on page 214, figure the cost of the leather in a pair of shoes that sells for $5.50. (b) Show the amount of cost added by the manufacturer, the wholesaler, and the retailer.
2. The tables in Illustrations Nos. 80 and 81 show that the retail margin included in the price of meat is 26 per cent. If a person purchases meat for 55 cents, how much of this price is the actual profit obtained by the retailer for the handling of the meat?
3. Suppose a manufacturer of flour contracts to sell 10,000 barrels of flour and to deliver them on December 1 at $5 a barrel. He plans to begin producing the flour on November 1. He therefore buys 45,000 bushels of wheat for delivery on November 1 at a market price of 85 cents a bushel. His estimated production costs are 75 cents a barrel. (a) What is his expected profit? (Assume that 4½ bushels of wheat will produce one barrel of flour.) (b) On November 1 the wheat is selling at $1 a bushel. If he had waited until November 1 to place his order, what would have been his profit?
4. A producer of apples gets 75 cents a bushel. The freight charges resulting from the transportation of the apples to a certain city amounts to 20 cents a bushel. The brokerage commission is 35 cents; the cost of insurance, 5 cents; the cost of storage and warehousing, 10 cents. The profit of the wholesaler amounts to 15 cents, and that of the retailer amounts to 35 cents. (a) What is the total cost of a bushel of apples to the consumer? (b) On the basis of the total cost, figure the percentage of each item of cost.

5. Two products, A and B, are manufactured by different companies. Product A is highly advertised and sells for 40 cents a package. Product B is not highly advertised and sells for 40 cents a package. The company that manufactures Product A produces and sells 1,000,000 packages at the following costs: materials, $250,000; labor, $50,000; other manufacturing expenses, $10,000; selling expense, $25,000; advertising expense, $25,000. The company that manufactures Product B produces and sells 200,000 packages. Its costs are as follows: materials, $50,000; labor, $8,000; other manufacturing expenses, $2,500; selling expenses, $12,000.

   (a) Figure the net cost of each unit of Product A and the net cost of each unit of Product B. (b) How do you account for the difference in the net costs?
6. Suppose eggs can be purchased in May at an average of 20 cents a dozen. Assume that the storage charges from the packing season in April and May until December amount to 7½ cents a dozen, payable at the time the eggs are taken out of storage, and that the market rate of interest is 6 per cent. At what price must the eggs sell in December in order that a net profit of 10 per cent will be made? (Do not consider any other expenses. Figure the interest charge from the end of May to December 1.)

COMMUNITY PROBLEMS AND PROJECTS

1. Consider some perishable product, such as milk, that is produced locally, and explain why the fresh product is not sold in a wider area.
2. Select some product that is sold locally. Trace the sources of all its ingredients, and make a report on the functions performed by all those who contributed to the production and the distribution of the product.
3. List various local businesses within a radius of your school that is designated by your teacher, classifying them according to the markets that are available to them.
4. If any products such as lumber, machinery, canned goods, clothing, farm produce, or the like are produced locally, find out the various channels of distribution through which a particular product goes from the time of its production until the time of its final use. Make a report on the process of distributing this product. List specifically the types of outlets through which the product is sold, and, if possible, use a map to indicate the area in which it is sold.

CHAPTER VIII

CREDIT RELATIONS OF BUYING AND SELLING

Purpose of the Chapter. As has been explained in a preceding chapter, the term *credit* has to do with obtaining money or some commodity or service by giving a promise to pay at a future date. There are definite obligations on the part of the one who extends the credit and of the one who obtains it. The use of credit (loans) in our monetary and banking system was studied previously. The discussion of credit in this chapter relates to the buying and selling of merchandise and services.

The most common type of credit granted is the privilege to buy merchandise without being required to pay for it until some future date. This type of credit is referred to as *purchasing on account* or *purchasing on the installment plan.* The person who makes the purchase obtains the credit; the person who sells the merchandise grants the credit. The purpose of this chapter is to explain the ordinary credit relations that exist between buyer and seller.

Section I

Kinds and Uses of Credit

Wholesale Credit. The very nature of the transactions between wholesalers and retailers makes the need for some kind of credit imperative. Requiring retailers to make their purchases in cash would be very inconvenient. Wholesalers therefore usually *sell on account* to retailers who have proved worthy of the extension of credit. The retailer buys merchandise, sometimes in a limited quantity, and is expected to pay when a statement of the account is sent to him. The granting of credit by a wholesaler thus permits the retailer to purchase goods and to sell at least part of them before he is required to make payment.

The wholesaler sometimes gives a *discount* as an inducement to buy, or more particularly as an inducement to pay promptly. Some common terms of discount and credit are given below. There are many variations of these terms of discount and credit, depending upon the locality, the type of business, and the customs of the trade.

1% discount in 10 days, net amount in 30 days
2% discount in 10 days, net amount in 30 days
2% discount in 10 days, net amount in 60 days
2% discount in 30 days, net amount in 60 days
2% discount in 30 days, net amount in 90 days
2% discount in 30 days, net amount in 120 days
3% discount in 10 days, net amount in 120 days

Retail Credit. Retail credit is ordinarily considered to be credit that is extended by the retailer to the consumer, whereas wholesale credit arises in transactions between the wholesaler and the retailer. The average person is more interested in retail credit than in wholesale credit.

Retail credit may be classified roughly as (a) *short-term credit* and (b) *long-term credit.* Short-term credit is credit extended on account. When the customer of a retailer buys merchandise, the sale is charged to his account. At the end of each month he is expected to pay for the purchases made during the month. A retailer usually submits a monthly statement to each customer. In most communities the practice is to require the customer to pay his account by the tenth of the month following that in which the purchases were made. Some stores, particularly food stores, expect customers to pay their accounts weekly. A discount is seldom allowed on retail purchases.

Long-term credit may be extended on account or through an installment plan. In the latter case the customer is required to enter into a formal contract. Such a contract is explained later in this chapter. The principal difference between short-term credit and long-term credit is that in the latter case the customer is given a longer time to pay. He is sometimes required to pay extra for this privilege, and he is often required to make regular small payments on the amount he owes.

Value of Credit. Some people openly boast, "We pay cash for everything." The ability to pay cash is commendable and desirable, but no one can predict when and under what circumstances he may need credit. The obtaining of credit is not a reflection upon one's character or capacity to pay. Obtaining credit under proper circumstances is a good test of one's character. It is important to everyone who expects to attain prominence in business or to build up the standing of himself or his family in the community. A man with poor credit usually loses his self-respect. He almost invariably develops a feeling that he does not have a fair chance in life.

Credit does not merely happen. It comes as the result of slow growth. It must be nurtured, fostered, strengthened, and improved. It is an asset of tremendous value to those who develop it over a long period of years. It can be destroyed easily; it is sensitive to abuse; and it usually continues only as long as it is justified. Credit is extended only to persons who deserve it and who have wisdom enough to protect it. It represents the willingness of others to accept a person's promise to pay under stipulated conditions.

Basis of Credit. A commonly recognized formula for determining the credit of a person or a business is the "three C's"—character, capacity, and capital.

Character is the first consideration. J. P. Morgan, the famous banker, is reputed to have said that he would lend more on an individual's character than on his capital resources. Wealth alone cannot determine one's credit. Because of the importance of character, one's reputation must be guarded carefully.

Capacity is merely another term for earning power. It represents one's ability to earn and to pay obligations when they become due. An individual may have an honorable character and perfectly good intentions of paying an obligation; but unless he has the ability or capacity to pay, he cannot pay satisfactorily. It is often more difficult to judge character than it is to judge capacity. Capacity, or earning power, can be measured reasonably accurately, but character is an intangible quality.

The third measuring standard, *capital,* applies only to people who have property. The amount of credit that individuals are entitled to receive varies greatly. A person with a temporary lack of earning power may be entitled to receive credit, provided he has good capital resources and a good character. Capacity and capital without character will, however, usually disqualify any credit applicant. The personal aspect of credit is extremely important.

Abuse of Credit. Credit may be used (a) for convenience in systematic buying or (b) to obtain something for the preservation of life or of happiness when a sufficient amount of money is not available to pay at the time the purchase is made. Credit obtained under the first condition is justifiable. In the second case, however, a careful study should be made to see whether the purchase is actually needed and whether the obligation can be met.

Some people are too willing to buy on credit just because credit is available. Merchants sometimes make credit "too cheap." In other words, they are willing to grant credit even though the payment of the obligation is doubtful. The propriety of buying an automobile on credit is doubtful when the payment of the obligation would mean the sacrificing of expenditures for food, clothing, and other necessities. The purchase on credit of an asset such as an automobile is, however, desirable if it will cause the family to avoid other wasteful expenditures. On the other hand, the dealer who encourages someone to accept credit in making a purchase but who does not consider the person's ability to pay is not fair to the purchaser. The user of credit should beware of the person who too willingly gives credit without investigation.

Many buyers are not good managers of their own incomes. They will accept just as much credit as will be extended to them. They do not look ahead and budget their incomes and expenditures. The wise credit manager will calmly and clearly give a prospective buyer reasons why he advises cautiousness and will give advice to his customers on the obligations that they should assume. The person who accepts credit should clearly understand his obligations.

Advantages of Credit to the Consumer. The credit privilege has certain definite advantages. In buying merchandise from a store, the purchaser is ordinarily given thirty days in which to pay. Particular regulations are governed largely by local merchants. The usual plan is, however, to render a bill to a customer on the first of each month for all purchases made during the preceding month. The bill is due immediately and should be paid within the first ten days of the month. If it is not paid within this time, the account becomes delinquent.

In addition to the advantage of buying merchandise without having to pay for it until a specified future time, the following are some of the specific advantages of using credit:

(a) The use of credit prevents loss. A person does not need to carry money with him when he goes shopping. He therefore is not so liable to lose money or to have it stolen. There is also less liability of mistakes in making change.

(b) Record-keeping is facilitated by the use of credit. Statements rendered serve as a basis for maintaining records and keeping a budget. This method is simpler than attempting to keep daily and weekly records through cash purchases.

(c) Although a person sometimes buys more freely on credit than he would if he were paying cash, this disadvantage is often offset by the advantage of leaving most of one's cash in the bank so that it will be safe and will not be spent foolishly.

(d) The use of a charge account usually results in payments by check. The checkbook stubs can be used as a basis for entries required in keeping accounts and a budget.

(e) The use of a charge account builds up a better relation between merchant and customer. Clerks and storekeepers soon learn to know and to appreciate the business of the person who has a charge account. That person will frequently get better consideration and better service than the person who buys only for cash.

(f) Charge accounts facilitate the ordering of merchandise by telephone.

Anyone who can be trusted to spend cash wisely can also be trusted to make purchases on credit. Neither plan—that is, spending cash or buying on credit—can be said to promote savings any more than the other. The growth of savings depends upon following a definite plan.

Remington Rand, Inc.

Illustration No. 86—The Credit Record Department of a Large Store

Advantages of Credit to the Merchant. As has been stated before, business could not be transacted without some form of credit. Merchants also recognize the advantages of credit in dealing with their customers. The following are some of these advantages:

(a) Credit develops permanent customers. It makes regular customers and creates a more intimate relation.

(b) As a rule, credit sales are larger than cash sales, although they are not quite so frequent as the latter. Customers usually buy in larger quantities when they do not have to pay immediately. The larger quantities last a longer time.

(c) Good credit relations develop confidence in a merchant and build goodwill.

(d) Customers who have the ability to pay patronize stores that extend credit, whereas bargain hunters sometimes seek cash stores.

(e) Credit permits a larger volume of business with less selling expense. Credit purchases are usually regular, whereas cash purchases in many types of stores are made periodically when the customers receive their salaries or wages.

The retailer who allows his customers to buy recklessly is not only abusing his credit relations, but also encouraging his customers to abuse their credit relations. Any merchant who encourages extravagance through urging customers to make thoughtless purchases finds quickly that he cannot collect the accounts that are owed him. He fails, and deserves to fail.

Procedure in Establishing Credit. Every person who attempts to obtain credit must realize that the one who is to grant it must have some information that will serve as a basis for extending credit. Because the latter is contemplating giving merchandise in return for a promise to pay, he has a right to obtain the information that he needs to determine the applicant's character, capacity, and capital. This information is for credit purposes only and will be kept confidential.

Applying for credit is no disgrace. The applicant should approach the merchant with an open mind and with a willingness to give the information that is desired. Most merchants are pleased to have an opportunity to discuss credit relations and to open accounts if credit is justified.

Illustration No. 87 shows a typical application for credit for customers of a department store. In some cases the forms are more complicated, but in general they require the same types of information.

Credit Agencies. In general there are two types of credit agencies: (a) agencies that provide credit information with regard to businessmen and companies, and (b) agencies that provide credit information with regard to individual purchasers.

Banks sometimes give confidential credit information on individuals and businesses. It is therefore important for a person or a business to maintain satisfactory relations with a bank if a good credit rating is desired. Information can be obtained from the local better business bureau as to whether there have been any complaints on the credit of a particular person or business.

LEDGER RECORD

ACCT. No. LIMIT

MEMBER OF
RETAILERS CREDIT ASSOCIATION
Application for Account

DATE

NOTIFIED

SPELL CORRECTLY. SURNAME FIRST, GIVEN NAME IN FULL. STATE IF SINGLE OR WIDOW

NAME OF HUSBAND Smith, Robert Allen — NAME OF WIFE Mary Ann

RESIDENCE ADDRESS 3948 Mission Street, San Francisco, California — HOW LONG 6 years PHONE None

FORMER ADDRESS 237 Holliston Street, Pasadena, California

HUSBAND'S OCCUPATION Salesman (POSITION) Fuller Brush Co. (FIRM) — WIFE'S OCCUPATION None (POSITION) (FIRM)

BUSINESS ADDRESS 1512 Van Ness Avenue — BUSINESS ADDRESS

HOW LONG PRESENT EMPLOY 5 years — HOW LONG IN CITY 6 years — HOME ☒ OWN ☐ RENT — OTHER PROPERTY

BANK Merchants National Bank (BRANCH) — COM. ☐ SAVGS. ☐ — BANK SIGNATURE OR NAME

COMMERCIAL REFERENCES F. C. Nash & Co. Dept. Store, Pasadena, Calif. — COMMERCIAL REFERENCES

" — "

" — "

PERSONAL REFERENCE Mr. F. L. Roth, Manager, Fuller Brush — NEAREST RELATIVE ADDRESS

AUTHORIZED BUYERS Mary Ann Smith

SEND STATEMENTS TO ☒ RESIDENCE ☐ BUSINESS — TOTAL AMOUNT CREDIT REQUESTED $150.00 — TERMS 30 days — SUBSCRIBER'S CODE No.

I CERTIFY TO THE ABOVE STATEMENTS AND AGREE TO PAY MY BILLS IN FULL IN SAN FRANCISCO DURING MONTH FOLLOWING PURCHASE. FOR THE PURPOSE OF HAVING CREDIT EXTENDED ME BY The Emporium

APPLICATION TAKEN BY HMK — SIGNATURE Robert Allen Smith

REMARKS

Illustration No. 87—An Application for Credit

Private credit agencies make a profit by collecting information and publishing confidential reports for the benefit of their subscribers, who are usually retailers. Each subscriber contributes to these reports by furnishing information and periodic ratings. Additional information is gathered from local newspapers, notices of change in address, death notices, and court records. Such information is valuable to the retailer in protecting himself from loss on accounts. If one of his customers moves, he will want to know of the change in address. If a customer dies, he will want to be sure that his claim is presented. If someone is taking court action against one of his customers, he will want to protect his own claim.

The National Retail Credit Association is composed of local associations in various cities. These associations are organized to co-operate in furnishing credit information. Credit reports can be submitted promptly to any subscriber.

The twelve hundred credit bureaus of the Associated Credit Bureaus of America, an affiliate of the National Retail Credit Association, maintain credit records on sixty million persons. These records are kept up to date through the co-operation of local bureaus. The information is quickly available to any member of a local bureau.

This huge network of credit-reporting agencies is beneficial not only to the merchant, but also to the individual who seeks credit. Anyone who is honest and who desires to maintain proper credit should be perfectly willing to have a report submitted on him. With this system of reporting credit information, it is difficult for any person to establish a bad credit reputation without the information being made available to other merchants who may want to extend credit.

There is another important source of information with regard to the credit of commercial houses and manufacturers. This agency is Dun and Bradstreet, Incorporated. A book of credit ratings is published regularly by this agency and sold as a service to subscribers. The service covers the entire United States. In addition, a subscriber can obtain a special report on any businessman or professional man in any part of the country. The reliability of this agency has been established through many years of effective service to all types of businessmen.

Community Credit Policy. It is desirable to have a uniform credit policy in each community so that all merchants will treat their customers alike and so that customers will become accustomed to the policy. The following credit policy was proposed by the merchants of one community:

(a) To standardize all terms, classifying accounts as follows:
   (1) Monthly charge accounts (Open Accounts)
   (2) Budget or deferred-payment accounts (time-payment accounts of short duration, that do not exceed ten weeks and on which no carrying charge is made)
   (3) Installment accounts (time-payment accounts of long duration, on which a carrying charge is made)

(b) To state the credit terms to the applicant for credit, stressing a definite due date

(c) To consider all accounts past due on the day following the definite due date

(d) To make no deviation from the credit terms

(e) When an account has not been paid in full within 60 days following the end of the month of purchase, to use at this point a uniform "term" letter

(f) To charge interest at the rate of not less than one-half per cent a month on all balances on monthly charge accounts that have been due for 60 days

(g) To use a credit application blank requiring the signature of the applicant, and carrying a notice of the interest charge

(h) To check *all* applicants for credit through the credit bureau *before* opening any new accounts, and not to open an account when the report is unfavorable

(i) To require a down payment of not less than 10 per cent on all installment, lay-away, or will-call sales

(j) To record all installment accounts with the credit bureau if they are not recorded with the county clerk and recorder

(k) To furnish to the bureau each month a complete list of all accounts that have been delinquent for 90 days (Example: January purchases would be reported on May first)

(l) To report promptly to the bureau all accounts that have been closed for various reasons; to report, at the time of repossession, all repossessions; and to report all unfair claims and any other special information that might affect credit standing.

Cost of Credit to the Seller. Merchants who sell on open account may be classified as follows: (a) those who have uniform prices for credit and for cash sales; (b) those who charge more for credit than for cash sales.

The extending of credit adds extra costs to every sale. The principal extra costs result from (a) the clerical work necessary for recording credit sales and collecting accounts, and (b) interest on the money that is invested in order to extend credit. Additional costs result from (a) occasional losses due to bad debts and (b) the tendency of credit customers to return goods for exchange.

These comments should not be construed to mean that a merchant who sells on credit must necessarily sell at higher prices than a merchant who sells for cash. If selling on credit results in greater sales than selling for cash, the increased sales may produce a greater profit. On the other hand, if a merchant does set his prices higher for credit sales and makes no concessions for cash sales, the person who buys for cash is penalized. When a merchant advertises "No additional charge on installment purchases," the person who buys for cash has a right to expect a discount.

Cost of Credit to the Individual. Any cost of credit is passed on either to the individual consumer on the basis of each sale, or to all buyers through generally higher prices.

Credit terms were discussed earlier in this chapter. They vary considerably; but through the efforts of credit associations, they are more or less uniform throughout any particular community. The common retail credit terms require the purchaser to pay his account on or before the tenth of the month following the month in which his purchases were made. Some stores grant an arbitrary credit period of thirty, sixty, or ninety days, especially on large purchases. Some purchases are made on this basis without an added charge, as in the case of regular installment sales.

Sometimes discounts are allowed to individuals in ordinary credit transactions. Common terms in such a case are "2 per cent ten days, thirty days net." These mean that, if the purchaser pays the amount within ten days, he may deduct a discount of 2 per cent from the amount of the bill; but if he does not desire to take advantage of the 2 per cent discount, he may pay the net amount at the end of thirty days. The person who sells on this basis is willing to forego 2 per cent of the sale value in order to obtain his money promptly. If the purchaser chooses not to take the 2 per cent discount, he is paying 2 per cent for the use of the money for twenty days. In other words, if he buys on these terms goods amounting to $100, he may take a discount of $2 at the end of ten days and therefore pay only $98. Suppose, however, that he has enough money to pay the bill but believes that he can use the money better in some other way. He therefore prefers to wait until the end of thirty days before paying the bill. By doing so, he pays $2 for using $98 for twenty days. If interest is figured on the basis of 360 days, he is paying interest at the rate of 36.72 per cent a year to use this money.

Responsibility for Debts. A young married woman opened charge accounts in two stores. Her purchases amounted to one hundred and fifty dollars. The husband became very indignant and refused to pay the debt. The stores sued for collection and won the suits. In most states the wife has implied authority to pledge her husband's credit for the necessaries of a household. Necessaries may include domestic service, medical attention, supplies, and clothing. Under some circumstances jewelry and furniture may also be included.

Unless a husband has given legal written notice that he will not assume responsibility for his wife's debts, he must pay the debts that she incurs. In the absence of specific instructions or of the publication of a legal notice, a merchant therefore has a legal right to sell on account to a wife and to expect payment from the husband.

The laws of most states place upon the parents the responsibility for the payment of debts incurred by their children in purchasing necessaries of life. Ordinarily, parents are not responsible for debts that their children have incurred by purchasing luxuries or other unnecessary articles.

TEXTBOOK QUESTIONS

1. In what way is buying on credit an indication of one's character and financial standing?
2. What are the "three C's" in the formula for determining credit? Explain each.
3. Under what two circumstances is credit ordinarily used by the average person?
4. (a) What is meant by making credit too cheap? (b) What is the effect?
5. Why does the National Retail Credit Association advocate a careful study of each applicant for credit?
6. What are the advantages to the consumer in using credit?
7. What are the five advantages of credit to the merchant?

8. List some of the information that an individual is required to give when he applies for credit.
9. What are some of the agencies through which credit information can be obtained?
10. Do all merchants charge extra for installment sales?
11. What are some of the extra costs involved in selling on credit?
12. Is it fair for a store to charge the same prices for cash sales and for credit sales?
13. How are the various types of accounts classified in the uniform community credit policy outlined in this section?
14. In most communities how is it possible for all stores to know whether you have paid your account regularly at one store?
15. Is a wife personally responsible for the debts she incurs, or is her husband responsible? Explain your answer.

DISCUSSION QUESTIONS

1. Some people consider that a credit bureau is unfair in reporting unpaid accounts. What is your viewpoint?
2. If you move to another city, how will a good credit rating that was established in your previous place of residence help you?
3. Some merchants solicit customers to buy on account. (a) Why do you think they do so? (b) How do they plan this solicitation?
4. Why is character more important than capital in establishing credit?
5. From the point of view of (a) the creditor and (b) the debtor, discuss some of the evils of encouraging people to use too much credit.
6. Why should merchants in the same type of business in the same city follow a uniform policy of extending credit?
7. Why is it unwise for a spendthrift to use credit?
8. Why has a creditor the right to know something about the income of a person who applies for credit?
9. Why do you think a merchant may want the name of your employer if you apply for credit?
10. If a merchant passes on to another merchant some credit information that is false and injures your credit rating, why should you have the privilege of bringing a lawsuit for damages?
11. If all credit customers in all types of businesses paid promptly, thus preventing any credit loss, how would this practice benefit you as a cash customer or a credit customer?
12. How do you think selling on credit could be (a) more costly than selling for cash? (b) more economical?

Section II

Installment Credit

Importance of Installment Buying. Estimates of the Government and of various associations disclose the fact that about 60 per cent of the yearly retail sales are credit transactions. About one third of these credit sales are made on the installment plan. Installment business is therefore important. It aids not only in the sale of finished products, but also indirectly in the sale of raw materials that go into these finished products. For instance, from 60 to 75 per cent of all new automobiles are sold on the installment plan. Because steel, fabric, rubber, and many other products go into the production of an automobile, the selling of automobiles on the installment plan increases the need for these raw materials.

Many other products besides automobiles are sold on the installment plan. Some of the common products sold thus are household appliances, musical instruments, and farm implements.

We have become dependent to a great extent upon the installment plan as a means of selling. In fact, it is doubtful whether installment sales could be stopped instantaneously without seriously affecting business conditions and the general welfare of the nation.

Types of Installment Contracts. Every time-payment contract provides an ironclad legal claim upon the merchandise until the obligation has been paid. Security for the deferred payment may take the form of (a) a chattel mortgage or (b) a conditional sales contract. Illustration No. 88 shows a chattel mortgage, and Illustration No. 89 shows a conditional sales contract. In most states the laws specify the particular form that must be used, whereas in a few states either form may be used.

Obligations on Installment Contracts. Some merchants will extend credit for sixty, ninety, or a hundred and twenty days without requiring the signing of a time-payment contract. Although a contract is not signed when credit is ex-

THE McALPIN COMPANY
Cincinnati, Ohio

County Hamilton State Ohio City Cincinnati Date January 3, 1939

CONSIDERATION ACKNOWLEDGED.—I do hereby grant, bargain, sell, convey and confirm unto THE McALPIN COMPANY (mortgagee) or assigns, the following described merchandise, to have and to hold said merchandise forever, provided, however, that I shall pay to the mortgagee or its assigns the full purchase price in installments on the day of each month that the installment becomes due, then this mortgage to be void.

DESCRIPTION AND TERMS

Item Thor Washing Machine Serial No. 625437 Cash Purchase Price $ 78.00

Less Down Payment Received by Louis P. Morton (Signature) $ 18.00

Balance to be paid as follows: Principal $ 6.00 BALANCE $ 60.00

Carrying Charges $ .30

Total $ 6.30 each and every month.

If I fail to make any monthly payment then all remaining installments may be declared due and payable, and upon failure to make any monthly payment, or all, if all are declared due, I agree to deliver said Merchandise as described, upon demand to the Company, or its assigns, and all payments made and the used Merchandise applied on purchase as described shall be retained by said Company, or its assigns, as stipulated damages. I Further Agree to take good care of said Merchandise and to be responsible for its loss by theft, fire or other casualty, and not to remove it from

1619 Buckeye Street (Name of Street) Cincinnati (City) Ohio (State) Melrose 2235 (Tel. No.)

unless I first obtain the written consent of said Company, or its assigns.

It is Understood and Agreed that no other agreement or guaranty, verbal or written, expressed or implied, shall limit or qualify the terms of this contract.

Not valid unless accepted by Dealer.

Accepted Paul C. Hillis, Treasurer Signed James L. Sherman (Customer)

Date January 3, 1939 Salesman Louis P. Morton (Salesman sign here)

Illustration No. 88—A Chattel Mortgage

tended over a long period of time, merchants often require regular weekly, biweekly, or monthly payments.

When a time-payment contract is used, the amount of each payment and the time of each payment are usually specified. The purchaser ordinarily signs a note and turns over to the merchant as collateral for security a conditional sales contract or a chattel mortgage. The signatures of the purchaser and the dealer must be witnessed. In most states, the contracts must be written in triplicate. One copy is kept by the purchaser; another copy is filed in some local recording office; and the original is sent to the finance company.

A *conditional sales contract* is essentially a lease. It holds the title to the property until the last payment is made. A *chattel mortgage* is a direct lien on the property. If the payments are not made in accordance with the agreement, the person who owns the mortgage may repossess the property. A comparison of the two types of contracts will show that they are very similar in many respects.

The purchaser must agree to do certain things. For instance, in the case of the purchase of an automobile, he must agree to keep the car free from taxes, liens, and encumbrances; and not to use the car for illegal or improper purposes, to remove it from the state without permission, or to transfer any interest in it.

Finance Companies. In the field of installment credit a particular type of financial institution has developed. It is often referred to as a *finance company*. In a sense it is a dealer or a bank that purchases from merchants the contracts signed by customers who buy on the installment plan.

CONDITIONAL SALES CONTRACT

3145
Contract Number

The undersigned seller hereby sells, and the undersigned purchaser or purchasers, jointly and severally hereby purchase(s), subject to the terms and conditions hereinafter set forth, the following property, complete with standard attachments and equipment delivery and acceptance of which is hereby acknowledged by purchaser, viz:

RADIO—Make Philco Model 165K Serial No. 12834

For a total time price of $ 105.40 (9), payable as follows: $ 10.00 (5) on or before delivery, leaving a deferred balance of $ 95.40 (8) payable at the offices of The Blank Acceptance Corporation to be hereafter designated in instalments of $ 7.95 (7-A), on the same day of each successive month, or as indicated in schedule of payments below, and commencing April 27, 1940; and the final instalment payable hereunder shall equal the amount of the deferred balance remaining due. Interest is due on instalments after maturity at the highest lawful contract rate, and if this contract be placed with an attorney for collection, 15% of the amount due hereunder as attorney's fees, or if prohibited, the amount permitted by law.

Date purchaser desires first payment to fall due.

Schedule of monthly payments

$ 7.95	1 Mo. hereafter
$ 7.95	2 Mos. hereafter
$ 7.95	3 Mos. hereafter
$ 7.95	4 Mos. hereafter
$ 7.95	5 Mos. hereafter
$ 7.95	6 Mos. hereafter
$ 7.95	7 Mos. hereafter
$ 7.95	8 Mos. hereafter
$ 7.95	9 Mos. hereafter
$ 7.95	10 Mos. hereafter
$ 7.95	11 Mos. hereafter
$ 7.95	12 Mos. hereafter

1. Title to said property shall not pass to purchaser until said amount is fully paid in cash.

2. No transfer, renewal, extension or assignment of this contract or any interest thereunder, or loss, injury or destruction of said property shall release purchaser from his obligation hereunder; assignee shall be entitled to all the rights of seller.

3. In the event purchaser defaults on any payment due on this contract or fails to comply with any condition of this contract or a proceeding in bankruptcy, receivership or insolvency be instituted against the purchaser or his property, or seller deems the property in danger of misuse or confiscation, the full amount shall be immediately due and payable; the seller's acceptance, after the full amount may have become immediately due and payable as hereinbefore provided, of any instalment or payment shall not be deemed to alter or affect the purchaser's obligations and/or the seller's rights hereunder with respect to any subsequent payments or default therein. Purchaser hereby authorizes any attorney-at-law to appear for said purchaser in any court of record in the United States, waive the issue and service of process, and confess judgment against said purchaser for any amount due hereunder in favor of seller or any assignee together with attorney's fees as hereinabove provided.

4. No warranties, expressed or implied, representations, promises or statements have been made by seller unless endorsed hereon in writing.

5. Purchaser shall keep said property free of all taxes, liens and encumbrances; shall not use same illegally, improperly or for hire; shall not remove same from the state without permission of seller; shall not transfer any interest in this contract or said property. The proceeds of any insurance, whether paid by reason of loss, injury, return premium or otherwise, shall be applied toward the replacement of the property or payment of this obligation, at the option of seller. Seller may insure said property against fire and theft, or any accidental physical damage to protect purchaser, seller or seller's assignee. Purchaser agrees to pay the premium upon demand and that on failure to do so, payment of said premium shall be secured by this contract.

6. Time is of the essence of this contract, and if purchaser default in complying with the terms hereof, or seller deems the property in danger of misuse or confiscation, seller or any sheriff or other officer of the law may take immediate possession of said property without demand (possession after default being unlawful), including any equipment or accessories thereto; and for this purpose seller may enter upon the premises where said property may be and remove same. Seller may resell said property, so retaken, at public or private sale, without demand for performance, with or without notice to purchaser (if given, notice by mail to address below being sufficient), with or without having such property at place of sale, and upon such terms and in such manner as seller may determine; seller may bid at any public sale. From proceeds of any such sale, seller shall deduct all expenses for retaking, repairing and selling such property, including a reasonable attorney's fee. The balance thereof shall be applied to amount due; any surplus shall be paid over to purchaser; in case of deficiency purchaser shall pay the same with interest. Seller may take possession of any other property in the above described property at time of repossession and hold same temporarily for purchaser without liability on the part of seller

7. Seller shall have the right to enforce one or more remedies hereunder, successively or concurrently. Purchaser hereby waives the right to remove any legal action from the court originally acquiring jurisdiction and waives all homestead and other property exemption laws. Any provision of this contract prohibited by law of any state shall as to said state be ineffective to the extent of such prohibition without invalidating the remaining provisions of the contract.

Executed in triplicate, one copy of which was delivered to and retained by purchaser, this 27th day of March, 1940
(Do not date on Sunday)

Purchaser Signs: H.A. Nieman (Purchaser's Signature) — (Title, if Company) — 3408 Vermont St (Street) — Covington (Town) — Kentucky (State)

Seller Signs: D.M. Cotton (Seller's Signature) — Modern Radio Store (Title, if Company) — 513 Madison (Street) — Covington (Town) — Kentucky (State)

G.W. Hughes (Witness) SIGN IN INK R.D. Durbin (Witness)

☞ In states where acknowledgment or affidavit is necessary for filing or recording, Notary Public will insert necessary acknowledgment or affidavit on reverse hereof.

Illustration No. 89—A Conditional Sales Contract

These notes are purchased by the finance company at a discount. For example, a person may purchase an automobile on the installment plan and sign a mortgage contract. The dealer who sold the car may then sell the contract to a finance company. In such case the person who purchased the car will be required to make payments to the finance company instead of to the dealer.

Typical Financing Charges. Frequently no extra charge is added to the selling price if merchandise is sold on open account on terms of thirty, sixty, ninety, or a hundred and twenty days. Sometimes, however, creditors add an interest charge on open accounts if the accounts are not paid within the time limit. The interest charge usually is about 6 per cent and is based upon the unpaid balance.

The financing charge on some installment sales is computed according to the following example: Mr. Jones makes a purchase of furniture amounting to $400 and agrees to pay $50 at the end of each month, plus interest at 6 per cent on the unpaid balance at the beginning of the month. At the end of the first month he pays $50 plus $2 interest. The unpaid balance is then $350. At the end of the second month he pays $50 plus interest amounting to $1.75, and he continues until all the payments have been made.

The usual plan of financing is to charge in advance a certain percentage based on the unpaid balance and the length of time during which regular installments will be paid. The table in Illustration No. 90 shows the typical percentages charged on contracts for such products as radios and refrigerators when installment payments are made monthly.

Percentage Added to the Original Unpaid Balance

MONTHS	0	1	2	3	4	5	6	7	8	9
0	....	....	....	....	6.0	6.5	7.0	7.5	8.0	8.5
10	9.0	9.5	10.0	10.5	11.0	11.5	12.0	12.5	13.0	13.5
20	14.0	14.5	15.0	15.5	16.0	16.5	17.0	17.5	18.0	18.5

Illustration No. 90—Percentages Charged on Installment Sales

The number of months allowed for making payment is the number in the first column plus the number in the columnar heading. For instance, if an original unpaid balance of $100 is to be paid in four monthly installments, the finance charge will be 6 per cent, or $6. The total amount to be paid will, then, be $106. If an original unpaid balance of $100 is to be paid in twenty-four months, however, the finance charge will be 16 per cent, or $16. The total amount to be paid in twenty-four installments will, then, be $116.

Terms of Payment. The percentage of down payment and the amount of time in which the debtor may pay vary according to the product, the amount of the down payment, and the policy of the finance company. The table in Illustration No. 91 provides a summary of the usual percentages of down payment and the usual maximum periods for making payment for particular types of merchandise.

When to Use the Installment Plan. Installment buying has its advantages and disadvantages. Some plans are good, whereas others are unsound. The misfortune of a single person as the result of using the installment plan does not necessarily prove that the plan is fundamentally wrong. The misfortune probably did not result from the installment purchase, but from a blunder on the part of the purchaser or the seller.

PRODUCT	USUAL PERCENTAGE OF DOWN PAYMENT	USUAL TIME ALLOWED THE DEBTOR TO PAY (MONTHS)
New automobiles	10 to 33⅓	12 to 24
Used automobiles	10 to 33⅓	6 to 18
Soft goods (textiles and perishables)	10 to 20	3 to 12
Furniture		
Department stores	10 to 20	6 to 18
Furniture stores	10 to 25	12 to 24
Refrigerators		
Department stores	5 to 10	12 to 36
Electrical appliance stores	5 to 10	12 to 36
Radios		
Department stores	10 to 20	12 to 24
Electrical appliance stores	10 to 20	12 to 24
Washing machines	5 to 10	12 to 24
Stoves	10 to 20	12 to 36
Jewelry	5 to 20	6 to 18
Men's clothing	10 to 25	3 to 12

Illustration No. 91—Down Payments and Time Allowed on Installment Sales

In some cases installment buying is harmful. For instance, buying luxuries on the installment plan is not justifiable; such items should be bought with money especially saved for the purpose. No wise home-manager would purchase expensive clothing or elaborate jewelry on the installment plan. A railroad engineer, however, would be justified in buying a good watch on the installment plan if it were needed in his work. If a radio is needed to entertain a sick person or an automobile is required for business, installment buying is permissible and usually justified.

In general, it is unwise to purchase luxuries on the installment plan. What constitutes a luxury is a debatable problem, for what may represent a luxury for one person may be a necessity for another. Circumstances must determine the case. For instance, an individual who has a mortgage on his home and is having difficulty in meeting all his obligations would be foolish to buy a radio or an automobile on the installment plan, for it is obvious that payments could not be made without sacrificing the well-being and the financial security of the family.

The age of a person and his expected income are vitally important in determining the advisability of buying on the installment plan. If a person is sure that his income will not be reduced, and if, on the contrary, it may be increased, he has some basis on which to plan the installment buying of substantial assets that are needed. On the other hand, if there is a chance that his income may decrease, buying on the installment plan will be a very doubtful procedure. Young doctors starting in their profession frequently find it necessary to finance the purchase of equipment through the installment plan. The assets that they buy are necessary for the practice of their profession.

Installment buying can be used frequently as a means of saving. It should, however, be used carefully and with common sense. For example, if one is furnishing a home, the purchase of furniture on the installment plan will be justifiable if the payments can be made without jeopardizing the budget. Using the installment plan will be better than spending all available funds to buy cheap furnishings, which would soon wear out and then have to be replaced.

Some families do not accumulate savings rapidly because their regular incomes are spent foolishly. If persons of this type would acquire substantial assets by assuming obligations under the installment plan, they might be able to save. For people who have never acquired the habit of saving, the installment plan can be an aid.

The seller of merchandise should be just as careful as the buyer in determining when the installment plan should be used. For instance, if Mr. Allen is contemplating buying an automobile from the Central Automobile Company, both the salesman and Mr. Allen should study carefully the latter's ability to pay for the automobile. Suppose that the automobile will cost $450. Mr. Allen has $100 that he can pay in cash. The most reasonable plan for the payment of the balance of $350 is $48 a month. Mr. Allen has been able, however, to save only $30 a month. It is obvious, therefore, that he cannot afford to buy the automobile unless he reduces his standard of living. If he makes the purchase, he will not only have to meet the payments of $48 a month, but also have to pay a license fee, repair bills, and other operating costs. If Mr. Allen were a salesman, however, and needed an automobile in his business, he would take into consideration any saving that would result from using his own automobile and any allowance that he might receive from his employer for using it.

Advantages of Installment Buying. The following are some of the recognized advantages of installment buying:

(a) Savings result if installment purchases are made wisely by people who otherwise could not save money and accumulate enough to purchase for cash.

(b) Necessities may be enjoyed before the full price is available for payment.

(c) Better and more substantial merchandise can sometimes be obtained by utilizing the installment plan instead of paying cash for cheap merchandise.

(d) Without the aid of installment buying, many young married people would be unable to furnish a home and start housekeeping.

(e) Sales are stimulated and mass production is made possible, consumer prices thereby being reduced.

Disadvantages of Installment Buying. The disadvantages of installment buying arise, not necessarily out of the faults of the system, but often out of its abuses. The following are some of the disadvantages of installment buying:

(a) Some people buy assets because of false pride. They are encouraged to buy more expensive assets than they can afford.

(b) When the number of dealers allowing installment purchases is limited, the person who wishes to make an installment purchase may have to accept an inferior product because the grade of goods he wants is not sold where he can make purchases on the installment plan.

(c) The person who buys on the installment plan pays interest at a rate of from 6 per cent to 25 per cent on the unpaid balance. He therefore pays more than he would have paid if he had purchased the merchandise for cash.

(d) Some people may overbuy unless they are given good advice by those from whom purchases are being made.

(e) "Credit competition" sometimes leads businesses to put customers under pressure in the hope of selling merchandise on "easy terms."

(f) Some merchants and dealers encourage buyers to use the installment plan because such a sale results in an additional income through the interest on the unpaid balance.

(g) Some users of the installment plan lower their standards of food, clothing, education, and environment in order to meet obligations on installment purchases.

It is evident that installment purchases should be made only on the basis of necessity and convenience after a careful study of needs and ability to pay. In general, installment buying is recommended only for accumulating worth-while assets.

Charges for Installment Service. In making a decision with regard to buying on the installment plan, it is not a question of whether the cost of buying in this way is fair or unfair; it is a question of whether the merchandise is needed sufficiently to justify paying the amount that is charged for the privilege of buying on this installment plan. In some cases the charges may be exorbitant; and yet in most cases they are reasonable when the costs of the finance company are taken into consideration. A list of the costs of operating one important finance company is given below. After these operating costs have been given consideration, an additional 2 per cent is added for profit.

(a) Interest on borrowed money
(b) Banking costs
(c) Insurance on loans
(d) Credit investigations
(e) Office detail
(f) Collections
(g) Repossession of property from defaulting buyers
(h) Storing, advertising, and selling repossessed merchandise
(i) Losses on repossessed merchandise
(j) Losses through defaults, conversions, or damaged merchandise
(k) Legal expenses
(l) General office overhead

When a person buys on the installment plan, he is therefore paying such miscellaneous costs as those listed. He is paying for more than merely the privilege of borrowing money. The following are typical installment charges on automobiles:

AMOUNT FINANCED	TOTAL CHARGE	MONTHLY PAYMENT	LENGTH OF CONTRACT
$100	$15.32	$ 9.61	12 months
150	17.28	13.94	12 months
200	21.88	18.49	12 months
250	27.32	23.11	12 months
300	32.76	27.73	12 months

Are Installment Costs Excessive? The preceding analysis of the costs that must be borne by a finance company provides some explanation of why the charge for installment buying seems excessive. The popular belief among buyers of automobiles and other equipment is that the finance business is largely one of banking. Because of the high charge the business appears to them to be simple and profitable. Competition has limited profit to a reasonably fair level. One should know what the real cost of buying on the installment plan will be, and then should decide whether he can afford to pay that cost.

Figuring the Cost of an Installment Purchase. There are numerous installment plans. Some of these reveal the true cost by making a charge, in the form of interest, on the unpaid balances. In such a case the actual cost of the merchandise to the purchaser is easy to figure. On the other hand, some plans involve discounts, fees, and carrying charges in order to conceal the real interest rate. The following is an example of how to figure the actual interest rate on a typical installment purchase when the rate is concealed. The example is based upon a study made by the Pollak Foundation for Economic Research.

A furniture store advertised a sofa on special sale of $79. The price could be paid at the rate of $9 down and $10 a month for seven months, with "no charge for the easy terms." A cash customer could get a $7 discount if he asked for it. The allowance of this discount meant, essentially, that an installment charge of $7 had been added on a sofa that was really priced at $72. One who purchased on the installment plan therefore had to pay an extra cost of $7. As the net price of the sofa was $72, the unpaid balance after the deduction of the $9 down payment was $63. The table below shows the basis on which the true interest rate was determined.

When one buys on the installment plan, he really borrows money because he owes a debt until it has been entirely paid off in installments. The table below shows that $63

MONTH	PRINCIPAL BALANCE	PAYMENT ON PRINCIPAL AT END OF MONTH	PAYMENT OF INTEREST AT END OF MONTH
1	$ 63	$ 9	$1
2	54	9	1
3	45	9	1
4	36	9	1
5	27	9	1
6	18	9	1
7	9	9	1
Totals	$252	$63	$7

Illustration No. 92—Figuring the Cost of an Installment Purchase was owed for one month, $54 was owed for one month, $45 was owed for one month, and so forth. A total of $252 was owed for one month. Seven dollars in interest was paid for the privilege of the installment purchase. To compute the yearly rate of interest, it was necessary to divide $252 into $7, and then to multiply the result by 12 because the total of the principal balances and of the interest payments were monthly figures. The formula for this computation may be stated as follows:

$$\text{Rate} = 12 \times 7 \div 252 = .33\tfrac{1}{3} \text{ or } 33\tfrac{1}{3}\% \text{ a year}$$

TEXTBOOK QUESTIONS

1. What is the difference between buying on account and buying on the installment plan?
2. Two general types of contracts are used in selling merchandise on the installment plan. (a) What are they? (b) When does the title pass in each case?
3. How is the seller protected under each type of installment contract?
4. (a) What types of products are most commonly sold on the installment plan? (b) Are these products sold on the installment plan to any great extent?
5. Why would you not recommend buying expensive luxuries on the installment plan?
6. How could the use of the installment plan result in a saving in buying furniture?
7. How does the installment plan force some people to save money?
8. What are some of the advantages of installment buying?
9. What are some of the disadvantages of installment buying?
10. When a new automobile is purchased on the installment plan, what is usually (a) the down payment required? (b) the time allowed for payment?

DISCUSSION QUESTIONS

1. How should installment buying be closely correlated with budgeting?
2. What effect do you think installment buying has in creating demand?
3. In what way do you think merchants who sell on the installment plan face difficulties during periods of decline and depression in the business cycle?

4. Why do you think employers sometimes investigate the credit of people who apply for work?
5. (a) Name two opposing social influences in installment buying. (b) Is there any remedy?
6. Some people are induced to buy refrigerators because of the slogan "25 cents a day will buy this refrigerator." What do you think of such a plan of buying?
7. A business advertises that it sells on the installment plan at no extra charge. (a) Is this practice fair to all customers of the business? (b) What should a cash customer expect?

PROBLEMS

1. On the basis of the example given on page 251, compute the annual interest rate on the purchase of a refrigerator that is sold for $165 with a down payment of $15 and installment payments of $10 a month for fifteen months, "no charge being made for the easy terms." Assume that a person paying cash could obtain the refrigerator for $150.
2. According to the model budget for a family of four on page 7, how much can a family with an income of $50 a week afford to pay on the installment plan for an electric refrigerator if (a) it wishes to continue depositing $2 a week in a savings fund, (b) 10 per cent of the allowance for food will be saved each week, (c) a saving of 25 cents a week on a twelve months' basis will be made in substituting the cost of electricity for the cost of ice? If the cost of the refrigerator is $150 plus a $15 carrying charge, how long will it take to make all the payments?
3. Mr. Fischer decides to buy an automobile that costs $610. Since he will receive $150 for his old automobile, he will have this amount as the down payment. The automobile dealer suggests that he sign a chattel mortgage and pay the remaining amount under a time-payment plan. The carrying charge, exclusive of insurance, is quoted as $29. The entire balance can be paid in ten equal installments at the end of the month, the payments to begin one month after the date of sale. Mr. Fischer decides instead to borrow from his bank the amount of the balance at 6 per cent interest, deductible in advance. He uses a Government bond as collateral. The loan is to be paid in one amount at the end of ten months. Compute the difference between the interest charge of the bank and the installment-service charge.
4. (a) On the basis of the table on page 245, compute the amount of a financing service charge that would be added to a balance of $135 that is to be paid in fifteen equal monthly installments. (b) How much would each monthly installment be?

5. Besides your other savings you wish to keep $100 in a special savings account. From this special savings account you take funds for the purchase of major equipment in the home. Because of a recent purchase the fund has been depleted and now contains only $20. The interest earned on the fund is 3 per cent a year, compounded annually. You are able to put into the fund $10 a month. You would like to buy a radio that sells at a cash price of $90. The carrying charges on the basis of a ten-month payment plan amount to $10. You decide to wait, however, until your special fund has been replenished so that you can pay cash for the radio instead of buying on the time-payment plan. What net rate of interest would you have paid if you had bought the radio on the ten-month payment plan?

COMMUNITY PROBLEMS AND PROJECTS

1. Obtain a credit application blank used by some local store or a store in a neighboring city. (a) Fill in as much of the required information as you can, and (b) write a report explaining why each item of information is needed by the store.
2. Investigate the policies of local stores in selling for cash and on credit. Learn (a) which ones have variations in price, (b) how much the difference is, and (c) what additional carrying charges are added in the case of credit sales.
3. Obtain the following information with regard to the purchase of an automobile: (a) the price f.o.b. the factory, (b) the delivered price, (c) the particular items and the amounts of the items that add to the cost in delivering the automobile, (d) the guarantee, (e) the service agreement, (f) the type of bill of sale used, (g) the carrying charge on the unpaid balance, and (h) the plan of paying the balance.
4. From local merchants, a local credit bureau, or some other local agency, obtain information with regard to (a) the percentage of merchandise sold on credit, (b) the average amount of credit losses, (c) the reasons for the credit losses, and (d) the local policies with regard to uniformity in granting credit.
5. Make a report on the sources from which local businesses obtain credit information. Explain how this information serves the local merchant and how it is also of benefit to every honest buyer of merchandise.
6. Select some local product such as a washing machine, furniture, a refrigerator, or a farm implement. Compute the extra costs of buying on the installment plan as contrasted with paying cash.

CHAPTER IX

LEGAL RELATIONS OF BUYING AND SELLING

Purpose of the Chapter. In our complicated society, practically every human action involves some legal right or responsibility. Our legal network is therefore intricate. People study for years to become lawyers and still do not have at their finger tips all the information that is recorded in the Federal and state laws. Everyone should, however, understand the elementary principles of legal relations, especially those pertaining to buying and selling, for everyone is engaged in either buying or selling activities. The purchase or the sale of any type of property involves a *contract*. A contract is an enforceable agreement between two parties that involves legal rights and responsibilities. It may be oral or written. The purpose of this chapter is to explain the nature of contracts and to give briefly an understanding of the legal relations of buyer and seller.

Offer and Acceptance. Whenever an offer has been made by one person and accepted by another, a contract has been made, provided the offer and the acceptance have been made in accordance with certain legal regulations. These regulations will be described later in this chapter. Unless a specific date is mentioned when an offer is to be withdrawn, the offer may be accepted within a reasonable length of time unless it is otherwise terminated. What may be considered reasonable will depend upon the circumstances. The interpretations of courts in such cases are not always uniform.

Oral Contracts Versus Written Contracts. For the sake of certainty and safety, all important contracts should be written. Many contracts do not need to be written, for the entire transaction is executed at the time the contract is made. Other contracts, however, must be written to be enforceable. Those that must be written usually pertain to real estate. In some states, however, a contract for the sale of merchandise above a certain minimum specified sum must be written and signed by both parties; whereas in other states the contract need be signed only by the person who agrees to accept and pay for the merchandise. In some states, contracts that require more than a year for fulfillment must be written.

Sales need not be in writing when the price is less than the amount designated in the law. As a rule, the minimum amount is five hundred dollars, but in some states it may be as low as fifty dollars. It varies, however, greatly in different states, ranging from thirty dollars to twenty-five hundred dollars. The Uniform Sales Act prescribes a minimum of five hundred dollars.

Learning to Recognize a Contract. Every paper should be read before it is signed. It may be called a memorandum, a sales slip, a purchase contract, or a note. In any case it represents a contract, and it will involve some obligation.

READ BEFORE YOU SIGN—KEEP A COPY

THE ABC BOOK COMPANY Date Mar. 15, 19..

Chicago, Illinois

Please enter my order for the following material

Standard History of the World - 12 Volumes

I agree to pay $60.00 for this material, payable as follows: $5.00 with the signing of this order and $3.00 each month thereafter, until the full amount is paid.

It is understood that title to all material furnished is to remain in The ABC Book Company until the agreed price above mentioned is entirely paid, and that a 90-day lapse in any payment renders the balance due and payable at once.

This order contains the whole agreement, is not subject to any verbal understanding with the representative, and cannot be canceled.

Date Mar. 15, 19..
Received as first payment the sum of $5.00
M. H. Henning
Representative

First payment to accompany application.

Signature Mark A. Hardin
Business Address 700 Edwards Bldg.
Residence 214 Woodward St.
City or Town Detroit, Mich.

Illustration No. 93—An Agreement That Is a Binding Contract

Illustration No. 93 shows an agreement to purchase a set of books. In Illustration No. 34 on page 75 is a promissory note. Each instrument is valid and binding upon the two parties to the contract. Each represents a promise to pay a certain sum of money at a certain time. Many persons recognize the responsibility of signing a promissory note, but fail to understand that the signature on any other type of contract is as binding as that on a note.

Read What You Sign. The National Better Business Bureau reports the case of a woman who bought some silk garments after examining them and specifying "Silk, No. 508." When the order blank was filled out by the salesman, he marked "Rayon, No. 507." When the package arrived, the woman blamed the company from which the merchandise was ordered. Regardless of the intention of the salesman, the woman was at fault for not having read the contract.

Reading a contract may prevent mistakes, misunderstandings, or fraud. For the following reasons every contract should be read before it is signed:

(a) To ascertain the exact responsibilities that are about to be assumed
(b) To prevent misunderstanding concerning what is being offered, what the costs will be, and when payment is to be made
(c) To ascertain the responsibility of the seller
(d) To protect oneself against the minority of merchants who sell by fraud and misrepresentation
(e) To assist honest businesses in detecting intentional or unintentional misrepresentations on the part of their salespeople
(f) To ascertain whether merchandise that is purchased may be returned

Unreadable Contracts. Some contracts are printed in very small type in the hope that they will not be read. The type, in fact, is so small in some contracts that it can scarcely be read. Many old forms of contracts are printed in this manner, although the businesses that use them are entirely honest. A person should not be misled by a contract that is printed in small type. He should insist upon taking time to read it.

Every contract should be examined carefully before it is signed. An honest and legitimate business will encourage the buyer to read the contract before signing, whereas an unscrupulous business may try to induce the buyer to sign before reading. An invitation to read a contract should always be accepted. The document may be presented in the hope that it will not be read. If there is any indication that an attempt is being made to prevent the reading of the contract, one should insist upon reading every detail.

Reasons for a Written Contract. The law of each state assumes that a person knows what he signs. Written contracts are desirable for the following reasons:

(a) To prevent misunderstanding. In a casual oral agreement there may be some misunderstanding with regard to price, terms of sale, or another element of the contract. The mere writing of a contract should cause each party to give more careful attention to the details than he could in the case of an oral agreement.

(b) To state the terms clearly. In an oral contract there may be apparent agreement; but if the contract is to be fulfilled later, some of the terms of the agreement, such as the quantity of the product to be delivered, the terms of payment, or the obligation of either party, may be forgotten.

(c) To provide an exact agreement. For instance, Mr. A may agree to furnish Mr. B all the eggs that the latter needs regularly each week. If Mr. B depends on receiving these eggs at a specific time each week or in a particular quantity, he may be inconvenienced by delivery at irregular intervals or in small amounts. In the absence of a written agreement, there would be no way of determining whether or not the contract was being fulfilled properly.

(d) To avoid litigation. One party to an oral contract may believe that he has a legitimate reason for bringing suit to enforce the carrying out of the agreement. If the contract were in writing, however, he would know more definitely his legal rights. Litigation is often the result of misunderstandings. Written contracts help to avoid misunderstandings.

(e) To prevent fraud. Although fraud is possible in written contracts as in oral contracts, a written contract provides better evidence in case there is an attempt to defraud. Statements in properly written contracts are enforceable, whereas statements in oral agreements are vague and often cannot be enforced.

(f) To provide evidence in the case of the death of either party to the contract. For example, Mr. A may lend one thousand dollars to Mr. B without requiring Mr. B to sign a note. If Mr. A dies and Mr. B wants to avoid his obligation, the heirs of Mr. A will have difficulty in proving the claim against Mr. B. A written contract left by Mr. A would provide suitable evidence.

Proper Contents of a Contract. The following is the essential information that is desired in a contract: (a) date and place of agreement, (b) names of parties entering into the agreement, (c) statement of the purpose of the contract, (d) statement of the money, services, or goods given in consideration of the agreement, (e) statement of the acts that are to be performed by each party, and (f) the signatures. Illustration No. 93 on page 256 shows a simple contract. The various elements in the contract should be observed.

Preventing Fraud and Misunderstanding. The following suggestions are offered to prevent fraud and misunderstanding in drawing a contract:

(a) Use simple words and expressions that will not be misunderstood. Do not allow the use of any word that might be misinterpreted.
(b) Deal only with those who are honest.
(c) In case of doubt with regard to a contract, consult a lawyer.
(d) In the absence of substantial proof with regard to oral agreements or supplementary agreements, only the agreements stipulated in the contract are enforceable. Do not leave anything to a general understanding. Be sure that every act to be performed is stated clearly in the contract.
(e) Do not sign a contract with the understanding that supplementary agreements will be made later. Be sure that all agreements are in the contract.
(f) Read the contract carefully before signing.

Bill of Sale. Bills of sale are used in selling many types of merchandise. In most states, but not all, bills of sale are required to provide evidence of the ownership of particular types of property. For instance, it is impossible in some states to obtain an automobile license without providing a bill of sale or a sworn statement as evidence of the ownership of the automobile. If the bill of sale is lost, it is possible to establish the ownership of the merchandise by going through the legal procedure of obtaining a sworn statement of ownership. The most common type of bill of sale is that used in selling automobiles. In many states, bills of sale of different types are required for new cars and used cars. Illustration No. 94 shows a typical bill of sale for a new car.

In most states in which a bill of sale is required, the transaction is not completed and legal until the contract has been recorded by the local recorder or other designated public official. The recording of a bill of sale prevents an unscrupulous seller from selling the same merchandise again to another buyer who has no knowledge that the merchandise has already been sold.

Uniform Sales Laws. The Uniform Sales Act has been adopted by almost every state. The purpose of the Uniform Sales Act is to establish some uniformity in the provisions of the sales laws in various states. When transactions take place between businessmen located in different states, many complications arise with regard to the contracts because of differences in the requirements and the interpretations of the sales laws in those states.

The following general provisions of the Uniform Sales Act serve as a guide in interpreting the legal relations of buying and selling:

(a) *Legality of sale.* For a contract to be legal, the sale must be legal. For instance, in some states it is illegal to sell on Sunday, and in some it is illegal to sell firearms.

(b) *Proof of acceptance.* One way of proving a sale is to produce evidence of a receipt and an acceptance of part of the goods.

(c) *Proof by partial payment.* A sale may be proved by showing evidence of having given a part payment.

(d) *Written proof.* Evidence of a sale is a written note or memorandum confirming the sale.

BILL OF SALE, in Duplicate

NEW MOTOR VEHICLE

Gen'l Code, Sec. 6310-5.

Know All Men by These Presents, *That* [1] The Grenat Motor Car Co.

Residing at 2200 Sycamore Street

Columbus, Ohio

*the Grantor...., do*es *hereby execute this Bill of Sale in Duplicate and deliver to* [2]

Milton L. Brown

Residing at 4724 Fourth Avenue

Columbus, Ohio

the Grantee...., the possession of the following described Motor Vehicle:

Manufacturer or Maker Plymouth Motor Car Co. *; Manufacturer's (Factory) No.* ......;

Engine or Motor No. P8-350199 *; other numbers* Chassis No. 18040228

Horse-Power 23.44 *; Description of Body* Coach, two-door Deluxe

Make Plymouth *; Type* Passenger Car *; Model* P8 (1938)

Other number or marks of identification thereon or on appliances attached thereto, ...

It is mutually understood that the contents, execution, delivery, acceptance or filing of this "bill of sale" in no manner affects or governs the rights, title and interest of either the transferer or transferee in and to the vehicle herein described or referred to, or in and to any chattel mortgage, note paid or unpaid purchase price, lease, lien, insurance policy, conditional sale contract, or any contract or agreement collateral or otherwise of any kind whatsoever, concerning such vehicle, the sole purpose of this "bill of sale" being to comply with Sections 6310-3 to 6310-14, inclusive, of the General Code of Ohio, and in order to evidence the fact that possession of such vehicle has changed on this day.

IN WITNESS WHEREOF, the said Grenat Motor Car Co. and Milton L. Brown

*ha*ve *hereunto set* their *hand this* 12th *day of* February *19*40

Witnessed by

Rose Fisher

Walter Green

The Grenat Motor Car Co.

A L Grenat

Manager

Grantor....

Milton L. Brown

Grantee....

Illustration No. 94—A Bill of Sale for an Automobile

(e) *"Let the buyer beware."* Except as indicated in points (f) and (g), the seller's statements of opinion or belief as to the value or merit of an article and his commendations used to induce a purchase are not warranties.

A *warranty* is a statement or an implied affirmation that the subject of a contract is as it is declared or promised to be. The statements that the seller uses merely to induce the purchase are called "puffs" or "trade talk" and should not be relied upon by the buyer. In the absence of fraud and of any special regulatory law, the principle of "Let the buyer beware" is followed. It is assumed that, if a person inspects an article before buying it, and if there is no fraud in the transaction, he should know what he is getting.

(f) *Buying by inspection.* When a buyer has an opportunity to inspect the goods, there is no implied warranty that the goods are of a particular quality. If the buyer does not inspect the goods, however, but relies largely on the judgment and honesty of the seller, there is an implied warranty (on the part of the seller) that the goods are of a satisfactory quality. The goods therefore must be suitable for the purpose for which they are sold.

(g) *Sale by sample.* When a sample is used to indicate the kind and the quality of the goods, the seller impliedly warrants the goods to correspond to the sample in kind and quality.

(h) *Sale by description.* When merchandise is purchased by description, such as specifications, the seller in making the sale impliedly warrants the goods to correspond to the description.

(i) *Remedies for breach of warranty.* There are different remedies in case of a breach of warranty. The following general recourses are open to the buyer: (1) to keep the goods and to deduct from the price the amount of the damages; (2) to keep the goods and to bring an action against the seller for damages; (3) to refuse to accept the goods and to bring an action against the seller to recover damages; (4) to rescind the contract and to refuse to receive the goods or, if the goods have been accepted, to return them to the vendor and to recover the price that has been paid.

(j) *Passing of title.* Two general rules govern the passing of the title when goods are sold, although there are exceptions in some states, especially with regard to such other goods as coal, wheat, or oil, of which any unit is considered to be the equivalent of any other unit. The two rules determining the passing of the title are: (1) Under a contract to sell *unascertained goods* the title will not pass until the goods have been ascertained; (2) under a contract to sell *ascertained goods* the title passes at the time when the parties intend it to be transferred.

Unascertained goods are goods in a lot that are not distinguishable from any of the others until an actual selection has been made. When the specific goods have been selected, they are said to be ascertained.

For instance, Mr. A agrees to sell Mr. B one hundred women's dresses at a specified price, the dresses to be selected by Mr. B from a display in Mr. A's exhibit rooms. Mr. B attempts to avoid fulfilling his contract by making the contention that the styles have changed and he does not wish to buy dresses that are out of style. Mr. B will not, however, be relieved of responsibility for fulfilling his contract. The title to the dresses could not have passed until Mr. B had personally selected them or, in other words, until the goods had been ascertained. Mr. B will therefore be forced to buy one hundred dresses, or to pay damages as a result of failing to buy.

On the other hand, if Mr. B had gone to Mr. A's exhibit rooms, had selected one hundred dresses, and had ordered them delivered within ten days, the title would have passed at the time the dresses were selected.

The determining of the intentions of the buyer and the seller sometimes presents a problem. It is therefore important for these parties to reach a definite agreement as to when the title will pass.

(k) *Place and time of delivery.* When the place of delivery of goods is not specified, it may be the seller's place of business or it may be fixed by the customs of the trade. For instance, when products are to be delivered for sale through a commission house, the custom of the trade may require them to be delivered at a certain warehouse or placed on a railroad siding for examination. The place of delivery of steel shipped on barges may be the water front at the destination. If no time is set for delivery, the vendor must make delivery within a reasonable time.

(l) *Acceptance.* The buyer is under duty to accept and pay for the goods, provided delivery of them is in accordance with the terms of the contract. The acceptance of the goods is indicated by (1) a specific indication that the buyer accepts the goods, (2) the use of the goods, or (3) the detention of the goods for an unreasonable length of time.

(m) *Enforceable agreement.* In the absence of any of the disqualifying factors indicated below, an exchange of assents constitutes an enforceable agreement, provided the assents are genuine. An agreement is not enforceable under any of the following circumstances:

(1) If there is a common mistake as to the identity of the subject matter. For example, assume that Mr. French offers to sell Mr. Thomas a team of horses. Mr. French has two teams of horses of the same general color and description. He has reference to one team that he is willing to sell, but Mr. Thomas has the other team in mind. There is a common mistake as to the identity of the subject matter.

(2) If fraud in the form of misrepresentation is present. Consider the following example: Mr. Allen intentionally misrepresents to Mr. Smith that he is acting as an agent for a certain producer of clothing. When the merchandise is delivered, Mr. Smith discovers that Mr. Allen is acting as the agent of an entirely different producer. Mr. Allen is guilty of fraudulent representation.

(3) If one person makes an agreement as the result of a threat or an act of violence. For instance, Mr. A induces Mr. B to sign a contract for merchandise under the threat that Mr. B's daughter will be abducted if he does not sign the contract. This contract is not enforceable, for it has been obtained by means of a threat of violence.

(4) If there has been undue influence to the extent that one person has not reached the agreement through the free exercise of his own judgment. For instance, consider the case of an aged woman who has inherited a small sum of money. A favorite nephew, after prolonged high-pressure selling, induces her to spend a major portion of her inheritance for a farm. Such a case would probably represent undue influence.

(n) *Delay in collecting.* The unreasonable delay of a creditor in bringing an action for a claim may result in the creditor's losing the right of taking legal action. The *statutes of limitations* in most states set a time limit after which a creditor cannot enforce a legal claim. For instance, in one state if an account is not collected within five years, the creditor cannot sue for the amount. If the debtor, however, has made at least one payment or promise to pay during the five years, the account has been revived or reinstated. Under such circumstances the period of time during which the creditor has the right to collect the account is counted from the date of the last payment or promise.

Protection of the Seller. If the buyer of merchandise fails to perform his part of the contract, the seller may select any one of the following remedies:

(a) *Sue for payment* (if the title has passed). When the buyer refuses or neglects to pay, the seller may sue for the price of the goods.

(b) *Sue for damages* (if the title has not passed). When the buyer wrongfully refuses or neglects to accept and pay for the goods, the seller may sue for damages. The amount of damages will usually be the difference between the contract price and the market price at the time and the place of delivery.

(c) *Rescind the contract.* When the buyer repudiates the contract, or when he cannot perform the contract or fails to perform it, the seller is allowed, under most laws, to rescind the contract by giving notice thereof.

Protection of the Buyer. If the seller fails to perform his obligations, the buyer has the choice of one or more remedies. These remedies are as follows:

(a) *Recover the goods or the value of the goods* (if the title has passed). When the seller wrongfully refuses or neglects to deliver the goods, the buyer may sue for the possession of the goods or for the recovery of the value that has been paid.

(b) *Sue for damages* (if the title has not passed). If the seller wrongfully refuses or neglects to deliver the goods, the buyer is entitled to damages for nondelivery. The amount of the damages is ordinarily the difference between the contract price and the market price at the time and the place of delivery. It may also include any other damages for loss resulting from the failure to fulfill the contract.

(c) *Insist upon the fulfillment of the contract.* The buyer has the right to sue for specific performance if damages will not be adequate compensation or if they cannot be computed. When the buyer sues for specific performance and wins the case, the seller is ordered by the court to carry out the original contract.

Voidable Contracts. A *voidable contract* is an agreement that may be enforceable but, because of a lack of one of the essentials of contracts, may be made inoperative by one or both of the parties. All contracts made by persons with unbalanced minds or by intoxicated persons are voidable. A minor (an individual who has not attained the legal age) can void any contracts made by him except those that were made for the purpose of obtaining necessary things, such as food and clothing. Even under such contracts the minor is responsible for only the reasonable value of the goods.

The contract of a minor may be rescinded by the minor. A contract made by a person with an unbalanced mind may be rescinded by the guardian of that person. A contract made by an intoxicated person may be rescinded by that person when he becomes sober. The fundamental reason for permitting minors to rescind their contracts is that they need certain protection in order that they will not be taken advantage of by unscrupulous persons. Contracts made with persons of unbalanced minds or with intoxicated individuals are voidable because these persons are not capable of guarding their own interests.

For instance, a youth of twenty bought an automobile. When he became of age, he returned the automobile and demanded his money. He was entitled to his money, for he had entered into the contract when he was a minor. As he disaffirmed the contract soon after he had reached his majority, he voided it. If he had failed to disaffirm the contract within a reasonable time after reaching majority, he could not have voided the contract.

Suppose the youth mentioned in the preceding example had agreed, while twenty years of age, to buy an automobile when he became twenty-one years of age. In this case the contract would not have been executed until after he had become of age. He would not have been liable unless he had ratified the contract after reaching his majority.

Garnishment. If a debtor refuses to pay, the creditor may in some states bring a legal action to force the payment of the debt. By an order of a court the employer of the debtor is required to pay to the creditor a certain percentage of the debtor's wages until the amount of the debt or the amount specified by the court has been paid. This procedure is called the *garnishment,* or the *garnisheeing,* of wages. The laws on garnisheeing wages vary in the different states. In some states, only a certain percentage of a person's wages can be collected in this way. In other states a worker cannot be forced to pay small debts through this process.

Replevin or Repossession. In Chapter VIII the two types of installment sales contracts were explained. When an article is sold under such a contract and the buyer later fails to live up to his part of the contract, the seller, in order to protect himself from loss, sometimes has the right to repossess the article. The legal action necessary is usually referred to as repossession. The law of replevin differs widely in various states. In some states the law permits the seller to repossess the property, and, regardless of the amount that has been paid, he need not compensate the buyer for anything that the latter has already paid. Under the laws of many states, however, the person who repossesses an article must, according to a definite plan prescribed in the law, compensate the buyer for any interest that the latter may have had in the article. Laws on the right of replevin are important from the point of view of the consumer. The consumer should know not only that they exist, but also his rights under those laws.

Bankruptcy. Some knowledge of bankruptcy laws is important. Because bankruptcy usually arises out of credit

ourt yesterday
er, Collector of
venue. He claims $316.12 as
ial security taxes for 1937 and 1938.

Man And Wife Bankrupts.

Albert W. Gerlaugh, coremaker, and his wife, Mrs. Mary L. Garlaugh, 6416 Chandler Street, Norwood, yesterday filed voluntary bankruptcy petitions. He lists indebtedness at $904.50, of which $300.98 is secured. Mrs. Gerlaugh reports the same secured indebtedness, plus $120.90 in unsecured claims. Joint assets are $100, representing household goods and an automobile.

Enter Bankruptcy Petitions.

Voluntary petitions in bankruptcy were filed in District Court yesterday by the following:

James Mark, last worker, Route 1, Portsmouth. Debts, $1,374; assets, $1,120, of which $1,100 represents value of real estate.

Ruford Vernon Moore, steel worker, 3702½ Rhodes Avenue, New Boston. Debts, $297.50; assets, $140.

Michael Parker, switchman, 710 East Pearl Street. Debts, $927.50; assets, $150.

Richard O'Brien, general pressman, 1010 York Street. Debts, $725.94; assets, $100.

Illustration No. 95—Notices of Bankruptcy

relations, it involves the buyer and the seller. There are two types of bankruptcy: *voluntary bankruptcy* and *involuntary bankruptcy*.

Bankruptcy laws are Federal laws usually administered through the United States district courts. A debtor may become a *voluntary bankrupt* by applying to a court for a judgment of bankruptcy. The court may discharge him from further claims after all his assets that are not exempt have been utilized in paying his debts. The circumstances under which a person may apply for voluntary bankruptcy are regulated by law.

An *involuntary bankrupt* is one who has been forced into bankruptcy by his creditors. Most persons, partnerships, and corporations owing debts that amount to one thousand dollars or more may be forced into involuntary bankruptcy. There are, however, a few exceptions. The law specifically excludes wage-earners, farmers, municipalities, railroads, insurance companies, banking corporations, and building and loan associations. A wage-earner is defined as an individual who works for wages or a salary and who earns a compensation not exceeding fifteen hundred dollars a year.

From this discussion it may be seen that voluntary bankruptcy is a means of protection for the buyer or debtor, whereas involuntary bankruptcy is a means of protection for the seller or creditor. Creditors often force a debtor into bankruptcy to avoid a greater loss that might result from allowing the debtor to continue in his former status.

The latest Federal bankruptcy law provides an opportunity for debtors of various types to apply to the proper court for special arrangements whereby they can pay their debts. From the point of view of the individual the most important provision of that law is the one that permits any debtor except a corporation to file a petition for the acceptance of a plan for the alteration or the modification of the rights of creditors, whether those creditors are holding debts secured by real property or other assets, or not secured by any assets. The court has authority to grant an extension of time or to rearrange a payment plan in view of future earnings. Therefore, a debtor who owes a debt secured by a mortgage on his home or on furniture may arrange a new plan of payment.

TEXTBOOK QUESTIONS

1. Must all contracts be written to be legal?
2. What types of contracts usually must be written?
3. Before signing a contract to buy goods, what questions should a person ask himself?
4. Does ignorance of the contents of a contract relieve one from responsibility?
5. Why should one read a contract before signing it instead of after signing it?
6. Is a sales slip a contract?
7. Why are written contracts more desirable than verbal contracts? (Name six reasons.)
8. What essential information is required in every contract?
9. What suggestions would you give as guides to prevent misunderstanding and fraud in writing contracts?
10. What is the Uniform Sales Act?
11. Are the laws pertaining to sales the same in all states?
12. What is meant by the term "Let the buyer beware"?
13. What is a warranty?
14. If there is a breach of warranty, what recourses are open to the buyer?
15. What evidence may there be that the buyer has accepted the goods? (Name three indications.)
16. What types of agreements are not enforceable as valid contracts?
17. What are statutes of limitations?
18. If a buyer of merchandise fails to perform his part of the contract, what three possible remedies does the seller have?
19. If a seller fails to perform his obligations, what may the buyer do to protect himself?

20. Give an example of a voidable contract.
21. Under what circumstances are parents responsible for the payment of the debts of their children?
22. What are the two types of bankruptcy? Explain them.
23. Under the Federal bankruptcy laws may a wage-earner be forced into involuntary bankruptcy?

DISCUSSION QUESTIONS

1. Why do you think a court will not enforce an agreement that has an unlawful purpose?
2. When is a verbal contract as binding as a written contract?
3. The statement is frequently made, "The best lawyers settle their cases out of court." If you had a case against someone, could you see any advantage in settling the case out of court?
4. From the study of this chapter why is it apparent that one should consult a lawyer to handle legal problems?
5. Mr. Jacobs insists that he will not fulfill a contract because he did not know all the contents of the contract when he signed it. His reason for not having read the contract carefully is that he finds it difficult to read fine print. He admits, however, that the signature on the contract is genuine. Is there anything he can do to avoid fulfilling the contract?
6. Why do you think some stores insist that customers return their sales slips or cash-register slips when they return merchandise or make a complaint with regard to merchandise?
7. You are given a sales demonstration in a store. During the demonstration the salesman tells you many ways in which his product is better than some other product. Later you find that what he has told you is not true. (a) Do his statements constitute fraud? (b) Have you any legal basis for returning the merchandise and demanding your money?
8. You received through the mail some literature with samples of cloth from which shirts are made. You test the cloth in various ways, including washing it and counting the threads in each square inch. You keep these samples and order five of the shirts for $5.25. When the shirts are delivered, you find that they are poorly tailored and that the cloth does not seem to be like that in the samples. One of the shirts is worn and then washed. It fades badly. Then you count the threads in each square inch and find that the cloth is actually inferior to that in the samples. What recourses have you?

PROBLEMS

1. Write a simple contract between you and someone else, in which you agree to perform some task.

2. Mr. Hughes agreed to construct a windmill on the farm of Mr. Williams. The contract required Mr. Hughes to furnish all the material, including the pipes. The contract also specified that the windmill should be completed within a reasonable length of time and that the windmill pumps should furnish plenty of water for Mr. Williams' cattle. Mr. Hughes worked only periodically on the construction. Mr. Williams complained several times. Finally, during the summer season, the dry weather caused a serious shortage of water. Because of the urgency Mr. Williams notified Mr. Hughes that he was canceling the contract, and then hired another person to construct immediately a pump that would furnish adequate water. Mr. Hughes sued for damages, claiming that Mr. Williams had no right to break the contract. What is your opinion? Why?
3. Mr. Ladley offered to sell Mr. Moore a house and lot for $7,000, $4,000 to be paid in cash upon the acceptance of the offer. On April 6 Mr. Moore mailed a letter to Mr. Ladley and inclosed a certified check for $4,000. The letter was delivered on April 10. On April 7 Mr. Ladley decided to withdraw the offer because he thought that the value of the property had increased. He wrote Mr. Moore withdrawing the offer. When Mr. Ladley received the check, he refused to accept it and returned it, claiming that the offer had been withdrawn. Mr. Moore brought a suit for breach of contract. Do you think Mr. Moore had any right to sue for breach of contract?

COMMUNITY PROBLEMS AND PROJECTS

1. Obtain information about the statute of limitations in your state as it applies to the collection of debts, notes, and other obligations. Show how this law affects the creditor and the debtor.
2. Obtain a copy of a chattel mortgage. Study it carefully and list the legal responsibilities (a) of the mortgagor and (b) of the mortgagee.
3. Investigate the legal procedure in your state with regard to collecting debts.
4. Obtain copies of the laws pertaining to bankruptcy, and if possible go to a Federal district court and examine some of the records of bankruptcy cases. (a) Write a report explaining the legal rights and responsibilities of a bankrupt. (b) Point out the rights of creditors.

CHAPTER X

GOVERNMENTAL AGENCIES OF CONSUMER PROTECTION

Purpose of the Chapter. Many of the agencies of the Federal Government, such as the Department of Commerce and the Department of Agriculture, have been developed to render service to business. Many of these services are, however, beneficial to the individual. In recent years many Federal agencies, as well as state and city governments, have entered into activities that are directly beneficial to the consumer. The purpose of this chapter is to enumerate these agencies and to indicate specifically the ways in which they can be used by the consumer.

United States Department of Commerce

Benefits to the Consumer. The primary purpose of the United States Department of Commerce is to serve business; and it publishes regularly information on production, sales, and prices. This information is of interest also to the consumer because it keeps him informed about the supply, the consumption, and the prices of the items that he needs. One of the most important activities of the Department is, however, the operation of the National Bureau of Standards, the functions of which are explained in the following paragraphs.

National Bureau of Standards. The functions of the Bureau of Standards that are of particular interest to the consumer are those that pertain to (a) the making of tests, (b) the establishment of standards, and (c) the control of weights and measures. The Bureau helps the consumer indirectly in many ways. Its purpose is not to regulate industry but to co-operate with industry and the consumer. One of the first functions of the Bureau of Standards has been to establish minimum requirements for purchases in various Federal departments. This function in itself has had an influence on the general standard of products offered for sale to the public.

Tests. The Bureau of Standards will make tests of products submitted by individual manufacturers and associations. It will also co-operate with manufacturers and associations in conducting research designed to establish standards and better processes of manufacture.

Classes of Testing Activity. The following classes of testing activity are within the scope of the National Bureau of Standards, but are subject to the judgment of the director:

(a) Fundamental tests for the National Government and state governments, or such tests to aid science, industry, or the general public
(b) Routine tests including the certification of weights, measures, materials, and devices, provided the work does not compete with that of commercial laboratories
(c) Referee tests or investigations to settle disputes when private laboratories are unable to agree
(d) Co-operative tests, the results of which are desired by the Bureau in co-operating with agencies

Under the policies of the Bureau the following tests are not permissible:

(a) Investigations of secret processes
(b) Tests of inadequately described materials
(c) Assays, analyses, and tests of methods already standard, for which private laboratories are equipped
(d) Unnecessary tests that cause duplication of work
(e) Tests that have as their primary object sales promotion

Standards of Quality. Most of the important national associations in industry co-operate with the Bureau of Standards. The standards established by the Bureau necessarily do not correspond to those established by national associations, although they usually do. The Bureau publishes a list of producers who are "willing to certify." This list is not broadcast, but will be sent to anyone upon request. The manufacturers whose names appear on the list signify their willingness to certify to purchasers, upon request, that the goods offered for sale by them are guaranteed to comply with the minimum standards and the tests established by the National Bureau of Standards. These manufacturers have the privilege of mentioning this certification in their advertising and of using it on their trade-marks and labels.

Illustration No. 96—National Bureau of Standards

The Bureau encourages manufacturers to adopt a distinguishing mark by which the purchaser will know that he is obtaining a product that measures up to the standards of the Bureau.

The standardization phase of the Bureau's activities may be summarized as follows:

(a) To bring commodity specifications of the United States Government to the attention of producers

(b) To list the "willing-to-certify" producers for the benefit of the producers and for the benefit of consumers who request the list

(c) To furnish all tax-supported institutions with copies of the list of "willing-to-certify" producers

It is therefore possible for a prospective purchaser, large or small, to obtain from the Bureau of Standards an analysis of the standard specifications for most products and a list of producers from whom products with these specifications can be obtained.

Simplification. Another important function in the establishing of standards has been to eliminate unnecessary variations in size, grade, color, shape, and nomenclature of products. The standardization of the sizes of bricks and bolts is a good example.

Labels. An outgrowth of standardization has been the use of identifying labels. The use of such labels is entirely voluntary. Although it may be promoted by manufacturers' associations, it has been the direct outgrowth of the activities of the National Bureau of Standards. The labels are self-identifying and represent a guarantee of quality. The values that accrue to the consumer are as follows:

(a) To identify a product that has been manufactured under recognized standards
(b) To give the "over-the-counter" buyer the same advantages as large-quantity buyers, who have their own laboratories and trained purchasing staffs
(c) To encourage other producers to comply with these specifications and standards

An Example. Just how does all this activity of the Bureau of Standards have an ultimate effect upon the consumer when most of the services of the Bureau are rendered in behalf of producers? Here is just one example: For many years manufacturers were making automobiles without regard to fuels and oils, while refiners were producing fuels and oils without regard to the automobiles that were consuming these products. In other words, the petroleum companies were furnishing fuels that were not economical for the type of engine that was being used in automobiles. Representatives of the two industries finally helped finance a research project through the co-operation of the Bureau of Standards. The result was that better gasoline was produced for the automobile used by the consumer. Estimates indicate that one hundred million dollars a year has been saved in gasoline as a result of this particular study.

United States Department of Agriculture

Functions. The United States Department of Agriculture administers the following acts that are of particular interest to the consumer: Food, Drug, and Cosmetic Act, Tea Act, Import Milk Act, and Insecticide Act. It also has authority to establish grades for farm products and meat.

The Tea Act and the Import Milk Act are concerned mainly with the wholesomeness of tea and milk. Standards of quality regulate the importation and the sale of these foods. The Insecticide Act is concerned mainly with the quality and the effectiveness of insecticides, fungicides, turpentine, and resin. When these products are sold in interstate commerce, they must meet the requirements of the Act and must be labeled accordingly.

Under the annual Appropriation Act, the Department of Agriculture is granted the authority to grade various farm products that are sold in interstate commerce. The grading of farm products should not be confused, however, with the setting of single standards for other foods coming largely under the control of the Federal Food and Drug Administration. The Federal Food and Drug Administration is one of the most important Federal agencies, for it administers the Federal Food, Drug, and Cosmetic Act.

Consumers' Guide

Illustration No. 97—A Product Inspected by the U. S. Department of Agriculture

New Food, Drug, and Cosmetic Act. On June 25, 1938, the new Federal Food, Drug, and Cosmetic Act became a law; but one amendment prevented some parts of the law from going into effect until later. As this act is a Federal law, it is effective only when products sold in violation of the law cross state lines. It is administered under the

Federal Food and Drug Administration. For the first time in the history of the country, poisonous cosmetics may be barred from interstate traffic; but certain cosmetics, such as hair dyes, that contain coloring that may cause irritation may be sold if they are marked with the proper warnings.

Any food that is injurious to health is barred from interstate commerce. Harmful ingredients may not be added to any food product. The Law makes it mandatory that harmful sprays on fruits and vegetables be thoroughly washed off before shipments of the products may cross state lines. Any type of food that may be contaminated during the process of manufacture or packing may be subjected to regulation and licensing by the Secretary of Agriculture in order to assure the wholesomeness of the product.

The new law permits the Food and Drug Administration to set minimum standards for foods after conducting public hearings. Strict control is granted over all forms of drugs and healing devices so that they will be labeled properly and will be free from false and fraudulent claims. All drug labels must bear adequate directions for use, as well as adequate warnings. The label on a nonofficial drug (a patent medicine) must declare the common name of the drug if there is one, the name of each active ingredient, and the quantity or proportion of each of a specified list of ingredients named in the Law. A drug that may be subject to deterioration must be marked accordingly on the label. New drugs intended for interstate sale must be examined and approved by the Federal Food and Drug Administration before the drugs can be sold.

The law specifically prohibits the following acts which are of particular interest to the consumer:

(a) The introduction or the delivery for introduction into interstate commerce of any food, drug, device, or cosmetic that is adulterated or misbranded

(b) The adulteration or the misbranding of any food, drug, device, or cosmetic in interstate commerce

(c) The receipt in interstate commerce of any food, drug, device, or cosmetic that is adulterated or misbranded, and the delivery or the proffered delivery thereof

(d) The giving of a guarantee that is false

(e) The alteration, mutilation, destruction, obliteration, or removal of the whole or any part of the labeling of, or the doing of any other act with respect to, a food, drug, device, or cosmetic, if such act is done while the article is held for sale after shipment in interstate commerce and results in the article being misbranded

Standard Grades for Canned Foods. The Secretary of Agriculture has the right to designate the grading standards for canned foods. These standards are designated as Grade A, Grade B, Grade C, and off grade. The products that are labeled with any one of the grades are up to the standards recognized by the Federal Government. Products that are designated as off grade must be wholesome foods, though they may not measure up to recognized standards in other respects. Standards have been established for such farm products as corn, peas, beans, and tomatoes, and are rapidly being extended to other foods. As standards are established for additional canned foods, the information can be obtained from the United States Department of Agriculture.

Milk Grading. There are a great many grades of milk on the market. There may sometimes be as many as five or six in one city. The same quality of milk may even be sold at different prices, because consumers are not aware of the difference. As the handling cost of low- and high-grade milk is exactly the same, the difference in cost should be only the additional amount paid the producer for better milk. Milk of the highest grade should be lowest in bacterial content and highest in percentage of butter fat. The housewife has a right to demand that her milk be labeled to show the bacterial content and the percentage of butter fat. The Department of Agriculture has authority, under the Food, Drug, and Cosmetic Act, to establish a single basic standard of quality of milk. However, the main functions of grading of milk are performed by the United States Public Health Service of the Department of the Treasury.

There are four grades of raw milk. The highest grade of raw milk is *certified raw*. The three most common grades of raw milk are A, B, and C. The highest grade of pasteurized milk is *certified pasteurized.* The most common grades are designated as A, B, and C. The use of these grades is promoted by encouraging local communities to adopt a milk ordinance based upon the standards recommended by the United States Public Health Service.

Meat Grading. The Department of Agriculture protects the consumer from unfit, adulterated, and misbranded goods and also makes it possible for the consumer to protect himself by demanding graded foods. For example, meats sold in interstate commerce must bear the United States meat inspector's purple stamp to indicate that the meat is safe for consumption. This certification does not, however, indicate whether the meat is tender or tough. There are four commonly used quality standards of beef: (a) prime, (b) choice, (c) good, and (d) commercial. The quality stamps are used in addition to the meat inspector's purple stamp.

Turkeys for Thanksgiving and Christmas markets are graded and marked when they are packed. Tags are put on the box or on the leg of the fowl in such a manner that they cannot be removed and changed.

The Department of Agriculture administers the grade marking through the Agricultural Marketing Serv-

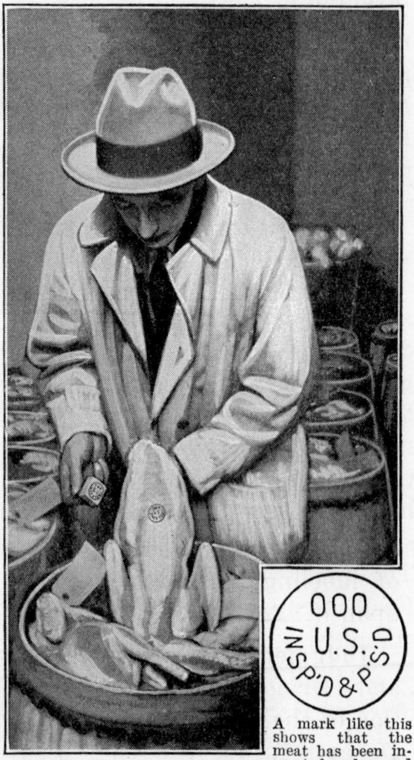

A mark like this shows that the meat has been inspected and passed as wholesome food.

Illustration No. 98—Inspecting and Stamping Poultry

ice. This service is being used in many of the large cities, and its use is gradually being extended. It will be extended just as rapidly as the consumer demands that he be told the grade of meat he is buying.

Eggs and Butter. There are also standards for eggs and butter. United States certificates showing the grade and the size are put on cartons when eggs are packed. The date of packing is also indicated for the protection of the consumer. The Federal law requires that butter contain at least 80 per cent butter fat; but even with this minimum, butter differs widely. It is therefore graded on a scientific basis. Butter with a score of 92 or higher is considered good.

The inspection and the grading of eggs and butter are under the supervision of the Department of Agriculture. Some local packers, however, use their own means of inspection and grading when eggs and butter are not sold in interstate commerce. The inspection and the grading of eggs and butter are not so general as those of meat. Consumers have a right to demand the labeling of eggs and butter. They can encourage the more widespread use of labeling by insisting upon it.

Judgments. The Food and Drug Administration of the United States Department of Agriculture regularly issues notices of judgments

The governmental stamp gives the grade.

Illustration No. 99—Grading and Stamping Beef

against manufacturers and distributors. These notices can be obtained from the United States Printing Office or the Department of Agriculture. They apply largely to adulterations and misbranding. The following is an example of one of the notices of judgment:

21033. Adulteration and misbranding of tomato catsup. U. S. v. 87 Cases and 100 Cases of Tomato Catsup. Default decrees of condemnation, forfeiture, and destruction. (F. & D. Nos. 29584, 29663. Sample Nos. 28467-A, 30126-A.)

These cases involved interstate shipments of tomato catsup which contained excessive mold and which was also found to contain added artificial color.

On December 6 and December 23, 1932, the United States attorney for the Northern District of Illinois, acting upon reports by the Secretary of Agriculture, filed in the district court libels praying seizure and condemnation of 187 cases of tomato catsup at Chicago, Ill. It was alleged in the libels that the article had been shipped in interstate commerce, in part on or about October 22, 1932, and in part on or about December 7, 1932, by the Summit Packing Co., from Wellesboro, Ind., and that it was adulterated in violation of the Food and Drugs Act. Subsequently the libels were amended to charge that the article was also misbranded.

It was alleged in the libels as amended that the article was adulterated in that it consisted in part of a decomposed vegetable substance.

Misbranding was alleged for the reason that the statement "Tomato Catsup," appearing on the label, was false and misleading and deceived and misled the purchaser, when applied to a product containing artificial color, which fact was not declared on the label.

On April 4, 1933, no claimant having appeared for the property, judgments of condemnation and forfeiture were entered, and it was ordered by the court that the product be destroyed by the United States marshal.

M. L. WILSON, *Acting Secretary of Agriculture*

Home Economics. In the Department of Agriculture there is a Bureau of Home Economics, which is charged with giving service to consumers, especially to those in the low-income groups. The duty of this Bureau is to aid the consumer in developing higher standards of living and in learning how to buy, manage, and save.

Consumers' Counsel. The Consumers' Counsel Division of the Department of Agriculture publishes biweekly a bulletin entitled *Consumers' Guide,* which is sent free to any interested individual. It includes official data of the Departments of Agriculture, Labor, and Commerce. Other current information is published in relation to prices, quality of commodities, costs, and efficiency of distribution. Consumers' Counsel is charged with the responsibility of disseminating information that is vital to the consumer.

Information on Production, Supplies, and Prices. An important function of the Department of Agriculture is to collect and disseminate regularly accurate information on production, supplies, and prices of farm products. Some of this information is made available through *Consumers' Guide,* mentioned above.

Federal Trade Commission

Functions. The Federal Trade Commission Act is the outgrowth of a demand for protection among competitors by the prevention of unfair methods of competition. The protection of the consumer was not originally the express purpose of the Act, although the consumer did benefit indirectly. An analysis of the decisions of the Commission shows that it protects the consumer as well as businesses. In other words, the prevention of unfair trade practices not only aids businessmen but also protects consumers. For instance, one businessman may make a complaint against another on the grounds that the latter is using unfair restraint in order to raise prices or that he is selling an inferior product under false specifications.

Complaints. A complaint may be registered with the Federal Trade Commission by an individual, a business, or an association. A letter of complaint may be submitted, stating the facts in the case. Some of the causes for complaint are adulteration, mislabeling, misleading selling schemes, false advertising, selling refinished goods as new, selling imitations of products, and otherwise misrepresenting an article to the extent that the business of a competitor will be damaged or the public misled. Loss or damage to a consumer or to a competitor is a justifiable complaint, but in any of these cases loss to a competitor is also loss to a consumer. Under the latest amendment the consumer gets more protection than under the original law.

The procedure in laying a complaint before the Federal Trade Commission is outlined in the following example: Dealer A discovers that Dealer B is selling a product that he is misbranding and misrepresenting. Dealer B is able to undersell Dealer A and therefore causes Dealer A a loss of business. As Dealer B is selling his product in interstate commerce, he is subject to the jurisdiction of the Federal Trade Commission. Dealer A writes a complete letter of complaint to the Commission. The latter asks for such additional information as it needs; or if the complaint is serious enough, it sends an investigator to get additional facts. The case will either be called for hearing or be dismissed. If it is called for hearing, both dealers will be called to testify. If a decision is rendered against Dealer B, the Commission will issue an order requiring Dealer B to cease from carrying on the unfair trade practice specified in the complaint.

Reports. A study of the annual reports of the Federal Trade Commission will give an idea of some of the unfair trade practices that are detrimental to consumers. Following is an example of a Federal Trade Commission report:

MISBRANDING PAINT

L. F. Cassoff, doing business under the names and styles of "Central Paint & Varnish Co.," "Central Shellac Works," and "Cumberland Paint Works," Brooklyn.—The respondent, following the issuance of Commission's complaint, waived hearing on the charges set forth in the complaint and consented to the order of the Commission to cease and desist in the violations of law charged in the complaint.

The Commission's order forbids the respondent from advertising paint with the words "Purest Paint, 50 per cent White Lead, 50 per cent Zinc," or similar phrases when the pigment of such paint is not in fact composed of 50 per cent lead and 50 per cent zinc. The order also forbids the respondent from causing its paint to be advertised, branded, or labeled with the phrases, "100 per cent Pure Ready Mixed Paint, Zinc Lead Linseed Oil," or "100 per cent Pure Lead and Zinc," or similar phrases, unless in each instance the pigment of such paint is, in fact, composed wholly of lead and zinc. The order further forbids the respondent from using any statement or representation as to the kind, class, or proportion of ingredients of any of its paint in advertising matter or on labels or containers thereof, except where such statement is true in fact. The respondent has filed a report with the Commission stating that it is complying with the order.

This case will serve to indicate some of the practices of which every consumer should be aware. Unless the consumer is protected by state or local laws, he will have to rely upon his own resources to protect himself against frauds in products that are sold locally and that do not enter into interstate commerce.

Control of Advertising. Effective May 22, 1938, the Federal Trade Commission Act was amended to provide for Federal jurisdiction over false advertising. Under this amendment it is unlawful for an advertiser to disseminate false advertising to induce the purchase of foods, drugs, devices, or cosmetics, or to participate in any other unfair methods of competition. Although this amendment is devised for the protection of honest businessmen, it directly benefits the consumer. Details of the amendment are given in Chapter XII.

United States Department of Labor

Bureau of Labor Statistics. The Bureau of Labor Statistics collects and publishes regularly data in regard to retail prices, wholesale prices, employment, wages, hours of work, and cost of living. It also publishes information that is helpful in the operation of consumer co-operatives.

From time to time the Department of Labor has maintained such advisory and information services as the Consumers' Project, which is no longer in existence. During its existence its objectives were (a) to stimulate interest in the problems of the consumer, (b) to review public policy so far as it relates to the consumer, (c) to suggest ways and means of promoting larger and more economical production of useful goods, and (d) to develop and maintian better standards of living.

Children's Bureau. Not all consumers are interested in the Children's Bureau because this Bureau is of particular interest only to parents. It provides literature on the health and the care of the family and is in a position to give advice on the problems of parents.

Other Public Agencies

United States Post Office Department. The inspectors of the United States Post Office Department are constantly checking fraudulent schemes that operate through the mail. Certain classes of mail may be opened for inspection, but first-class mail may not be opened except with the authority of a search warrant issued by a court. If fraudulent letters are sent through the mail, the complaint must therefore be taken to court to provide authority for searching through any other letters of a similar kind. You may, for instance, be invited through the mail to get in on the ground floor of some new business venture. You may be offered an opportunity to invest your money so that you will earn five times your investment in the first year. If you are confined to your home because of a physical handicap, you may be invited to do work at home and thus "get rich quick." Such schemes as these are investigated by the postal inspectors.

The protection of the United States Post Office Department is limited because (a) much damage can be done before someone complains and the post office inspectors investigate a particular case, and (b) slowness and tediousness mark the procedure before post office inspectors can open mail. Furthermore, this protection does not cover any frauds except those that go through the mail.

Securities and Exchange Commission. The Securities and Exchange Commission is a Federal agency that has control and supervision over the prospectuses and the literature used by corporations in selling securities. This governmental agency thereby provides a means of protection to the consumer.

Public Health Service. The Public Health Service is a part of the function of the Department of the Treasury.

The principal activity is the prevention of disease and the protection of health. Close co-operation is provided with medical, dental, nursing, and other social service groups, and with schools and governmental bodies of states, counties, and cities. For instance, one of the activities of the Public Health Service has been to set up standards for milk and to promote the adoption of a standard milk ordinance in cities. This Service deals largely with groups rather than with individuals.

Department of the Interior. The Bituminous Coal Commission, which was created by an act of Congress in 1937, is now the Bituminous Coal Division of the Department of the Interior. The Consumers' Counsel Division of the Department of the Interior has been established for the purpose of looking after the interests of consumers to prevent them from being at the mercy of the employers, the workers, and the distributors of coal. Attempts are made to assure fair competition, adequate wages for miners, suitable working conditions for miners, reasonable prices of coal, the conservation of coal resources, and an adequate supply of coal. Literature pertaining to the qualities and the uses of coal and to means of protection from unfair practices is available from the Consumers' Counsel Division. The Counsel will welcome complaints against practices that jeopardize the interests of consumers.

State and City Protection. In some states laws have been set up for grading the quality of such items as fruits and vegetables. Many states and cities have set up regulations for controlling the quality of milk and other foods sold in local markets. The health departments of those states and cities require products to measure up to specified standards. Most cities require the regular inspection of scales and measures. Many other local regulations tend to protect the consumer.

.... 1939
CITY OF CINCINNATI
DEPARTMENT OF SAFETY
PUMP
EXAMINED AND SEALED
I. VAN CLEEFF,
Supt. Markets, Weights, Measures
Office, Sixth and Plum Sts.
Market House
Phone CHerry 5300, Line 303
Cincinnati, O.

Illustration No. 100—A City Inspector's Seal

State Control of Advertising. There are numerous state laws that represent barriers against dishonest advertising. Probably the most famous law is the *Printers' Ink* Model Statute. The following is the Model Statute:

Any person, firm, corporation or association who, with intent to sell or in any wise dispose of merchandise, securities, service, or anything offered by such person, firm, corporation or association, directly or indirectly, to the public for sale or distribution, or with intent to increase the consumption thereof, or to induce the public in any manner to enter into any obligation relating thereto, or to acquire title thereto, or an interest therein, makes, publishes, disseminates, circulates, or places before the public, or causes, directly or indirectly, to be made, published, disseminated, circulated, or placed before the public, in this State, in a newspaper or other publication, or in the form of a book, notice, handbill, poster, bill, circular, pamphlet, or letter, or in any other way, an advertisement of any sort regarding merchandise, securities, service, or anything so offered to the public, which advertisement contains any assertion, representation or statement of fact which is untrue, deceptive or misleading, shall be guilty of a misdemeanor.

The following twenty-five states have adopted it:

Alabama	Nevada
Colorado	New Jersey
Idaho	New York
Illinois	North Dakota
Indiana	Ohio
Iowa	Oklahoma
Kansas	Oregon
Kentucky	Rhode Island
Louisiana	Virginia
Michigan	Washington
Minnesota	Wisconsin
Missouri	Wyoming
Nebraska	

The following thirteen states have substitute laws patterned after the *Printers' Ink* Model Statute:

Arizona	Pennsylvania
California	South Carolina
Connecticut	South Dakota
Maryland	Tennessee
Massachusetts	Utah
Montana	West Virginia
North Carolina	

Public Testing Departments. The testing departments of cities, counties, states, and universities provide an important means of protection to the consumer, even though this means of protection may be rather indirect. Any agency that makes tests and sets up standards usually causes producers to attempt to meet those standards, even though there is no law requiring such action. In some cities, counties, and states there are definite testing departments

Chicago Board of Health

Illustration No. 101—A Public Testing Laboratory

that are used to judge the quality of goods which, being sold locally, do not come under the jurisdiction of the Federal Government. Local laws and ordinances frequently place restrictions on such perishable foods as milk, fruit, and eggs. If a dealer does not live up to the standards of the law, the consumer has recourse to the proper local authority, to whom he may complain.

Many of our leading colleges and universities maintain laboratories that are used for testing materials and foods brought to them by consumers and by business concerns.

Most of the reports are confidential and are available only to the person or the business that requested the test. Nevertheless, this service is one means of determining whether one is getting his money's worth in a product.

TEXTBOOK QUESTIONS

1. What functions of the National Bureau of Standards are of the most interest to consumers?
2. What testing service is performed by the National Bureau of Standards?
3. What is meant by the list of manufacturers "willing to certify"?
4. In what way does the National Bureau of Standards aid in the program of standardizing products?
5. What functions are served when manufacturers use labels which indicate that their products measure up to the standards of the National Bureau of Standards?
6. What classes of testing activity are within the scope of the National Bureau of Standards?
7. What laws administered by the Department of Agriculture are of primary interest to the consumer?
8. Under what circumstances does the United States Department of Agriculture have jurisdiction?
9. (a) What are some of the canned farm products for which grades have been established? (b) What are these grades?
10. In what way does the United States control the sale of poisonous cosmetics?
11. How does the new Federal Food, Drug, and Cosmetic Act affect the labeling of drugs?
12. Does all milk conform to the standards recommended by the United States Public Health Service and bear the corresponding grade marks?
13. What two services of the Department of Agriculture in connection with meat aid the consumer?
14. What is the minimum amount of butter fat that butter must contain if it is to be sold in interstate commerce and is to conform to governmental standards?
15. What recourse has the Department of Agriculture if a person adulterates or misbrands food that is sold in interstate commerce?
16. What service is rendered by the Bureau of Home Economics of the Department of Agriculture?
17. (a) What is the main function of the Federal Trade Commission? (b) How does this function aid consumers?
18. Who may register a complaint with the Federal Trade Commission?

19. May a complaint be registered with the Federal Trade Commission because of loss or damage suffered by a consumer?
20. In what way does the Federal Trade Commission have control over advertising?
21. What is one of the main ways in which the United States Post Office Department protects consumers?
22. In what way does the Securities and Exchange Commission protect the individual?
23. How does the Public Health Service of the Department of the Treasury aid the consumer?
24. What is the *Printers' Ink* Model Statute?
25. What public testing agencies besides those of the Federal Government serve consumers?

DISCUSSION QUESTIONS

1. How does the fact that the National Bureau of Standards helps to establish standards for governmental purchases help all of us?
2. How do the tests that are made by the National Bureau of Standards for individual manufacturers help all consumers?
3. In what way does the standardization program of the National Bureau of Standards help you as a buyer?
4. How does the use of specification labels of the National Bureau of Standards force manufacturers to comply with the standards established by the Bureau?
5. (a) How does the grading and the inspection services of the Department of Agriculture aid the consumer? (b) How can you as an individual benefit from these services?
6. Is the consumer benefited by the Federal Food, Drug, and Cosmetic Act if a product that he buys is made locally?
7. On which would you place more reliance: an advertisement of a particular product, or the label on the product?
8. How do you think the standards set up by the Department of Agriculture for grading milk will help a local consumer of milk, although there are no local laws with regard to milk?
9. Why do you think it is especially important that meat be inspected?
10. Many local packers of meat utilize the inspection service of the Department of Agriculture, although they are not required to do so. Why do you think they use this service?
11. (a) In what way does false advertising affect the consumer? (b) In what way does it affect a competitor?
12. Point out why the consumer cannot expect everything that comes through the mail to be free from fraud.
13. Formerly there were many advertisements of remedies that claimed to cure cancer and epilepsy. What do you think is the status of such advertising under recent laws?

PROBLEMS

1. Read the labels on foods that are purchased during one entire week for use in your home. (a) List the specific information on the labels that indicates quality and contents. (b) Find out which foods measure up to governmental standards, and tabulate the standards that are indicated on the labels.
2. Examine the products in your medicine cabinet at home. Study the labels, and find out whether the products comply with the regulations of the Federal Food, Drug, and Cosmetic Act. List under the name of each product the contents and the quality; whether or not artificial coloring or adulteration is present; and other similar facts.
3. On the basis of the study of this chapter, write a report setting forth a summary of what you believe are the shortcomings of the various governmental services in relation to consumer protection. Indicate what you consider would be suitable remedies.
4. From a magazine or a newspaper obtain an advertisement giving a rather complete description of a food, drug, cosmetic, or device. Analyze the advertisement to see whether it, in your opinion, violates the Federal law.

COMMUNITY PROBLEMS AND PROJECTS

1. Investigate the regulations in your community for maintaining the quality of milk.
2. Write a report on the legislation that you believe your local, state, or National Government might enact to help protect consumers.
3. Obtain a copy of a report of a judgment rendered by the Food and Drug Administration of the Department of Agriculture. (a) Make a summary of the findings in a particular case involving a violation of the Food and Drugs Act or the new Food, Drug, and Cosmetic Act. (b) Report the benefits that accrued to businessmen and to consumers from this judgment.
4. Investigate the activities of your state department of agriculture or any other state department that is regulating the production, the advertising, and the labeling of products sold within the state. Indicate the benefits that accrue to the buyer and the seller.
5. Obtain a copy of one of the latest reports of the Federal Trade Commission involving an unfair trade practice. (a) Summarize the decision, and point out the reasons for the complaint. (b) Give your conclusions as to the benefits of the activities of the Federal Trade Commission.

CHAPTER XI

PRIVATE AGENCIES OF CONSUMER PROTECTION

Purpose of the Chapter. Besides the governmental agencies that have been organized to serve the consumer, there are many private agencies. It is impossible to discuss in the short space of one chapter all the functions performed by such agencies. Nevertheless, every buyer should know something about the more important private agencies that can be called upon for protection and guidance in buying. The purpose of this chapter is, therefore, to point out some of these agencies and to discuss their functions.

Better Business Bureaus

Purpose. The better business bureaus of the United States were originally organized as a means of protecting businessmen. Most of the bureaus have, however, expanded into agencies that protect the general public and especially the consumer.

One function of a local better business bureau is to check carefully the practices of local businesses in order to prevent any unfair trade practices. Standards are usually specified for truthful advertising and fair public relations. The local bureau also investigates the various promotional schemes of new businesses that enter the community. Some local better business bureaus conduct newspaper campaigns to warn people against fraud and deception. Illustration No. 102 shows examples of some of the warnings that are published regularly in local newspapers by the Cincinnati Better Business Bureau.

Many of these bureaus investigate soliciting schemes and promotional schemes. Anyone has the privilege of calling the local better business bureau for information and advice. In many communities the members of the bureau will not contribute to any soliciting scheme until the scheme has

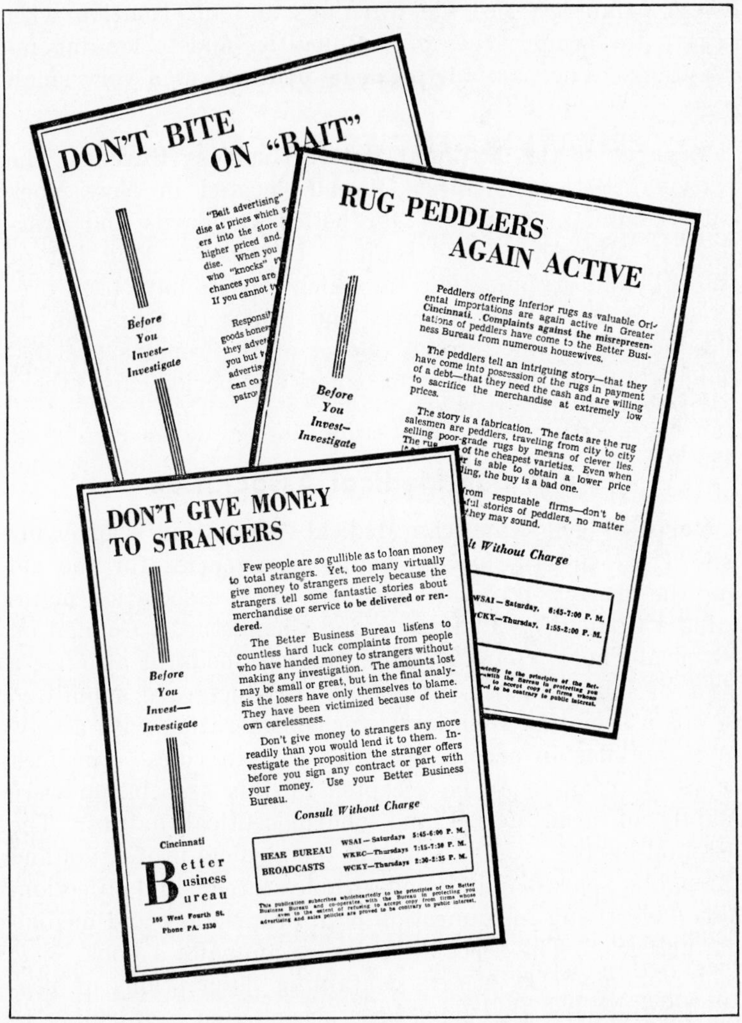

Illustration No. 102—Warnings Published by the Cincinnati Better Business Bureau

been approved by the bureau. Consumers can protect themselves if they will get in touch with the bureau immediately whenever there is any question of an unfair trade practice.

The National Better Business Bureau publishes various pamphlets specifically for the benefit of the consumer.

These pamphlets provide warnings and information with regard to specific types of commodities and to lending institutions. The pamphlets can be obtained at a very small cost.

Reports of the National Better Business Bureau. The National Better Business Bureau, located in New York City, conducts campaigns for better standards and practices in advertising and selling. It issues a long list of subjects and organizations on which reports have been prepared. A list of the reports and copies of them can be obtained from the Bureau. Some of the reports are distributed to publishers of newspapers and periodicals; others are for general distribution.

American Medical Association

Purpose. The American Medical Association is probably one of the most respected nonpublic agencies for the aid and the protection of the consumer. This association maintains a Council on Pharmacy and Chemistry, a Council on Physical Therapy, and a Committee on Foods; it also has a staff of laboratory investigators. Products are submitted to this association voluntarily for consideration with a view to acceptance in accordance with certain rules. The first types of products to be accepted by this association were mainly of a medicinal and pharmaceutical nature. The original purpose was "to protect the medical profession and the public against fraud, undesirable secrecy, and objectionable advertising in connection with proprietary and medicinal articles." The association issues annually a book, *New and Nonofficial Remedies,* containing descriptions of proprietary articles that have been accepted as conforming to the rules of the association.

Seals of Acceptance. There are two seals of acceptance of the American Medical Association. One is the seal of the Council on Pharmacy and Chemistry, and the other is the seal of the Committee on Foods. Illustration No. 103 shows these two seals. When either seal appears on the label of a product or in the advertising of the product, it indicates that the product has been approved and accepted as meeting the rules of the respective body. No remuneration in any form is accepted for this work; the expense is borne entirely by the American Medical Association.

Foods. Manufacturers whose food products are accepted by this association are allowed to advertise them as "accepted by the Committee on Foods of the American Medical

Illustration No. 103—Seals of the American Medical Association

Association." The association reports that but a small proportion of food products that have been submitted have been rejected. The reasons for refusal to accept products are always given in the reports of the association.

Reports. The American Medical Association issues reports on its investigations. These reports are available to anyone who subscribes to the publications of the association. The accepted foods and drugs are announced in the journal of the American Medical Association.

American Dental Association

Accepted Dental Remedies and Dentifrices. The Council on Dental Therapeutics of the American Dental Association publishes a list of accepted dental remedies and dentifrices. This list contains descriptions of proprietary articles that seem to be of sufficient importance to warrant their inclusion. The Council has established rules and regulations for observ-

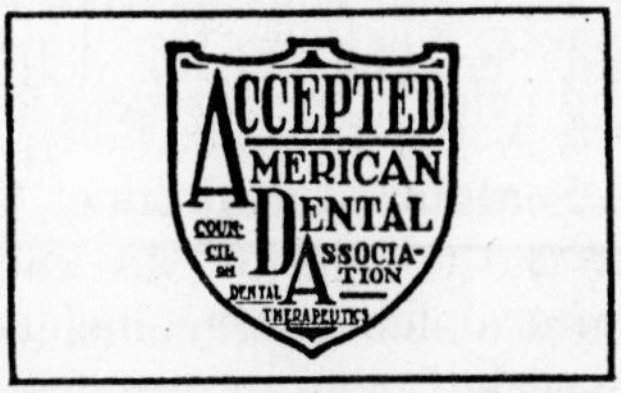

Illustration No. 104—The Seal of the American Dental Association

ance in examining and accepting dental remedies and dentifrices. Not only the remedy or the dentifrice itself must be acceptable, but the advertising also must be approved. A manufacturer whose remedy or dentifrice is accepted may use the seal of acceptance of the council in his advertising and on the label of his package. Several tooth pastes and tooth powders have been accepted, but it is significant to know that not a single mouthwash has been accepted.

National Board of Fire Underwriters

Laboratories. The National Board of Fire Underwriters maintains laboratories that are operated on a nonprofit basis for the purpose of giving information on the merits of materials and appliances that may involve hazards of life, fire, theft, or accident. The laboratories are known as the Underwriters' Laboratories, Inc.

Tests. Tests are conducted in the laboratories on the basis of predetermined standards. Information on these standards may be obtained by writing to a testing laboratory of the National Board of Fire Underwriters. The major work of the laboratories consists in inspecting various materials and appliances to ascertain whether they meet the minimum standards. The board publishes annually a list of important appliances and materials, such as electrical appliances, fire-protection appliances, oil and gas appliances, and automotive appliances, that have been approved by it.

Label. The consumer can profit from the services of the underwriters' laboratories by purchasing only equipment or material that has been approved. Approved equipment and material can be determined from the published lists and also from the labels on the products. A product that bears the label of an underwriters' laboratory has been inspected and approved in the factory in which it was produced.

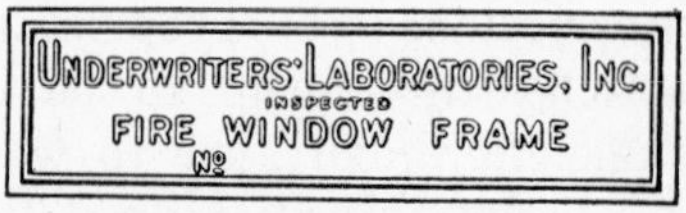

Illustration No. 105—A Sample Label of the Underwriters' Association

American Standards Association

Purpose. The American Standards Association includes in its membership practically all the standardizing agencies, associations of manufacturers, associations of producers, and private laboratories, as well as a great many educational organizations and private business concerns. Membership is open to anyone who is interested in standardization. The association is founded upon the principle that "commercial contracts transferring the ownership of commodities must be based on dimensional standards and quality specifications that are mutually satisfactory to the buyer and seller. National recognition of such standards will remove misunderstandings and expedite commercial standards." It is evident from this statement that the functions of the association are closely related to the consumer as well as to the producer.

The American Standards Association has organized an Advisory Committee for Ultimate Consumer Goods. This committee co-operates with various interested groups, such as the American Home Economics Association and the National Retail Dry Goods Association. The purpose is to develop reliable standards and the use of grades on labels of goods sold to the ultimate consumer.

Publications. The American Standards Association publishes a yearbook and a monthly bulletin. The yearbook contains a report of the activities of the association and lists of new standards that have been developed. The monthly bulletin provides current information with regard to progress in the standardization, the certification, and the labeling of products.

The consumer may purchase the literature of this association. Specification of the standards for any product that has been standardized by the association can be obtained at a nominal cost.

American Home Economics Association

Functions. The American Home Economics Association has devoted some of its main efforts to the education and the protection of the consumer by furnishing buying information and by encouraging suitable legislation and the use of proper standards. The association publishes a monthly magazine and bulletins on buying and the protection of the consumer. Most of the information pertains to such topics as food, clothing, health, and legislation.

Magazines and Newspapers

Testing and Advisory Services. Magazines and newspapers have been performing an untold amount of service for the average consumer. Some of the publishers of these maintain testing laboratories, and others have advisory or consultation services for the benefit of consumers. The following are some of the laboratories and services maintained by the publishers of national periodicals:

Good Housekeeping Institute and Bureau
Household Searchlight
McCall's How-to-Buy Service
Parents' Magazine Consumer Service Bureau
Physical Culture Institute of Nutrition
Crowell Publishing Company

Purposes. Some of the testing laboratories have been developed to ensure truthful advertising in the magazines and to encourage the respect of the reading public. Although some consumers may question the value of such testing laboratories, nevertheless they do provide one additional means of evaluating products that are advertised in periodicals.

Advertising in a magazine which sponsors a seal is not necessarily a prerequisite to issuing a seal. For instance, in the case of the seals issued by Good Housekeeping Institute or Bureau, only about 25 per cent of the manufacturers whose products are on the tested and approved list advertise in Good Housekeeping magazine. Along with their work in the testing of products, some of the publishers, through their periodicals, also give their readers guidance in the technique of purchasing.

Approval of Products. These organizations deal chiefly with products intended for the ultimate consumer. Approval is usually based on inspection, laboratory tests, and

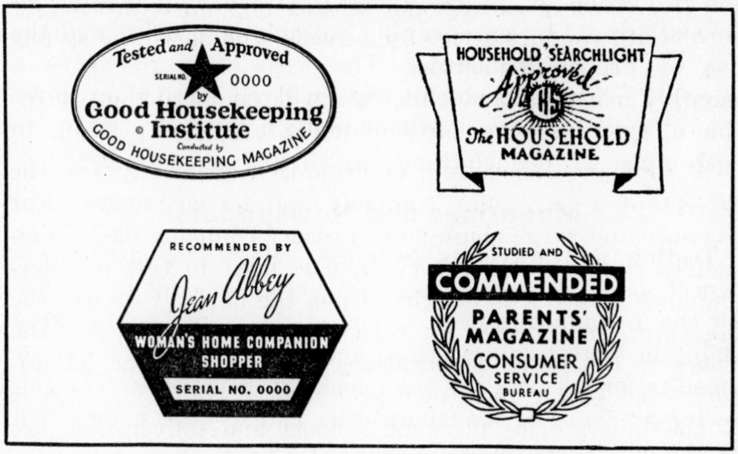

Illustration No. 106—Seals Issued by Magazines

service tests. Products are ordinarily not graded; they are either approved or disapproved. Most of the testing laboratories issue a seal or a label that may be used on the product and in advertising. Most of the publishers of periodicals also issue lists of approved products for the benefit of readers. One of the greatest results of the activity of these organizations has been to eliminate extravagant advertising claims.

There are many testing agencies now available, including governmental testing agencies. Regardless of the fact that the testing agencies of magazines may not be considered independent, they have rendered a unique and valuable service to consumers. This is particularly true in the testing of household appliances and cosmetics by Good Housekeeping Institute and Bureau.

Private Laboratories

Types and Services. In a discussion of private agencies for consumer protection, it is desirable to include various types of laboratories that test foods and other merchandise. Such laboratories may be classified as follows:

(a) Laboratories maintained by private companies for testing their own products and purchases

(b) Laboratories of some schools and universities that will conduct a test for anyone who is willing to pay a fee for the service
(c) Private laboratories that will do testing on a fee basis for anyone who submits a product

A company laboratory is organized primarily for the benefit of a particular company and its customers. For instance, one large chain-store grocery company has a completely equipped laboratory that is used to test all merchandise before it is bought. Upon the basis of its test the laboratory authorizes or rejects any proposed purchase. Some of the great corporations operate scientific laboratories for testing their own products.

The laboratories of some schools and universities are operated only for the benefit of the institutions, but occasionally the facilities of such a laboratory are available to any client who is willing to pay an established fee.

There are numerous laboratories that the individual or any organization can utilize by having tested various types of products, ranging from foods to chemicals, clothing, and heavy machinery. The National Bureau of Standards of the United States Department of Commerce publishes a directory of commercial testing laboratories and college research laboratories. This directory indicates the types of commodities that can be tested by each laboratory. Some of these laboratories will test items such as clothing, shoes, or food for a fee ranging from one dollar to ten dollars.

Raising Standards. The proving grounds and the testing laboratories of our large corporations indirectly affect the consumer, for they tend to raise standards of quality. For example, the automobile manufacturers have large proving grounds used to test new devices and new models of automobiles before they are offered for sale. If this testing were not conducted, the consumer in many cases would not get his money's worth. He would do the experimenting rather than the producer. Producers usually feature in their advertising certain tests that have been made on the proving grounds or in the laboratories. The wise buyer will weigh the results of such tests.

Consumers' Research Organizations

Nature and Functions. There are at least three organizations that solicit membership on a fee basis and furnish members with bulletins and buyers' guides. These organizations are as follows:

Consumers' Research, Inc., Washington, New Jersey
Consumers Union, Inc., 17 Union Square West, New York, New York
Intermountain Consumers' Service, Inc., 1016 South Clarkson Street, Denver, Colorado

Such organizations are operated on a nonprofit basis for the benefit of their members. The membership fee is reasonable. Their services are within the reach of most consumers.

Because of the potential liability of damage suits, organizations such as these must confine the dissemination of their findings largely to their own members, who pay for the services. For instance, if one of these agencies were to make an error in some analysis or to issue a misstatement with regard to some product, the general dissemination of this information to the public would be damaging to the manufacturer of the product that was the subject of the report. The producer would have a just claim for damages against the reporting agency. When the information is furnished as a professional service, however, the only one who can complain is the subscriber. These organizations are therefore able to escape legal attacks by those whose products are tested.

The direct benefit of these organizations is therefore limited largely to the subscribers. As these organizations are operated only for members, however, they have greater freedom in making tests and in reporting the information to their members.

Consumers' Research, Inc. Consumers' Research is the outgrowth of what was originally a small club for the study of consumers' goods. Consumers' Research is now a large national organization with extensive laboratory facilities at its plant at Washington, New Jersey, and elsewhere. It is not affiliated with any other organization. It is operated on a nonprofit, noncommercial basis for the benefit of those who subscribe to its advisory services on technical and scientific questions relating to consumers' goods. Since the subscription fee is reasonable, the services of Consumers' Research are within the reach of most consumers.

Because there is a possibility of damage suits, an organization such as Consumers' Research finds it desirable to confine the issuance of a part of its findings to those who sign a formal application blank and pay for its services. If Consumers' Research were to make an important error or issue a misstatement unfavorable to some widely distributed product, the general dissemination of this information to the public at large would be damaging to the manufacturer of the product that had been reported on, and the producer would have a right to enter a suit for damages against Consumers' Research. The direct benefits of an organization of this type are therefore limited largely to the subscribers to the service. Since Consumers' Research is operated only for its subscribers as ultimate consumers, the organization has great freedom in making tests and reporting its findings.

Consumers' Research tests products which are most widely distributed and most inquired about by those who use its services. The bulletins of the organization consist of (a) monthly *Bulletins* containing reports on products

Illustration No. 107—Tests Being Conducted by Consumers' Research, Inc.

that have been tested; (b) a *General Bulletin*, issued quarterly, containing similar material but available to anyone, whether subscribers or not; and (c) an *Annual Cumulative Bulletin* of over two hundred pages, which furnishes a comprehensive summary of previous findings.

Products that have been examined and reported on are classified on the basis of quality as (a) recommended, (b) intermediate, or (c) not recommended. The fact that a particular product is not listed in a bulletin usually means that the product has not yet been examined. The following is a portion of a report pertaining to electric lamp bulbs. Only the products that have been examined and recommended are mentioned in this partial report.

ELECTRIC LAMP BULBS [1]

Greatest economy, with usual rates for electric energy, is obtained by the use of standard bulbs with rated life of 1,000 hours. In some cases, it is even more economical to use an "overrun" bulb; for example, a 115-volt bulb on a 120-volt line. Bulbs of longer life are uneconomical except in particular locations where avoidance of frequent replacements is important enough to warrant acceptance of considerably lower efficiency. Large-size bulbs produce more total light per watt than small sizes (for example, a 60-watt bulb produces more light than three 25-watt bulbs at a saving of 66⅔% in bulb cost and 20% in energy cost) but more wattage than needed for illumination should, of course, not be used merely to obtain higher efficiency.

Preliminary tests indicate that the recently introduced fluorescent lamps, with rated life of from 1,500 to 2,000 hours, are approximately twice as efficient, in light production, as the ordinary filament lamps. They must be operated through special auxiliary devices, and require special sockets. Both the lamps and the auxiliaries are at present rather high in price, as are the industrial and home-lighting fixtures so far introduced for use with them. The stroboscopic effect of these lamps may be found disagreeable by some.

A. Recommended

G. E. (General Electric Co., Nela Park, Cleveland) 10¢. 500-hr. rated life. At average rates for electricity, produced light at practically same overall cost as *Mazda* 1,000-hr. lamps.

Hygrade (Hygrade-Sylvania Corp., Salem, Mass.) 15¢. 1,000-hr. rated life.

Mazda (General Electric Co.) 15¢. 1,000-hr. rated life.

Mazda (Westinghouse Lamp Co., 150 Broadway, N. Y. C.) 15¢. 1,000-hr. rated life.

---

[1] Quoted by special permission from *Consumers' Research Bulletin, Annual Cumulative Number*, issued by Consumers' Research, Inc., Washington, New Jersey, September, 1939.

Consumers Union, Inc. Consumers Union provides services similar to those of Consumers' Research. The annual subscription fee covers twelve monthly reports and an annual buying guide. Legislation, labor problems, and health problems are discussed in the reports.

Illustration No. 108—Test Being Conducted by Consumers Union, Inc.

The monthly reports of Consumers Union, in addition to giving general information, provide specific ratings of products. Products are rated (a) best buys, (b) also acceptable, or (c) not acceptable. The following is an example of the rating of men's raincoats:

MEN'S RAINCOATS [1]

Best Buys

Ward's Cat. No.—5336 (Montgomery Ward). $3.98 plus postage. Cotton fabric with rubber back. Waterproof. Weight, 22 oz. Available in medium gray only, which faded in sun. Ventilators and pockets, but "wrist straps" not adjustable.

Raynster So Lite No. MA 611 (U. S. Rubber Products, Inc., Passaic, N. J.). $5.50. Cotton fabric with rubber back. Waterproof. Weight, 23 oz. Appeared to be nearly identical with Ward's—5336. Ventilators and pockets, but "wrist straps" not adjustable.

Also Acceptable

Top Hat (fabric by Du Pont; coat by Spatz Bros., NYC). $7.95. Rubber with silk back. Waterproof. Weight, 18 oz. Smallish pockets. Fabric deteriorated somewhat in sunlight.

Gooseskin Raingard Style 050 (Arrow Importing Co., Cleveland). $9.75. Fabric similar to that in *Top Hat*. Waterproof. Weight, 20 oz. Deteriorated somewhat in sun.

Mansbrooke Horco-Silk (Hodgman Rubber Co., Framingham, Mass.). $12.50. Rubber impregnated silk. Waterproof. Weight, 12 oz. Lowest tensile strength and tore most easily of all coats tested. Well cut.

---

[1] Quoted by special permission from *Consumers Union Reports*.

Goodyear (Goodyear Rubber Mfg. Co., NYC). $4.95. Rubber with cotton back. Waterproof. Weight, 27 oz. No ventilators or wrist straps. Small pockets. Tensile strength uneven, and rather low in filling.

Ward's Cat. No.—5302. $1.89 plus postage. Heavy rubber, with cotton back. Weight, 38 oz. Resistance to tearing higher than that of lighter coats. Rubber surface cracked in creases. Waterproof. Not well cut. Acceptable because of price.

Alligator Featherweight (Alligator Co., St. Louis). $13.75. Oiled cotton. Fabric waterproof, but water penetrated seams. Weight, 23 oz. Good tensile strength but once ripped tore easily. Generously cut. Heavier "Alligator" oiled cotton coats, presumably of similar material, available for as low as $5.50.

Topcoat Style, Heavier and Hence Not Entirely Comparable:

Sears' Rain-O-Shine Cat. No.—7460 (Sears Roebuck). $3.95 plus postage. Cotton face and back, cemented together with rubber. Shoulder seams double-stitched but rain seeped through them. Weight, 51 oz. No ventilators. Somewhat skimped dimensions. Very strong material which did not tear easily.

Intermountain Consumers' Service, Inc. Intermountain Consumers' Service, Inc., is organized under the laws of Colorado. It provides advice, opinions, and scientific testing information in relation to commodities and services that have been investigated by the organization. Membership is accepted on a subscription basis. The *Consumers' Buying Guide* is issued in installments during the year.

Other Agencies

New England Council. In 1925 the governors of six New England states authorized the use of a New England quality label. This label can be used on products that are produced in New England if these products are packed to conform to official standards approved by the council. Illustration No. 109 shows this label.

Illustration No. 109—The New England Quality Label

To protect the reputation of the label, each state department of agriculture maintains an inspection service.

The service inspects and grades the products on which the label is to be used. The products are not required to be graded in these states, but they must be graded if the label is to be used. It is used largely on such products as fruits, vegetables, butter, eggs, jelly, maple products, honey, and poultry.

Associations of Producers. The American Gas Association, the American Canners' Association, the Illuminating Engineers' Society (I. E. S.), and many other organizations have established standards of their own. Many of these standards correspond to the Federal standards. The associations issue labels of approval, which may be used only after products have been tested and approved.

Publications. There is so much literature available for the aid of the consumer that it would be impossible and impractical for the average individual to collect and use all this information. The following are, however, some suggestions of literature that will be especially helpful:

The American Consumer, 205 East Forty-Second Street, New York City
Better Buymanship booklets, Household Finance Corporation, 919 North Michigan Avenue, Chicago, Illinois
The Consumer, Consumers National Federation, 110 Morningside Drive, New York City
Bulletins of the National Better Business Bureau, Chrysler Building, New York City
Consumers' Digest, Consumers' Institute of America, Inc., Washington, New Jersey

Consumers' Research, Inc., formerly published *Consumers' Digest,* but a separate organization has been established to handle the publication. The *Digest* is not a confidential publication. It is sold on newsstands. It contains a list of recommended products, but does not give the names of those that are not recommended.

Other items of literature have been mentioned previously in this chapter. Additional types of literature that provide buying information are the shopping guides and the specific merchandise information of some of the leading stores in large cities.

TEXTBOOK QUESTIONS

1. What are some of the functions performed by the better business bureaus in promoting fair trade practices?
2. Who may utilize the services of a better business bureau?
3. What are the functions of the reports that are issued by the National Better Business Bureau?
4. What are the two committees of the American Medical Association that help to protect the consumer?
5. How can anyone obtain the advantage of the services rendered by the American Medical Association?
6. When a product has been accepted by a committee of the American Medical Association, how can a consumer distinguish this product from others?
7. What is the significance of the fact that a dentifrice bears the seal of approval of the American Dental Association?
8. For what purpose are the laboratories of the National Board of Fire Underwriters operated?
9. What two main functions are performed through the tests conducted in the laboratories of the National Board of Fire Underwriters?
10. How can a buyer identify a product that has been tested and approved by a laboratory of the National Board of Fire Underwriters?
11. On what principle was the American Standards Association founded?
12. How does the American Home Economics Association benefit the consumer?
13. Name five magazines, or periodicals, in connection with which some type of testing laboratory is maintained.
14. On what assumption are the testing laboratories of periodical publishers usually established for the benefit of consumers?
15. What is usually the means of identifying a product that has been tested in a laboratory operated by a periodical publisher?
16. What three types of private laboratories are there?
17. What are the three main private agencies organized on a membership basis to provide information for consumers?
18. What products are tested by Consumers' Research, Inc.?
19. Why does Consumers' Research have considerable freedom in making tests and reporting the results?
20. How does the New England quality label help buyers in New England?

DISCUSSION QUESTIONS

1. How does the American Medical Association help to protect consumers, even though only a small percentage of products is approved by this association?
2. On which would you place the greatest reliance: a test made by the American Medical Association, a test made by Consumers' Research, the testimonial of a user, or a laboratory test made by the manufacturer? Why?
3. When products have been examined and disapproved by the American Medical Association or Consumers' Research, why do the reports of the tests fail to perform a widespread service?
4. How do the laboratories of the National Board of Fire Underwriters save money for all of us?
5. "The activities of the American Standards Association save many thousands of dollars each year." Do you think this statement is true? Why?
6. What are some possible limitations on tests that are made in the laboratories maintained by publications in which manufacturers advertise?
7. Some people assert that the scientific laboratories maintained by periodical publishers are operated for the benefit of manufacturers and therefore render little service to buyers. Do you think this assertion is true? Why?
8. Some manufacturers oppose such organizations as Consumers' Research, Inc., and Consumers Union, Inc., whereas others approve them. How do you account for the difference in attitude?
9. Why do you think some manufacturers organize an association and use a seal indicating that products of the members of that association meet certain requirements?
10. It is not likely that, at the time of purchasing any ordinary product, the consumer will use the service of a testing agency. How might he, however, use such a service to his advantage?
11. In what way do you think the scientific accuracy of a consumer research organization might be limited?
12. Some of the reports issued by consumer research organizations are often a year old and sometimes older. Are these reports valuable? Discuss.

PROBLEMS

1. Study a daily newspaper and cut out all advertisements (a) that may violate the principles under which better business bureaus operate, and (b) that conform to standards set up by the American Dental Association, the American Medi-

cal Association, or any other agency mentioned in this chapter. Paste these advertisements on sheets of paper, and submit them with your comments.

2. Prepare a complete list of the products that are advertised in a current issue of some popular magazine. Opposite the name of each product, indicate whether there is any seal, label, certified test, or testimonial used to indicate the standard of quality of the product. Indicate the specific proof that is given.
3. Make a list of food products and drugs that you find bearing seals or labels of approval. Indicate the particular seal or label for each product. If you find any seals or labels with which you are not acquainted, inquire about the conditions under which these are awarded.

COMMUNITY PROBLEMS AND PROJECTS

1. Obtain all the information you can on the services of the American Medical Association in aiding the consumer. Write a synopsis of your findings in the form of a report.
2. Investigate the services that are performed by some periodical publisher in testing and approving products and in issuing information for the benefit of consumers. Write a report on your findings, and evaluate the services performed.
3. Collect samples of labels and seals of approval used on various products. Paste each label or seal on a sheet of paper with an accompanying discussion of the basis on which it is awarded and its use as a guide to consumers.

CHAPTER XII

HOW THE CONSUMER IS INFLUENCED IN BUYING

Purpose of the Chapter. People who have goods for sale make an appeal to every one of the human senses. Everywhere one goes, one is asked to see, hear, feel, taste, or smell certain sales inducements. If a person allows this array of pleasing sensations to be his sole guide in the selection of goods and services, he is often at the mercy of people who know how to influence the emotions. The ordinary buyer is an amateur dealing with professional salespeople. The only way for him to be sure that he is getting his money's worth is to think for himself and to analyze all sales messages and all products critically. The purpose of this chapter is (a) to analyze buying motives, (b) to explain advertising and selling influences, (c) to point out some of the pitfalls in buying, and (d) to establish safe principles for guidance in buying.

Section I

How the Consumer Is Influenced by Advertising and Selling

The Amateur Buyer. Just what is a consumer? There are individual buyers and industrial buyers. The individual buyer is generally spoken of as the consumer because he is the person who finally eats, wears, lives in, or otherwise uses the things that industry produces for him. Everyone of us is an ultimate consumer. We should therefore analyze the influences that lead us to buy.

The industrial or business buyer makes most of his purchases for resale, but is a consumer of such items as fuel and supplies. The purchaser for an established and efficient business buys more or less scientifically. At least, buying is his profession. He may be influenced emotionally; he probably is influenced in this way by advertising and by promotional schemes. But he follows some organized procedure.

Advertising, in our present economic system of profit-making, is one of the most vital influences on the consumer. The great mass of population constitutes a group of amateur purchasers who are subjected to professional sales pressure. Every producer is crying his wares in an effort to obtain the attention and the personal favor of such purchasers. Each advertiser is competing not only for the consumer's attention and favor, but also against hundreds and thousands of other advertisers.

Who Pays the Cost of Advertising? Some economists contend that all advertising is wasteful because it influences people to buy when they should be allowed to make their own choices without such an influence. It is true that some advertising is wasteful; but, on the other hand, if one makes an honest analysis of the situation, he will see that without advertising it would be impossible to have mass distribution. Without mass distribution it would be impossible to have mass production. Without mass production it would be impossible to have manufacturing processes improved to such a high degree as we now are accustomed. Without improved manufacturing processes it would be impossible to have many of our commonly accepted necessities produced at a low cost. For instance, in 1922 a few thousand people with radio sets costing from $100 to $500 could make their friends envious by receiving radio programs. There are now more than 26,000,000 homes equipped with radio sets, which have cost in some cases as low as $5 or $10 a set. Advertising and mass production have brought about this change.

Sometimes critics cite examples of manufacturers who are able to produce and sell an item, such as a razor, for $5, $10, or $15. These critics attribute the high cost to advertising. One of the reasons for the high cost is patent protection, which enables the producer to get the price he wants. Lack of competition is another factor. Furthermore, during the early stages in the introduction of a product, it is necessary to charge a higher price to carry the burden of advertising until mass production results in lower production costs. Without advertising, a large market would not be created; low production resulting in high production costs would therefore tend to keep the price at a high level. In normal unrestricted advertising and trade, however, when new competing products come onto the market, additional advertising causes wider use; and, through competition and mass production together, a lower price is made available to the consumer.

It is true that, in the case of luxuries such as exclusive clothes and cosmetics, advertising costs may run unusually high; but when one buys a luxury, he is not necessarily looking for value. When one analyzes commonly advertised commodities, he finds the advertising cost rather low. For instance, in the case of a well-known shirt, only 64/100 of a cent goes into public information about it. In the case of a well-known brand of soup, only 36/1000 of a cent on each can is spent for advertising.

Purposes of Advertising. Advertising is the lifeblood of many businesses. These businesses have discovered that to stop advertising for any great length of time means a loss in sales. This fact proves conclusively that the consumer is influenced by advertising, whether the advertising is good or bad.

Advertising has proved to be a business necessity in our present economic system. In some form or another it is necessary in order to promote a wide distribution of products. A wide distribution of products, in turn, promotes greater production and results in lower costs. The formal purposes of advertising are as follows:

(a) To make an immediate sale of a product
(b) To educate the consumer to have a higher regard for a product
(c) To induce the consumer to buy one product in place of another
(d) To turn a natural desire into an actual want
(e) To increase the frequency of purchases
(f) To raise the level of necessity by educating consumers to feel that former luxuries are now necessities

Psychology of Selling. The professional seller is a trained psychologist. He understands human behavior and the workings of the human mind. He presents his product so that it will attract attention, create desire, convince the consumer of its worth, and cause him to act by purchasing it. The following steps therefore constitute the psychology of the selling process: (a) attracting attention, (b) creating desire, (c) causing conviction, and (d) obtaining action. These steps are followed in advertising as well as in personal selling.

Types of Sales Appeal. There are two general types of sales appeal. The first is known as the *emotional,* or *human-interest, appeal;* the second, as the *rational,* or *reason-why, appeal.* Professional sellers refer to these respectively as the *short-circuit* and the *long-circuit appeal.*

Experience has proved that, in the selling of many commodities, the emotional appeal is more effective than the reason-why appeal. The emotional appeal influences the buyer through suggestion. He is not invited to deliberate, consider, or compare; he is made to feel that the article that is advertised will please his senses or satisfy his desires.

The reason-why appeal is referred to as the long-circuit appeal because it requires a careful presentation of facts that appeal to conscious deliberation. This type of appeal must present logical reasons why the product should be purchased.

Within these two general classes of sales appeal, there are numerous appeals used by advertisers to stimulate sales. The following is a list of twelve that are commonly used in advertising all general types of products:

(a) Health
(b) Maternal affection
(c) Appetite and taste
(d) Attraction of the sexes
(e) Economy
(f) Comfort, pleasure, and luxury
(g) Ambition
(h) Beauty and appearance
(i) Efficiency
(j) Safety
(k) Vanity, pride, and fashion
(l) Sympathy

The way in which the advertiser utilizes an appeal depends upon whether the appeal is emotional or rational. For instance, if clothing is sold purely for the sake of beauty or appearance or with the purpose of enabling the buyer to imitate someone else, the appeal is highly emotional. On the other hand, if the advertiser of men's clothing points out how attractive clothing and a good appearance will help a man in business, the appeal is somewhat rational.

Illustration No. 110 shows an advertisement with an emotional appeal. Illustration No. 111 shows one with a reason-why appeal. Compare the two. Determine which one actually tells enough to enable the reader to determine the merits of the product.

"And Every One Stopped and Stared . . . !"

•

Time: EASTER MORNING.

Place: ANYWHERE.

Principal· A YOUNG MAN.

As he strolled along the street, every one stopped and stared—stared at his modish new suit. The suit stood out from all the rest. Only "The Tailor Shop" can fashion such a suit that will make all your friends envy you.

Illustration No. 110—An Emotional Appeal

Be *sure* that your DOLLARS buy comfort, quality, and style!

You can afford to pay 5 or 10 per cent more for a finely tailored suit from "The Tailor Shop." For this small extra margin we give you (a) pure virgin wool cloth, (b) a selection from 100 weaves of cloth, (c) a suit made to fit *you*, (d) repair service for one year, and (e) free pressing service once a week for six months.

Illustration No. 111—A Reason-Why Appeal

Experts in selling and advertising study very carefully the appeals that are most effective in selling products. They find that some appeals are satisfactory for men, whereas they cannot be used satisfactorily with women; and vice versa. Style, for example, is an important consideration in selling shoes to women, whereas it is not so important in selling them to men. Many tests will show that men consider the quality of shoes before style, whereas women make style the paramount consideration. In choosing an appeal to be used, the seller or the advertiser must therefore consider the prospective buyer.

Results of Advertising. Does advertising pay? It certainly does. The fact that advertising does pay is proved by the successful selling of advertised products and by the fortunes that have been built as the result of good advertising programs. It can also be proved by an analysis of the effects on consumers. For instance, the following analysis [1] shows the partial results of an examination of one thousand college students. When the test was administered, students were requested to associate a particular product with a trade name. The table shows the results.

880 out of 1,000 mentioned "Eastman" for camera.
771 out of 1,000 mentioned "Singer" for sewing machine.
757 out of 1,000 mentioned "Campbell" for soup.
748 out of 1,000 mentioned "Arrow" for collars.
746 out of 1,000 mentioned "Waterman" for fountain pens.
436 out of 1,000 mentioned "Life-Savers" for 5-cent mints.
430 out of 1,000 mentioned "Sunkist" for fruit.
419 out of 1,000 mentioned "Diamond" for dyes.
396 out of 1,000 mentioned "Gillette" for razors.
389 out of 1,000 mentioned "Ivory" for soap.

High-Pressure Salesmanship. Some salesmen attempt to sell merchandise or services regardless of whether or not the merchandise or the services are needed. Sometimes no attempt is made to find out what the customer needs or wants. Such tactics are referred to as *high-pressure salesmanship.* The wise consumer will not tolerate these tactics. The consumer should either build up a strong defense against such tactics or patronize stores that have trained employees to interpret his needs and wishes.

How to Develop Sales Resistance. Just what can the average buyer do to assure himself that he is being treated fairly? What can he do to investigate? The sources of

---

1 Adapted from *The Leadership of Advertised Brands* by George Burton Hotchkiss and Richard B. Franken. Doubleday, Page & Company, 1923.

protection are mentioned in preceding chapters. The following specific suggestions are helpful:

(a) *Buy, but do not allow yourself to be "sold."* Adopt a scientific attitude in buying. Insist upon detailed facts and pertinent information. Be sure that you obtain specific information with regard to quality, efficiency, cost, ingredients, and net contents.

(b) *Do not depend upon reputation.* Do not give too much consideration to trade names. In the absence of an indication of grades and the ability to make a test or to formulate a reasonable judgment, a known brand is better than an unknown brand. In some instances, however, you may pay more for a branded product just because it is highly advertised under a trade name. A trade name is not necessarily the final guarantee of quality.

(c) *Study advertisements.* View with suspicion any advertisement that avoids facts and talks only in terms of generalities or makes emotional, extravagant claims.

(d) *Examine the product carefully.* Learn to know what you are buying. Look at the label and determine the ingredients, the net contents, and the quality. Labels on packages are usually more reliable than advertising. Laws governing labeling usually specify what must be stated on the label, but laws governing advertising merely state what must not be put into the advertising.

(e) *Take an active interest in your buying.* The United States Department of Agriculture will furnish notices of judgments against manufacturers of food and drug products. In addition this Department issues various bulletins. Other information can be obtained from private agencies and from many of the periodical publishers.

(f) *Report unfair practices.* The better business bureaus stand ready to investigate misrepresentation and other unfair practices in advertising and in selling. Report fraudulent advertising to the proper bureau.

TEXTBOOK QUESTIONS

1. Explain what is meant by the term *consumer*.
2. Who pays the cost of advertising?

3. What are the six purposes of advertising?
4. Is the advertising cost of luxuries high or low as compared with the same cost of most other products?
5. Why does the professional seller usually have an advantage over the inexperienced buyer?
6. What four fundamental steps constitute the psychology of the selling process?
7. (a) What are the two general types of appeal that advertisers and sellers use in encouraging people to buy? (b) What are the differences between them?
8. Name at least five specific appeals.
9. Show how the fact that advertising pays has been proved through a test based upon the memory of trade names.
10. What are some suggestions on developing sales resistance?
11. What is high-pressure selling?

DISCUSSION QUESTIONS

1. How do you account for the fact that many of the advertisements published in magazines and newspapers are evidently not truthful but do obtain results?
2. If we were to eliminate all forms of advertising, would we be able to obtain better and cheaper goods?
3. "Advertising has converted many luxuries into necessities." Explain this statement.
4. "An uneducated person is a toy in the hands of an advertising expert." Explain this statement.
5. When an advertiser is trying to sell a piece of mechanical equipment to women, he finds that emotional appeals are rather effective; but when he sells the same equipment to men, he finds in general that rational appeals are more effective. How do you account for this difference?
6. Which type of appeal should be more effective in attempting to sell to a truly educated person?
7. More than a billion dollars is spent each year for advertising. If advertising were discontinued, could we expect to buy the same goods in the same quantities for one billion dollars less?
8. Manufacturers have a strong incentive to use trade names and to advertise their products extensively under these names. (a) Is the use of trade names beneficial? (b) Why do you think wholesalers use trade names?
9. Can you justify buying advertised goods when unadvertised goods cost less?
10. When you buy clothes, what appeals influence you most?
11. What do you think of a statement such as this in an advertisement: "Used by the best families"?

Section II

How to Interpret Advertising

Honest and Dishonest Advertising. Every buyer must recognize the fact that, although the majority of advertisers are honest, some are unscrupulous. Substantial and well-established business concerns recognize the fact that honesty, in advertising as well as in other relationships with consumers, must be the basis of permanent success. The publishers of magazines and newspapers recognize the fact that dishonest advertising reacts unfavorably against their publications as well as against the products advertised. Because of the importance of advertising, the Federal Government and also state governments have passed laws on this subject. One of the most effective promoters of honesty in advertising is the National Better Business Bureau and its affiliated organizations.

Forces in Improving Advertising. A great many forces have helped to improve advertising. The consumer has benefited primarily from this improvement. The advertiser also has benefited because truthfulness in advertising has helped to develop a greater confidence on the part of consumers. There are occasional trends, however, that cause the public to lose confidence. The wide use of paid testimonials, for instance, has drawn severe criticism from the public. The attacks of one industry on another or of one company on another through advertisements have created additional distrust. In time, however, most of these practices disappear. On the whole, present-day advertising is far above the level of that of fifty or even ten years ago.

The following are some of the important forces that have helped to create more truthful advertising:

(a) Better business methods
(b) Efforts of publishers
(c) Legal methods
(d) National Vigilance Committee
(e) Better business bureaus
(f) Association of National Advertisers
(g) American Association of Advertising Agencies

Better business methods have been the outgrowth of various trade associations, large businesses, and some of the more modern business codes. Various groups have established regulations of their own in relation to fair trade practices. These regulations include truthful advertising.

Magazine and newspaper publishers have raised the tone of advertising by setting certain standards of advertising, by eliminating particular types of advertising, and by investigating and testing through their own bureaus. Some publishers approve and even guarantee articles and services that they advertise.

In Chapter X the *Printers' Ink* Model Statute is mentioned as a barrier against dishonest advertising. This statute has been adopted in its original form in twenty-five states and in a modified form in thirteen additional states.

Since 1912 the affiliated advertising clubs have adopted a campaign for truth in advertising. In that year a National Vigilance Committee was appointed. The purpose of the committee is to eliminate objectionable and dishonest advertising and to promote higher ethics in the field of advertising. The committee gives wide publicity to its activities and encourages the enforcement of laws. Higher standards of ethics are encouraged among the members, and publications are urged to scrutinize advertising.

The better business bureaus are largely an outgrowth of the National Vigilance Committee. The various local bureaus, which are principally in the large cities, are affiliated with the National Better Business Bureau, of New York City. The purpose of a better business bureau is to protect the seller as well as the buyer. The bureau scrutinizes advertising and selling schemes carefully. It investigates complaints and aids in the prosecution of fraudulent schemes. Anyone has the privilege of reporting a complaint to a better business bureau. The National Better Business Bureau issues bulletins for the benefit of its members and the general public.

Good Advertising of Foods. The American Medical Association, through its Committee on Foods, has been instrumental in developing higher standards in the advertising of foods. The principles laid down by this association can be applied in general to all forms of advertising. The following is a brief summary of the general criteria of good advertising advocated by the Committee on Foods of the American Medical Association:

(a) The common name of the food should be used in the advertising; or if the product is sold under a trade name, the ingredients should be identified properly in the order of their decreasing proportions.
(b) Any statement of the physical, chemical, nutritional, or physiological properties or values of the food should be truthful and should be expressed in simple terms that the public can understand.
(c) Good advertising is free from false implications.
(d) It does not create incorrect or improper inferences with regard to foods, or lead to such comparisons between foods.
(e) It attempts to promote sales solely on the merits of the food article itself.
(f) It discusses nutritional values, but avoids specific claims concerning health.

For many years advertisements for goods purchased by manufacturers have been phrased in terms giving exact descriptions of those goods. At present some advertisers of consumers' goods are featuring in their advertisements pertinent statements on standards, specifications, and performance.

It is true that much advertising is far from being educational. The publishers of reliable newspapers and magazines scrutinize the advertisements that they accept and attempt to eliminate obviously fraudulent statements. The better business bureaus in some cities give publicity to stores that deliberately misrepresent their wares. In spite of these activities, however, the buyer must learn to read advertising critically if he expects to obtain information that is worth while.

Testimonials. It is common knowledge that debutantes, society leaders, political figures, film stars, and many other people prominently before the public eye have been guilty of selling their names and photographs for use in the testimonial advertising of various products. They have been paid in money, publicity, or other forms. In fact, there are agencies that make a business of arranging contracts with clients who are willing to sell their names and photographs for such purposes. Obviously, testimonials that are obtained and used promiscuously cannot be sincere. In evaluating testimonials, one must therefore take this common practice into consideration. If a consumer is going to judge a testimonial upon its merits, the testimonial should come from a person qualified by experience, training, and integrity.

Disapproved Advertising. The preceding discussion has mentioned various types of unscrupulous advertising. The following represent types of advertising that are reported by the Federal Trade Commission as meeting with its disapproval:

Patent medicines for incurable diseases
Appliances for the correction and the cure of bodily deformities
Anti-fat remedies
Hair restorers
Lotions, creams, and various other toilet preparations, advertised as capable of making impossible improvement in personal appearance
So-called puzzle advertisements that offer valuable inducements
Advertisements soliciting manuscripts and articles on which a copyright or a patent may be obtained
Lottery schemes disguised in countless ways
Matrimonial advertisements

Unfair Advertising. The truth-in-advertising movement is spreading each year. It is spreading rapidly because advertisers and publishers are realizing that consumers are insisting upon a higher type and a more truthful form of advertising. The Association of National Advertisers and the American Association of Advertising Agencies have established the following criteria of unfair advertising:

(a) False statements or misleading exaggerations
(b) Indirect misrepresentation of a product or a service through the distortion of details, either editorially or pictorially

(c) Statements or suggestions offensive to public decency
(d) Statements that tend to undermine an industry by attributing to its products, generally, faults and weaknesses true only of a few products
(e) Price claims that are misleading
(f) Pseudo-scientific advertising, including claims that are insufficiently supported by accepted authority or that distort the true meaning or application of a statement made by professional or scientific authority
(g) Testimonials that do not reflect the real choice of a competent witness

Federal Control of Advertising. An amendment to the Federal Trade Commission Act, which became effective on May 22, 1938, provides for Federal jurisdiction over false advertising. Among other forms of control, that amendment provides for the following, which are significant to the consumer:

(a) In general, all unfair methods of competition in commerce, as well as unfair or deceptive acts or practices, are declared unlawful.
(b) It is unlawful to disseminate false advertising in order to induce purchases of foods, drugs, devices, or cosmetics.
(c) Publishers, radio broadcasters, advertising agencies, and other advertising mediums are relieved from liability under the Federal Trade Commission Act unless they refuse to furnish the Commission with the name and the address of the manufacturer, packer, distributor, seller, or advertising agency that has accused the dissemination of such advertisements.
(d) False advertising is defined as being "misleading in a material respect," including the failure to reveal facts as to consequences that may result from the use of the advertised commodities.
(e) Products marked and labeled under the Meat Inspection Act are not covered by the new Act because the consumer is provided protection.

Some Absurdities of Advertising. Let us consider some of the tactics of those who write advertisements that are supposed to educate consumers and to induce them to buy.

Demands are placed upon the writers of advertising copy to use devices that will build up the maximum amount of emotion. Note just a few of the irrational appeals that are used: Turn to a page of a popular magazine and you will find the picture of a beautiful young woman with a statement that Miss So-and-So uses Such-and-Such face powder; turn to another page and you will see pictured an attractive young woman who is supposed to convey the idea that, if a particular product is good enough for her, it is good enough for you; turn to another page and you will find a grotesque picture warning you against dire results if you do not use a certain disinfectant or mouthwash. Search for statements relating to performance, quality, ingredients, and actual results.

Shallow Statements. Pictures are not the only devices used to convey certain emotional impressions. Headings, slogans, verse, and humorous quotations also serve that purpose. Here are some examples of slogans:

"The Standard of the World"
"The Most Beautiful Car in America"
"It's the Best"
"It Can't Be Beat"
"The Perfect Dentifrice"
"The Best Shoe Available"
"The Unusual Watch"
"Our Product Is Recognized as the Best"
"Better Than Any Others"

Do any of these convey definite assurance of quality, performance, or value? The answer is "No."

Headings are interesting. Slogans sometimes catch the eye. Verse and humorous statements are frequently amusing. But these should not be allowed to influence buying. One should read the advertisement carefully, and then learn something about the quality of the product, the contents, the cost, and the performance.

It has been said that the public likes to be fooled. Most buyers are influenced by tradition, and many lack the incentive to investigate for themselves. Instead of taking the initiative, they wait until the seller does so. Flattery and the appeal to envy often induce a prospective purchaser to buy without consideration of quality, cost, or utility.

Read Advertisements Carefully. In the face of all the money-getting activities of advertisers, the consumer is liable to become confused, discouraged, and skeptical. His first means of protection is to learn to read and to understand advertisements. He must distinguish between exaggerated, meaningless statements and honest, meaningful statements; between emotional appeals and rational appeals. If he does not learn to distinguish between nonsense and fact, he will be at the mercy of the professional advertiser.

An advertisement may not be intentionally dishonest. The person who wrote it and the company that sponsors it may be entirely honorable, but they may have been overzealous in their statements. Misleading statements in advertising are, however, usually the direct result of exaggeration, false implications, paid testimonials, and sometimes false association through the use of photographs or illustrations. One should always seek out the answers to the following questions:

(a) What does the product contain?
(b) Is it harmless?
(c) Is it beneficial?
(d) How long will it last?
(e) How economical is it?
(f) Do I need it?
(g) How does its price compare with the prices of similar products?
(h) Are any of the advertising statements evasive or misleading?
(i) What proof is used to back up the statements?

TEXTBOOK QUESTIONS

1. Name some of the types of advertising that are disapproved by the Federal Trade Commission.
2. (a) In what way does an advertiser benefit from truthfulness in advertising? (b) In what way do all advertisers benefit?
3. What are some of the important agencies or forces that have helped to create more truthful advertising?

4. What magazine has sponsored legislation against fraudulent advertising?
5. (a) What is the National Vigilance Committee? (b) What is its purpose?
6. What are some of the services rendered by better business bureaus?
7. Why is testimonial advertising often frowned upon?
8. (a) What jurisdiction does the Federal Government have over advertising? (b) By what agency is control over advertising administered?
9. Give examples of the irrational use of appeals in advertisements.
10. Give some examples of shallow, meaningless statements used in advertising.

DISCUSSION QUESTIONS

1. What information do you gain from superlative terms such as "best," "greatest," and "most modern" that you find in advertisements?
2. "Some advertisements are honest in content, but the products that are advertised are harmful." (a) Discuss this statement. (b) Do you think this situation is possible?
3. On whose testimonial for a certain medicine would you place the greatest amount of confidence: (a) the American Medical Association, (b) the superintendent of a hospital, (c) a patient who has used the medicine, (d) a foreign doctor, (e) a chemist in the laboratory in which the medicine is produced? Explain your answer.
4. What do you think hinders publishers from being strict in the enforcement of honesty in advertising?
5. Which do you think has more influence on the buyer: (a) the information on the label of a package containing a particular product; or (b) the advertising of the product that appears in magazines, newspapers, and other mediums?
6. Discuss some of the advantages and the disadvantages of brands or trade names from the point of view of the buyer.
7. What do you think of this guarantee: "We guarantee this product to give you satisfactory results"?
8. In your opinion why is it to the advantage of the Association of National Advertisers and the American Association of Advertising Agencies to establish criteria of unfair advertising?
9. How may testimonial advertising of athletes sometimes serve a useful purpose?
10. What may be at least part of the objective of advertising cigarettes on the same pages as the comic strips of Sunday newspapers?

Section III

Cautions Against Frauds in Advertising and Selling

Beware. Every consumer should be aware of the fact that there are always a few unscrupulous people who are trying to take advantage of others. Such persons devise schemes to obtain money dishonestly. Often these schemes are merely glittering promises that are never fulfilled; in other cases they represent devices of deliberate deception. The following discussion will disclose some typical frauds.

General Types of Frauds. The National Better Business Bureau and the local better business bureaus are active in suppressing frauds of various types. The Federal, state, and local governments are also constantly trying to break up dishonest practices. In the following paragraphs some typical frauds condemned by the National Better Business Bureau are explained.

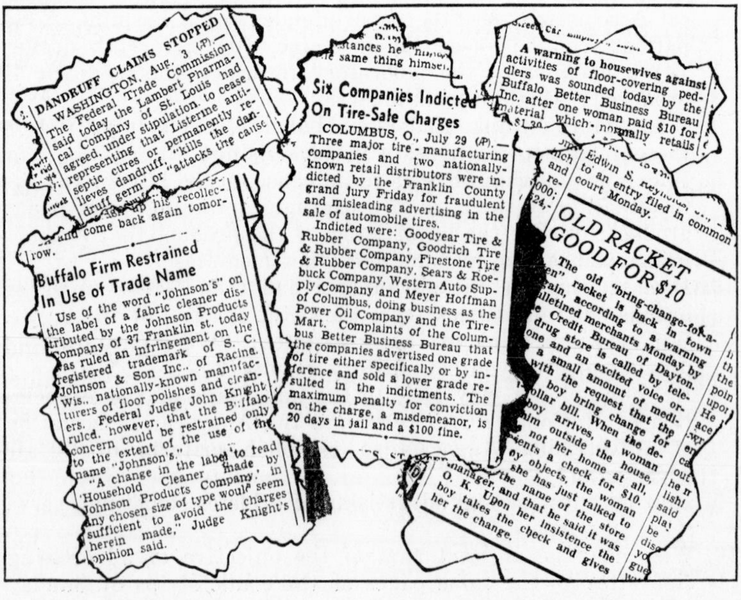

DANDRUFF CLAIMS STOPPED

WASHINGTON, Aug. 3 (AP).—The Federal Trade Commission said today the Lambert Pharmacal Company of St. Louis had agreed, under stipulation, to cease representing that Listerine antiseptic cures or permanently relieves dandruff, "kills the dandruff germ" or "attacks the cause

Buffalo Firm Restrained In Use of Trade Name

Use of the word "Johnson's" on the label of a fabric cleaner distributed by the Johnson Products Company of 37 Franklin st. today was ruled an infringement on the registered trademark of S. C. Johnson & Son Inc., of Racine, Wis., nationally-known manufacturers of floor polishes and cleaners. Federal Judge John Knight ruled, however, that the Buffalo concern could be restrained only to the extent of the use of the name "Johnson's."

"A change in the label to read 'Household Cleaner made by Johnson Products Company,' in any chosen size of type would seem sufficient to avoid the charges herein made," Judge Knight's opinion said.

Six Companies Indicted On Tire-Sale Charges

COLUMBUS, O., July 29 (AP).—Three major tire-manufacturing companies and two nationally-known retail distributors were indicted by the Franklin County grand jury Friday for fraudulent and misleading advertising in the sale of automobile tires.

Indicted were: Goodyear Tire & Rubber Company, Goodrich Tire & Rubber Company, Firestone Tire & Rubber Company, Sears & Roebuck Company, Western Auto Supply Company and Meyer Hoffman of Columbus, doing business as the Power Oil Company and the Tire-Mart. Complaints of the Columbus Better Business Bureau that the companies advertised one grade of tire either specifically or by inference and sold a lower grade resulted in the indictments. The maximum penalty for conviction on the charge, a misdemeanor, is 20 days in jail and a $100 fine.

A warning to housewives against activities of floor-covering peddlers was sounded today by the Buffalo Better Business Bureau Inc. after one woman paid $10 for material which normally retails

OLD RACKET GOOD FOR $10

The old "bring-change-for-a-...en" racket is back in town ...gain, according to a warning ...lletined merchants Monday by ...e Credit Bureau of Dayton. ...drug store is called by tele...one and an excited voice or...a small amount of medi...with the request that the ...boy bring change for ...ollar bill. When the de...boy arrives, a woman ...im outside the house, ...not her home at all, ...ents a check for $10. ...oy objects, the woman ...she has just talked to ...the name of the store ...ger, and that he said it was ...Upon her insistence the ...kes the check and gives ...change.

Illustration No. 112—Some Examples of Frauds

Work-at-home schemes. Nearly a million dollars was contributed by approximately twenty-five thousand people to two concerns operating work-at-home schemes. These concerns advertised widely that they would pay from fifteen to fifty dollars weekly to people who would color photographs at home during their spare time. Many of the advertisements began with these words: "Earn money at home." The concerns induced prospective home-workers to enroll in a short course of instruction, the tuition for which was thirty-five dollars or more. The majority of those persons who enrolled paid their tuition, but received no employment because they "failed" to complete the course. In this case an investigation should have been made before the money was paid.

Literary bureaus. Some so-called literary bureaus are willing to examine any manuscript, criticize it, and submit it to a market in return for a fee. Apparently it does not matter what the author writes, for the fee seems to be the main thing in which such a bureau is interested.

The National Better Business Bureau reports the experience of having a person write an illiterate and ridiculous story and submit it to three so-called literary bureaus. One of these bureaus responded as follows: "Your story was chosen by our manuscript department. I want to extend my personal congratulations. The way you have carried out your plot and handled your wording shows me your ability as a writer." The bureau then offered to prepare the manuscript for publication in return for what appeared to be a reasonable sum of money. It also told the author that it would reserve a twenty per cent commission in case the story was published.

Another bureau responded to the same author and indicated a willingness to help prepare the story for publication. It stated, "The story is hardly in shape to be brought to the attention of the publishers." It told the author that the story needed revision and correction, for which there would be a charge of thirty-five dollars.

Become a talking-picture actor. Advertisements have presented in glowing terms the possibilities of employment in the motion-picture industry. The reader of such an advertisement is encouraged to believe that the opportunity is open to him if he will merely undertake the training that is advertised.

An investigation made by the National Better Business Bureau disclosed that the producers of motion pictures are experiencing no difficulty in obtaining actors and do not anticipate any shortage in this respect. Furthermore, the producers believe that it is impossible to learn acting by correspondence.

Puzzle bait. Puzzle contests, which were formerly common, are rapidly dropping out of use because of their disrepute. They are frowned upon particularly by the Federal Trade Commission. In certain publications and localities, however, they are still used.

The common type of undesirable puzzle contest is that in which an automobile or cash is offered for solving what proves to be a rather simple puzzle. The unsuspecting contestant soon discovers, however, that he is expected to do much more before he even begins to approach the possibility of earning a prize. He is required to buy something, to sell something, or to obtain subscriptions for a publication. The sponsor of the contest usually requires him to continue this type of work for a long period of time in the hope that eventually he will drop out of the contest and will no longer be a contestant for the final prize. The last barrier between the contestant and the prize is a final test, which is sufficiently difficult to eliminate practically all contestants.

Publishers have begun to realize that contests of this type are detrimental to advertising and to the publications in which they appear. They are very damaging to public confidence.

Help wanted. Classified advertisements in some publications lead readers to believe that certain positions are available. The following advertisement is typical:

> STEAMSHIP POSITIONS—Positions on ocean liners to Europe and Orient. Good pay. Experience unnecessary.

The advertiser in this case was interested in selling a booklet outlining the procedure and the qualifications necessary to obtain a position on an ocean liner. Other advertisers hope to sell lists that explain how applicants can qualify for positions. Others offer training by correspondence upon the payment of a fee. Investigation usually discloses that there is no shortage of workers in any of the positions advertised.

Fictitious schools. All honorable and legitimate correspondence schools have been handicapped by unscrupulous correspondence schools, many of which have never existed in fact. Every new opportunity for education has brought with it at least a few schools that have been interested only in obtaining tuition fees from students. The fictitious telegraph schools, business schools, aviation schools, and schools of beauty culture provide some interesting examples. Legitimate schools, chambers of commerce, departments of education, publishers, and better business bureaus have coöperated in attempts to stamp out such unscrupulous schools; but in spite of these efforts new schools of the same nature are organized and operated at least for a short while.

Schools of this kind are frequently characterized by high-pressure salesmanship in obtaining students, fabulous promises of opportunities, and glaring statements that are impossible to prove. Some of the schools consist of no more than one or two people with a small office. Before enrolling in any correspondence school that is not known, a prospective student should investigate the school through some agency such as the better business bureau, the chamber of commerce, or the department of education in the state in which the school is located.

Puff sheets. The so-called puff sheet is supposedly a nationally known magazine, but is actually a special publication in which the promoters promise to publish, in return for a certain fee, an article extolling the good qualities of an individual. Solicitations for puff sheets are often made by telephone or telegraph in order to avoid possible action by postal authorities for using the mails to defraud. Many prominent men have paid from fifty to one thousand dollars to have their photographs and a write-up published in a magazine that supposedly has a large circulation, but that actually has little, if any, circulation.

Fictitious charitable solicitations. Numerous frauds have been promoted in the name of charity, often without the knowledge of the particular charitable institutions mentioned. The promoters use the name of a charitable organization and promise to collect a certain amount of money. They then proceed to put on an intensive campaign and collect a great amount of money, in some cases turning over to the charitable organization only 10 or 20 per cent.

Numerous solicitation schemes are conducted over the telephone to cover up identity. The promoters know that out of a certain number of calls they can expect some results. If the person solicited complains, they merely let him alone. The promoters are often afraid to solicit by mail because of Federal laws and city ordinances.

Frauds and Deception in Merchandising. Fortunately, most businessmen are just as honest as any other group of people; but, as there is always a number of businessmen who use deceptive practices, the buyer must beware. The following discussion presents some examples of deception used in advertising and merchandising.

Secondhand furniture sale. A furniture company, particularly one dealing in secondhand furniture, may rent a vacant house and then advertise that the family has moved and that the furniture must be sold immediately at sacrifice prices. The house is stocked with furniture. When people come to buy or to attend the auction, the furniture is sold at prices much higher than would ordinarily be obtained. In many communities there are laws against such a practice.

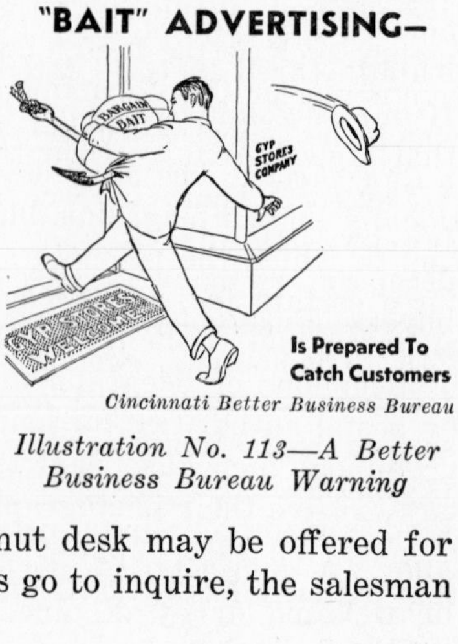

Cincinnati Better Business Bureau

Illustration No. 113—A Better Business Bureau Warning

Bait. It is a common practice in furniture stores and in many other types of stores to advertise a few genuine bargains. For example, a walnut desk may be offered for twelve dollars, but when buyers go to inquire, the salesman immediately begins to try to sell more expensive furniture. Upon inquiry he will state that he is sorry but the last twelve-dollar desk has been sold. He may be truthful; but the deception often lies in the fact that just a few of the genuine bargains were available and they were used as bait to draw people into the store. In some cases the bait is not even available for a few customers. The same practice is often carried out in other types of stores.

Misleading terminology. Investigation has often disclosed that so-called linen stationery advertised and sold as such is nothing more than paper stationery with a linen finish. So-called engraved stationery sometimes sold by letter shops and department stores or by direct mail is often nothing more than printed stationery.

Labels. There are as yet no ironclad regulations governing the labeling of many products to indicate the exact specifications. The buyer should therefore be sure to find out what he is buying. If clothing is supposed to be made of wool, find out what kind of wool has been used and whether it is pure wool or a mixture. If one is buying maple sirup, he should know whether he is getting pure maple sirup or a mixture of maple and cane sirup. If one is buying linen, he should know whether he is definitely getting linen or cotton or some other kind of fabric. Many of the so-called Oriental rugs sold by sidewalk shops, at amusement centers, and by house-to-house peddlers are manufactured in the United States from cheap materials. If one is going to buy an Oriental rug, he should realize that a good, genuine Oriental rug is expensive.

Jewelry. There is probably more deception in selling jewelry than in selling any other commodity. Much of this deception is made possible by ignorance on the part of buyers. Pure gold, for instance, is 24 carat, referred to as 24K. The common qualities of gold that is satisfactory for jewelry are 10K, 14K, and 18K. Pure 24-carat gold is seldom used. Much jewelry that is sold, including watches, is gold-filled or made of rolled gold plate. Jewelry of this kind is made of a base metal, such as brass or some other alloy. A gold plate is attached to the surface by brazing or welding, or by dipping the base metal into a molten gold alloy. An electric process is also used for depositing the gold on the base metal. The electric process is often referred to as gold-plating. Gold-plated jewelry usually contains the least amount of gold.

Silverware. Reliable merchants clearly distinguish between silver, silver-plated ware, and "silver" sold under such trade names as German Silver and Liberty Silver. So-called German Silver and Liberty Silver do not contain any silver. They are made of special alloys. Sterling silver is not pure silver, but it contains 925 parts of silver to 75 parts of copper. Silverware made of a solid silver alloy should indicate the amount of silver that it contains. For instance, sterling silver should be 925/1000 fine silver, but a piece of solid silver might contain 800/1000 fine silver. Silver-plated ware is a base metal coated with silver, usually deposited by an electric process. Genuine hand-wrought silver should be constructed by hand from a flat piece of silver.

Jewels. There is probably more deception in the selling of jewels than any other item of jewelry. One must first be aware that there are many synthetic or artificial stones. As the average individual cannot detect a synthetic stone from a genuine stone, he should buy his jewelry only from a reliable jeweler. The quality of diamonds is determined (a) by the kind of diamond, (b) by the weight, (c) by the cutting, and (d) by the flaws or degree of perfection. The kind of diamond is usually determined by the color or the lack of color. The best diamonds are supposedly clear and colorless. Some of the cheaper diamonds have a tinge of yellow. The color of surrounding objects will, however, often be reflected in the diamond and give it a bluish white cast or sometimes a yellow cast. It is therefore very difficult for the average person to judge the value of a diamond. The buyer must therefore depend largely upon a reliable jeweler.

TEXTBOOK QUESTIONS

1. Name some general types of frauds that are condemned by the National Better Business Bureau.
2. What is the so-called puzzle-bait advertising?

3. Why are help-wanted advertisements in some publications often frowned upon?
4. How are secondhand furniture sales sometimes deceptive?
5. Why is bait advertising of stores considered to be deceptive?
6. Give some examples of misleading terminology used in describing merchandise.
7. Give some examples of deception in selling gold jewelry.
8. What is German Silver?
9. Is sterling silver pure silver?
10. What are the factors that determine the quality of a diamond?

DISCUSSION QUESTIONS

1. How do you think you might distinguish a legitimate literary bureau from an illegitimate one?
2. What do you think of a school that advertises, "We guarantee a job at twenty-four hundred dollars a year after the completion of our course"?
3. How would you investigate an advertisement that holds out a great promise for future success in earning if instruction is taken in a particular institution?
4. Suppose that the head of your school is approached by an editor who promises to publish a write-up of the head of your school in his magazine upon the payment of one hundred dollars. Discuss the case.
5. Give some examples of terminology that is used in describing merchandise but that does not tell all the facts. Explain why some information is withheld.
6. How would you buy diamonds in order to avoid deception?
7. Explain why one should look carefully for the information stamped on pieces of silverware that are to be purchased.

PROBLEMS

1. In magazines or newspapers in your home find advertisements that contain appeals to (a) health, (b) beauty, (c) economy. Paste these on a sheet of paper, and write opposite each advertisement a brief notation indicating how the appeal is emphasized.
2. Bring to class an example of one of the types of advertisements disapproved of by the Federal Trade Commission. Indicate the source. Write a report giving your views as to whether the advertisement deserves to be placed in this classification or whether it is honest.
3. Bring to class two advertisements of similar products, one giving few or no specific facts and the other containing several facts. List for each advertisement the specific facts that

are given with regard to the product. If none are given, indicate the fact. If it is impossible to find two advertisements of similar products, select advertisements of different products and then complete the same work.

4. Bring to class a list of trade names taken from one current issue of a popular magazine. Opposite each name describe the corresponding product in a single sentence. Place a check mark before each of those trade names familiar to you.
5. Bring to class an advertisement that, in your opinion, illustrates one or more of the criteria of unfair advertising established by the Association of National Advertisers and the American Association of Advertising Agencies.
6. Bring to class an advertisement containing a testimonial that, in your opinion, is not sincere and that probably has been purchased. Give your reasons for your opinion.

COMMUNITY PROBLEMS AND PROJECTS

1. In many communities various groups of people—for instance, persons who contribute to charitable organizations—find that their names have been placed on "sucker lists," which are sold or lent for all types of soliciting. Soliciting bureaus often solicit contributions on a commission basis. Investigate to see if there are any such listing agencies in your community. Find out for what groups they conduct solicitations.
2. Investigate some promotional scheme in your community, and make a report on its merits. If possible, obtain some information from the investigation department of your local chamber of commerce, from your retail credit bureau, or from your better business bureau.
3. (a) From five magazines or newspapers make a list of all the high-sounding titles and terms used in advertising products. This list should include meaningless, but attractive, slogans and descriptive terms. (b) After listing these, analyze their truthfulness, their intent, and their usefulness from the point of view of the buyer.
4. If your community has a better business bureau, investigate the services available from this bureau. Also obtain a story of a service that has been performed locally to protect the public. Write a report on your findings.
5. Obtain a copy of a guarantee, and analyze the provisions of the guarantee. Prepare a report on its true value.
6. Learn from a magazine or a newspaper publisher what regulations are placed upon the acceptance of advertisements. Ask specific questions with regard to how the truthfulness of advertising is judged and investigated. Write a report of your findings.

CHAPTER XIII

METHODS AND TECHNIQUE OF BUYING

Purpose of the Chapter. Preceding chapters have attempted to present a background of information that everyone needs in learning where to obtain buying information and how to analyze influences on buying. Before taking up the study of buying specific products, it is necessary to learn something about the general technique of buying. The purpose of this chapter is to correlate and to apply the information presented in preceding chapters and to prepare for a study of the buying of typical products. This chapter therefore deals with the technique of shopping, of evaluating products, and of determining values. The principles discussed are applicable to all types of buying.

Comparison. At the time of purchase the buyer seldom has an opportunity to make comparisons. When there is opportunity for it, comparison may be made casually and hastily, or it may be well thought out and reasonably scientific. The more scientific the procedure, the more chance the buyer has of getting value for his money.

Intelligent buying demands the development of a consciousness of differences between products. One of many products may be good. Two products may be very similar. It is frequently difficult to determine the better of two products even under the most careful scrutiny. When such is the case, there is little danger of making an unwise selection.

What Is a Bargain? A bargain is not a bargain unless what one buys is needed and serves satisfactorily the purpose for which one buys it. Bargain hunters sometimes waste more money than thrifty purchasers who buy when they need merchandise. The habitual bargain hunter is sometimes inclined to buy something in anticipation of needing it, whereas he may never need it.

Legitimate Bargains. The following paragraphs explain types of bargain sales that are conducted by reputable stores. The buyer must learn from experience what stores really offer bargains when such sales are conducted.

Remnants are merchandise, usually yard goods, that a merchant is anxious to sell to avoid a loss. A remnant is a bargain if the total price paid for the piece is less than the cost of the actual quantity of goods needed. Buying a large remnant that cannot be used is not a bargain. *Mill ends,* short lengths of goods purchased by the merchant from a mill, are sometimes included in such sales.

Soiled goods placed on sale may be returned goods, shelf-worn goods, or sample merchandise. Such goods may represent true bargains; but if the merchandise requires dry cleaning or repairing, this additional cost should be taken into consideration.

Pre-season sales usually give the customer the advantage of obtaining seasonable merchandise in advance of the regular season. The merchandise is offered at a reduction in price in order to encourage the consumer to buy a little earlier. If one has the money to spend at that time, a saving will result.

Pre-inventory sales are conducted by merchants to reduce their stocks so that merchandise can be converted into cash and need not be carried over into a new season. Such a sale also helps to reduce the work of checking the inventory. Bargains can usually be obtained at these sales.

Out-of-season sales are sales of merchandise at the close of a season. For instance, summer clothing is often put on sale in July and August so that the merchant can clear out his stock and need not carry it over into the next summer season. Genuine bargains can be obtained at these sales if the clothing is of a color, a design, and a style that can be worn satisfactorily during the following summer. Extreme styles will, however, go out of date by that time.

Odd-lot sales are sales of odd sizes and irregular merchandise, such as seconds. The odd lots may consist of apparel of unusual sizes that the merchant cannot sell. A person can usually get a bargain at such a sale if the clothing is suitable in size. Irregular clothing or seconds should be examined carefully to see whether the flaws materially affect the value of the merchandise.

Sales of *surplus stock* sometimes result from the overproduction of mills or the overbuying of the merchant. The merchant may buy a special lot of merchandise from a mill at a low price and offer it as a sale, or he may attempt to unload his shelves to stimulate business during the regular season. Such sales usually provide bargains if the merchandise is what the buyer needs.

Questionable Bargains. The following paragraphs point out some questionable bargains. Although they may be legitimate, they should be considered with caution.

Auction sales are not always sales at which one will find bargains. There are two types of auctions. One is the kind in which an auctioneer closes out stock. The other is the continuous auction of regular merchandise. In neither case can one be assured of a bargain. He should be fairly familiar with values before attempting to bid on any product.

Fire sales and *bankrupt sales* in many communities are subterfuges to create a sensational sale. In some communities newspapers will not accept advertising for such sales unless the sales are legitimate. Where there are better business bureaus, such sales are scrutinized carefully. In many communities, however, frequent fire sales or bankrupt sales by the same store can be recalled. Some of these sales seem to last indefinitely. At legitimate fire sales or bankrupt sales, one may find bargains.

So-called *direct selling* is not always direct selling. Many stores and house-to-house agents claim that they have direct connection with manufacturers and are therefore able to sell at lower prices. If one understands the economics of marketing, he will see that direct selling does not necessarily reduce costs. In evaluating merchandise sold in this manner, one should ignore claims of saving and inspect the merchandise.

Buying at *wholesale* is not always what it appears to be. If someone offers to sell you at wholesale, you can be sure that the procedure is an unfair trade practice and should be looked upon with skepticism. If a standard product is bought in this way at a reduced price, it probably is a bargain; but chances are that no service or repairs can be obtained through any legitimate retailer. So-called wholesale outlets for the consumer are often subterfuges.

Cincinnati Better Business Bureau

Illustration No. 114—Goods Bought at "Wholesale" May Not Be Bargains

When to Buy. The preceding discussion of various types of sales gives some ideas as to when to buy. For instance, it is easy to observe that seasonal goods usually run through a definite cycle in price level. When offered in advance sales, they are usually sold at reduced prices. The buyer who is especially interested in the style of his clothing can frequently take advantage of such sales. At the beginning of a season style goods sell at the highest prices. As the season progresses, the prices are gradually lowered, for merchants hope to dispose of their goods before the end of the season.

There are important price cycles for many other products. For instance, in cities in which coal is used for heating purposes, it is usually sold at its lowest price in April and May and at its maximum price during the winter months. It sells at a low price in the spring and the summer because then the rate of consumption is low and dealers are anxious to make sales and deliveries.

Fresh fruits and vegetables usually sell at the cheapest prices during the summer. The prices of canned goods are lowest soon after the canning season. Illustration No. 115 shows the seasonal trends in the prices of some of the most common food products. This illustration shows that there is a variation in the high and the low prices of different products. As one might suspect, products that are most difficult to store have wide fluctuations in price.

Some Policies in Buying. In determining how to buy, let us think in terms of shopping procedure. The saving of time, energy, and money are the points to be considered in shopping procedure. The saving of money may be the primary consideration of one buyer, whereas the saving of time may be an important consideration of another. For instance, the buyer may save time and energy by ordering by telephone, but he may pay extra for delivery service and may not get the benefit of personal selection.

Consumers' Guide

Illustration No. 115—Seasonal Price Trends of Common Foods

Buying in large quantities rather than in small quantities usually is desirable, provided the large quantities are needed. People who buy small lots of groceries from day to day, or even several times a day, are causing an economic waste of time and are paying more per unit than persons who buy in larger quantities. A housewife will, however, find it desirable to buy food in small quantities if larger quantities would spoil before they could be used.

Seasonal buying and quantity buying go hand in hand. In other words, if a person decides to enjoy the advantage of buying canned goods when prices are low, he must buy a relatively large quantity in order to profit by the reduced prices. Many families buy whole cases of canned foods at the end of the canning season and store these for use during the winter. Others buy potatoes in large quantities and store them in a place where they will not spoil. Such persons are able to take advantage of the saving made possible by the reduced prices.

The size of the package is an important element in the cost. Obviously, it costs more to put a certain food product into ten small cans than it does in one large can. In some instances, therefore, the cost of the package is an extremely important factor. Some foods that are ordinarily offered for sale in packages can be bought more economically in bulk. This factor will be studied in detail in a later chapter.

No definite rules can be laid down for buying, because there are many variables. Different quantities must be bought for families of varying sizes. The quantity to be bought will depend upon the amount of money available and upon the peculiar needs of the family. The following is, however, a list of recommendations for guidance in buying foods and household supplies:

(a) Buy in as large quantities as can be stored conveniently and used without waste from spoilage.
(b) Keep informed of the regular prices of staple foods and household supplies in order to gauge the savings that will be possible through taking advantage of special sales.
(c) Watch market conditions and know whether the general price trend is upward or downward. Take advantage of seasonal low points and of rising markets for quantity buying.
(d) Consider the value of time and effort, as well as money,
    (1) When deciding between charge-and-delivery and cash-and-carry stores.
    (2) When deciding whether to buy in large or small quantities.
    (3) When deciding whether to buy in bulk or in packages.
(e) Keep on hand an emergency supply of foods that will provide at least one meal on short notice. A larger supply, however, is usually advisable.

Where to Buy. The selection of a suitable market is an important factor in determining how to buy. Some of the indications of a good place at which to buy are as follows:

(a) A wide range of varieties, sizes, and qualities
(b) Labels and standards that aid in making intelligent selections
(c) Shopping conveniences that save time and energy
(d) Fair prices based on the quality and the service
(e) Services such as credit and delivery
(f) Reliability
(g) Courteous treatment

Returning Merchandise. Many merchants are confronted with the serious problem of accepting or rejecting merchandise that is returned by buyers. Sometimes this problem arises through the fault of the buyer; at other times it results from that of the seller. Usually the buyer is indirectly at fault because of his failure to examine the merchandise carefully before buying. Sometimes merchandise is returned because the buyer feels he has been misled.

When merchandise is returned, most stores accept it as a matter of policy provided it has not been used or damaged by the purchaser. The customer has no legal right to return merchandise unless he made the purchase with that understanding. An exception may be made when the merchandise is not in accordance with the implied, the stated, or the written warranty. In such a case the merchant must accept the return of the merchandise.

Merchandise should be returned in good condition to protect the store from a loss. The returning of merchandise has become a wasteful and unfair practice in many communities. The ordinary returning of merchandise should be considered as a privilege that should not be abused.

Trade Names. The modern development of science has brought with it a variety of new products, many of which are but imitations sold under trade names. For example, artificial silk is not silk; its common trade name is *rayon.* In addition to these synthetic products there are variations in products made from the same basic material. Advertisements and labels that describe products may not, and probably do not, disclose the particular quality unless it is of the best.

Wool cloth, for instance, may be made from (a) long fleece, (b) short fleece, or (c) part wool. The dictionary defines parchment as the skin of a sheep. Parchment paper and parchment lamp shades, however, are very seldom made of skin; they are usually made of paper. Chinaware usually does not come from China; the word designates a type of clay from which the pottery is made. The product may or may not be better than a similar product made in China. Silverware is not sterling silver, but usually plated ware. Sterling silver is solid silver. For other examples of trade names of furs and fabrics, refer to Chapter XV.

Grade Designations. Until uniform grade standards have been established and are used for all products, it is impossible to rely upon the existing grade designations without knowing what those grades mean. Much of the terminology in use means one thing to the seller, but a different thing to the buyer. If the buyer takes the words at their face value, he is frequently misled into believing the goods to be of a grade higher than they actually are. Furthermore, the terminology is made confusing by the wide variation in its use. In other words, buyers and sellers do not speak the same language. When this situation exists, grade designations are of very little value.

For instance, if Mr. Jones, the neighborhood grocer, buys *fancy* asparagus, he gets the sixth, or poorest, grade. If he buys *extra fancy* asparagus, he obtains the fifth grade. The highest grade, however, is designated as *colossal.*

One would suppose that the *first* grade of butter is the best grade, but as a matter of fact it is the third grade when compared with governmental standards. To get the best grade of butter, one has to buy the *extra* grade. Similar confusing grades are used for other products.

Such grade designations differ according to the products. It is therefore impossible for the average person to understand all the details of grade designations without making a study of the matter. Bulletins on this subject are available through the Federal Government and through various associations organized by consumers. Chapter XIV provides more detailed information on grade designations.

How to Read the Label. The buyer should read labels carefully to obtain information with regard to (a) the weight or the volume, (b) the grade or the quality, and (c) an analysis or a description of the contents. The labels of some private agencies have been discussed previously.

As was explained in a preceding chapter, the Federal Food and Drug Administration protects the consumer from obtaining adulterated and misbranded products. Under the Federal law the labels on foods and drugs must not mislead consumers. For instance, if an article is artificially colored, this fact must be indicated on the label. All imitations must be definitely indicated. Ingredients in imitations must be declared. Although an imitation product may be wholesome, it is usually inferior to the genuine product. If the consumer is to realize the full benefit of such protection, however, he must learn to read labels accurately.

Suppose, for example, that you ask for a bottle of vanilla and are handed a bottle marked "Vanillin Extract." What does this name mean? It really means that the bottle contains a flavoring material that is a synthetic coal-tar product, whereas the genuine product is made from the vanilla bean. If the extract is colored to imitate genuine vanilla extract, this fact should be indicated on the bottle. The names of some other products are also misleading.

If you ask for egg noodles and are given a package merely labeled "Noodles," you are not getting what you requested. Egg noodles must contain egg solids to the extent of 5½ per cent by weight. Plain noodles contain no egg products.

When you buy jams, jellies, and preserves, do the labels on the containers mean anything to you? Do you expect to get pure fruits and sugar? If you wish to be sure to obtain a product containing nothing but pure fruit and sugar, you should buy one that has a label indicating what you desire. The product should contain not less than 45 per cent of fruit and not more than 55 per cent of sugar. It should not be an imitation and should not be artificially colored or flavored. If it is a pure food, it will not contain glucose, or pectin, or any other added ingredient. If preserves contain only 25 per cent of fruit with 75 per cent of sugar, water, additional pectin, and acid, you are paying largely for sugar and substitutes instead of for fruit. Many other examples could be cited, but the main purpose of this discussion is to point out the necessity for studying labels.

Specifications on Labels. The Federal Trade Commission now has the power to prevent deception in packaging and labeling and also has the power to prevent fraudulent claims on labels. These powers apply only to products sold in interstate commerce. The new Federal Food, Drug, and Cosmetic Act might be considered to be a companion act to the Federal Trade Commission Act. It not only makes it unlawful to sell harmful foods, drugs, and cosmetics in interstate commerce, but it also provides many new regulations governing the labeling of those products.

Under the new Federal Food, Drug, and Cosmetic Act, standards are being developed as rapidly as possible for foods that are sold in interstate commerce. When these standards have been established, they will have the full force of law and will require that a definite statement of contents be placed on labels.

Various state laws set definite standards for products sold within the corresponding states and require definite specifications on the labels. Through the demands of buyers, reliable specifications are being used to an increasing extent on many goods not covered by Federal and state laws. Unless these specifications are understood, however, they are of no value. If the standards are those prescribed by some association or by the Government, they can be relied upon. If they merely represent the standards of manufacturers, they cannot be used as a guide in determining quality. For instance, a grade that one manufacturer might designate as Superb may actually be a relatively low grade.

Various organizations are co-operating in establishing voluntary labeling so that the consumer will be enlightened as to quality. For instance, the Consumer-Retailer Relations Council is gradually developing specifications for the labels on many items sold through dry goods and department stores. This council is composed of several organizations representing consumers, as well as of the National Retail Dry Goods Association and the National Better Business Bureau.

The Committee on Foods of the American Medical Association advocates that specific information be given on the labels of all foods. The information recommended for the ideal type of label is shown in Illustration No. 116. This label can be used as a guide in examining others.

IDEAL LABEL FOR FOODS

(Skeleton outline for main panel faces)

COMMON NAME OF FOOD

*(Statement of added minor ingredients)

Example:

RICE FLAKES

*(Flavored with sugar, malt and salt)

—OR—

FANCIFUL TRADE NAME

*(Descriptive statement identifying ingredients)

Example:

BLANCO

*(Sugar, dried fruit, eggs and milk)

ADDITIONAL INFORMATION OF A SPECIAL CHARACTER

NET CONTENTS

NAME OF MANUFACTURER, PACKER, OR DISTRIBUTOR

*NOTE: Ingredients arranged in order of decreasing proportions.

Illustration No. 116

The contents indicated on labels are also important, for the size of the container is frequently misleading. Deceptive containers are now illegal if the products are sold in interstate commerce. In examining a label, one should look for the following information:

(a) Specific descriptive statements
(b) Facts regarding quality
(c) Facts regarding quantity
(d) Grades or other similar designations
(e) Certificate or other mark of approval

Trade-Marks. A trade-mark is used for one purpose only: to encourage people to ask for the product again after using it the first time. The manufacturer of an established brand therefore usually strives to fulfill certain standards that the consumer will expect to obtain when he buys the product. In the absence of information that would permit comparison, the recognized brands of reputable producers are usually more reliable than other brands. If other information is available, however, the brand on a product should not be used as the only means of comparison. Furthermore, the branding of a product may cause a purchaser to pay more than he would have to pay for another product of an equivalent quality.

Personal Inspection. Personal inspection is the most common method used by consumers in buying products. It is valuable only so far as the consumer is capable of comparing one product with another and rationally deciding which represents the greater value. Personal inspection requires a personal knowledge of materials, workmanship, style, finish, and age. A detailed discussion of tests that will aid in personal inspection is given in a subsequent chapter.

Trial Use. Purchasing on the basis of sample is more common in the case of products of small-unit value than in those of high-unit value. Obviously, the purchasing of an article with a high-unit value requires careful consideration because such purchases are made infrequently. In buying a product such as an automobile, the consumer should make the trial before the purchase rather than afterwards. In buying a food product, the consumer may try out a small sample before buying a larger quantity. Occasionally it is possible to try out a free sample before buying, and in some cases it is possible to return a product if it is not satisfactory. A decision based on trial is valuable only to the extent of the purchaser's knowledge of what standards to expect. The other points mentioned in this chapter should therefore be considered during the trial of a product. When there is an opportunity for trial, take advantage of it.

Advertising. Advertising may or may not be a desirable source of information on a product. It is, however, one of the most common sources of information and should therefore be considered seriously. The purchaser is usually unconsciously, and often consciously, influenced by advertisements. In reading advertisements for information on products, a person must remember that two types of appeal are used by advertisers. One appeal is to the emotions so as to encourage buying without thinking; the other is to the sense of reasoning. When the latter type of appeal is used, the advertisement should tell specifically what a product will do and how it will do it.

In studying an advertisement for information on a product, there is therefore only one type of information to be considered. That is the information that tells specifically and frankly what the product is, what it will do, and how it will do it. This information should then be considered in the light of the scientific information that is at the disposal of the consumer for comparing this product with others.

Demonstration. Demonstrations were formerly considered to be applicable only to mechanical products; but they are now applied to food products, pharmaceutical products, and cosmetics. In watching the demonstration of a cosmetic, one should ask oneself, "What will be the effect?" rather than merely, "How is it done?" In watching a demonstration of a food product, such as baking powder, the buyer should ask himself, "In what way does this product differ from other products?"

In observing demonstrations of mechanical appliances, it is usually possible to make comparisons. No wise purchaser will select the first make that he has examined. He should watch the demonstration of more than one make. The more demonstrations he observes, the greater chances there are that he will get his money's worth. Through a demonstration of a mechanical appliance, for instance, he gets specific information with regard to original cost, performance, cost of operation, length of life, amount of service, guarantee, workmanship, finish, and chance of obsolescence. If possible, the information obtained from a demonstration should be supplemented by that obtained from unbiased users of the product being considered.

A person may not be sufficiently familiar with workmanship and finish to be able to judge a single product, but a comparison with other similar products will give some basis for judgment. The free service furnished with an appliance can be evaluated definitely. The cost of extra service is very important. The amount that other users of the product have had to pay for service is measurable.

Obsolescence is one of the important elements to be considered. In many cases obsolescence occurs when the manufacturer of the product has gone out of business. Under such circumstances it usually becomes difficult or impossible to obtain replacements or proper service for the product. Such a product is referred to as an "orphan."

Salespeople. The prospective buyer should remember that the primary objective of a salesperson is to sell something. Before he buys, he should therefore have a reasonable conception of what he wants. He should not buy the first article he sees unless it measures up to his expectations in every detail. Furthermore, he should know clearly the distinction between high-pressure selling and courteous, considerate selling.

Intelligent salespeople can and will give information if it is demanded. Sales propaganda should, however, not be confused with real sales information. One should distinguish between glowing terms that paint a beautiful picture without telling what the product will do for the prospective buyer and facts that show what it has done for others.

The prospective buyer should ask questions and see that his questions are not avoided. If, in examining a product, a person does not readily observe what he wants to know, he should ask the salesperson. The failure of the latter to give a satisfactory answer will be based on lack of knowledge or on unwillingness to tell the truth.

Information from the Producer or the Distributor. The well-informed agent or salesperson will usually be able to give the desired information about a product. If a person wishes to buy a product that he will use frequently, or one that will cost a large sum of money, he should determine definitely the quality and the value of the product. If he cannot get this information from the agent or the salesperson, he should write to the producer or the distributor. He may ask for information on performance records, guarantees, specifications, and tests.

Laboratory Tests. Laboratory tests of products are conducted by numerous governmental and private agencies. Tests of this type and the services that can be obtained through such agencies are described in Chapters X and XI. To a limited extent individuals can make simple tests in their own homes. Some tests of the latter type are mentioned in Chapter XV.

TEXTBOOK QUESTIONS

1. Enumerate some bargains that are genuine bargains if they are legitimate.
2. Enumerate some types of so-called bargains that are often questionable.
3. (a) What kind of special sale is advantageous to the person who is interested in style? (b) What kind of sale is advantageous to the person who is not interested in style?
4. As a season progresses, why do merchants gradually reduce the prices of their seasonal merchandise?
5. Are the price cycles for various products the same?
6. What is the result of buying frequently and in small quantities?
7. Under what circumstances is it desirable to buy food in small quantities?
8. How can the person who has surplus funds take advantage of the price cycle in buying foods?
9. Under what circumstances has a buyer the right to return merchandise?
10. What are the criteria by which you can select a good place at which to buy?
11. (a) Can trade names be followed as guides in buying? (b) In what way?
12. What handicap is there in relying on grade designations?
13. What special types of labels are helpful guides to consumers although they do not show any specifications?

14. What kind of information is sometimes provided on the labels of clothing?
15. What information does the Committee on Foods of the American Medical Association recommend be placed on the labels of all foods?
16. Why are trade-marks used?
17. Name some products that can be bought on the basis of trial use.
18. How effective is advertising as a guide in determining the quality of a product?
19. Why would you not want to buy an "orphan" product?

DISCUSSION QUESTIONS

1. Some people are interested in style and are not particularly concerned with price. They buy when a product is at its highest price. How do after-season sales and special sales benefit such people?
2. Name some of the reasons why you should expect to pay less when you deal at cash-and-carry stores.
3. To what extent does experience in buying and using commodities serve as an adequate guide in making purchases? (a) Suppose an article is expensive and will normally last many years. Will the consumer's experience in buying that article be of any value to him? (b) Suppose an article of a relatively low price is used frequently and bought rather often. Will the consumer's experience in buying that article be adequate as a guide? (c) Suppose an article such as tooth paste is bought frequently. Will the consumer's experience in buying that article be a suitable guide in making purchases?
4. What are some of the limitations to the benefits derived from buying in order to take advantage of low prices during price cycles?
5. On Saturday a man and his wife buy groceries from a cash-and-carry store and haul them home in their automobile. During the week the wife needs miscellaneous supplies. She telephones another grocery and has the supplies delivered. What do you think of this practice?
6. Mrs. Jones prides herself on buying only nationally advertised goods. (a) What do you think of her practice? (b) Is she following good judgment? Why?
7. A woman bought a dress but later found another made from the same pattern and cloth in a different store for two dollars less. How do you account for the difference in price?
8. How would a knowledge of the nutritional values of foods aid in budgeting family purchases of food?

9. Discuss the advantages and the disadvantages of trade names.
10. What do these grade names mean to you: Fancy, Grade A, Extra Fancy, Superb?
11. If you went into a strange grocery store for the purpose of buying peas, and found on the shelf two brands of peas, one of which was well known to you and the other was not known, what procedure would you follow in buying? Why?
12. (a) Name some products that do not lend themselves to trial use before the purchase is made. (b) Why do they not?
13. (a) In what ways do you think you could rely on the opinions of your friends and neighbors in buying? (b) In what ways do you think it would be unwise to rely on their opinions?

PROBLEMS

1. Take a label from a can, and, on the basis of the ideal type of label recommended by the American Medical Association, reconstruct the label to make it conform to the specifications of the association. Use a separate sheet of paper for your new sketch of the label.
2. Examine some advertisements of clothing in magazines or newspapers, and select one. Submit a report on the facts that are disclosed with regard to quality, grade, and other definite specifications.
3. Examine advertisements of household equipment such as food mixers, cooking stoves, electric cleaners, and washing machines. Write a report on the basis of one of the advertisements. Point out what specific facts are available that will guide a buyer, or what information should have been given.

COMMUNITY PROBLEMS AND PROJECTS

1. Over a period of a week examine all the products purchased by your family, and determine how many products are marked with (a) the seal of some organization such as the American Medical Association or the Good Housekeeping Institute, (b) governmental standards, (c) manufacturer's standards. List also any unintelligible grade markings and any superlative statements on quality.
2. Find out how many products in a local store are marked with (a) the seal or the label of some organization such as the American Medical Association or the Good Housekeeping Institute, (b) governmental standards, (c) the standards of some organization. List also some unintelligible grade markings and some superlative statements on the quality of other products.

CHAPTER XIV

HOW TO BUY FOODS

Purpose of the Chapter. The buying of foods is an important business problem in every family. It is not possible in a short time to make a detailed study of standards and methods of buying, and of each type of food. There are many varieties of food and many variations in quality. If a person expects, however, to spend his money wisely, he should understand certain fundamentals with regard to quality and the technique of buying. The purpose of this chapter is, therefore, to point out some of the most common problems relative to the buying of food and to discuss ways in which these problems may be solved.

Section I

Buying Packaged Foods

Standards of Canned Foods. As rapidly as standards for foods are established by the Federal Government, all foods sold in interstate commerce must measure up to these standards. Standards have been established for such canned foods as peaches, pears, peas, tomatoes, apricots, and cherries. The new Federal Food, Drug, and Cosmetic Act provides for establishing, as rapidly as possible, standards for many other foods. After standards have been established for a canned vegetable, any food of that type entering into interstate commerce that does not measure up to the lowest standard must have printed on the label the words "Below U. S. Standard. Low quality but not illegal." A canned fruit that does not measure up to the lowest standard must bear on its label "Below U. S. Standard. Good food—not high grade." These regulations do not yet govern products that are not sold in interstate commerce. Additional regulations have been established, however, by various associations of canners and by state governments.

This discussion should not lead to the assumption that everyone must buy the best grades of canned food. In fact, canned food of the lowest grade is wholesome, but it is not suitable for all purposes. For example, the lowest grade of canned fruit may have the same proportions of fruit and juice as the higher grades; but the fruit may not be uniform in size, color, or maturity. Some of the fruit may be broken. There may be halves and quarters instead of whole fruit or halves. The better grades are ordinarily used for fancy desserts and salads, while the lowest grade is usually satisfactory for pies and other pastries. For the average family the higher grades are not recommended. The same principles apply to canned vegetables.

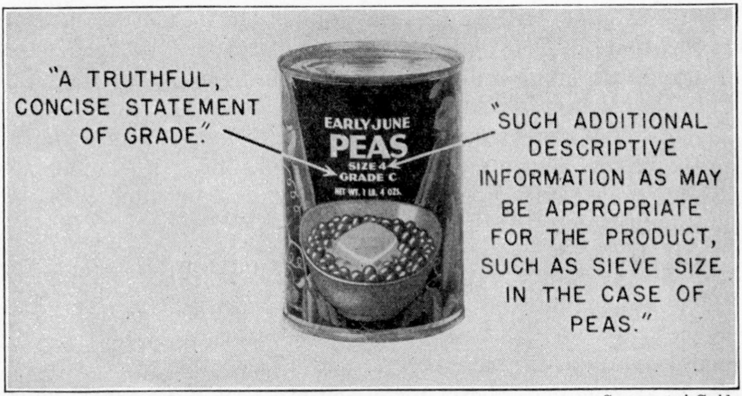

Consumers' Guide

Illustration No. 117—An Intelligible Food Label

Adulterated Foods. In general, the Federal Food, Drug, and Cosmetic Act prohibits the sale of foods that contain a poisonous or otherwise harmful substance, or that contain any decayed substance. Some foods naturally contain a certain amount of harmful substance; but if such foods are ordinarily not injurious to health, they may be acceptable. Manufacturers are prohibited from abstracting a valuable constituent from a food and substituting partially or totally some other substance. If a product has been damaged or if it is inferior, that fact must be disclosed. If any substance has been added or mixed to increase the bulk or the weight, or to reduce the quality or the strength so as to make the food appear of greater value, that food is considered to be adulterated. In general, a food may not contain a coal-tar coloring unless that fact is certified according to the law. There are also other minor regulations.

It must be borne in mind that, if a food is manufactured and sold within the boundaries of a particular state and is not shipped to another state, it is not subject to these regulations but may be subject to state regulations.

Misbranded Foods. Under the Federal Food, Drug, and Cosmetic Act a food is considered to be misbranded under any of the following conditions:

(a) If its labeling is false or misleading in any particular.

(b) If it is offered for sale under the name of another food.

(c) If it is an imitation of another food, and its label does not bear, in type of uniform size and prominence, the word *imitation* with, immediately thereafter, the name of the food imitated.

(d) If its container is so made, formed, or filled as to be misleading.

(e) If it is in a package that does not bear a label (1) showing the name and the place of business of the manufacturer, the packer, or the distributor, and (2) containing an accurate statement of the quantity of the contents in terms of weight, measure, or numerical count. Under clause (2), however, reasonable variations may be permitted, and exemptions as to small packages may be established, under regulations prescribed by the Secretary of Agriculture.

(f) If any word, statement, or information that is required, by or under authority of the Act, to be placed on the label is not prominently shown thereon.

(g) If the food purports to be one for which a standard has been established, but fails to conform to that standard.

(h) If the food is one for which a standard of quality has been established, but it falls below that standard and does not bear a label indicating the substandard grade.

(i) If the label fails to bear the common or usual name of the particular food.
(j) If the food is fabricated from two or more ingredients, and the label fails to indicate these ingredients.
(k) If the food purports to be or is represented for special dietary uses, but its label does not bear such information concerning its vitamin, mineral, and other dietary properties as the Secretary determines to be, and by regulations prescribes as, necessary in order to inform purchasers fully as to the value of the food for such uses.
(l) If the food contains any artificial flavoring, artificial coloring, or chemical preservative, but its label does not state that fact.

These regulations do not apply to a product manufactured and sold within a particular state; but state laws, if there are any, do apply to such a product.

Grades of Canned Fruits. Under the Federal Food and Drug Administration, standard grades have been established for canned fruits. The grade markings do not appear on the labels of all canned fruits, but they do appear on the labels of many. The purchaser has a right to demand canned fruits that have such markings; in fact, he should insist upon them as a protection.

The table in Illustration No. 118 provides an explanation of the grades for canned fruits. This method of indicating grades is commonly known as the ABC method of grading. Other methods have been established by various associations, canners, and distributors; but there is no particular uniformity among the standards set up under these methods.

Grades of Canned Vegetables. The United States Department of Agriculture has established standards for such products as canned corn, peas, beans, and tomatoes. New standards are being established constantly. The table in Illustration No. 119 describes various grades. Many canners are voluntarily labeling their products according to these designations.

Canned fruits and vegetables of the fancy grade are uniform in size, color, and texture. They represent the perfect portion of the crop. The choice fruits and the extra-standard vegetables are next best, while the standard products rank third. The better grades are usually packed in better juice. Additional designations are used in grading such products as asparagus, corn, and peas.

GRADE	QUALITY	COLOR	FORM	SIZE	SIRUP WHEN PACKED
A (fancy)	Very best	Very high	Free from blemishes; mature but not overripe	Very uniform and symmetrical	From 40 to 70 per cent sugar, depending on acidity of fruit
B (choice)	Fine	High	Free from blemishes; mature but not overripe	Uniform, symmetrical, usually smaller than A	From 30 to 55 per cent sugar
C (standard)	Good	Reasonably good	Reasonably free from blemishes; reasonably uniform in ripeness	Reasonably uniform and symmetrical	From 14 to 30 per cent sugar, or water pack
Sub-standard	Second	Below standard	Below standard; not uniform	Below standard; not uniform	Below standard for sirup or water pack

Illustration No. 118—Quality Grades for Canned Fruits

GRADE	QUALITY	COLOR	FORM	SIZE	LIQUOR
A (fancy)	Finest; of uniform quality	Uniformly good	Uniform; very tender	Uniform	Clear or only slightly turbid
B (extra standard)	Sound; of good stock	Practically free from under-colored parts	Practically uniform; tender	Practically uniform	May be some discoloration
C (standard)	May be field run of good stock	May be slightly discolored	Some may have been broken in processing	Need not be uniform	May be somewhat turbid
Sub-standard	Second	Below standard	Below standard; not uniform	Below standard; not uniform	Below standard; not clear

Illustration No. 119—Quality Grades for Canned Vegetables

Meaningless Designations. Consumers should not be misled by such designations as Extra Special, Exquisite, Superb, Supreme, Superior, Select, Our Best, or any other designation that has no recognized meaning. These are terms selected by packers or distributors. Consumers should look for standard designations such as Grades A, B, and C, or Fancy, Extra Standard, Choice, or Standard. If the contents of the can have been graded according to size (as in the case of beans or peas), the size number should be observed. The size number (1, 2, 3, or 4) will not indicate the specific size, but it will provide a basis for judging the relative size.

If a canner or a distributor marks foods according to the governmental grades, the foods must conform to the governmental standards for these grades. In one year, however, Grade A may not indicate exactly the same quality as it did in another year. For instance, if a crop of peas produced in one year is of unusually high quality and the crop of the next year is of a generally low quality because of growing conditions, the Grade A peas in the second year will not be of exactly the same quality as the Grade A peas of the previous year. The crop for any particular year is divided into various grades that are relative to one another. This fact is largely true also of size designations. Therefore, grades and sizes are not always the same.

Consumers' Guide reports a survey made by a group of consumers in answer to the question, "Does the price mark on canned foods tell the quality of the product?" The survey was based on an examination of about one hundred and fifty cans of peas, corn, and tomatoes, which had been purchased at different stores in the regular manner. The cans did not bear grade markings of the Federal Government; some of them bore various meaningless grade designations. The cans were opened, and the vegetables were examined on the basis of governmental standards. The study disclosed definitely that paying a high price for a canned food that is not graded according to governmental standards does not necessarily ensure obtaining a good product. Another investigation by *Consumers' Guide* disclosed the fact that canned green beans of almost uniform quality were distributed by the same company in two different cans of the same sizes, and were sold in the same stores in Washington, D. C. One can was priced at thirteen cents, whereas the other was priced at only eight and a third

PRICE CLASS	SUB-STANDARD	GRADE C	GRADE B	GRADE A
17½ to 20 cents	......	4 cans	3 cans	......
15 to 17½ cents	......	7 cans	4 cans	......
12½ to 15 cents	2 cans	3 cans	8 cans	1 can
8 to 12½ cents	8 cans	6 cans	1 can	......

Illustration No. 120—The Price Does Not Indicate the Grade

cents. The price of the beans therefore was no indication of their quality.

The table in Illustration No. 120 is an analysis of forty-seven cans of peas that were purchased at prices ranging from eight cents to twenty cents a can.

It is evident from this analysis that price was no indication of quality. There was only one Grade A can of peas out of the forty-seven, this particular can having been bought for thirteen cents. In the higher-priced groups there were no cans of Grade A.

Furthermore, the labeling of the cans provided no guide to quality. Six of the cans were marked Fancy, but four of these were of Grade B and two of Grade C. Brand names were also unreliable. For example, four cans were branded in identically the same way; but one was of Grade A, two were of Grade B, and the fourth was of Grade C. Although brand names proved unreliable in this case, they are not, however, disqualified as guides in all cases. If a person learns to depend upon a particular brand name as indicative of good quality, purchasing under that name is probably more satisfactory than attempting to follow miscellaneous grade designations that are meaningless.

Determining the Quality of Canned Foods. The average buyer of canned foods finds it difficult to rely upon his own judgment in determining quality. Some large buyers of canned foods employ experts to perform this function for them. Nevertheless, a person has an opportunity to determine quality largely by comparison. The following is a check list of items that should be considered in determining the quality of canned foods:

Open space in can	Crispness
Gross weight of contents	Flavor
Volume of juice	Maturity
Weight of juice	Percentage of whole food
Net weight of food	Tenderness
Absence of defects	Uniformity of size
Clearness of liquor or juice	Uniformity of color
Character of liquor or juice	Nature of blemishes
Color of food	Units per can
Consistency	

These simple observations can be made at home. A comparison of one can of food with another is the best way of making an analysis. For instance, when two cans of peas are compared, the poorer grade may show these defects:

(a) Lack of uniformity in size
(b) Lack of uniformity in texture
(c) Overmaturity or undermaturity
(d) Discolored liquor
(e) Too much liquor in proportion to food
(f) Poor color
(g) Broken pieces
(h) Poor flavor

Sizes of Cans. When canned goods are bought, the size of the can and the quality of the contents must be considered. There is so much variation in the sizes of cans that the buyer should familiarize himself with them. Even though he is acquainted with the sizes in general, unusual shapes of cans may sometimes mislead him. Cans ordinarily used for fruits and vegetables are in the following sizes:

NUMBER OR NAME OF CAN	AVERAGE NET WEIGHT	APPROXIMATE CUPFULS
Buffet or Picnic	8 oz.	1
No. 1	11 oz.	1⅓
No. 300	14 oz.	1¾
No. 1 tall	16 oz.	2
No. 303	16 oz.	2
No. 2	20 oz.	2½
No. 2½	28 oz.	3½
No. 3	33 oz.	4
No. 5	3 lb., 8 oz.	7
No. 10	6 lb., 10 oz.	13

Illustration No. 121—Sizes of Cans

Some foods may be advertised at "four cans for 25 cents." This statement does not mean anything unless one knows the exact size of the can. If a can appears not to be of standard size, it should be compared with a can of standard size on the merchant's shelf. This comparison will help in determining the relative contents of the can that is not of standard size.

Usually the larger the can, the less one pays proportionately for the quantity of goods bought. For instance, if a person buys a vegetable in No. 2 cans, he probably pays from two to four cents a pound less than if he bought the same food in No. 1 cans. If he buys fruit in No. 2½ cans, he probably pays from three or four cents a pound less than if he bought the same fruit in No. 1 cans.

One should watch for cans of unusual sizes, for they are sometimes misleading. For instance, a special can used by some companies appears to be much the same as the No. 2 standard-size can. The average person cannot discover the difference because the can is just slightly shorter and a little less in diameter than the No. 2 can. It holds, however, three or four ounces less. In spite of its smaller capacity it is often advertised at the same price as the No. 2 can. The can is known to the trade as No. 303. It is, of course, labeled correctly according to the weight of the contents. It is evident from this discussion that one should learn to read labels and to recognize the sizes of cans.

Relative Values According to Sizes of Cans. Another important consideration in buying canned foods is the amount that should be purchased. It is not economical to buy a large can if part of the contents will spoil before they can be used. Illustration No. 122, which is based upon a study made in a large city, shows the relative price a pound for canned goods bought in cans of different sizes. This table can be used as a guide in determining the fairness of prices in comparison with the sizes of cans. For instance, if cut beans in No. 1 cans cost 9.1 cents a pound, the price should be 6.6 cents a pound when the beans are purchased in No. 2 cans. The absence of figures in some of the columns indicates that products are seldom packed in those sizes.

The buyer usually chooses a No. 1 can or a No. 2 can. He should pay approximately 25 per cent less a pound if he buys the larger can. As the difference between sizes becomes greater, the percentage difference in the price per pound becomes greater.

ITEM OF FOOD	COMMERCIAL GRADE AS INDICATED BY DISTRIBUTOR	PRICE PER POUND (CENTS)				
		8- OR 9-OUNCE CAN	NO. 1 CAN	NO. 2 CAN	NO. 2½ CAN	NO. 3 CAN
Vegetables:						
Beans, cut	Extra standard		9.1	6.6		
Beans, cut	Standard		8.7	5.0		
Beans, Lima	Extra standard		14.0	10.0		
Corn	Fancy		10.9	9.2		
Corn	Extra standard		9.1	6.6		
Corn	Standard		8.2	5.0		
Peas	Extra standard		14.0	10.0		
Tomatoes	Fancy			10.1		
Tomatoes	Extra standard		10.0	7.0		8.2
Fruits:						
Apricots	Choice	16.0	12.5		12.3	
Cherries	Choice		12.5		12.3	
Fruit salad	Choice		17.0		14.4	
Grapefruit	Fancy	12.5		10.0		
Peaches	Fancy	14.0	12.5		9.1	
Pears	Fancy		15.0		11.2	
Pineapple, sliced	Choice	22.2			8.9	
Pineapple, sliced	Fancy		13.0		9.6	

Illustration No. 122—Price per Pound of Foods in Cans of Various Sizes

Packaged Foods Versus Bulk Foods. When buying certain types of groceries of a staple or semistaple variety, the consumer must choose between bulk and packaged goods. In recent years there has been a definite trend toward selling goods in packages, although many of the same foods are still available in bulk. Such foods as dried fruits, dried beans, butter, lard, crackers, tea, and coffee are still available in bulk. Packaged foods have the advantage of greater sanitation, convenience in handling, and ease of identification. On the other hand, bulk goods usually cost somewhat less. Their quality is often as good as that of the packaged foods.

If the consumer does not wish to buy bulk goods, his problem is to decide what size of package to purchase. If the contents of a large package can be consumed before they spoil, the large package is often more economical than a small one. In a comparison of purchases made in the same stores on the same days over a period of two years, the saving that resulted from buying in large packages ranged from 8 to 38 per cent, depending upon the quantity purchased and the difference in size of the packages.

Guideposts in Buying Canned Goods. In the purchase of canned fruits or vegetables, the following procedure is suggested for determining values:

(a) Determine how much canned food should be bought at a time. If your requirements at any one time can be filled by one large can, do not buy two small ones, for the cost in the latter case will be greater. If your budget will permit the purchase of a number of cans at one time, buy at special sales in dozen lots or in case lots.

(b) Watch the appearance of the can. If the can is dirty, discolored, or rusty, examine it carefully. If the can has a small hole in it, do not accept it. If the ends are flat or slightly drawn in, but there is no noticeable flaw, the can is probably all right. If the ends are bulged, however, or if one end bulges out when the other is pressed, the food has probably spoiled.

(c) Decide what use you wish to make of the food. Lower grades of canned foods are often suitable for combination dishes, whereas the better grades may be more desirable for other purposes.

(d) Read the labels carefully. Note the designation of size, weight, and grade, and any descriptive terms used. Compare the product with other similar products to determine the value.

(e) Evaluate the cost by comparing the product with two or more similar ones after the specifications of each product have been determined.

(f) When the can is opened, note the condition of the food and observe whether the quality is what you expected. If there is any doubt as to whether the food is good, return it to the merchant as soon as possible. Keep it in its original container if possible, but do not wait too long before returning it.

(g) Shop in more than one place, and compare products at home. Learn where the best values can be obtained.

TEXTBOOK QUESTIONS

1. Do the standards established for canned foods by the Federal Government appear on the labels of all canned foods?
2. What are the names of the four Federal grades of canned fruits?
3. State the differences between the first and second grades of canned fruits.
4. If the Federal Food and Drug Administration has established standards for a canned food, how must the label be marked if the product does not measure up to the lowest standard but is sold in interstate commerce?
5. Under the Federal Food, Drug, and Cosmetic Act, what is the regulation with regard to the sale, in interstate commerce, of foods that contain poisonous matter?
6. Are all canned foods sold in the United States now under the jurisdiction of Federal law?
7. Name at least three ways in which a food may be considered to be misbranded under the Federal Food, Drug, and Cosmetic Act.
8. Are canned fruits and vegetables of the lower grades undesirable for use as foods?
9. What are the names of the four Federal grades of canned vegetables?
10. What are the five main factors on the basis of which canned vegetables are graded according to quality by the Federal Government?
11. What are the distinguishing characteristics of canned vegetables of the third grade?
12. Name some meaningless grade designations.
13. Does experience in buying prove that there is a relation between the price and the quality of canned foods?
14. Name the criteria by which the quality of canned foods can be determined.
15. Why should the consumer be familiar with the sizes of cans?
16. Is it always economical to buy a large can rather than a small one?
17. What are the advantages of buying packaged goods?
18. What is usually a disadvantage of buying packaged goods?
19. Name seven points in a procedure suggested for determining the values of canned fruits and vegetables.

DISCUSSION QUESTIONS

1. Is a canned vegetable of Grade A (according to the Federal Government standards) that is sold under a particular brand name the same in quality as another canned vegetable of the same grade that is sold under a different brand name?

2. (a) In your opinion how useful are the standards established by the United States Department of Agriculture? (b) What will determine their future usefulness?
3. Do you think a store has any advantage in selling merchandise that is marked according to standard grades?
4. What do you think is meant by Grade AA, which appears on the label of a canned food?
5. Explain a procedure that you would suggest for comparing canned foods on the basis of quality and value.
6. Why should a person beware of cans that have unusual sizes or shapes?
7. One advertiser announces, "Three cans for 25 cents." Another announces, "Three large cans for 28 cents." What do these advertisements mean?
8. "A small can of corn is a more economical purchase for some families than a large one, but a large can is a more economical purchase for others." Explain this statement.
9. Why do you think many stores are now selling most foods in packages?
10. Suppose that, in examining a can of peas, you find the peas to be as follows: firm; fairly uniform in color; tender; only occasionally broken; fairly uniform in size; and in a slightly dull-colored liquid. What do you think would be the grade of this can of peas?
11. Suppose that, in examining a can of peaches, you find the peaches to be as follows: firm and crisp; uniform in color; very tender; practically uniform in shape and size; and in a sweet, clear liquor. How would you grade this can of peaches?

Section II

Buying Perishable Foods

Safeguards in Buying Meat. The important, and difficult, problem in the purchase of fresh meats is judging the quality. Very few buyers know how to judge the quality of meat. Although the average buyer must depend upon the recommendation of his local meat dealer, he should at least become familiar with the various cuts of meat. Information on the cuts of meat can be obtained from the United States Department of Agriculture.

For the buyer of meats some safeguards have been provided. In many communities, for instance, there are ordinances that require certain standards in the marketing of meats.

Inspection of Meat. All meats sold in interstate commerce must bear the stamp of inspection of the United States Department of Agriculture. This stamp therefore appears on almost all meat except that intended for local consumption. Illustration No. 98 on page 279 shows the type of stamp used. This stamp is an indication that the meat was wholesome when inspected, but does not indicate specific quality.

Grading of Meat. The grading of meat has been gradually extended, although what has been done applies largely to the grading of beef. Packers are not required to have their meat graded by the United States Department of Agriculture. The grading of meat is therefore entirely voluntary on their part. If consumers are not obtaining graded meat, however, they have the privilege of demanding it from local dealers. If graded meat is demanded, packers will be more likely to furnish this service.

The official grades of beef established by the United States Department of Agriculture are listed as follows in their order of excellence: U. S. Prime, U. S. Choice, U. S. Good, U. S. Commercial, U. S. Utility, U. S. Cutter, and U. S. Canner. The first four grades are the most common. The illustration on page 280 shows graded beef.

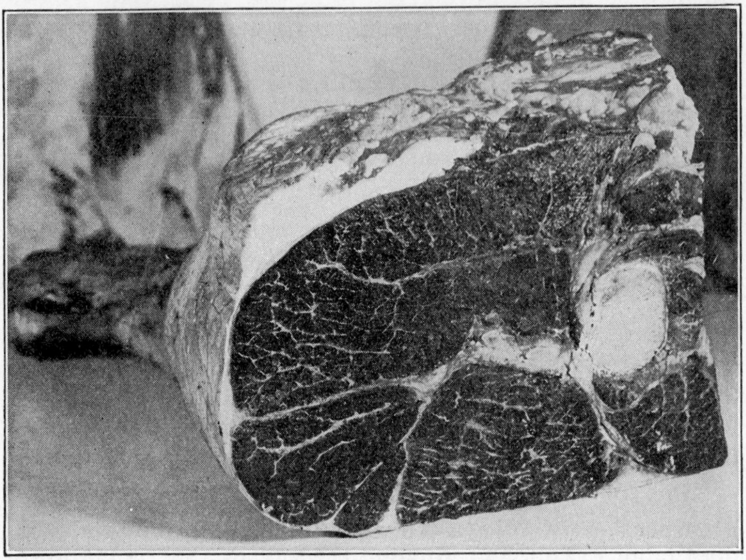

Illustration No. 123—Good Grade of Beef with Streaks of Fat

Quality Characteristics of Beef. Prime beef is practically perfect, and choice beef is difficult to distinguish from prime. Good beef is very desirable. Most beef sold is, however, of the medium (U. S. commercial) grade. This grade has a large amount of bone and a small amount of fat in proportion to flesh. Furthermore, the flesh and the fat are inclined to be less firm than those in other grades.

The characteristics that are desirable in beef are (a) light cherry red color; (b) velvety appearance; (c) firmness and fine grain; (d) absence of muscle tissue; and (e) evenly distributed fat that is brittle, creamy white, and flaky. The distribution and the kind of fat are probably the best characteristics by which to judge meat. If the fat does not cover the surface evenly and is not firm, this fact is assurance that the meat is not of a better grade. The consumer should not hesitate to buy meat that has considerable firm fat on it, for good fat indicates quality.

Veal and Calf Meat. *Veal* is the name applied to the meat of a young calf not more than twelve weeks of age. The meat of an older animal, for instance, from three to ten months in age, is referred to as *calf meat.* The grades of veal are prime, choice, good, medium, common, and cull. There is seldom any prime veal to be sold.

Good veal is finely grained, firm, somewhat moist, and light pink. The lighter the flesh, the better the meat. The exterior of the better grades of veal is covered with a thin layer of white fat. A good quality of calf meat is firm, finely grained, velvety, and light tan or reddish in color. The exterior should be covered with a generous amount of creamy white fat.

Lamb and Mutton. Lamb comes from animals that are from twelve to fourteen months old. The meat of an animal that is more than fourteen months old is considered mutton. Lamb is sold principally during April, May, and June; but practically no mutton is sold in this country.

Lamb and mutton are firm and finely grained if the quality is high. The color varies from pink to dull red according to age. The fat of a young lamb is creamy and slightly pinkish. It becomes white as the animal grows older.

Pork. Pork is inspected in the same way as beef and is marked with the same type of Federal inspection stamp. Although there is no governmental grading of pork, packers usually have their own grades, which are numbered one, two, and three.

Most pork comes from hogs that are from seven to twelve months old. Pork of high quality has a grayish pink color. The flesh is firm and finely grained, and the fat is firm and white. Smoked ham and bacon of high quality are firm, have a thin layer of fat, and have a smooth skin.

Dressed Poultry. Practically all dressed turkeys and a great many dressed chickens and ducks are graded by the Federal Government. This grading service is available to any producer at a cost of only one cent a bird. The governmental grade mark is put on each box in which the dressed fowl are packed and is printed on a tag attached to each bird. Besides bearing the grade mark, each tag states whether the bird is young or old. The grades for dressed poultry in general are as follows:

U. S. Special indicates a commercially perfect specimen. The supply of such dressed poultry is limited, and the price is correspondingly high.

U. S. Prime or No. 1 indicates poultry that is well fleshed and fattened, and practically free from pin feathers, skin tears, and other defects.

U. S. Choice or No. 2 indicates poultry that is fairly well fleshed and fattened, but may have slight defects such as skin tears or discolorations.

U. S. Commercial indicates poultry that is not well fleshed and fattened, and has more defects than poultry of the other grades.

Dressed chickens are sold in wholesale lots by grade, but they are seldom tagged. The crates in which they are packed are, however, tagged according to grade. The quality of dressed chickens can be judged as follows:

(a) If the bird is young, the breastbone is flexible, the feet and skin are soft, and the claws are short and sharp.

(b) If the bird is old, the breastbone is brittle and frequently rough. The skin is coarse, and the claws are long and usually dull. The presence of long hairs also indicates age.

(c) The female fowl is usually more tender than the male. The fowl that is plump and well rounded is of good quality.

(d) Fresh poultry of a high quality is plump, fat, and firm. Storage poultry is frequently flabby and dull in color.

Milk. Dairy products include milk, cream, butter, eggs, and cheese. The consumer may choose from among several grades of raw or pasteurized milk. The price of milk varies according to the grade, the grades usually being designated as A, B, and C. However, certified milk is of a higher grade. These grades are approved by the United States Public Health Service. Milk sold in cities is usually pasteurized. Grade A pasteurized milk is produced under more sanitary conditions and has a lower bacterial count than Grade B. Grade C milk must be labeled "cooking milk."

Departments of health in most cities have established rigid systems for controlling the inspection and the grading of milk. The standards set up by these communities are usually patterned after those of the Federal Government.

Cream. There are four classes of cream: heavy cream, whipping cream, medium cream, and light cream. They rank according to their content of butter fat, which may test from 36 per cent to 18 per cent.

Butter. The United States Department of Agriculture maintains a service for grading butter. Butter is classified as follows: dairy butter, which is made on the farm; creamery butter, which is made in the creamery or factory; packing-stock butter; ladled butter; process or renovated butter; and grease butter. In the scoring of the first three classes, maximum ratings are given to various factors in the following manner: flavor, 45 per cent; body, 25 per cent; color, 15 per cent; salt, 10 per cent; package, 5 per cent; total, 100 per cent. Butter that scores about 93 or 94 per cent is fine, sweet, fresh, mild, and clean. Any butter that scores below 75 per cent is classified as grease butter and is considered unfit for food. Only butter scoring 92 per cent or above may be marked with the certificate of quality issued by the United States Department of Agriculture. Except in case of butter that is sold under certification, the score of the butter sold in most retail stores is not easily available for the consumer. Any butter that contains less than 80 per cent of butter fat is an adulterated product and cannot be sold legally.

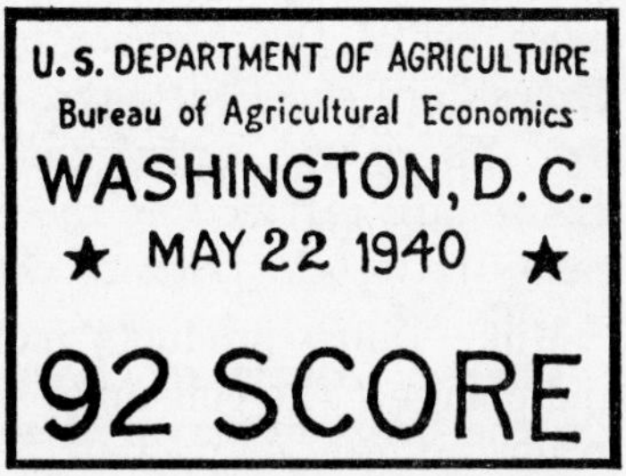

Illustration No. 124—A Governmental Grade Mark for Butter

Eggs. In many markets eggs are sold in cartons bearing a seal showing the date of grading and the inscription U. S. Specials or U. S. Extras. These inscriptions mean that on the date the eggs were sealed, they were examined by a

Consumers' Guide

Illustration No. 125—A Merchant Selling Graded Eggs

Federal Egg grader and were classified on the basis of size, condition of the shell, size of the air cell, and condition of the yolk and the white. To be graded as U. S. Specials, eggs must be of the highest quality. Those graded as U. S. Extras are excellent eggs, but are of a slightly lower quality. There are additional grades of eggs, but only two grades are certified by the Federal Government. Eggs may range in weight from 24 ounces to 17 ounces a dozen.

Cheese. American cheese is classified on several bases. On the basis of flavor it may be classified as fresh, mild, or aged; on the basis of texture, as close, medium close, or open; on the basis of color, as uncolored, medium-colored, or highly colored. The final scoring represents the combined ratings on the basis of the various factors. For instance, a particular cheese may be scored as follows: flavor, 30 per cent; texture, 40 per cent; finish and appearance, 20 per cent; color, 10 per cent; total, 100 per cent. The grades and corresponding scores established by the

Federal Government are as follows: U. S. Extra Fancy, a score of 95 or more; U. S. Fancy, a score of 92 to 94; U. S. No. 1, a score of 89 to 91; U. S. No. 2, a score of 86 to 88; U. S. No. 3, a score of 83 to 85.

Quality of Fresh Fruits and Vegetables. The factors that are considered by the United States Department of Agriculture in establishing standards for grading fresh fruits and vegetables include: (a) degree of ripeness; (b) uniformity in size and shape; (c) color; (d) freedom from injuries caused by mold, decay, freezing, cuts, bruises, worms, insects, or plant diseases.

Grades of Fresh Fruits and Vegetables. Although the number and the names of grades established for the different varieties of fresh fruits and vegetables differ somewhat, the classification is, in general, as follows: best grade, U. S. Fancy; next grade, U. S. No. 1; third grade, U. S. No. 2. Many states have adopted their own grades, but most of these conform to the standards established by the United States Department of Agriculture.

Many fruits and vegetables, especially berries and green vegetables, are so perishable that their desirability decreases rapidly. Hence it is often not possible for the retailer to offer such products for sale according to grades. If, however, such fruits and vegetables have been graded and the original grading is known, the consumer can judge the quality by considering the degree of freshness. Less perishable products, such as potatoes, apples, and citrus fruits, are sold in some retail markets according to grades.

Citrus Fruits. As graded citrus fruits are likely to be found in retail markets, they can be discussed in more detail. Citrus fruits are graded for quality and also for size. Oranges, for example, run in size from 80 to 324. The number indicates how many are in a crate. Illustration No. 126 shows the number of oranges in a crate, the approximate diameter of each orange, the approximate weight of a dozen, and the volume of juice in each dozen.

A pound of Florida oranges usually yields about one cup of juice. Navel oranges, however, ordinarily yield less juice.

SIZE OF ORANGE AND NUMBER IN CRATE	APPROXIMATE DIAMETER OF FRUIT [1]		APPROXIMATE WEIGHT PER DOZEN [2]		APPROXIMATE VOLUME OF JUICE PER DOZEN [3]		
	FLORIDA ORANGES	CALIFORNIA ORANGES	FLORIDA ORANGES	CALIFORNIA ORANGES	FLORIDA ORANGES	CALIFORNIA NAVEL ORANGES	CALIFORNIA VALENCIA ORANGES
	Inches	*Inches*	*Pounds*	*Pounds*	*Cups*	*Cups*	*Cups*
Large:							
80	...	3¾	...	10.4	...	8.5	...
96	3⅝	3⅝	10.0	8.8	...	...	...
100	...	3½	...	8.4	...	7.1	...
126	3¼	3⅛	7.6	6.7	9.9	...	7.1
Medium:							
150	3⅛	3	6.4	5.6	7.1	5.7	...
176	3	2⅞	5.4	4.8	5.9	4.2	...
200	2⅞	2¾	4.8	4.2	...	...	...
216	2¾	2⅝	4.4	3.9	4.8	3.4	4.0
Small:							
250	2⅝	...	3.8	...	4.2	...	...
252	...	2½	...	3.3	...	2.9	3.5
288	2½	2⅜	3.3	2.9	3.5	...	...
324	2⅜	2¼	3.0	2.6	2.8	...	...

[1] The data for Florida oranges have been obtained from the Bureau of Agricultural Economics, United States Department of Agriculture; those for California oranges, from the California Fruit Growers Exchange.
[2] The approximate net weight of 1 crate of Florida oranges is 80 pounds; that of a crate of California oranges, 70 pounds.
[3] These data have been obtained from the Food Utilization Section of the Bureau of Home Economics.

Illustration No. 126—Juice Content of Oranges of Various Sizes and Weights

As a general rule, citrus fruits that have smooth, thin skins have more juice than the varieties that have thick skins.

The relative economy of buying different sizes of oranges depends upon the price according to the most important element to be considered in buying. For instance, if the quantity of juice obtainable is the most important element in buying oranges for a specific purpose, the No. 126 Florida oranges would be cheaper at 50 cents a dozen than the No. 250 oranges at 25 cents a dozen.

Potatoes. Potatoes constitute one of the main items of diet of most families. They therefore deserve special attention in the family budget. The following are some of the points to be considered in buying potatoes:

(a) Are the size and the shape desirable?
(b) Is the surface smooth and firm?
(c) Are there any imperfections?
(d) Are the potatoes graded?
(e) Are they sold by weight?
(f) What variety is best?

Deep eyes, irregular shapes, and broken skins are productive of waste when the potatoes are prepared for cooking. It is more economical to buy potatoes of a uniform size with a smooth, firm skin, provided the price is not excessive in proportion to the prices of other grades. If the buyer doubts whether he is getting full measure, he should remember that potatoes ought to weigh sixty pounds to the bushel.

The most economical time to buy potatoes is, of course, in the fall. If sufficient money is available and if the potatoes can be stored so as to keep properly, a considerable saving can be effected by purchasing a large quantity. Most city buyers, however, find it more economical to purchase potatoes in small quantities, for then there is less chance of shrinkage and decay.

After the variety that is most suitable for a particular need has been determined, the next step is to select the grade. In many markets potatoes can be purchased according to grade, especially if they are still available in their original containers. The grade is often indicated on the container. The desirable grades are U. S. No. 1 and U. S. No. 2. The finest grade, of course, is U. S. Fancy. Potatoes of inferior grades may be more economical if they are to be used for certain purposes or if they can be purchased at exceptional bargain prices. The important thing to remember, however, is that not only the price and the variety of the potatoes, but also the purpose for which the potatoes are intended, determine the relative economy.

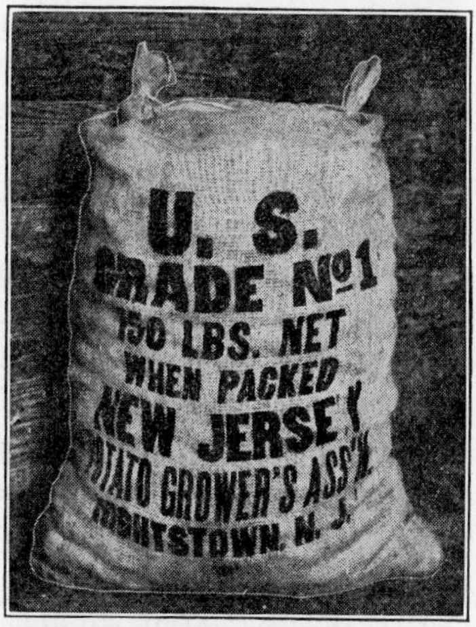

Illustration No. 127—A Bag of Graded Potatoes

Very few people can recognize potatoes by name. When the names are known, however, the following information can be used as a guide in selecting potatoes according to use:

NAME	USE
Triumph (Red Bliss or Bliss Triumph)	For steaming and for salads
Rose (Spaulding Rose or Early Rose)	For steaming, for salads, and for French frying
Irish Cobbler	For most cooking purposes
Early Ohio	For all general purposes, including baking
Rural	For all general purposes, including baking
Green Mountain	For all general purposes, including baking
Russet Burbank (Idaho)	Especially good for baking or frying

Cold-Storage Foods; Frozen Foods. The consumer must recognize that cold storage is a factor of economy for him. This service also provides a greater variety of foods in those seasons when particular foods are not produced in large quantities. The person who insists upon buying fresh foods instead of cold-storage foods must expect to pay higher prices.

Frozen foods are now common in large cities. The purchase of frozen delicacies, such as fine fruits and vegetables, is still a luxury for most people.

Rules for Buying. When buying foods, it is, of course, desirable to determine the specific purposes for which they are wanted. The highest grade of food is not always the most suitable, and it frequently is not economical. If a lower grade of food is satisfactory and is more economical, that is the grade to buy. The better grades of food must, however, be used in determining fair prices for the lower grades. The following are a few marketing rules that will save money in buying fresh fruits and vegetables:

(a) Make your own selection; do not order by telephone. Buy in small quantities unless you have a cool, dark place for storage.

(b) Fruits and vegetables that are in season in the nearest marketing area are cheapest in price and often best in quality.

(c) Do not handle fruits and vegetables unnecessarily. Handling increases spoilage and the retailer's overhead, both of which represent costs that must be passed on to consumers.
(d) Avoid the purchase of foods that show decay. Distinguish between blemishes that affect only appearance and those that affect eating quality.
(e) Whenever possible, buy by weight instead of by measure.
(f) Do not always buy the best; but buy the grade that is wholesome, economical, and suitable for the purpose for which the food is intended.
(g) Buy from more than one merchant. Compare prices and quality.
(h) Determine the relative values obtained from a particular merchant, or from various merchants, by testing the foods at home.

How to Spend the Food Dollar. A preceding chapter on budgeting shows food budgets for families of various sizes. The wise buyer will learn what constitutes adequate menus for the food budget of his family. He will then apportion the food budget so that the necessary food values will be included.

Home economists who are acquainted with food values have made various studies to determine the minimum amounts that a family should spend for various types of

FOOD REQUIRED	COST	FOOD REQUIRED	COST
6 lbs. meat and fish	$1.50	18 qts. or cans milk	$1.80
1½ doz. eggs	.45	¾ lb. cheese	.15
6 lbs. graham bread	.60		
5 lbs. flour	.15	12 lbs. potatoes	.20
1 lb. cracked wheat	.08	5 lbs. carrots or squash	.15
1 lb. oatmeal	.07	3 lbs. cabbage or greens	.15
½ lb. macaroni or rice	.04	5 lbs. apples	.20
⅓ lb. crackers	.06	1 doz. oranges	.20
		1 jar canned fruit	.12
2 lbs. butter	.60	1 lb. dried beans	.08
1 lb. lard or oil	.20	2 lbs. bananas	.12
1 lb. peanut butter and		1 can peas or corn	.10
bacon	.30	1 lb. dried fruit	.10
coffee, salt, etc.	.50	2 cans tomatoes	.20
Total cost of food for four people for a week			$8.12

From *This Problem of Food,* The Public Affairs Committee, Inc., New York City

Illustration No. 128—A Weekly Food List for a Family of Four

foods in order to obtain the proper nourishment. The food list shown in Illustration No. 128 is recommended for a family of four that has a reasonably low income. The prices are those that prevailed in Seattle, Washington, during April, 1939, and will, of course, vary according to the general price level. Tables such as this help to determine how to spend wisely the money available for food.

TEXTBOOK QUESTIONS

1. What are the usual local safeguards provided for the buyer of meat?
2. What means is used to protect the buyer of meat that is sold in interstate commerce?
3. What are the official grades of beef?
4. Of what grade is most of the beef that is sold in local markets?
5. Name the characteristics of a good piece of beef.
6. What are the characteristics of good veal?
7. During what months is lamb principally sold?
8. What are the characteristics of good lamb and mutton?
9. Is pork inspected and graded in any way?
10. What are the characteristics of good pork?
11. What grading service is provided for dressed poultry?
12. Is U. S. Prime or No. 1 the best grade of turkey?
13. How can the quality of dressed chickens be judged?
14. What are the three common grades of milk?
15. What are the four classes of cream?
16. What are the factors by which butter is judged?
17. What percentage rating must butter have before it may bear the certificate of quality issued by the United States Department of Agriculture?
18. What percentage of butter fat must butter contain in order to avoid being classified as an adulterated product?
19. (a) What two grades of eggs are certified by the United States Government? (b) What does the certification on the label mean in each case?
20. What factors are considered in rating cheese?
21. What quality factors are used by the United States Department of Agriculture in grading fresh fruits and vegetables?
22. What grades of fresh fruits and vegetables are recognized by the United States Department of Agriculture?
23. Why cannot the consumer depend upon the grades assigned to some fresh fruits and vegetables?
24. On what basis should one buy citrus fruits: weight, juice, size, price?

25. In addition to the variety what are some of the other points to consider in buying potatoes?
26. What kind of information is helpful to a family in determining how to buy food so as to have a balanced diet and at the same time adhere to its food budget?

DISCUSSION QUESTIONS

1. Explain the limitations and the inadequacies in the use of United States inspection stamps as guides in buying perishable foods, such as meat.
2. If a piece of beef has a dark, dull red color and is very lean, how would you classify it according to quality?
3. Does the size of the animal indicate the quality of beef?
4. If lamb is offered for sale in December, is it young lamb? Give the reason for your answer.
5. Some buyers insist upon obtaining lean pork. What do you think of this demand?
6. How do you think you could distinguish a young dressed fowl in a meat market?
7. In some communities it is impossible to obtain milk that has been graded and marked according to standards. How do you account for this situation?
8. A dairy company advertises Grade A cream. What kind of cream is this?
9. Discuss some of the difficulties in making sure that you buy good butter.
10. Explain some of the dangers of relying on grade marks on packages of eggs.
11. Have you ever seen graded fresh vegetables? If so, where were they seen, and how were they marked?
12. Why do you think it is difficult to enforce the use of quality standards for fresh fruits and vegetables?
13. Some foods, such as oranges and nuts, are stamped with trade-marks and occasionally with grade marks. What is the advantage of each type of marking?
14. Potatoes must be known by variety in order to be judged. Why is this knowledge necessary? Explain your answer.
15. The honesty of the merchant is the greatest aid to the buyer of fresh fruits and vegetables. Why is this statement true?
16. What services help consumers to have well-balanced diets throughout the year?

PROBLEMS

1. If a No. 1 can of food sells for 10 cents and a No. 2 can sells for 15 cents, what is the price of a pound in each case?

2. Canned tomatoes were advertised by one store as selling at 13 cents a "large can." Another merchant advertised a "large can" for 14 cents. The tomatoes were of approximately the same quality. Investigation disclosed, however, that those advertised in the first case were packed in No. 1 tall cans, whereas those advertised in the second case were packed in No. 2 cans. Was there any difference in the price of a pound? If there was, which can was the cheaper?
3. On the basis of the price of a pound of cut beans, lima beans, corn, peas, and tomatoes, as shown in the table on page 361, figure the percentage of added cost by buying a No. 1, rather than a No. 2, can.
4. If Florida oranges are packed 216 to a crate and sell for 30 cents a dozen, what should be the price of California navel oranges of the same size if they are bought on the basis of juice content? (Use the table on page 372.)
5. If California oranges that are packed 150 to a crate sell for 40 cents a dozen, what should be the price of a pound of these oranges? (Use the table on page 372.)

COMMUNITY PROBLEMS AND PROJECTS

1. On the basis of the weekly food requirements of a family of four, which are shown in Illustration No. 128 on page 375, and on the basis of current prices, set up a food diet for your family, assuming that the amount consumed by each person in the family is equal to one fourth of the price established for each item in this table.
2. Make a list of the various grades used to designate the quality of canned foods sold in a local grocery store. Indicate which foods bear recognized Federal grades.
3. Compare the contents of two or more cans of beans or of some other product. Note the price, volume, weight, taste, and other factors that can be used in determining the quality and the value. Make a comparative report on the quality and the price. Use the brand names to distinguish the products that you compare.
4. Collect a variety of labels from cans of similar products. Make a list of the information shown on the labels, and report your conclusions as to what criteria can be followed in evaluating these foods on the basis of the information given on the labels.
5. From a local retail grocer, meat market, or wholesaler, obtain information with regard to the approximate monthly price level of some particular commodity. Draw a chart, or construct a table, indicating the seasonal trend of prices for that product.

CHAPTER XV

HOW TO BUY CLOTHING, FABRICS, AND SHOES

Purpose of the Chapter. There are numerous items of apparel that the average person buys, and there is still a greater variety of fabrics purchased for the household. Several volumes would be required to present a detailed analysis of the procedure involved in buying these various products scientifically. The purpose of this chapter is, however, to present (a) guides for use in buying clothing, (b) information for use in analyzing and judging cloth, (c) simple tests that can be performed in the procedure of buying fabrics, and (d) simple chemical tests that can be performed in the home. Helpful guides for buying shoes are also included.

Labels on Clothing. Some manufacturers of clothing use labels indicating the standards set up by the United States Bureau of Standards. Some of the trade associations require their members to use labels indicating the quality of the clothing and the working conditions under which the clothing was manufactured. A truly informative label will provide information on such points as yarn used, thread count, color fastness, shrinkage, special features of the material, design, construction, methods of cleaning, labor conditions of manufacture, and laboratory tests.

Look for the following specific types of labels:

(a) General statements of "preshrunk," "will not shrink," "completely shrunk," or "fully shrunk" may be true, but their meanings are not definite. The Texturized process for woolen fabrics and the Sanforized process for cotton or linen fabrics are reliable processes when indicated on labels.

(b) The seal of approval of the American Institute of Laundering is important as a guide in determining color fastness, shrinkage, and construction.

(c) The label of the National Association of Dyers and Cleaners indicates whether that association has approved the merchandise as to serviceability from the point of view of cleaning.
(d) Look for fabric identification labels. For instance, determine particularly whether the label indicates the percentage of wool in the garment.
(e) The use of a brand name is important in identifying merchandise, provided the buyer has had previous experience with clothing purchased under that brand. Merchandise made under a private brand label for a particular store, even though it has been made by a manufacturer of a well-known brand, may not necessarily measure up to the specifications of the well-known brand. Some privately branded merchandise may, however, be better than similar merchandise sold under a well-known brand.
(f) Special labels with regard to workmanship may disclose the types of seams, the method of sewing, the inner construction, the type of hem, or other features.
(g) Many buyers consider it important to look for union labels or other labels indicating the working conditions under which the clothing was manufactured.
(h) Any other kind of so-called protective label is meaningless unless the label indicates definitely what protection is provided.

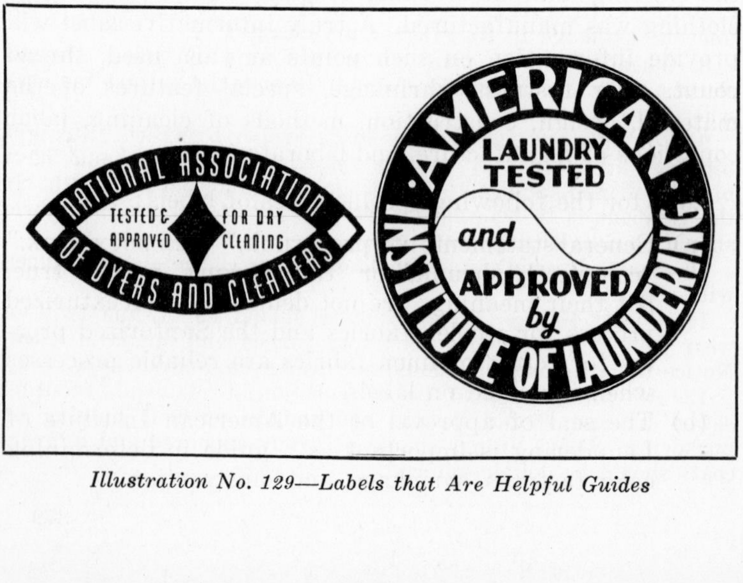

Illustration No. 129—Labels that Are Helpful Guides

Determining the Quality of Clothing. The following suggestions, taken from *Stretching the Clothing Dollar* of the Household Finance Corporation, provide guides in examining some types of garments to determine their quality:

1. Look for labels or ask questions concerning the specific directions for the proper method of handling the garment. How many trips to the dry cleaner will it survive? Will it require frequent pressing? Will it wash? Is the color fast? Is the finish permanent? Is the garment guaranteed against shrinking out of fit?

2. Look for the inside story which is told by the width and stitching of seams, hems, bindings around neck and cuff.

3. Pull the seams to test their strength. Note the quality of the thread used. Silk or very fine mercerized cotton thread should be used for silk, rayon, and wool. Cotton thread should be used on cottons and linens.

4. In dresses, lingerie, and garments made of lightweight fabrics, small stitches, about fourteen to the inch, are an indication of conscientious workmanship.

5. Hems should be generous enough to allow for possible future lengthening.

6. The intelligent shopper buys garments only after an actual try-on, not by size mark. A try-on is always important, but is especially so in the purchase of inexpensive clothes, for only in this way can the buyer be sure that the garment was not skimped. Stretch, bend, reach, move about, and sit down to be sure there is no tightness, that shoulders are comfortable, and that other details of fit and tailoring are properly worked out.

7. The fabric in all parts of the garment should be cut along the same way of the material. A combination of lengthwise and crosswise cutting of fabric may indicate skimping and may cause uneven shrinkage in washing or dry-cleaning.

8. When buying a plaid or striped suit or dress, observe sleeves, pockets, collars, and seams to be sure the pattern matches where pieces meet.

9. Bindings and facings should be properly applied. Straight bindings are good only on straight edges. Curves should have bias or shaped facings to ensure good fit and smooth finish. If the garment is to be washed, the binding as well as the fabric should be color-fast to washing.

10. Seams in men's suit should be hand-felled, taped, or piped with silk.

11. Pocket linings in men's suits should be of fine twill to wear well, and the edges should be turned and double-stitched Notice the stitching. It should be close, even, and smooth.

12. All linings should be of substantial material, securely sewed in, and should lie flat and smooth without bulging or puckering. Sleeve linings should be firmly anchored and in overcoats should be double-stitched.

Distinguishing Fabrics. A knowledge of fabrics is important in buying clothing and household materials. The identification of the fibers in a fabric is of first importance. The next most important task is judging the quality and value of the fabric. The selection of a particular weave will depend largely on taste and style. As a general rule, tightly woven cloth is more durable than cloth that is loosely woven.

Wool. Wool has a resiliency that cotton does not have. Woolen cloth that contains some cotton is heavier and harder than cloth containing only wool. It may therefore be stronger, but it will soil readily and fade more easily.

Cotton. Cotton is nonabsorbent, soils easily, and is more inflammable than wool. Cotton is, however, purified and treated chemically to make it absorb moisture readily. Ordinary cotton is dull and limp as contrasted with wool or linen.

Linen. Linen is characterized by its smoothness, crispness, and luster. Cotton is frequently a substitute for linen.

Silk. Pure silk is the strongest fiber known. If a piece of silk cloth splits or breaks after brief wear, this fact is definite indication that the cloth is not pure silk. Many good pieces of silk are spoiled because chemicals are put into the cloth when it is dyed.

Rayon. Although rayon is sometimes called artificial silk, it should not be classed as silk. It is a textile in a class by itself. It can be distinguished from silk by physical comparison. Rayon has a higher luster than silk; and, although heavier, it is weaker. Its fibers are also coarser than those of silk. Rayon feels stiffer and is less elastic than silk. Cloth made of it is usually cheaper than silk cloth.

Trade Names of Fabrics. Different fibers are frequently combined to form fabrics. Silk and cotton, for instance, are combined to form fabrics sold under the following trade names: A. B. C., Aledo, Fairy, Seco, Sello, Silcot, Tezzo.

Rayon is the general name applied to a synthetic fiber that is produced from a cellulose base. In the early stages of the production of this fiber, some of the manufacturers referred to it as "artificial silk" because its high gloss and some of its other features make it somewhat similar to silk. Although this fiber is now generally sold under the recognized name of *rayon,* it is given various individual trade names, many of which are derived from the process by which it is produced. The following are some of the trade names of rayon: Acetate, Baronette Satin, Celanese, Luminette, Lustron, Milo Sheen, Trico Sham, Tricollette. In some respects these fabrics are superior to silk, whereas in others they are inferior. As a matter of fact, they are in a class by themselves and should therefore be clearly distinguished from silk.

The following list contains additional trade names for fabrics. For each trade name the real name is indicated.

Trade Name	*Real Name*
Canton fabrics	Cotton and silk mixtures
Daisy cloth	Outing flannel
Gloria	Silk warp and worsted
Grass cloth, Chinese grass cloth, grass linen, Canton linen	Ramie fiber (China grass)
Hospital gauze	Cheesecloth
Kapock	Fast-color drapery fabrics
Leatherette, Fabrikoid	Artificial leather
Linen-finish suitings	Mercerized cotton yarns used to give a linenlike finish
Metalline	Imitation of metal cloth
Mungo	Remanufactured wool made from rags
Palm Beach cloth	Cotton warp with mohair filling
Rajah	Pongee type of material
Ripplette	Seersucker
Sateen, or satine	Mercerized cotton fabric in satin weave
Snia-fil	Artificial wool
Velveteen	Fabric with short cotton pile made in imitation of silk velvet
Viyella flannel	Cotton and wool in equal amounts mixed before spinning

Trade Names of Furs. Furs used as clothing provide one of the best examples of the use of trade names. Many of the furs sold under trade names are good, but some are of a very poor quality. The following is a list of some of the common types of furs sold under trade names:

Trade Name	*Real Name*
Arctic Seal	Rabbit
Australian Chinchilla	Australian Opossum
Australian Seal	Rabbit
Baffin Seal	Rabbit
Baltic Leopard	Australian Rabbit
Bay Seal	Rabbit
Beaverette	Rabbit
Buckskin Seal	Rabbit
Caracul	Lamb
Chinchilla Squirrel	Squirrel
Chinchillette	Rabbit
Ermiline	White Rabbit
Ermine	Weasel
Erminette	White Rabbit
French Beaver	French Rabbit
French Chinchilla	Hare
French Leopard	Hare
French Mole	Rabbit
French Seal	French Rabbit
Galiac	Lamb
Hudson Bay Seal	Rabbit
Hudson Seal	Muskrat
Kalinsky	Weasel
Lapin	Rabbit

Simple Store Tests for Fabrics. Many complicated tests of fabrics can be conducted in laboratories, and simple tests can be made in the home; but most buyers have to depend upon a casual examination in a store. Tests of the last type must be simple and easy to perform. The following are a few tests that may be used in a store:

(a) *Creasing fabrics.* If a fabric is folded lengthwise and crosswise, the sharpness of the crease indicates the kind of fiber present. Creasing the fabric also provides an opportunity to examine it more closely to distinguish a mixed weave from a weave made of one kind of fiber. Linen folds more readily and holds creases longer than cotton. Cotton creases more readily than wool or silk, which will spring back into its original form. The scratching of the edge of the fold will frequently disclose whether the cloth has been weighted, that is, impregnated with a substance to fill the pores and to add weight.

(b) *Examining yarns.* If a piece of fabric has a rough edge, some of the threads may be raveled loosely between the fingers and examined carefully to determine whether there is a mixture of fibers.

It is easy to distinguish wool from cotton by creasing and by additional tests indicated in the following discussion. Silk or wool may be combined with any one of several other fibers. If the threads are raveled, it is easy to distinguish the silk or the wool from the other fiber.

Frequently cotton and linen are woven together, as, for example, in materials for towels. The linen threads may run in one direction and the cotton threads in another; they are rarely twisted together. Another test to distinguish linen from cotton is to note the relative stiffness and luster. Cotton is limp and dull, whereas linen is stiff and lustrous.

Rayon is frequently combined with cotton or silk. Rayon and cotton are easily distinguishable because of their relative luster. Rayon and silk can be distinguished easily by the degree of fineness.

(c) *Examining fibers.* The kind of fiber in a certain cloth can be determined by raveling off a piece of yarn and untwisting it. Some yarns may be made of two or three different fibers. Untwisting will show the kind of fiber better than breaking the yarn abruptly or attempting to compare yarns. This test is most practicable for examining the yarn in a garment. A piece of yarn can usually be obtained, for instance, by taking a thread from the inside of the pocket or from along a seam. When wool yarn is untwisted, the fibers appear kinky and have a resiliency that is absent in cotton.

When there is considerable nap on cloth that is of a cotton and wool mixture, the wool nap can be distinguished from the cotton. If a moistened finger is passed over the nap, the cotton will absorb the moisture and lie flat, whereas the wool will spring back into its original position.

Rayon can be distinguished from silk by untwisting the yarn to see if there is a difference in the fineness, the softness, and the strength of the fibers.

Linen can be distinguished from cotton by untwisting the yarn and pulling it apart slowly. The linen will usually come apart in long pointed strands, whereas the cotton will break more abruptly with brushlike ends.

These tests are not reliable in the case of some novelty cloths, in which there is an unusual mixture of fibers. Some novelty cloths contain as many as five types of fiber. For them a more thorough test is required.

(d) *Determining weighted cloth.* The finish of a piece of cloth is extremely important. The discovery of weighting in cloth will frequently be an indication of the relative quality and strength of the cloth. Many cotton fabrics are put through elaborate weighting processes. The thread is impregnated with starch and with another filler, such as chalk, China clay, or magnesium. When the cloth is finally pressed between rollers, it will not be substantial, although it may appear to be so. It will lose its beauty when it is washed and worn. The filling in cotton cloth can be detected by rubbing a piece briskly to dislodge the filler.

The substances used for weighting silk cloth are usually added to the filling (the crosswise yarns) so as not to impair the lengthwise strength. Weighted silk will stay creased lengthwise better than it will crosswise. In fact, the continued lengthwise creasing of weighted silk may cause the cloth to split.

Tests That Can Be Performed at Home. It is frequently possible for the buyer to test a piece of cloth at home. Tests at home should, however, supplement those performed in the store. The most satisfactory tests that can be performed at home are as follows:

(a) *Lye test.* Wool and silk are animal fibers. Either may be distinguished from vegetable fibers in the following manner: Place a sample of the cloth in a granite pan or a porcelain cooking dish, and pour over it a solution of one tablespoon of lye to one-half pint of water. Cover the container and boil the contents for fifteen minutes. At the end of that time animal fiber will be completely destroyed, but vegetable fiber will remain. This test reveals the presence of such vegetable fibers as cotton, linen, or rayon.

(b) *Acid test.* Another simple test will give the reverse effect. It requires the use of a hot iron and a 2 per cent solution of sulphuric acid. It is as follows: Place a drop of acid in the center of the sample, and then place the sample between layers of heavy paper. Press the cloth with a hot iron. If cotton or any other vegetable fiber is present, the cloth will burn black and become brittle. Rub the cloth between the fingers. The cotton or other vegetable fiber will disintegrate and leave merely the wool or the silk.

(c) *Counting the threads.* The closeness of the weave is an important factor in the durability of different grades of cloth. This is determined by counting the number of warp and filling threads in each inch. The counting can be done best with the aid of a microscope. A special instrument is sometimes used. Anyone can make a count, however, by laying off a one-quarter inch of the cloth and, with a magnifying glass, determining the number of threads in each direction.

U. S. Bureau of Home Economics

Illustration No. 130—Making a Thread Count

With the aid of a microscope another test may be made to determine whether yarns are of uneven size, lumpy, or fuzzy. Smooth, uniform yarns are desirable except in novelty cloth. In this test several samples of the cloth should be used, and the threads in the yarns counted, so that the average quality of the cloth can be determined.

A relatively expensive cloth may prove to be cheaper, in the long run, than a cloth that costs less. For instance, in the case of sheets, the warp (or lengthwise yarns) has been found to range from 44 to 109, while the filling (or crosswise yarns) ranges from 47 to 97. A cloth with a warp count of 80 and a filling count of 55 might be only 10 per cent cheaper than one with a warp count of 109 and a filling count of 97, but the more expensive cloth might last almost twice as long as the cheaper.

(d) *Burning test.* If cotton yarn is woven with woolen yarn, it is easy to ravel the cloth and burn the separate pieces of yarn for comparison. Cotton burns with a flash and leaves no deposit. Wool burns more slowly and gives off an odor similar to that from burning hair or feathers.

Combinations of silk and cotton yarns are easy to identify. The yarns should be burned separately. The cotton will burn with a flash, leaving no deposit, whereas the silk will burn more slowly and will form a bead at the end. Weighted silk, however, acts differently in some cases.

Unweighted silk burns like wool, whereas weighted silk usually retains its form. Rayon burns like cotton. It is therefore possible to determine good silk from weighted silk or imitation silk.

(e) *Test of tensile strength.* Tensile strength is important and is used frequently as a selling point, but it should not be taken as the sole measure of quality. It is difficult to obtain a suitable test of tensile strength without some kind of equipment. Special scales are available for measuring the amount of weight required to break threads. Crude scales can sometimes be constructed. One can, however, make a rough test by stretching the cloth till it breaks, or by breaking one of the threads in the hands. Several different threads should be tested in measuring tensile strength.

(f) *Washing test.* The laundering test is one of the most important, especially in the buying of wash clothes and household fabrics. A careful check should be kept on the length of life of a particular brand of sheet, shirt, or other item. The brands that wear longer should be given favor in future purchases.

(g) *Sun test.* The only way for a consumer to protect himself from unsatisfactory dyes is to take a sample of the fabric home and to submit it to conditions similar to those under which it will be used. A very satisfactory test is to place the fabric where it will be exposed to the sunlight and then to cover part of it with a piece of cardboard. The cardboard should be removed occasionally, and the change in the color of the exposed part should be observed. A portion of the fabric should also be washed to determine whether the cloth fades or loses its original luster.

Evaluation Guide for Buying Shoes. Even experts admit that it is difficult to detect poor leather and substitutes for leather in shoes. For many years American buyers have demanded style in preference to comfort. It has been estimated that only 14 per cent of the women and 40 per cent of the men wear shoes that are correctly fitted. In buying shoes, it is therefore important to consider more than style and appearance.

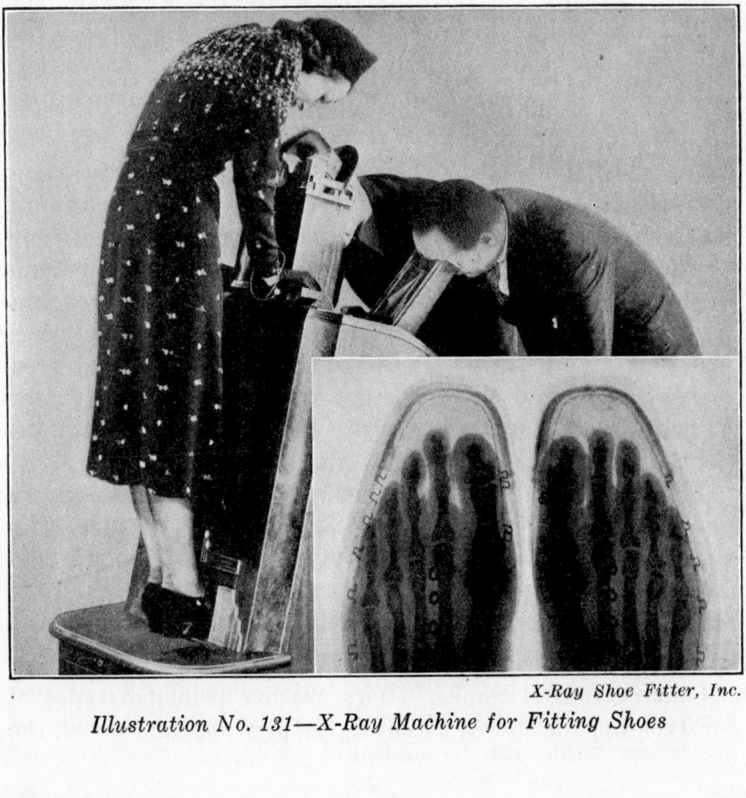

X-Ray Shoe Fitter, Inc.

Illustration No. 131—X-Ray Machine for Fitting Shoes

In the selection of shoes, design is the most important consideration, for it regulates comfort. A person can sometimes afford to sacrifice quality in order to get a shoe of the proper design to give him comfort. Because of the importance of this consideration, a person should buy shoes only from a merchant who is qualified to fit them properly.

Workmanship and materials are sometimes given less consideration than design. Style may have a greater influence than workmanship and materials in determining cost. The value of a shoe should, however, be determined largely on the basis of quality with only a reasonable consideration for style.

One of the greatest mistakes made in buying shoes is to choose them without regard to the purpose for which they are needed. For instance, school children may look better in lightweight calfskin shoes with thin soles; but a more durable leather will give longer wear, and a thicker sole will ensure greater comfort. If a woman is to be on her feet much during the day, she will not want to wear shoes with extremely high heels. Climate and type of occupation often must be taken into consideration in deciding between shoes that are cut low and those that have higher tops.

Cost of Shoes. In respect to cost there are three general classes of shoes: high-priced, medium-priced, and low-priced. There should be little doubt about the construction of high-priced and low-priced shoes. High-priced shoes, almost without exception, are made of a better quality of leather than low-priced shoes and by one of the better processes. Low-priced shoes are usually made of lower grades of materials and by a cheap process. The middle group is the one that causes confusion for the buyer.

The price of a shoe is governed largely by the process of manufacture, the quality of the leather, and the style. If a manufacturer has given special attention to style, it is possible that the buyer may be attracted by a shoe that has been made by a cheap process and of low-grade material. These various factors will be discussed in detail.

Construction of Shoes. There are five principal types of construction for shoes: the *welt*, the *McKay*, the *turned*, the

Littleway, and the *stitchdown.* The difference between them lies in the process by which the sole is attached to the upper. This process is the manufacturer's most important problem and has an important relation to the quality of the shoe. There are still other types of construction, which may be classified according to the process of attaching the sole to the upper. These are the *standard screw,* the *pegged,* the *nailed,* and the *cemented.* The nature of each of these four types of construction is obvious from the name. The five principal types that have been mentioned previously are briefly described in the following paragraphs. Some of these require as many as two hundred and ten operations.

The *welt* construction is used on about 40 per cent of American-made shoes. It is especially good for shoes that are subject to heavy wear, such as school shoes and work shoes. In this type of construction the sole and the upper are joined by being stitched to a narrow strip of leather called the welt. Illustration No. 132 shows an example of this construction. The welt shoe can be identified by examining the inside and lifting the lining, if there is one. The inside should be smooth. If tacks or thread can be felt or seen, the shoe has not been made by the welt construction. Shoes constructed in this manner are relatively easy to repair provided the welt is strong.

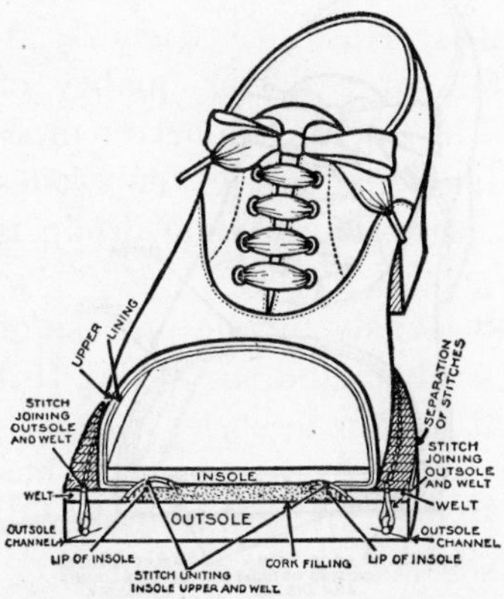

Illustration No. 132—A Section of the Welt Shoe

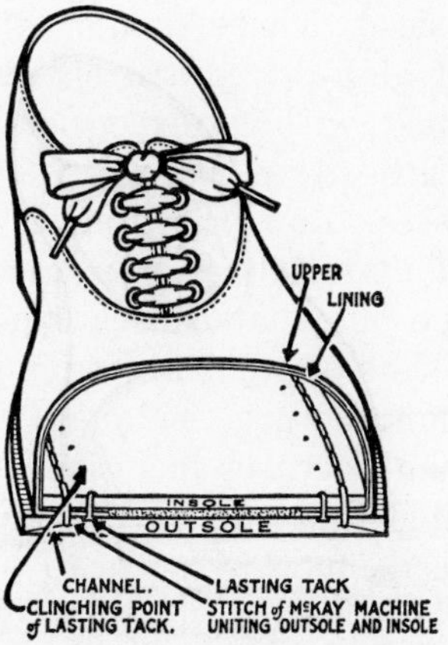

Illustration No. 133—A Section of the McKay Shoe

The *McKay* construction is used for medium- and low-priced shoes, particularly women's shoes. About 35 per cent of all American-made shoes are made in this manner. The insole and the outsole are fastened together with tacks and are then stitched. The stitches on the inside are covered by a thin lining. The stitching on the outside is hidden in a channel that is made by splitting the outsole. Illustration No. 133 shows an example of this construction. McKay shoes are made generally for women and children. Such a shoe may be identified by lifting the lining. The sewing and the tacks near the edge will then be evident. In some cases the stitching and the tacks may hurt the feet.

Shoes made with *turned* soles comprise about 15 per cent of all American-made footwear. This type of construction is used especially in the manufacture of high-grade boots, shoes, and slippers for women and children. It and the Littleway method are considered the best types. No insole is used. The outsole is channeled and sewed to the upper. Illustration No. 134 shows an example of this construction. When the lining of a turned shoe is lifted, the seam should be evident in the groove at the edge of the sole. This type of shoe can be distinguished from the McKay type because the sewing in the former case is farther from the edge of the sole.

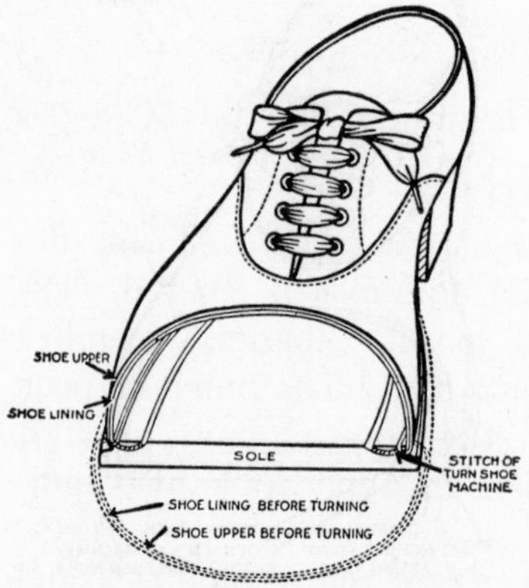

Illustration No. 134—A Section of the Turned Shoe

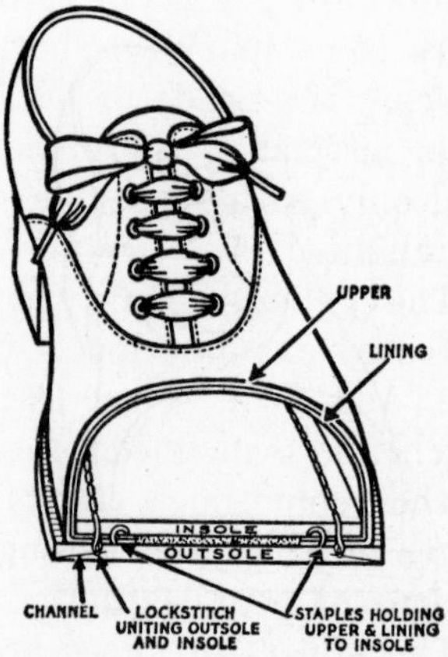

Illustration No. 135—A Section of the Littleway Shoe

The *Littleway* method is somewhat similar to lower grades of construction, although the staples do not come through the insole. It is used in the manufacture of shoes for women and children and also for athletic wear. Work shoes are sometimes manufactured by this method. Illustration No. 135 shows an example of this type of construction. The Littleway process can be distinguished from the McKay process by the absence of tacks or staples on the surface of the insole.

Many children's shoes are made by the *stitchdown* process. In this process the upper is stitched to the insole and the outsole. This method produces a very satisfactory shoe for small children. Illustration No. 136 shows an example of this type of construction. Shoes made in this way can be identified by the smooth insole and by the inner edge of the welt, which shows on the outside of the sole when the upper is pushed back.

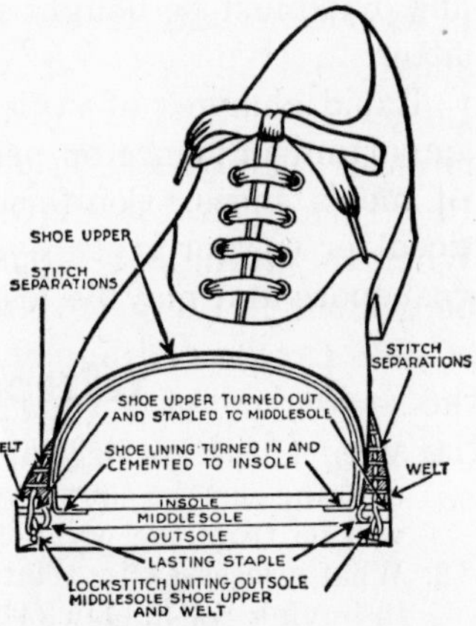

Illustration No. 136—A Section of the Stitchdown Shoe

Kinds of Leather. The average person is not in a position to judge the specific quality of leather. Furthermore, there is no mark on shoes to indicate the grade of leather. It is advisable, therefore, to deal only with reputable shoe merchants.

The general quality of leather can, however, be detected by examination. Good leather is closely fibered, flexible, and firm. Poor leather is loosely fibered, stretches much, and is inclined to break when bent. The finish on poor leather sometimes cracks when the shoe is bent. Rough edges on soles and a rough finish on uppers are also indications of poor leather.

The uppers of shoes are made from many qualities and kinds of leather. Calfskin is probably the best kind for the uppers of dress shoes. Various other heavy skins are used as substitutes. Many varieties of special leathers are coming into use. These include the skins of reptiles, deer, ostrich, and kangaroo, and many substitutes for them. The buying of shoes made of novelty and special leathers also presents difficulties. Again, the only safe method is to buy from reputable dealers.

Comfort Versus Style and Cost. One of the most important considerations in buying shoes is to get the right size and shape. Sometimes style must be ignored, at least partially. The arch, the lining, the size, and the shape are far more important than style. Failure to buy properly fitting shoes may cause ill health and physical deformity. Wise buyers realize that shoes cannot be bought like other clothing, but must be bought with the advice of a capable shoefitter.

Rapid changes of style in women's shoes often have an important influence on price. Style also influences the price of men's shoes. Comfort should never, however, be sacrificed for cost or style, even though comfortable shoes may cost more and may be less stylish than other shoes.

TEXTBOOK QUESTIONS

1. What labels are helpful guides in determining (a) how well clothing can be laundered and (b) how serviceable clothing will be from the point of view of cleaning?
2. What processes in relation to shrinkage are reliable guides in buying washable clothes?
3. What is the standard trade name for all types of fabrics made from cellulose, which are sometimes incorrectly referred to as artificial silk?
4. Name at least three trade names of furs that are really rabbit fur.
5. How can one prove definitely that silk cloth has been weighted?
6. How can silk be distinguished from rayon?
7. Explain the creasing test.
8. Explain how yarns may be tested.
9. Explain the lye test.
10. Explain the acid test.
11. Explain the burning test.
12. What tests can be used to determine whether cloth will hold its color?

13. (a) What are the three general classes of shoes with respect to cost? (b) In what general ways do shoes of these classes differ?
14. Name the principal types of shoe construction in the order of the quality of the process.
15. By examining shoes, how can the average person determine the quality of the leather?
16. How can the quality of the leather in shoes be determined by examining the edges of the soles or the finish on the uppers?
17. What is considered to be the best type of leather for the uppers of dress shoes?
18. What is the most important element to consider in buying shoes: style, quality of leather, comfort, color, price? Why?

DISCUSSION QUESTIONS

1. (a) Should you always buy clothing of the best grade? (b) How can you determine which is the best grade? Discuss your answers to these questions.
2. Cloth is creased several times; the fold is then scratched with the fingernail; and a white dust is loosened. What does this test disclose?
3. On the basis of the discussion in this chapter, explain the steps that you feel are practicable in buying your own clothing.
4. Even though some of the tests explained in this chapter cannot be conducted in a store at the time a purchase is to be made, how are they helpful to the buyer?
5. Women are generally considered to have more trouble with their feet than men. Why do you think this condition exists?
6. From your observations what is your opinion of the effect of style on the price and the wearing quality of shoes?
7. Does the manufacturer's price indicate the quality of a pair of shoes? Explain your answer.
8. What care do you think should be exercised in buying shoes from the stock of a bankrupt store?
9. State some advantages of buying all your shoes at the same place.

PROBLEMS

1. A person buys two summer suits. One suit can be laundered, but the other must be dry cleaned. The suit that can be laundered costs $12 and is expected to last two years. It will have to be laundered eight times during each summer at a cost of 50 cents each time. The other suit costs $20

and is expected to last three years. It will have to be dry cleaned four times during each summer at a cost of $1 each time. Figure the yearly cost of each suit, considering that the original cost in each case is divided equally over the number of years during which the suit will be worn.

2. Window curtains of a particular kind cost $1.60 a pair and will wear, on the average, twenty-four months; window curtains of another kind cost $2.10 and will wear, on the average, thirty-six months. Which represents the more economical purchase on the basis of months of wear?
3. Bring to class a newspaper or magazine advertisement showing merchandise bearing some quality designation of a type mentioned in this chapter.
4. Obtain samples of three different kinds of fabrics. Cut them into squares of approximately one inch. Paste them on a sheet of paper, and opposite each write an explanation of why you have classified the fabric as you have.
5. Obtain two different pieces of cotton fabric. Cut them into pieces approximately two inches square. Paste them on a sheet of paper, and opposite each give your opinion of the strength and the general quality of the fabric. Give an analysis of the thread count by marking off a one-inch square on each piece and counting the number of threads running lengthwise and crosswise.

COMMUNITY PROBLEMS AND PROJECTS

1. Obtain samples of two pieces of cloth that are supposed to be all wool or to contain part wool. Conduct tests in your home to determine whether the cloths are made of wool. Submit a report giving the results and your conclusions.
2. Obtain samples of at least two pieces of cloth that are supposed to be silk. Conduct tests in your home to determine whether the cloths do contain silk. Report the results of the tests and your conclusions.
3. Obtain samples of at least two pieces of cloth of a similar nature. Make a thread count for each piece of cloth. Submit your samples with a written report of your findings.
4. Compare four pieces of similar cloth by subjecting them to the sun test or the washing test. Submit the samples with a written report on your procedure and the results.
5. Bring to class an advertisement of a fur coat, and try to determine from the list given in this book the exact kind of fur that is being advertised.

CHAPTER XVI

HOW TO BUY APPLIANCES AND AUTOMOBILES

Purpose of the Chapter. The purchase of a household appliance or of some mechanical product is an important problem in the average home, for it involves a major expenditure. As such a transaction occurs less frequently than the purchase of food and clothing, the householder obtains relatively little practice in buying appliances and mechanical goods. It is important, therefore, to know in advance how to proceed wisely. In a book of this kind it is impossible to discuss all household appliances and mechanical products, but the more important types will be considered.

Buying Household Ranges

Seal of Approval. All the gas-burning appliances that are tested and approved by the American Gas Association bear the laboratory seal of that association. This carries the name of the association and states that the appliance fulfills national requirements. These standards relate to safety, construction, and performance. This seal not only guarantees that the appliance on which it appears complies with safety requirements, but also ensures efficient operation. There is no guarantee of quality beyond these assurances.

Examining a Gas Range. Not all gas ranges bear the seal of approval of the American Gas Association. The absence of this seal is not, however, a definite indication of poor quality. In buying a gas range, the purchaser should consider the following points:

(a) Is the product manufactured by a reliable company?
(b) Will the range fit into the space available?
(c) Is the seller of the range dependable for prompt installation and service?
(d) Is the product well constructed with regard to surface, movable parts, legs, and the like?

(e) Is the oven of the proper size and height, and does it have suitable shelves and broiler?
(f) In what way does this range surpass other comparable makes?
(g) Is there complete combustion of gas?
(h) Are there any special features?

Asking Questions. The purchaser should not be satisfied solely with his examination of the product. He should ask questions and observe whether he is given intelligent answers. The following questions should be asked:

(a) What is the cost of operation?
(b) Is any guarantee in printed form issued by the manufacturer or the dealer?
(c) Is the oven properly insulated to conserve heat and to prevent excess heating of the kitchen?

Selecting an Electric Range. The problem of buying a range is much the same whether the range uses wood, coal, electricity, or any other fuel. Essentially the same questions can be asked with regard to all types of ranges, but additional points should be observed and additional questions asked in buying an electric range. For instance, the purchaser should learn all that is possible about the switches and the general operation of the stove. The length of life of the heating unit and the type of electric current required are also important items of information. In buying any type of range, the purchaser should learn what results other people have obtained from using the same make.

Buying Refrigerators

Factors in Performance. A study of the Federal Consumers' Advisory Board discloses the fact that there are five points to be considered in the satisfactory performance of refrigerators. These apply to ice-storage refrigerators as well as to electric refrigerators. They are discussed in the following paragraphs:

(a) *Temperature that the refrigerator will maintain.* Tests disclose that the following temperatures are necessary to preserve particular types of food under average conditions:

Milk, milk dishes, butter, broth, desserts	Not over 45° F.
Uncooked meats, poultry, covered jars of salad material	Not over 47° F.
Berries, cooked meats	Not over 48° F.
Cooked vegetables, eggs, fats, left-overs	Not over 50° F.
Uncooked fruits and vegetables	Not over 52° F.

(b) *Cost of operation.* When one considers the cost of operation of a refrigerator, he must take into consideration the following factors:

(1) Actual tests that show the cost of ice, electricity, gas, or kerosene at a constant room temperature
(2) The rate of depreciation of the refrigerator (Five or ten per cent of the cost of the refrigerator can be considered the expense of each year)
(3) Cost of repairs (Warranties, guarantees, and service contracts should be considered carefully)
(4) The durability of construction can be judged by the rigidity of the frame, the quality of the insulation, and the quality of the hardware. The National Association of Ice Industries recommends corkwood as being one of the best insulation materials. The efficiency of insulation, however, cannot be measured entirely by the type of material used. Actual tests are more reliable

(c) *Storage space and freezing capacity.* Manufacturers of ice-storage refrigerators construct them so that the ice compartment has a definite relation to the food-storage space. In better refrigerators the food-storage space is greater in proportion to the ice compartment than it is in refrigerators of lower grades.

In considering mechanical refrigerators, one should determine the amount of food-storage space, the amount of shelf space, the rate of freezing, and the capacity of freezing. The rate and the capacity of freezing should be measured at a definite room temperature. In some mechanical refrigerators, fast freezing will cause the freezing of certain foods in the refrigerator and therefore will spoil them. On the other hand, some of the refrigerators have a freezing compartment as an added feature for housewives who wish to freeze meats and other foods.

Weighing Values. A refrigerator should not be bought merely on the basis of advertisements or sales talks. As it represents an important investment in the average household, its purchase should be considered carefully. The following points should be thought over before the selection is made:

(a) How much will the refrigerator be used if it is purchased?
(b) What will be the original cost and the operating cost?
(c) Does the model selected measure up to acceptable standards of performance?
(d) Will electricity (or gas, ice, kerosene, or water) be available for operating the refrigerator?
(e) Is the saving from food spoilage a justification for buying the refrigerator?

In comparing refrigerators for the purposes of making a selection, the buyer has a right to ask questions and should insist upon being given satisfactory answers. The following are some of the questions that should be asked the salesman:

(a) What temperature does the refrigerator maintain?
(b) If the refrigerator is operated by electricity (or gas or kerosene), what is the rate of freezing?
(c) What is the cost of operation?
(d) What assurance is there of proper installation and maintenance by the factory or the dealer?
(e) Is there a guarantee? If so, what are its exact provisions?
(f) Is a cross section of the insulation available for examination?
(g) Will fruit acids damage the interior?

There are many special types of refrigerators. The most common refrigerators, however, are those that use ice, electricity, or gas. In purchasing any refrigerator, it is important to know the cost of operation. In case of a more modern type, such as the electric or the gas refrigerator, the cost can be computed easily in advance. Information on costs of operation can be obtained from certain testing agencies, from friends who own refrigerators, and from manufacturers and dealers. The important thing is to obtain a refrigerator that will have a long life, can be operated economically, and will maintain an even temperature. The average temperature of a modern type of refrigerator should not exceed 45 degrees in the milk compartment and 50 degrees in the food compartment, when the outside temperatures average 80 degrees with occasional periods of 90 degrees or higher.

Quietness of operation is important in the mechanical refrigerator. Although it may be quiet when new, it may later become noisy. The experiences of others with the same make will aid the purchaser. Another consideration is the assurance of adequate service. Service will depend upon the reliability of the manufacturer and the distributor. A buyer should be assured that he can get adequate service.

Buying Other Mechanical Equipment

Principles of Selection. The mechanical equipment of a modern home frequently includes such items as electric cleaners; electric mixing machines; electric, gasoline, or water-power washing machines; and many other labor-saving appliances. The problems involved in purchasing labor-saving equipment are much the same in every case. The electric washing machine is an excellent example. The following are some of the important points to consider when one buys an electric washing machine:

(a) Is the machine made by a reliable manufacturer?
(b) Is service assured through the local dealer?
(c) What results have others obtained from using the same type of machine?
(d) Are the mechanical parts safe, and is the operation of the machine simple?
(e) Will the agitator injure the types of fabrics that will have to be washed in the machine?
(f) Will the noise and the vibration be undesirable?
(g) Can the machine be moved easily?
(h) Can the tub be drained easily, and is the opening large enough to prevent clogging?
(i) Is the tub durable, and can it be cleaned easily?
(j) Is a wringer or an extractor preferable?
(k) If the wringer is used, is there a safety device?

(l) Is the motor made by a reliable manufacturer; is it of the proper voltage; and can it be operated on the current that is available?
(m) Are the working parts enclosed to ensure safety?
(n) Are there any special features?
(o) Is the actual time required for adequate cleansing comparable to that required by two or more similar machines?
(p) Is the machine of adequate size and capacity to handle the work for which it is being considered?

Investigation. If the machines that are being considered have been used by friends, helpful information can be obtained. Additional definite information should be obtained from the salesman. The following questions are appropriate:
(a) What is the cost of operation?
(b) What care does the machine require?
(c) Will any parts need to be replaced occasionally?
(d) How long will the machine last?
(e) Is there any guarantee?
(f) What service can be expected?

Price should be considered as a relative matter. A machine that sells for fifty dollars may be a bargain as compared with one that sells for forty. All the factors of quality, length of life, and cost of operation must be taken into consideration with price. Whenever possible, the choice should be based on comparison.

Buying Automobiles and Automobile Supplies

Types of Automobile Engines. As a general rule, an automobile with high power in proportion to its weight will give the better performance as to speed and acceleration, but will not operate so economically as an automobile with low power in proportion to its weight. Furthermore, a high-speed engine normally will not last so long as one with less power.

Analysis of Values. Prospective buyers should learn to weigh the value of one product as compared with that of another. It is true that a purchaser can virtually shut his eyes and buy any one of several automobiles and yet get one that will give satisfactory performance. On the other hand, he should not pay more than is necessary to get what he wants. Some analysis should therefore be made so that actual values can be compared. A prospective buyer should select the automobile that not only has the largest number of points that appeal to him but also will be of the greatest benefit to him.

Let us examine, for example, the check sheet prepared by Mr. Thompson, a prospective purchaser of an automobile. This check sheet is shown in Illustration No. 137. Forms such as this are made available by some automobile manufacturers, but they can be compiled by anyone. The danger of using a check sheet prepared by a producer is that it may be constructed with the idea of influencing a person to buy the product of that company.

Mr. Thompson used this check sheet in evaluating the desirable features of three automobiles that were within the range of price that he could afford to pay. He used a check mark to indicate each factor that he approved on each automobile. For instance, from the point of view of Mr. Thompson, Automobile A had the most dependable brakes. In comparison with those on the other automobiles, he considered the brakes on this automobile to be sufficiently superior to justify approving the brakes on only the one car.

The final summary shows that Automobile A had fifty-four points that were approved, and that Automobiles B and C had forty-four and thirty-three respectively. Mr. Thompson selected Automobile A, although other people might select Automobile B or Automobile C. Some features outweigh others. One factor may be important to one person, but not important to another. For instance, if the gas consumption of Automobile C were much more economical than that of Automobile A, a person who was thinking largely in terms of economy would give favorable consideration to Automobile C.

This same type of evaluation can be used for all kinds of mechanical equipment and for many other products that are purchased by the average consumer. If the buyer does not follow a formal plan of checking various features, he can do so mentally.

FACTORS FOR EVALUATING AUTOMOBILES

Check the Factors that Have Been Approved in Examining Each Automobile

	Car A	Car B	Car C
Dependability:			
Air Cleaner	√	√	
Automatic Shock Absorbers	√	√	√
Good Braking System	√		
Adequate Cooling System	√		√
Close-fitting Doors	√	√	
Quick-starting Engine		√	√
Frame		√	√
Repair Parts	√	√	
Reputation of Maker	√	√	
Service	√	√	
Economy:			
Lubrication		√	√
Service	√	√	√
Fuel Consumption		√	√
Oil Consumption		√	√
Quality of Finish		√	√
Safety:			
Body Construction	√		√
Braking System	√		
Bumpers	√	√	√
Frame		√	√
Headlights		√	√
Headlight Dimmer Control	√		
Horn	√	√	
Instruments	√	√	√
Locks		√	√
Safety Glass	√		
Speed	√		
Steering Apparatus	√	√	√
Vision	√	√	
Appearance:			
Side View	√	√	
Front View	√	√	√
Rear View	√	√	√
Body Hardware (Interior and Exterior)	√	√	
Bumpers	√		√
Color	√		√
Fenders and Mud Guards	√	√	
Finish	√		√
Interior	√	√	
Running Boards	√	√	√
Comfort and Smoothness:			
Accelerator	√	√	√
Adjustable Front Seat	√	√	
Arm Rests		√	
Heat Control	√		
Automatic Shock Absorbers	√	√	√
Clutch	√		
Ventilators	√		
Foot Rest	√		
Power	√		√
Rubber Mountings	√	√	
Seats and Cushions	√	√	
Silent Gears	√	√	
Wheelbase	√		
Springs	√		
Ease of Control:			
Clutch	√		
Door Locks	√	√	
Engine	√		
Foot Controls	√	√	
Instruments		√	
Light Switches			√
Starting System	√	√	
Steering Apparatus	√	√	√
Transmission			√
Turning Radius			√
Vision	√	√	√
Other Factors:			
Automatic Clutch	√		
Free Wheeling	√		
Pick-up			√
Cruising Speed	√	√	
Frequent Change in Design	√	√	√
Price	√	√	√
Total Points Approved	54	44	33

Illustration No. 137—A Check Sheet for Evaluating Automobiles

Gasoline and Oil Consumption. The consumer should know that every automobile burns more gasoline at a high rate of speed than it does at a reasonable rate of speed. Furthermore, there is a difference among automobiles. Some will burn more gasoline than others at certain rates of speed. The chart in Illustration No. 138 shows the quantity of gasoline burned by each of five different automobiles at varying rates of speed. For each of these automobiles the most economical rate of speed is between twenty and thirty miles an hour. When a person is selecting an automobile on the basis of economy, he will want to consider gasoline and oil consumption.

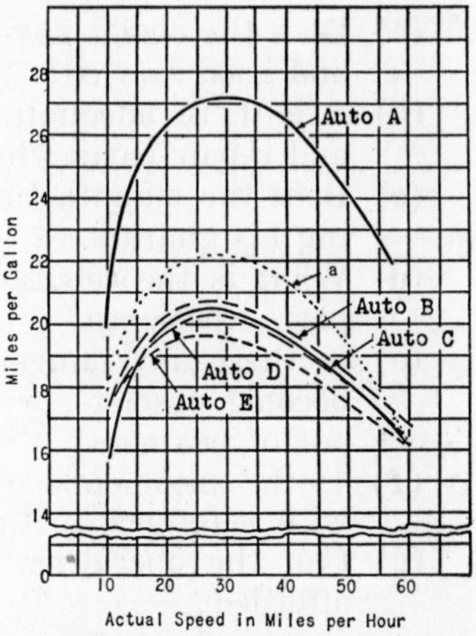

Reprinted from *Consumers' Research Bulletin*, February, 1939, by special permission of Consumers' Research, Inc., Washington, New Jersey

Illustration No. 138—Gasoline Consumption

Every automobile must consume a certain quantity of oil because oil lubricates the mechanism. Nevertheless, some automobiles consume excessive quantities of oil. For instance, the following table shows the quantity of oil consumed by each of five automobiles in the same price class:

Oil Consumption

Automobile A	1,670 miles on a quart of oil
Automobile B	1,180 miles on a quart of oil
Automobile C	990 miles on a quart of oil
Automobile D	880 miles on a quart of oil
Automobile E	830 miles on a quart of oil

Illustration No. 139—Oil Consumption

General Factors to Be Considered. Although the engine of an automobile is the matter of first importance, there are many other important factors. The check list on page 404 shows the points to be investigated in purchasing an automobile. Riding comfort, ease of driving as well as of starting and stopping, safety, and reasonable economy of operation are important factors. Still other considerations are as follows:

(a) Does the dealer have a reputation for fair treatment and good service?
(b) Are there adequate facilities for obtaining service and repair parts where the automobile will be used?
(c) Does the manufacturer have a reputation for fulfilling his guarantee?
(d) What is the reputation of the automobile based on past experience?
(e) Is there any danger that the automobile will soon become obsolete or that the manufacturer will go out of business?
(f) Is the automobile within a satisfactory price range with reference to the budget?
(g) Can the operating expenses of the automobile be afforded?

Automobile Depreciation. For practical consideration, depreciation of an automobile and loss from obsolescence are the same. When a person drives a new automobile out of an agency and takes the title to it, he suffers a loss due to obsolescence, although the automobile has not depreciated because of wear or deterioration. If the automobile were to be resold immediately, the owner would have to accept a price lower than that he paid. Depreciation, on the other hand, results from wear.

If an automobile is used for business purposes, the Federal Government will allow the owner, in computing his income tax, to deduct depreciation to the extent of one fourth of the cost during each of the four years after the purchase. In other words, the Federal Government recognizes that an automobile used for business purposes normally serves its useful life in four years.

Most people find that it is most economical to trade in a car at least every three or four years. Although an automobile may have been driven less in three years than another was driven in two, it is a common practice in the automobile industry to allow less for the automobile that has been driven three years than for the one that has been driven two. This practice is based on the fact that the older model has become more obsolete than the one that has been out only two years.

Two automobiles that were purchased at the same price may not have the same trade-in value because one of them may have a greater rate of depreciation. The greater rate of depreciation arises from the fact that cars of this make are not readily salable as secondhand or used automobiles. If one is interested in owning an automobile that has a relatively good trade-in or secondhand value, he should consider this fact when he purchases a new car. In general, the higher the purchase price of the car, the greater the percentage of depreciation and the greater the total amount of depreciation. Consumers' Research publishes yearly figures on the depreciation of automobiles.

Figuring the Initial Cost. The actual cost of an automobile is usually greater than the advertised cost. The advertised cost is ordinarily stated "f.o.b. the factory." This term means free on board at the factory; that is, the buyer is expected to pay the shipping costs. A handling charge, and frequently a charge for extra equipment, must be added to the factory price. It is difficult to determine what is included in the handling charge. This charge may range from 10 to 35 per cent of the factory price, depending to some extent upon where the automobile is delivered. Sometimes the price quoted on an automobile does not include the cost of spare tires, bumpers, and other equipment that the average driver considers necessary. All these additional charges should be investigated before an order for an automobile is signed.

New Devices. Many automobile manufacturers make it a practice each year to install new devices that will help in competing for business. They hope that the new devices will be an improvement and that purchasers will want automobiles in which these new devices have been installed. Frequently so much emphasis is placed upon these relatively insignificant devices that the buyer overlooks other undesirable characteristics. The wise buyer will not be too eager to accept a new device and certainly will not allow a single new device to outweigh all other considerations in the choice of an automobile. The check sheet on page 404 will help a person to weigh values without placing too much emphasis on a new device. Sometimes new devices prove to be unsatisfactory and are discontinued by manufacturers after one or two years.

Automobile Supplies. Tires, oil, and gasoline represent the major operating costs of an automobile. The problem of buying automobile supplies, of which these are the chief items, is so important that technical information should be obtained from some authoritative source. Consumers' Research, Incorporated, and other testing agencies are in a position to furnish such information. Large companies and some public institutions have their own testing laboratories for guidance in buying these supplies.

The most expensive product is not necessarily the best; but cheap tires, oils, or gasolines are frequently not economical. Some cheap oils may damage the engine, and some cheap gasolines may cause the formation of carbon and a loss of power. A number of the more expensive gasolines, however, are not adapted to high-speed and high-compression engines. The only safe guide in buying automobile supplies is to learn from authoritative tests what products measure up to reasonable standards. Two or three of the better products should then be selected for regular use.

TEXTBOOK QUESTIONS

1. If a gas-burning appliance bears the seal of the American Gas Association, what can you assume with regard to the quality of the appliance?
2. If a gas-burning appliance does not bear the seal of approval of the American Gas Association, is that fact an indication that the appliance is of a poor quality?
3. What are eight points to be considered in buying a gas range?
4. What additional factors should be considered in buying an electric range?
5. What is the maximum temperature that should be permitted in a refrigerator to preserve (a) milk, (b) cooked meats, (c) uncooked fruits and vegetables?
6. What four factors with regard to cost should be considered before selecting a refrigerator?

7. What are seven questions that you would ask a salesman if you were buying a refrigerator?
8. What are at least six points to be considered in buying an electric washing machine?
9. What information would you expect to obtain from a salesman if you were buying a household appliance, such as a washing machine?
10. In addition to the factors listed on the check sheet on page 404, what others should be considered in selecting an automobile?
11. (a) What is depreciation of an automobile? (b) What is obsolescence?
12. Why can the owner of a two-year-old automobile usually get a better trade-in allowance than the owner of a three-year-old automobile, even though the latter car has been driven less? Assume that both cars are in the same condition.
13. Do all automobiles consume about the same quantity of gasoline and of oil at the same speed?
14. Which cars usually depreciate more rapidly: (a) low-priced cars or (b) high-priced cars?
15. What usually accounts for the difference between the advertised price of an automobile and the delivered price?
16. Why should one give relatively little attention to the sales emphasis placed on a new device on an automobile?

DISCUSSION QUESTIONS

1. How does the seal of approval of the American Gas Association protect a purchaser against inferior materials in a gas appliance?
2. Discuss the importance of selecting a household appliance made by a reliable manufacturer and of purchasing it through a reliable dealer.
3. Discuss the type of guarantee that you think would be acceptable if you were buying an electric refrigerator.
4. If you were examining an enameled gas range with a view to buying it, what information do you think you should rightfully expect the salesman to give you?
5. When you try to investigate the performance of an electric refrigerator, you find that styles in refrigerators change so frequently that it is impossible to form any conclusions unless a comparison is made with older models of the same refrigerator. What are some of the factors that could be investigated in order that you might base some of your conclusions on the experience of those who are using older models?

6. A dealer advertises the sale of the electric refrigerators of a bankrupt manufacturer at 75 per cent of the cost. (a) Would you consider such an electric refrigerator to be a bargain? (b) Would you buy one? Give your reasons.
7. From your knowledge of copper, enamel, and aluminum, what do you think would be the advantages and the disadvantages of washing machines made from each of these three kinds of materials?
8. What do you think are the factors that determine a good electric cleaner?
9. What would you consider to be the factors by which the quality of an electric toaster could be measured?
10. Discuss repair service as a factor in buying an automobile.
11. In proportion to the original cost of the automobile, a large secondhand automobile can be purchased for less than a small used automobile of the same age. Why is this true?
12. (a) Discuss the merits of some of the claims in relation to new devices on automobiles. (b) In buying an automobile, to what extent would you be influenced by new devices?

PROBLEMS

1. A family that has a savings budget of $10 a month wishes to buy an electric refrigerator. The payments will amount to $10 a month for twelve months. The increase in the electric bill will average 85 cents a month. Past experience discloses that the average amount spent for ice during the warm weather is $12 a year. The family does not want to withdraw anything from its savings fund to use in paying the monthly installments. (a) Can a plan be worked out satisfactorily? (b) If the refrigerator will cost $120 and can be used no more than twenty years, do you think it will be a wise investment? Under what circumstances?
2. The Williams family keeps a record of the costs of ice used during the warm weather in one year. These costs are as follows: April, $3; May, $3.25; June, $3.40; July, $4.50; August, $4.25; September, $3.15; October, 75 cents. Omitting any consideration of food savings, the Williams family tries to decide whether to buy an electric refrigerator. Investigation discloses that a family that has been using the type of refrigerator that is being considered paid an average monthly electric bill of $2.35 before buying the electric refrigerator, but has paid an average monthly electric bill of $3.45 since buying the electric refrigerator. From the point of view of costs of operation, would the purchase of the refrigerator result in a saving or an added expense for the Williams family?

3. On the basis of the check list on page 404, prepare a check list for use as a guide in purchasing an electric food mixer.
4. A company that uses a large number of automobiles finds that the average costs per mile for the operation of each automobile are:

Gasoline and oil	$0.0148
Garage rent	.0026
Repairs	.007
Insurance	.0013
Depreciation	.0156

(a) What should be the annual cost of operating an automobile that is driven 30,000 miles during the year? (b) On the basis of the costs listed above, what should be the monthly cost of operating an automobile if the owner drives the car about 10,000 miles a year and trades it in on a new automobile at the end of three years?
5. If insurance on an automobile costs $40 a year, gasoline and oil cost 1.29 cents a mile, and repairs average .52 cents a mile, what is the average yearly cost if the automobile is driven 8,000 miles a year and is traded in at the end of three years at an allowance of $200? Assume that the automobile originally cost $740.

COMMUNITY PROBLEMS AND PROJECTS

1. On the basis of the check sheet on page 404, investigate at least two automobiles. Write a report on your findings. In your report reproduce the check sheet. Explain your procedure, and justify your conclusions as to which is the better automobile.
2. Obtain all the advertising literature that you can on two competitive household appliances. On the basis of the information that is available, write a report in which you compare these appliances.
3. From two local businesses that sell competitive types of a household appliance, find out the installation service, the repair service, the adjustment service, and the guarantee offered by each. Without considering the quality of either make, write a report giving your conclusions as to the reliability of each make on the basis of the services and the guarantee.
4. Obtain samples of written guarantees on various types of household appliances. Study these guarantees. Write a report pointing out their advantages and their inadequacies as protection for the buyer.

CHAPTER XVII

HOW TO BUY FURNITURE AND FLOOR COVERINGS

Purpose of the Chapter. Many items make up the furnishings of the average household. The purchase of furniture and floor coverings is an important problem. These items are not purchased often; but when they are purchased, they deserve careful consideration, for they will be used a long time. The primary purpose of this chapter is to establish a few fundamental standards by which furniture and floor coverings can be judged without the necessity of a technical analysis. Another purpose of the chapter is to indicate means of judging the proper amount to be spent for furniture and floor coverings on the basis of various budgets and homes of different sizes. In this respect the chapter correlates closely with that on budgeting.

Following a Definite Plan. The householder should *buy* furniture and not allow himself to be *sold* furniture. In furnishing a home, it is desirable to know in advance the space to be filled and the amount of money that may be used. Of course, the ideal situation is one in which the funds available will permit the furnishing of all the rooms adequately. In many cases, however, the budget must be stretched considerably to buy the bare necessities.

Deliberation will help to eliminate unwise buying. There are two extremes to be avoided. One is a disproportionate expenditure for a few pieces of furniture at the sacrifice of other necessary pieces. The other extreme is the buying of unsatisfactory furniture at a low price in order to obtain a full suite.

The suitability of furniture depends largely on personal taste. Good judgment can, however, be formed by studying color combinations, by considering the space that is available, by observing the furnishings in other homes, and by examining the furniture in several stores.

What Is a Good Furniture Wood? The type of wood has an important relation to the price of furniture. It also has an important relation to the quality and the wearing features. Some woods crack easily and show scratches readily. Those that are soft show marks easily. Others are subject to warping when exposed to moisture.

The ideal wood for furniture possesses enough hardness to resist normal wear, yet it is sufficiently soft to be worked with ordinary tools without splitting. It should also be subject to minimum swelling and shrinkage. The natural grains are attractive, although no wood is perfect in this respect. Some woods have one desirable feature, but lack some other. The problem resolves itself into getting the best wood one can afford at a reasonable price.

Kinds of Woods. Walnut is almost an ideal wood for furniture because it combines beauty, strength, and durability. There are various grades of walnut, most of which are good. Oak is a good wood for furniture because it is solid and substantial. It is so hard that it is not subject to scratching, as are many of the other woods.

Gum is one of the most widely used of the American hardwoods. It is used frequently by itself and in many cases in combination with other wood. It is not so desirable as the two previously mentioned woods because it is softer and is subject to scratching and warping.

Birch, maple, beech, chestnut, and cherry are also good woods for furniture. Mahogany is excellent, but most of it is imported and is therefore costly, although it is often not so costly as walnut.

The softer woods, such as poplar, spruce, and pine, are not so desirable for furniture because of their relative lack of durability and beauty.

The average person who is not familiar with woods cannot rely upon his own judgment in distinguishing them. In selecting a piece of furniture, he should therefore be sure to observe whether it is made of more than one piece of wood, how much of it is solid, and what parts are made of veneer. Ask what kind or combinations of wood are used in its construction.

Veneer. As a general rule, but not always, furniture made of a solid wood is more expensive than a comparable piece made wholly or partially of veneer. Solid wood can be carved. If it is scratched or chipped, there is no danger, as in the case of veneer, that a thin surface layer of wood will be penetrated. The use of veneer, however, is not necessarily an indication of low quality.

Veneer consists of two or more thin layers of wood glued together. Veneer makes it possible to use a good piece of wood for the surface of furniture and a cheaper piece for those parts underneath the surface. Large panels and the tops of large tables are less liable to warp if they are made of veneer than if they are of a solid wood. Cheap veneer may blister, however, because moisture loosens the glue. It also may develop checks and cracks.

The mechanical construction of a piece of furniture may be perfect, but the beauty of the piece may have been lessened by carelessness in matching the grain of the veneer in a panel. The beauty of the grain in the wood is one indication of quality, whereas the careful matching of the grain tends to indicate good workmanship. Illustration No. 140 shows how veneer is matched in creating attractive designs. Unusual designs may be created in this way. Drawer fronts, doors, and table tops made of veneer often have beautiful patterns.

Illustration No. 140—Well-Matched Veneer

When examining a piece of furniture, the purchaser should look underneath and inside it if possible. He should notice ends that can be examined. A place that is not covered with varnish and stain is preferable for examination. It is easy to distinguish veneer from solid wood because veneer is composed of two or more thin layers of wood with the grains crossing. The purchaser should find out whether the furniture is made of just one kind of wood or of more than one kind.

The quality of veneer depends largely on (a) the care used in gluing, (b) the number of layers, and (c) the kind and the thickness of the veneer. The only way in which a casual observer can judge the quality of the gluing is to observe whether the veneer is coming loose in any place. This test is not absolute, however. It is often easy to determine the number of layers. When other factors are not considered, the veneer with the greater number of layers is the better piece of veneer. Illustration No. 141 shows five-ply and three-ply veneer. Although it is too much to expect the average person to be able to judge the quality of the wood used in a veneer, he can usually detect the thickness of the surface veneer. If this veneer is too thin, it will scratch easily or absorb moisture.

Color or Stain. Furniture is frequently advertised as having "walnut finish" or "maple finish." These terms do not indicate the kind of wood or veneer. They merely indicate the kind of stain that has been used. The wood may be, and probably is, entirely different. A walnut stain, for instance, may be given to furniture made of pine; but this treatment does not improve the quality of the wood.

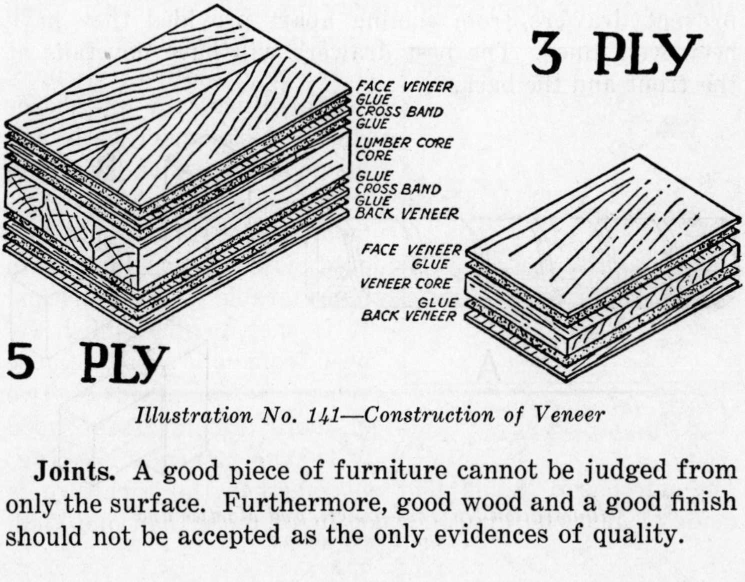

Illustration No. 141—Construction of Veneer

Joints. A good piece of furniture cannot be judged from only the surface. Furthermore, good wood and a good finish should not be accepted as the only evidences of quality.

The back of any cabinet will give clues as to the quality of workmanship. The purchaser should notice whether it has been nailed or screwed and whether the work has been done poorly or neatly. The back posts of chairs and beds should be scrutinized carefully to determine how they have been put together. All points where there will be stress and strain should have been reinforced when the furniture was manufactured. Fastening joints together with glue, nails, or screws usually does not provide adequate strength. Corner blocks, which should have been fastened with screws and glue, are important because they add considerable strength.

In the accompanying illustration, the example designated as A shows the dowel type of construction; that designated as B shows the mortise and tenon type of construction. Both types are desirable, for they help to strengthen furniture. Sometimes a combination of the two is used. Example C in Illustration No. 143 shows how a chair joint is frequently put together, and example D shows the assembled joint. Combinations of A and B are sometimes used by employing the dowel with the mortise and tenon. Examples E and F show a typical dovetail joint and dado joint used in the construction of drawers. These joints prevent drawers from coming apart provided they have been well glued. The best drawers will have dovetails at the front and the back.

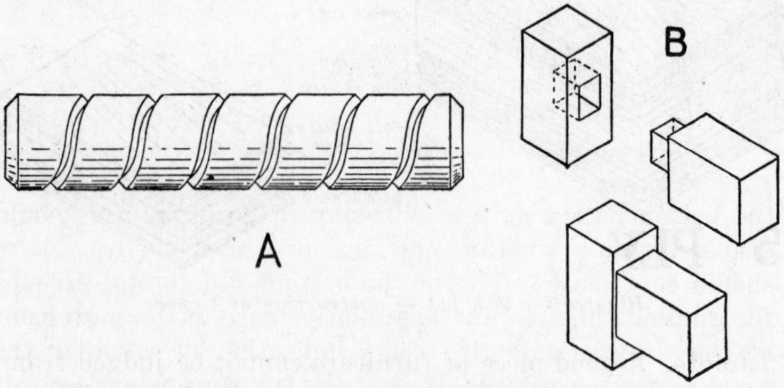

Illustration No. 142—Dowel, and Mortise and Tenon Construction

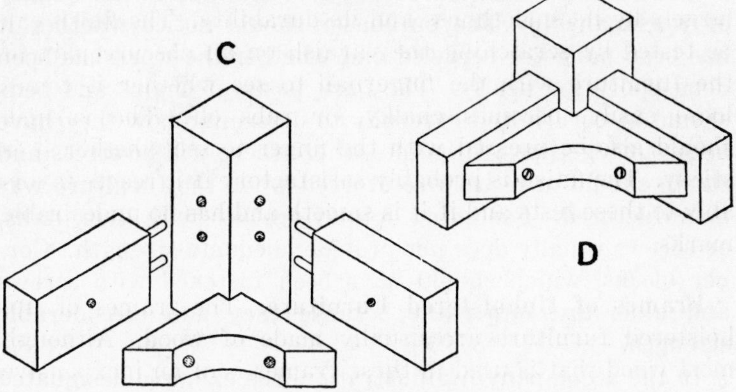

Illustration No. 143—A Good Chair Joint

The drawer is one of the best indications of care in the construction of a piece of furniture, for many things can be observed from the drawer but not elsewhere in the same piece of furniture. The purchaser should observe whether

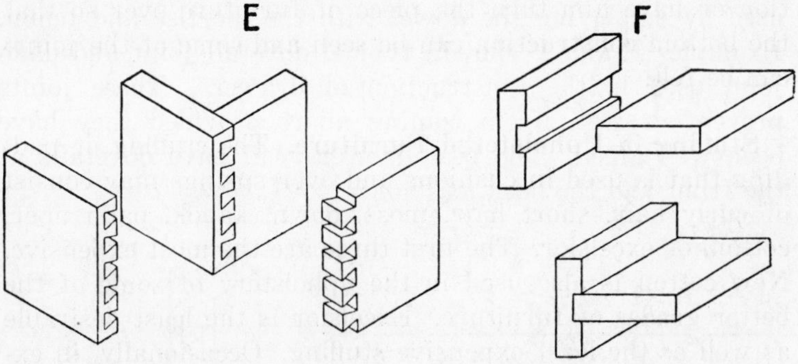

Illustration No. 144—Good Construction for Drawers

the bottom is strong and will stay in position. He should also determine whether the drawer slides easily. There should be a center slide for the bottom and special grooves for guiding the drawer. The relative ease in the movement of the drawer will give some indication of whether the wood is well seasoned. If it sticks or jams when new, it probably will be worse later.

Finish. The finish of a piece of furniture can be judged largely by its smoothness and its durability. The finish can be tested by scratching the varnish on an obscure part of the furniture with the fingernail to see whether it comes loose easily, becomes chalky, or rubs off. The varnish should also be pressed with the finger to see whether it is sticky. The finish is probably satisfactory if it reacts favorably to these tests and if it is smooth and has no undesirable marks.

Frames of Upholstered Furniture. The frames of upholstered furniture are usually made of wood. Although most wood that is used in these frames is of an inexpensive variety, it must be strong and free of knots and cracks to avoid breaking. Ash, birch, and hard maple are used frequently.

The joints of upholstered furniture must be as carefully made as the joints of any other furniture, even though they may be covered. If possible, the purchaser should have the salesman display a cross section of the construction or have him turn the piece of furniture over so that the bottom construction can be seen and some of the joints can be felt.

Stuffing in Upholstered Furniture. The stuffing or padding that is used in cushions and over springs may consist of curly hair, short hair, moss, down, kapok, palm fiber, cotton, or excelsior. The first three are the most expensive. New cotton is also used in the upholstery of some of the better grades of furniture. Excelsior is the least desirable as well as the least expensive stuffing. Occasionally, in exceptionally low-grade furniture, shredded paper has been used. Before buying, therefore, it is wise to examine carefully any mattress or upholstered piece of furniture and to obtain some definite assurance of what has been used for stuffing.

In many states the law requires the labeling of bedding material. If there is a label on a piece of furniture that has upholstery stuffed with cotton, the buyer has the assurance that the cotton used is new.

Coverings of Upholstered Furniture. The coverings of upholstered furniture are made of animal fibers, vegetable fibers, or leather. Woven fabrics may be a combination of animal and vegetable fibers. The animal fibers used for furniture coverings include silk, wool, mohair, and horsehair. The vegetable fibers include cotton, rayon, flax, hemp, and jute. In general, any upholstering material made from an animal fiber will wear longer and will have a better gloss and color than a material made from a vegetable fiber.

Leather is used to a limited extent for upholstering. Good leather is relatively expensive. Some of the modern artificial leathers are very durable.

Pile and Weave of Floor Coverings. The best rugs and carpets are those with (a) the thickest pile and (b) the closest weave. The thickness of the pile depends upon the length of the yarn that protrudes through the base of the fabric and forms the surface. The closeness of the weave in any rug or carpet can be checked by counting the rows on the back. Thirteen rows of tufts to the inch are used in the highest grade of Wilton rug. Ten or twelve to the inch are generally used in a good Axminster rug. A rug with only five rows of tufts to the inch cannot be expected to give good service and should be sold at a low price.

Types of Woven Rugs. The thickness of the pile, the closeness of the weave, the height of the pile, and the quality of the wool are more important than the type of weave. The types of weaves are as follows:

(a) *Cut-pile* carpets and rugs, including Oriental, Chenille, Wilton, Axminster, and Velvet.
(b) *Loop-pile* carpets and rugs, including Brussels and Tapestry weaves.
(c) *Flat-weave* rugs, such as those made of linen, cotton, wool, pulp fiber, and grass, which may be used either side up because both sides are alike.

Carpets and rugs in the first two groups mentioned above will stand the greatest amount of wear.

Another consideration is the particular quality of the rug that is being purchased. Still another is beauty. Some purchasers of rugs are willing to sacrifice a certain amount of quality for beauty. The following discussion points out the characteristics and the merits of individual types of rugs.

Oriental rugs are the most costly of all floor coverings. The value of an Oriental rug can be determined only by an expert. A good Oriental rug will last a very long time. The so-called glossy Oriental rugs have been washed chemically to create the sheen on the surface. These will not wear so long as an unwashed Oriental rug.

Chenille carpets and rugs are not common among the better grades, but they are the most luxurious and will wear a long time because of the densely packed pile.

The *Wilton* rug used to be considered the standard for high-grade rugs and carpets, but such rugs are now produced in low grades as well as high grades.

The *Axminster* is considered excellent for all purposes. Many of the better rugs on the market today are Axminsters.

A *Velvet* rug does not require so much wool yarn as an Axminster because it is made by a more simple method of manufacture. Although Velvet rugs are cheaper to produce, the better grades are very durable.

Brussels carpets and rugs are seldom seen for sale in stores now. They have somewhat the same characteristics as Wiltons except that their pile is uncut. The surface is constructed of tightly looped wool. Some machine-made hooked rugs are manufactured in very much the same manner as the Brussels rug.

Tapestry rugs are made in a manner similar to Velvet rugs except that the pile is left uncut. Such a rug is sometimes referred to as a *Tapestry Brussels.* These rugs often resemble hooked rugs.

Some of the so-called *American Oriental* rugs are misnamed. They are often made in the same way as Wilton, Axminster, and Velvet rugs and are treated so that they have a surface sheen like that of washed Orientals. Many of the American Orientals have patterns copied from genuine Orientals. The value of an American Oriental rug is based upon its weave and not upon the fact that it is called an Oriental.

As *flat-weave* rugs are made of various types of materials, the quality of such a rug depends upon (a) the material used, (b) the thickness, and (c) the firmness of the weave.

Jute and hemp are used largely for the backing of cut-pile and loop-pile rugs and carpets. Jute is cheap and strong, but will decay if it becomes damp. Paper yarns are sometimes used. These are strong when dry but become weak when wet.

Standards for Carpets and Rugs. The National Bureau of Standards has set standards for some types of carpets and rugs. As an example, a summary of those standards for Axminster rugs and carpets is as follows:

(a) The fabric must be woven from the best quality of filling wools with a cotton warp and a filling of jute. All weaving must be even and neat.

(b) The yarn must be elastic and uniform in diameter and strength.

(c) The pile must be evenly and thoroughly dyed with fast dyes.

(d) The weight per carpet yard (27 inches wide and 36 inches long) must not be less than 39.5 ounces, made up approximately as follows: 17.3 wool pile, 5.1 cotton, 17.1 jute. There must not be a variation of more than 5 per cent in the total weight, 5 per cent in the amount of wool, or 10 per cent in the amount of cotton or jute.

(e) The sizing in the rug or the carpet must not be greater than 10 per cent of the total weight.

A leaflet explaining standard specifications for some types of rugs and carpets can be obtained from the National Bureau of Standards and can be used as a guide in examining rugs. If a label on a rug indicates to what extent the rug conforms to Federal standards, the buyer has a good means of judging the quality.

Label of Approval on Rugs. Rugs should be examined to see whether they bear the label of the Institute of Carpet Manufacturers of America. If a rug bears this label, its quality conforms to the strict specifications of that institute.

Rug Cushions. The length of life of any rug or carpet can be prolonged through the use of what is called a *rug cushion.* Such a cushion, which is placed under the rug or the carpet, prolongs the life of the rug.

Fiber Rugs. Fiber rugs are usually made of a composition of paper pulp. The pulp is given special treatment so that the rugs will be hard and durable. Sometimes the pulp is combined with wool and other materials. The wearing qualities of a rug of this type depend largely upon the toughness of the fiber. In purchasing such a rug, one should therefore examine the fiber carefully with the fingernail to judge its toughness.

Another important consideration is whether the rug will hold its color under wear. Unless the color design has been stamped into the rug, it will probably wear off easily.

Linoleum. The use of such a wide variety of materials results in a great difference in quality. Some of the materials that go into the making of linoleum are cork, burlap, linseed oil, flax, cotton, rosin, and dyes. These materials in various combinations are mixed together and heated. They are then spread upon burlap by various processes. After ageing or baking, they develop a hard, rubbery surface.

The linoleum industry has rather generally adopted standard gauges of thickness. The price therefore usually varies in relation to the thickness and the pattern. The most expensive types of linoleum are inlays and special kinds resembling tile.

Felt-Base Rugs. A kind of floor covering that is similar to linoleum is made of felt, asphalt, and paint. The asphalt is placed on a felt base, and durable paint is then applied. The final product is relatively inexpensive and can be obtained in a great variety of sizes. It is not so durable as linoleum. Unless the surface is preserved carefully, the paint will wear off. Some types of felt-base floor coverings are not much more durable than painted paper impregnated with tar. The quality of a felt-base floor covering can be judged by the thickness, the tearing strength, and the durability of the paint on the surface.

TEXTBOOK QUESTIONS

1. What two extremes are to be avoided in buying furniture if it is necessary to budget the expenditures carefully?
2. What are the characteristics of a good wood for furniture?
3. (a) What is considered to be almost an ideal wood for furniture? (b) What is one of the most common American hardwoods? (c) What are some additional desirable woods for furniture?
4. Which is usually the more expensive: furniture made from solid wood or furniture made from veneer?
5. Which is better for panels: solid wood or veneer?
6. What decorative advantage has veneer?
7. (a) Upon what does the quality of veneer depend? (b) In what way can one judge the quality of veneer?
8. What type of construction should be used to strengthen the posts of chairs and beds?
9. What type of construction should be used to fasten the corners of drawers in furniture?
10. What qualities should the wood in the frames of upholstered furniture possess?
11. (a) What are the most common types of stuffing used for upholstered furniture? (b) Which are the best? (c) Which is the least desirable?
12. (a) What are some of the better upholstering materials? (b) From what type of fiber are they made?
13. Does the use of an imitation leather indicate inferior quality in upholstered furniture?
14. What are the distinguishing characteristics of good rugs and carpets?
15. Is there any distinguishing mark that can be used as a guide in buying rugs?
16. What criteria determine the wearing quality of fiber rugs?
17. (a) What are the most durable types of linoleum? (b) What factors regulate the price of linoleum?
18. In what way do felt-base rugs differ from linoleum?

DISCUSSION QUESTIONS

1. What are some of the dangers of buying extreme furniture of the modern type?
2. What do you think would be a good policy to follow in buying furniture for a home in which there are children?
3. How would you judge the value of a piece of furniture if it contained (a) oak and poplar? (b) walnut and gum? (c) gum and pine?
4. "If a piece of furniture contains veneer, it is not of high quality." Discuss this statement.

5. If you were asked to examine a piece of furniture and to pass judgment on the merits of the finish, on what would you base your judgment?
6. As the first step in judging the quality of a piece of furniture, one expert on the selection of furniture advocates removing and examining the drawer. What information is disclosed in this way?
7. What do you think would be some guides in judging the covering of upholstered furniture?
8. Discuss some of the factors that determine the suitability of a rug.
9. Explain how the back of a rug will indicate the quality of the rug.
10. What information pertaining to the quality of furniture should one be able to obtain from a furniture salesman?

PROBLEMS

1. If a living room is twenty feet long by fourteen feet wide and has no obstructions protruding into it, how much will be the cost of having a rug made from strips of carpeting that are twenty-seven inches wide and cost $2.50 a yard? There is to be a border of fifteen inches around the rug, and six strips of carpeting are to run lengthwise with the room. If a fraction of a yard is needed, the charge for a full yard must be used.
2. A kitchen is eight feet wide by eleven feet long and has no obstructions protruding into it. Linoleum is available in strips three feet wide. Compute the cost of linoleum for the kitchen if the price is $1.25 a yard and the strips are to run lengthwise with the room.

COMMUNITY PROBLEMS AND PROJECTS

1. Make a comparison of several different types of rugs on the basis of the information given in this chapter. Analyze the prices, and form conclusions in relation to values. Indicate for what purpose each type of rug is suitable.
2. Make an analysis of the furniture in your home on the basis of (a) the kind of wood in the furniture, (b) the kind of construction used in the drawers and in strengthening the legs of chairs and tables, and (c) the use of veneer or solid wood. On the basis of the illustrations in the textbook, determine what kinds of joints have been used.
3. From some lumber company get a quotation of prices on various woods.

CHAPTER XVIII

HOW TO BUY DRUGS, COSMETICS, SOAPS, AND DENTIFRICES

Purpose of the Chapter. Although the major problems of the individual are obtaining food, clothing, and shelter, his personal welfare is affected by many other items that he purchases. Many of these items are luxuries that are bought with the full knowledge that they are not really needed. Cosmetics, in many respects, are luxuries although—as will be seen later—some of them do serve useful purposes.

The purpose of this chapter is to discuss the problems relative to drugs, cosmetics, soaps, and dentifrices on the basis of available facts and from an enlightened but fair point of view.

Supervision by the Federal Government. The Federal Food, Drug, and Cosmetic Act, which was enacted on June 25, 1938, represents the first instance of Federal control over cosmetics. It extends governmental control over drugs and curative devices, although in some cases there had previously been a certain amount of state control over the manufacture and the sale of these items.

Under the provisions of the Act the term *drug* applies to articles recognized by the official United States Pharmacopoeia, the official Homeopathic Pharmacopoeia of the United States, the official National Formulary, or any supplement to any of them. The term also applies to (a) articles intended for use in the diagnosis, cure, mitigation, treatment, or prevention of disease in man or other animals; (b) articles (other than food) intended to affect the structure or any function of the body of man or other animals; and (c) articles intended for use as components of any articles specified in the other classifications.

The so-called health devices governed by the Act are instruments, apparatus, and contrivances for use in the diagnosis, cure, mitigation, treatment, or prevention of disease in man or other animals. The term also applies to devices that affect the structure or any function of the body.

The term *cosmetic* applies to articles intended to be rubbed, poured, sprinkled, sprayed on, introduced into, or otherwise applied to the human body for cleansing, beautifying, or altering appearance. In addition, the term applies to articles intended for use as components of such cosmetics. The Act does not, however, govern the sale of soaps.

Adulterated Drugs. Under the Federal Food, Drug, and Cosmetic Act, a drug is considered to be adulterated under any of the following circumstances:

(a) If the drug consists in whole or in part of any decayed substance.
(b) If it is prepared, packed, or held under unsanitary conditions whereby it may become contaminated or rendered injurious to health.
(c) If the container of the drug is composed of any substance that may render the contents injurious to health.
(d) If the drug contains coloring that has not been certified under the regulations of the Law.
(e) If the strength, the quality, or the purity of a recognized drug differs from the standard established for that drug.
(f) If the drug is mixed or packed with any substance that reduces its quality or strength.

Misbranded Drugs. Under the Federal Food, Drug, and Cosmetic Act, a drug is considered to be misbranded in any of the following cases:

(a) If the package fails to disclose the name and the place of business of the manufacturer, the packer, or the distributor.
(b) If the package fails to give an accurate statement of the contents in terms of weight, measure, or numerical count.
(c) If any statement required under the Law does not appear prominently on the label so that it is likely to be read and understood by the ordinary individual under customary conditions of purchase and use.

(d) If the drug may be habit-forming and does not bear on its label the statement, "Warning—May be habit-forming."

(e) If the drug is one not designated entirely by an official name and fails to bear the common name. If it contains two or more ingredients, the common or usual name, as well as the quantity, of each ingredient must be given.

(f) If the label fails to give adequate directions for use or warning against misuse.

(g) If the drug is a recognized one and is not packaged and labeled properly.

(h) If the drug is one liable to deterioration and is not packaged and labeled according to the regulations of the Food and Drug Administration.

(i) If the container is made, formed, or filled so as to be misleading.

(j) If the drug is an imitation of another or is offered for sale under the name of another.

(k) If the drug, when used according to the directions on the label, will be injurious to health.

Reading the Labels on Drugs. In some states there are laws requiring the labeling of drugs, including patent medicines, to indicate the specific ingredients. The purpose of such laws is to let the consumer know what he is getting for his money and whether there is anything in the drug that may be harmful to him. What may be harmful to one person may not be harmful to another. Identifying the contents, however, provides a safeguard.

Seldom is it possible for an individual to prescribe his own treatment through the use of drugs. He should not even rely upon statements on labels. If he has an ailment, he certainly should not be influenced by such vague claims as "wonder worker," "magic," "infallible," "new discovery," "builder," "anti-apoplectic," "anti-pneumonia," and many others. Such vague claims may be legally permissible, but many of them have no definite meaning. Such drugs are investigated every year by the Federal Food and Drug Administration, and many are condemned. One needs only to consult a reputable physician to learn, for instance, that there is not yet any known cure for epilepsy or apoplexy. Certainly there is no known manufactured drug that will cure either disease.

Probably some of the greatest dangers to the average person arise from the promiscuous use of prepared cures that have been bought over the drugstore counter as casually as chewing gum is purchased. A doctor will give one advice on the proper remedy. One should not take a chance in using a product that may be of questionable value or definitely harmful.

The following criteria are suggested for the selection of drugs:

(a) Rely upon a dependable doctor for prescribing the proper drugs.
(b) Learn from your doctor the names of manufacturers of dependable drugs and buy under brand names the drugs manufactured by those companies.
(c) Be skeptical of new drug concoctions until your doctor has assured you of their accepted use.
(d) The preceding criteria are more dependable than the advice of a drug clerk. The drug clerk may not know any more about particular drugs than you do.
(e) Obtain what information you can from labels.

Drug Advertising. One should not only read drug labels intelligently, but he should also read drug advertisements intelligently. He should avoid seeking a magic cure. When a good cure for an ailment is discovered, it will certainly be used by the medical profession.

When epidemics, such as the influenza epidemic, sweep over the country, many new cures and preventives are thrown onto the market with flagrant claims and loud praise.

Some manufacturers of patent medicines advertise their medicines under high-sounding names, such as "Life Balm," in the hope that the names will create a favorable impression toward the products. Photographs of the manufacturers are often used in the advertising to indicate the authenticity of the products. Sometimes signatures are used to distinguish these products from so-called fake competitors. Such means of proof, however, are often of no particular importance.

The responsible physicians of the United States will not lend their signatures for the endorsement of a questionable product. Some manufacturers therefore obtain the photograph and the written endorsement of some foreign physician and use these in advertisements published in the United States.

Warnings About Drugs. Even though we now have Federal control over drugs and health devices sold in interstate commerce, the average consumer should exercise caution in buying drugs. The following warnings are therefore offered:

(a) Some drug preparations are harmless concoctions, but have no real value.
(b) Even though some drug preparations are more or less harmless for the purposes that they are recommended, such drugs may be harmful if taken without the advice of a physician.
(c) Some drugs may be harmless to certain individuals, but harmful to others. Follow the advice of a physician in taking prepared medicines.
(d) Follow the advice of a physician in selecting a suitable antiseptic.
(e) Beware of drugs sold under mysterious names.
(f) Beware of drugs with all-inclusive claims as to their uses.
(g) Avoid drugs with meaningless but elaborate statements as to their contents or usefulness.
(h) Question the contents of any drug if only some of the ingredients are listed on the label.
(i) Beware of any drugs that are to be taken internally to reduce weight. Most of these are injurious.
(j) Undoubtedly most drugs carried by the average store are sold in interstate commerce and therefore come under the provisions of the Federal Food, Drug, and Cosmetic Act. There may be some drugs sold in certain states that do not enter into interstate commerce and therefore are not governed by Federal law.

Adulterated Cosmetics. Under the Federal Food, Drug, and Cosmetic Act, a cosmetic is considered to be adulterated in any of the following cases:

(a) If it contains any substance that is poisonous or injurious to users under the conditions prescribed on the label or under such conditions of use as are customary. This section of the Law does not apply, however, to coal-tar hair dye, the label of which bears the following conspicuous warning: "Caution—This product contains ingredients which may cause skin irritation on certain individuals, and a preliminary test according to accompanying directions should first be made. This product must not be used for dyeing the eyelashes or eyebrows; to do so may cause blindness."

(b) If the cosmetic consists in whole or in part of any decayed substance.

(c) If it has been prepared, packed, or held under unsanitary conditions whereby it might have become injurious to health.

(d) If its container is composed in whole or in part of any poisonous or injurious substance that may render the contents injurious to health.

(e) If it is a cosmetic, other than a hair dye containing coal-tar coloring, that has not been certified according to the Law.

Misbranded Cosmetics. Under the Federal Food, Drug, and Cosmetic Act, a cosmetic is considered to be misbranded under any of the following circumstances:

(a) If its label is false or misleading.

(b) If the package fails to bear the name and the place of business of the manufacturer, the packer, or the distributor.

(c) If the package fails to provide an accurate statement of the contents in terms of weight, measure, or numerical count.

(d) If any statement required by the Law is omitted from the label.

(e) If any statement required by the Law is not printed prominently and in such terms as to permit it to be read and to be understood by the ordinary individual under customary conditions of purchase and use.

(f) If the container has been made, formed, or filled so as to be misleading. For example, thick glass jars sometimes contain very little material.

Are Cosmetics Safe and Useful? On the whole, the cosmetic industry is legitimate and honorable, but it gets a bad reputation because of some unscrupulous manufacturers. Most of the products are of high quality and are safe to use. They are produced under scientific methods with unquestioned safety.

The cosmetic industry also suffers disrepute because some people are allergic to various ingredients. In other words, some individuals are hypersensitive to substances that are not harmful in the least to the majority of persons. Such an ingredient may cause a skin irritation to a few persons, but may be used daily by others without injury. When one considers the great number of ingredients included in cosmetics, it can easily be seen how some of these ingredients may cause irritation to at least a few users.

The preparations that are most liable to contain dangerous ingredients are hair dye, hair tonics, dandruff removers, hair beautifiers, freckle removers, skin peelers, skin bleaches, depilatories, and personal deodorants. Many of these will cause the hair to fall out or the skin to become irritated.

To go into an elaborate discussion of the advertising and the labeling of cosmetics would be futile because most people buy these products regardless of the irrational claims in advertisements and on labels. Most people buy beauty preparations in the hope that they will become or will remain beautiful. Advertisements that contain testimonials of attractive women or photographs of glamorous persons merely add to the self-satisfaction of the individuals who buy those products. Such advertising has principally one purpose: to satisfy certain human emotions. As a result most cosmetic advertising appeals to the emotions rather than to the reason of the buyer.

What Cosmetics Will Do and What They Will Not Do. Price alone is not an adequate guide to quality or effectiveness in the purchase of cosmetics. Many preparations available at reasonable prices contain pure ingredients that are helpful. Unless a cosmetic serves a definite purpose as a drug, its real purpose is to keep the skin moistened. Any other purposes claimed for it are questionable.

A study of cosmetics involves many points of view. In this study there is no attempt to decide whether cosmetics should or should not be used. The following lists point out what cosmetics will do and what they will not do. These statements are based upon available scientific facts.

WHAT COSMETICS WILL DO

(a) A cosmetic preparation is primarily a protection for the skin from the ravages of weather and time. It may help to prevent defects and deficiencies, but it will not cure them.

(b) The massage that accompanies the application of cosmetics is helpful in delaying the formation of wrinkles.

(c) The application of a cosmetic has a temporary effect on the outer skin but has no permanent effect.

(d) The skins of most people have excretions of fat that tend to lubricate the skin. These are washed away by soap and water. A cosmetic will help to replace them.

(e) Some lotions for the hands and the face will form a protective coating and help to retain natural oil and moisture, thereby encouraging the healing of chapped hands and face.

(f) If astringent lotions are strong enough, they will temporarily keep pores from functioning.

(g) Any make-up preparation that temporarily coats the skin will serve as a slight protection in addition to enhancing the appearance, provided it is applied properly.

WHAT COSMETICS WILL NOT DO

(a) No cosmetic will bring about a permanent change in the nature of the skin. The general nature of one's skin depends largely upon the health and the cleanliness of the individual and upon inherited characteristics.

(b) Wrinkles in the skin are caused by the effect of emotions and expressions on the face. The folding of tissues gradually causes wrinkles that cannot be erased by the application of oils or creams. Wrinkles can be avoided or partially removed by prolonged rest and relaxation and by a conscious attempt to avoid frowning and other unusual facial expressions. Such treatment is effective only in the case of young persons, however.

(c) No cosmetic can nourish or feed the skin.

(d) An astringent lotion, although producing a slight contraction of cells, will not shrink the pores. Sometimes these lotions cause annoying irritation.

Cautions About Cosmetics. When one studies the things that cosmetics will and will not do, he does not get the complete picture. The following is a summary of cautions on the use of cosmetics:

(a) Beware of preparations that contain a lead compound because such a compound may cause serious poisoning. Fortunately some preparations advertised as being radio-active do not have any radio-active substances in them. If they did, the preparations would be injurious.

(b) There are no creams that are known to grow hair.

(c) Nearly everyone is allergic to some kinds of preparations. To find out whether one is allergic to a certain cosmetic, apply it to a small area as an experiment.

(d) Only those skin-bleaching compounds that bleach the surface are safe. Their effectiveness is slight and slow. Bleaches that loosen the outer skin cause irritation and possible poisoning. Many of them contain mercury, which is dangerous to the human body.

(e) Skin peelers or freckle removers that require the removing of layers of skin are considered very dangerous, especially when used by the average individual.

(f) There are several types of hair dyes that will cause irritation and possible poisoning to some individuals. The safest procedure is to consult a dermatologist or some other expert on the use of such dyes.

Selecting Soaps. Bath preparations and toilet soaps may rightfully be considered to some extent as cosmetics because all these products have a related nature.

Bath salts are usually nothing more than water-softeners that have been colored and perfumed. They usually have no beneficial effect upon the skin; sometimes they may injure the skin by causing excessive dryness. Bath oils form an emulsion in water. The only real purpose of bath oils is to provide perfume and to prevent excessive drying of the skin.

Soaps used on the skin or the hair should be mild or neutral. Such soaps will prevent irritation of the skin and excessive drying of the skin. The most that a toilet soap can do is to cleanse efficiently. An inexpensive mild or neutral soap will serve the purpose; but if the family budget will permit, one may indulge in soaps that are perfumed and colored, and can be obtained in small bars or in unusual shapes. These soaps, however, do not have any additional advantage for the consumer.

There are numerous soaps, such as floating, castile, transparent, hard-water, grit, liquid, tar, and medicated. Grit soaps contain an abrasive for removing grease and stains. Hard-water soaps contain oils that lather well in hard water. Certain medicated soaps may have a slightly additional antiseptic value, but all soaps have a good antiseptic value because the lather washes away germs. In considering toilet soaps, one must bear in mind the two fundamental purposes of such soaps: (a) to cleanse and (b) to be mild or neutral. There are no other important considerations.

It is important for the housewife to become familiar with the various types of soaps that can be used for different purposes. For instance, silk, rayon, and wool require neutral soaps and careful handling. Laundry soaps, bleaches, and powders should be used with a full knowledge of their intended purposes.

Buying Dentifrices and Mouthwashes. There are many good dentifrices on the market that are honestly labeled and advertised. It is true that one usually pays a pretty high price for a small tube of dentifrice. There are some people who claim that the price is exorbitant. By pointing out that certain ingredients can be obtained and mixed together to form a good dentifrice, they attempt to prove that the consumer is cheated. If one wishes to prepare his own dentifrice, he may use ordinary salt, soda, or magnesia. Any of these will make a satisfactory tooth powder. Nevertheless, if the consumer is willing to have the ingredients prepared and mixed for him, properly flavored and packaged, and finds that it is more advantageous to pay the price than to prepare his own dentifrice, no one can object to this procedure.

One should not expect too much of the dentifrice he uses. Tooth paste cannot do the work of a dentist in caring for the teeth. The *Journal* of the American Dental Association says: "On the basis of available evidence, the functions of a dentifrice are limited to its aid in mechanically cleaning the surfaces of the teeth when used with a tooth brush." No dentifrice can effectively clean the hidden areas of the teeth. As these are the real danger spots, the teeth should be inspected regularly by a dentist.

Medical and dental authorities seem to agree that there is no real way for a dentifrice to preserve the teeth, to act as an antiseptic, or to serve as a medicinal cure. As a cleansing agent, however, a dentifrice will help to keep the teeth free from decay.

Most dental preparations are composed of common ingredients, such as chalk, soap, salt, baking soda, borax, magnesia, glycerine, alcohol, saccharin, oils, water, flavoring, and color. Claims on the labels and in the advertising of dentifrices shoud be considered in the light of the latest medical knowledge.

As was explained in Chapter XI, the Council on Dental Therapeutics of the American Dental Association issues a list of dentifrices that are acceptable. The manufacturers of these products may use in their advertising and on their labels the seal of acceptance of the American Dental Association. The list is changed from time to time as new products are added or other products are dropped. The rules for the use of the seal are as follows:

1. The Seal may be used in advertising, in circulars, and on packages after the product has been made acceptable to the Council and after the acceptance has been announced in the *Journal*; or, in special cases, before the acceptance is announced, at the discretion of the Council.

2. The Seal is to be used only in conjunction with advertising of claims allowed by the Council.

3. The Seal, if it appears on the package, must be the only seal of such character, and must not appear in conjunction with the seal of any other investigative group, unless approval for such display has been obtained from the Council.

4. The Seal is to be used without comment of its significance unless such consent has been previously approved by the Council. A statement proposed for such use follows: "The Seal of acceptance denotes that (product named) and advertisements for it are acceptable to the Council on Dental Therapeutics of the American Dental Association." The Council will not object to any statement which is wholly in accord with its own definition of the significance of the Seal. In all cases, the statement must be approved by the Council before it is used.

5. The size of the Seal in advertising shall not exceed one and one-half inch in height or diameter, and shall in no case be larger than an illustration of the trade package, excepting for use in connection with exhibits at the meetings of the American Dental Association or of its recognized component societies, when a Seal up to twelve inches (12″) in height or diameter may be used.

6. Should the product for any reason become unacceptable, all use of the Seal must be discontinued within six months of date of announcement to the manufacturers of action taken by the Council.

The council does not approve so-called antiseptics that are recommended as mouthwashes. It feels that the general use of mouthwashes can be considered to serve no intrinsic purpose except to clean the mouth, largely through rinsing. Many doctors and dentists recommend a salt solution or a salt and soda solution as an effective mouthwash or gargle.

TEXTBOOK QUESTIONS

1. By what Federal law is the sale of drugs and cosmetics regulated?
2. By what department of the Federal Government are drugs and cosmetics regulated?
3. What is the definition of a health device?
4. What is the definition of a cosmetic?
5. In what respect does the Federal Trade Commission have any jurisdiction over the sale of drugs and cosmetics?
6. To what extent may drugs contain artificial coloring?
7. What warning must be placed on the label of a drug that may be habit-forming?
8. What instructions with regard to use must be placed on the label of a drug?

9. Name the five criteria that are suggested for the selection of drugs.
10. Give three or more warnings about the use of drugs.
11. Name two conditions under which a cosmetic may be misbranded.
12. Although the Federal Law does not prevent the sale of coal-tar hair dye, what must be placed conspicuously on the label of such a hair dye?
13. What are at least three of the things that a cosmetic will do for the skin?
14. What will cosmetics not do?
15. Give at least three cautions that should be observed in using cosmetics.
16. What essentially is a bath salt?
17. What are the desirable characteristics of a good toilet soap?
18. What warnings would you give about the use of soap for washing various fabrics?
19. What basis is there for the contention that so-called mouthwashes have an antiseptic value?

DISCUSSION QUESTIONS

1. The Federal Law governing drugs and cosmetics applies only to goods sold or intended for sale in interstate commerce. To what extent, however, are all consumers protected?
2. Do you think that ordinary cold cream comes under the regulations of the Federal Food, Drug, and Cosmetic Act?
3. Many patent medicines have in the past been manufactured according to secret formulas. Do you think that it is necessary now for the labels on these patent medicines to show the formulas?
4. Suppose that a person buys nose drops for a cold and, after using them frequently, finds that the membrane of his nostrils has become inflamed and seriously injured. Has he any basis for complaint?
5. Do the regulations of the Federal Law that relate to drugs make it unnecessary for a person to consult a physician as frequently as he did formerly?
6. Manufacturers of drugs and cosmetics have been blamed for diseases or ailments that resulted from the fact that certain persons were allergic to particular ingredients in the drugs or the cosmetics. Discuss this situation.
7. Why do you think the Federal Food, Drug, and Cosmetic Act permits the sale of coal-tar hair dye provided the proper warning is placed on the label?
8. In your opinion may an advertisement for a cosmetic legally assert that the cosmetic will eliminate wrinkles in the skin?
9. Will mouthwashes tend to eliminate bad breath?

PROBLEMS

1. Remove the label from some cosmetic used in your home, or copy the information from the label. Submit the label or the information with a written report indicating to what extent you believe that the label conforms with the Federal Law and to what extent it fails to conform with the Law.
2. Obtain the label from an empty medicine container that you find at home, or copy the information from such a container. Submit the label or the information with a report on the following: (a) ingredients, (b) quantity, (c) instructions, (d) warnings, and (e) any other important information. Point out any ways in which you think the label violates the Federal Law.
3. From among your family and acquaintances make a list of the persons whom you know to be allergic to drugs or cosmetics containing certain ingredients. Explain the results.

COMMUNITY PROBLEMS AND PROJECTS

1. From your local druggist find out approximately what portion of his packaged drugs come under the regulations of the Federal Government and what portion are manufactured and sold within the state.
2. It is said that price is no indication of the quality of cosmetics. Verify or disprove this statement by a personal investigation.
3. Investigate to see whether your own state has a law controlling the advertising, the labeling, and the selling of drugs and cosmetics. Report the significant points of the law if there is one.
4. From the United States Department of Agriculture obtain an example of a case that involved condemnation of a drug on the basis of adulteration. Report the reasons for the condemnation, and mention any other points of significance in the case.

CHAPTER XIX

FINANCIAL PROBLEMS OF OBTAINING A HOME

Purpose of the Chapter. Everyone must have some means of shelter. The problem of the family is to decide whether to rent or lease a house or an apartment, or whether to buy or build a house. To own a home or not to own a home is the question to be decided. Most people have an inborn desire to own a home; but not everyone is justified in buying.

A home should be selected on the basis of a cool and calm consideration of investment principles and the earning power of the family. Very few people purchase a home for cash; most people must depend on some person, bank, association, or insurance company for a loan to finance the purchase. The purpose of this chapter is to present information that will serve as a guide in determining whether to buy, lease, or rent; how much to invest in a home; and what type of financing plan to use.

Section I

Renting, Leasing, or Buying a Home

Advantages and Disadvantages of Renting or Leasing. The first consideration in paying for the temporary use of a home, whether a house or an apartment, is to determine the advisability of renting as compared with leasing. Renting a home gives a person greater freedom to move and to take advantage of decreases in rentals as conditions change. A person who anticipates having to move because of a change in his work should probably not sign a lease unless he is required to do so in order to obtain the use of a particular piece of property. Renting may make it impossible to get desirable property because the owner may want to be sure that he will have a tenant for a reasonable length of time.

A person who rents is also subject to the necessity of moving if the owner wants the property for some other purpose. In most states, however, the custom or law requires the property owner to give at least thirty days' notice. If legal action is necessary to force the renter to move, still more time will be required before the property must be vacated.

Cost of Renting. There is, of course, a limit to the amount of money that one should spend for rent. This fact has been emphasized in a preceding chapter on budgeting. As one's income increases, the percentage spent for rent should decrease.

Illustration No. 145 shows the rent paid by various occupational groups in a large city (Chicago). These figures are for families consisting of a husband and a wife.

Income Group	Average Monthly Rent							
	Amount				Percentage of Income			
	All Occupations	Wage Earners	Clerical Workers	Bus. & Prof.	All Occupations	Wage Earners	Clerical Workers	Bus. & Prof.
$ 500 to $ 750...	$22.90	$20.60	$26.10	$26.90	43.5	39.0	49.9	51.7
750 " 1,000...	22.80	20.70	25.60	29.20	31.3	28.4	34.9	40.6
1,000 " 1,250...	26.00	23.20	28.20	32.30	27.9	24.9	30.2	34.6
1,250 " 1,500...	28.10	25.90	30.50	33.00	24.8	22.9	27.0	29.2
1,500 " 1,750...	30.80	28.50	32.50	35.50	23.1	21.3	24.4	26.8
1,750 " 2,000...	34.20	31.00	36.20	38.20	22.1	20.0	23.5	24.7
2,000 " 2,250...	36.80	33.50	37.70	41.60	20.9	19.0	21.4	23.8
2,250 " 2,500...	40.60	36.00	41.20	45.80	20.5	18.2	20.8	23.1
2,500 " 3,000...	42.10	37.20	43.30	45.60	18.8	16.5	19.3	20.4
3,000 " 3,500...	47.40	39.20	46.90	51.50	17.9	14.7	17.7	19.6
3,500 " 4,000...	53.60	44.00	52.80	56.70	17.3	14.2	17.1	18.4
4,000 " 4,500...	55.40	40.70	55.20	58.40	15.8	11.5	15.7	17.1
4,500 " 5,000...	64.90	44.40	57.00	64.70	16.4	11.2	14.4	16.4

Illustration No. 145—Rent Paid by Families Living in a Large City

When the rentals are equal, the cost of living in an apartment is usually less than that of living in a house. A person who rents a house usually has to pay for such items as heat, light, water, and the care of the yard; whereas one who rents an apartment frequently has such items included in the rental.

Things to be Investigated. In renting or leasing, a person should be careful to select the location and the type of house or apartment that is consistent with his earning power and the standards of living of his family. The following are some of the points that should be investigated:

Location	Other equipment, such as shades, curtains, and awnings
External appearance	Renovations and repairs
Internal appearance	Privileges of the yard
Size and location of rooms	Character of the neighborhood
Heating and lighting	
Laundry	
Plumbing, ventilation, and sanitary conditions	

When to Lease. If a person is considering leasing property, he should give particular attention to the time of year and general business conditions. In a period of depression rentals of property are low; but these rents will not continue during times of prosperity. A depression is therefore a good time to negotiate a lease. A long-term lease obtained during a depression is advantageous because of the future tendency of rentals to rise. The making of a short-term lease during a period of prosperity is advisable because of the future possibility that rentals will be lowered.

In some communities most leases expire at a definite date, usually in April or May. In other cities there is no uniformity; leases are made at any time and are terminated in various months. When all leases in a community terminate at the same time, the tenant is handicapped in finding a new location and in obtaining aid in moving. It is therefore advisable for a tenant to set his own date for the termination of the lease.

Length of the Lease. Many families find that it pays them to select a home carefully with the intention of occupying it for several years. By leasing for a long period, they can reduce moving costs and become better established in the community. By staying in one place a long time, a family has an opportunity to develop a garden and to improve the property. Landlords are usually willing to keep property in good repair if the tenants indicate a desire to stay a reasonable length of time. People who lease property will therefore usually find it advantageous to obtain a lease for one year with the privilege of extending the lease one or more years.

Advantages of Owning a Home. A writer in the *Economist* has pointed out the following advantages of owning a home: an inspiring adventure, a civic education, the development of a better credit rating, personal enjoyment, the development of a definite purpose in life, the acquisition of a background and prestige, the acquisition of security, the development of stability, and the development of thrifty habits.

Regardless of the advantages that may be claimed for owning a home, one should approach the problem cautiously because, even though it may be desirable to own a home, it may be unwise to buy or build a house.

When to Buy. A person who is planning to buy a house should consider the following four factors in determining when to make the purchase:

(a) The economic and financial status of the family
(b) General economic and business conditions
(c) The particular community and its stage of development
(d) The season of the year

Success in acquiring a home depends not only upon selecting the right kind, but also upon choosing the right time to buy. If one can afford to buy, the best time to buy is during times of declining prices when most people cannot buy.

The price of property is governed largely by supply and demand. In times of prosperity, when many people are eager to buy, property sells at high prices. Calm judgment will warn a person not to "follow the crowd" in buying a home and going into debt during times of prosperity and high prices. When prices and wages drop, it is difficult for the average family to finish paying for a home. Ordinarily the best bargains in property can be obtained during periods of decreasing prices. A person who hopes to buy a home should therefore save during periods of prosperity and buy when property sells at more reasonable prices.

Sometimes property in newly developed communities is sold at exorbitant prices just because the communities are new. It is not advisable to pay an exorbitant price for a home in such a community, nor is it wise to buy in a community that is declining.

As people ordinarily move in the spring, much property is offered for sale at that time. During the other seasons of the year the demand is less. The fall and the winter are good times of the year to buy property.

Costs of Owning a Home. The desire of many people to buy a home comes from the fact that they see their money being paid out in rent without any permanent acquisition of property. The determination to put an end to this constant payment of rent sometimes causes people to buy a house when the venture is not financially wise. In the first place, the time may not be an opportune one in which to buy; and in the second place, the income of the family may not be sufficient for the size of investment that will be required.

The question of buying a house should be analyzed carefully; it is a matter that is closely tied up with the budget. The following elements in the cost of acquiring and maintaining a home should be studied:

(a) Payments on the principal of the loan
(b) Payments of interest
(c) Taxes
(d) Assessments
(e) Repairs, general upkeep, and depreciation
(f) Insurance

If a person wishes to figure all the costs incidental to owning a home, he should also include interest on the money that he has invested. For instance, if one has two thousand dollars invested in a home, that money is not earning interest as it would if it had been put into some savings account or invested in some security. If the interest that could be earned on this amount in a savings account is 3 per cent a year, the owner of the house is foregoing the earning of sixty dollars a year in interest. This is legitimately a cost of owning the home.

Capacity to Pay. If a person buys a house for cash, he should not invest so much that he must use all the funds that he has laid aside for use in an emergency. For instance, if he uses all his cash to purchase a house, he may not have any reserve to use in case of a serious illness or some other emergency. A person who acquires a house by means of borrowed money makes a serious mistake if he buys beyond his capacity to pay the interest charge on the loan. If the loan is too great, he may become discouraged because of the necessity of cutting down the level of living and of thus depriving his family of necessities that are required to maintain health. He may even lose the house through foreclosure.

In buying a house or renting, many young people gamble to the extent of assuming that their earnings will increase. They therefore undertake a greater obligation than they should. If future earnings do not become greater, or if they become less, discouragement inevitably results. One of the first questions that should arise in the mind of a prospective renter or purchaser is the percentage of earnings to be expended in providing the home. The family budget should therefore be considered carefully.

The amount that a person may spend as the interest and the principal on a loan on a home is always a question. The amount of the expenditure must depend upon the family budget, which should always be prepared before any plan for buying a home is accepted. Studies have been made to determine reasonable amounts that should be spent in acquiring a home. The President's Conference on Home Building and Home Ownership has shown that builders, realtors, and lenders of money estimate that about 23 per cent of the assured income of a family may safely be spent in buying a home.

The Home as an Investment. Buying a house should be looked upon as making an investment. Payments of rent, however, constitute expense. If regular payments are made on a house, they represent (a) interest expense and (b) payments on the principal. If a person who has been renting a house decides to buy it, he will be required to make greater expenditures than those required formerly in renting. If it has not been possible for him to save money regularly in the past, it will probably not be possible to finance the purchase of the home. Some people do, however, undertake such a purchase because they are then forced to follow some definite plan of saving. The purchase of a home may result in systematic saving in order to pay for the investment.

Minimum Cash Investment. As will be explained later in this chapter, there are many ways of financing the purchase of a home, but usually a person must pay part of the original price in cash.

Until recent years all conservative financial advisors have recommended that a person who buys a home should pay 20 to 25 per cent of the purchase price in cash. As will be explained in a later part of this chapter, it is frequently impossible to obtain a first-mortgage loan of more than 50 or 60 per cent of the value of a house. The difference must be paid in cash, or an additional loan must be obtained from another source. The plans developed under the Federal Housing Administration permit a minimum cash investment of from 10 to 20 per cent. These plans will be explained later.

Causes of Default on Loans. Regardless of its advantages the ownership of a home should be undertaken with careful forethought. The President's Conference on Home Building and Home Ownership made a study of the reasons why people have been unable to pay for their homes. The following, reported in *Home Finance and Taxation,* are the principal causes of default on loans on homes:[1]

(a) Unemployment
(b) Too heavy investment
(c) Installment purchase
(d) Excessive principal payments
(e) Business losses
(f) Stock market losses
(g) Depreciation of the building
(h) Domestic difficulties
(i) Increase in taxes, or special assessments
(j) Illness or death
(k) Neighborhood changes
(l) Bank failure

---

[1] Reprinted, with permission, from *Home Finance and Taxation,* Volume II of the publications of the President's Conference on Home Building and Home Ownership.

The meanings of most of these causes are obvious. Let us discuss, however, the significance of the causes designated as (b), (c), (d), (g), and (k). Some people invest too much in a home and consequently do not have enough money for other purposes. Others assume a debt that is more than they can afford to pay. In such cases the installment payments on the home are more than can be made from the income. Other people are so eager to pay off the debt rapidly that they pay more than is necessary on the principal and find themselves without funds in an emergency. Sometimes the debt incurred is to be paid off in a few years, whereas it should be distributed over a longer period of years. A house may depreciate so rapidly that it requires unusual repairs and replacements. Instead of a neighborhood improving in character, it sometimes becomes undesirable and the value of the property consequently decreases.

TEXTBOOK QUESTIONS

1. What are the advantages of renting as compared with those of owning a home?
2. What are some of the disadvantages of renting as compared with those of owning a home?
3. What are some of the things to be investigated when a person is contemplating renting or leasing a home?
4. Why is it usually cheaper to live in an apartment than in a house, provided the rentals are the same?
5. When is it desirable to make (a) a short-term lease? (b) a long-term lease?
6. What are some of the advantages of a long lease?
7. What are some of the advantages given for owning a home?
8. What six elements in the cost of buying and maintaining a home should be considered?
9. In determining one's ability to carry the financial burden of buying a home, what six questions should one answer?
10. What percentage of income is considered the maximum amount that one may safely spend in buying a home?
11. What is the minimum percentage of the purchase price that conservative financial advisors have recommended as the cash payment at the time a home is purchased?
12. In what way is the purchase of a home an investment?
13. Name the twelve principal causes of default on loans on homes.

DISCUSSION QUESTIONS

1. Give your opinion as to whether each of the following individuals should own or rent a home, provided each can afford to buy: (a) a traveling salesman, (b) the owner of a retail store, (c) the sales manager of a district office, (d) the office manager in a local manufacturing plant. Give reasons for your answers.
2. A young couple find that it is possible to make a down payment on a home and to pay the principal, the interest, and the taxes with the money that is ordinarily spent for rent and the additional amount that is placed in a savings account each month. They consider that they can save more by investing in a home than they can by paying rent and accumulating a savings fund. Do you agree with them? Give your reasons.
3. (a) Why is location an important factor in selecting a house to rent or to buy? (b) Are the considerations the same in both cases?
4. Explain how the characteristics of a neighborhood are important as a factor in selecting a house for renting or buying.
5. Give some of the advantages and the disadvantages of buying a house during a depression.
6. Mr. Moore, who is considering the purchase of a house, finds in an old community a house that is better constructed and otherwise more desirable than a newer one in a recently developed community. The two houses are offered at the same price. What do you think are some of the factors that he should consider in determining which house to select?
7. Discuss what you consider to be the merits of buying a home on the assumption that one's income will increase to such an extent that the debt can be paid off.
8. Explain some of the circumstances under which renting a home would be more economical than buying one.
9. Under what circumstances might a person be justified in paying 30 to 40 per cent of his income for the purchase of a home?
10. Under what circumstances do you think a person would be justified in making a down payment of only 5 or 10 per cent of the purchase price of a home?

Section II

How Much to Spend for a Home

Analysis of Costs. The table in Illustration No. 146 on page 449 shows the first-year cost of financing a home. This information was collected for prospective home owners by the Bureau of Standards of the United States Department of Commerce. The various income groups are listed according to the approximate cost of the home that a person in each income group can afford. This table assumes that an initial cash payment of 20 per cent of the total value will be made when the home is purchased.

The fact is recognized that families having the same annual income may not be able to devote the same amount toward purchasing a home. For example, a family having four or five children and living in a city may not be able to put much aside for buying a home; but another family with only one or two children and located possibly in a small village can afford to apply a larger proportion of its income for the same purpose.

The following is an explanation of the items appearing in the table:

Item 1. Value of house and lot. The value of the house and the lot is the basis upon which the expenses in this table have been computed. The value of the lot will usually be from 8 to 20 per cent of the total amount.

Item 2. Annual income. Because of the wide variation the incomes have been grouped. No rule can be set that will apply to all classes. It is assumed in this table, however, that the value of the house and the lot will be between 1⅔ and 2½ times the annual income. For example, a family with an income of $3,000 could expect to pay from $5,000 to $7,500 for a home. The average amount to pay for a home will be about double the annual income.

Item 3. First cash payment. The cash payment should not be below 20 per cent of the value of the house and the lot. It should be much higher if possible. The greater the down payment, the better, for the financing is then simpler and the cost is less. Occasionally a home can be purchased

1. Value of house and lot ...	$3,000	$4,000	$5,000	$6,000	$7,000	$8,000	$9,000	$10,000
2. Annual income	1,200 to 1,800	1,600 to 2,400	2,000 to 3,000	2,400 to 3,600	2,800 to 4,200	3,200 to 4,800	3,600 to 5,400	4,000 to 6,000
3. First cash payment (20% of value)	600	800	1,000	1,200	1,400	1,600	1,800	2,000
4. Amount of loan (80% of value)	2,400	3,200	4,000	4,800	5,600	6,400	7,200	8,000
5. Amount of yearly payments	300	400	500	600	700	800	900	1,000
A. Interest (6%) ...	144	192	240	288	336	384	432	480
B. Amortization	156	208	260	312	364	416	468	520
6. Taxes and assessments (2%)	60	80	100	120	140	160	180	200
7. Insurance (.5%)	15	20	25	30	35	40	45	50
8. Upkeep (1.5%)	45	60	75	90	105	120	135	150
9. Total first-year cost (5 plus 6, 7, 8)	420	560	700	840	980	1,120	1,260	1,400
A. Expense (5-A plus 6, 7, 8)	264	352	440	528	616	704	792	880
B. Saving (9 minus 9-A)	156	208	260	312	364	416	468	520

Illustration No. 146—The First-Year Cost of Financing a Home with a down payment of less than 20 per cent, but even under normal conditions a down payment of 20 per cent is dangerously low for many people. It is unwise to make so small an initial payment unless there is a good margin for saving. When there is a shortage of money for lending purposes, the loan is difficult to obtain if only a small down payment can be made. Furthermore, the interest charge at such a time is high.

Item 4. Amount of loan. After the amount of the initial cash payment has been deducted from the value of the house and the lot, the difference represents the amount of the loan.

Item 5. Amount of yearly payments. In this table the yearly payments are the same in amount. Under some plans of financing, however, the payment is reduced as the loan is paid off. Item 5A represents the amount of each payment that is applicable as interest; and item 5B, the amount that is applicable as amortization of the principal. With a small down payment the interest rate is usually higher than with a large down payment. If it is necessary to obtain a second mortgage, the interest rate is less favorable.

The interest rate will depend upon local conditions at the time the loan is made. It is generally considered best to pay off a loan on a home within fifteen years or less. If interest rates are unfavorable at the time the loan is to be made, the loan can be obtained for a short time in the hope that it can be renewed later at a lower rate.

Various plans of financing require weekly payments, semimonthly payments, monthly payments, semiannual payments, or annual payments. The plan of payment should be fully understood before any contract is signed.

Item 6. Taxes and assessments. Local taxes on real estate usually range from 1½ to 2½ per cent of the market value of the property. Occasionally there are assessments against the property for a sidewalk, a street, lights, or other facilities; but ordinarily the assessments on residential property are not high. In this table 2 per cent has been allowed for taxes and assessments.

Item 7. Insurance. Fire insurance rates rarely amount to more than ½ per cent of the value of the house. The allowance made in this table is liberal because it has been figured on the basis of the value of the house and the lot.

Item 8. Upkeep. The cost of maintaining a home will vary considerably, depending upon the condition of the property, the age of the house, and the type of construction. The yearly cost of maintenance may, however, be estimated reasonably at 1½ per cent of the total value.

Item 9. Total first-year cost. The total first-year cost of the home includes the total annual payment plus taxes, assessments, insurance, and upkeep. Item 9A represents the yearly expense. The difference between the total cost for the year and the total expense is the saving (item 9B). In other words, this is the amount of investment that the buyer has accumulated during the first year. The rest of his money has been used for interest and the various expenses of maintaining the house. Item 9A is therefore equivalent to the rent of the house.

Buying Compared with Renting. Whether to buy or to rent a home is the problem of each individual. A person frequently rents because (a) he desires freedom of movement, (b) he is unable to arrange a plan of financing a home, (c) he believes that it is cheaper to rent, (d) he doubts the investment value of owning a home, or (e) he does not care to assume the obligation of paying for a home. If a person needs a permanent home and can buy it, the following table will serve as a guide in comparing the cost of buying a home with the cost of renting one:

1. Annual income..	$1,200 to 1,800	$1,600 to 2,400	$2,000 to 3,000	$2,400 to 3,600	$2,800 to 4,200	$3,200 to 4,800	$3,600 to 5,400	$4,000 to 6,000
2. First-year cost of buying a house	420	560	700	840	980	1,120	1,260	1,400
A. Expense ..	264	352	440	528	616	704	792	880
B. Saving ...	156	208	260	312	364	416	468	520
3. Annual cost of renting a house								
A	240	300	360	420	480	540	600	660
B	270	360	450	540	630	720	810	900
C	300	390	480	570	660	750	840	930
D	360	450	540	630	720	810	900	990

Illustration No. 147—Comparison of Cost of Buying with Cost of Renting

Items 1 and 2 have been taken from the table on page 449. Items 3A, 3B, 3C, and 3D are examples of rental costs. These can be compared with item 2A. In making a comparison, one should answer the following questions:

(a) Ignoring the possible future reduction in expense and increase in saving, is it justifiable to pay this much for the privilege of owning a home?
(b) Can the total expenditure designated as item 2 be provided for safely out of the budget and yet a margin for additional savings be left?
(c) Would it be better to wait a few years and accumulate a greater saving for an initial down payment, thereby reducing the first-year cost?
(d) Is there any likelihood that the annual payments could not be continued?
(e) Will the expense be adequately offset by the advantages of owning a home?

Let us consider some of the examples in Illustration No. 147. If a person with a salary of $1,300 a year can rent a house for $240 (item 3A), there will be no saving in buying a home. If, however, he has to pay $270 a year (item 3B), there will be a slight financial advantage in buying a home, although some of the disadvantages may outweigh this advantage. If he has to pay rent amounting to $360 a year (item 3D), there will be a considerable financial advantage in buying a home.

To Build or Not to Build. It is just as common to make errors in building a house as in buying one. Eagerness to own a new house should not be allowed to interfere with one's good judgment in evaluating the purchase of a house that has been used or one that has been recently built and is being offered for sale. In building a house, one should consider the following points:

(a) Time at which to build
(b) Requirements of the family
(c) Selection of good plans
(d) Selection of a reliable contractor
(e) Written contracts with regard to construction
(f) Financing plan for the home

The same principles involved in buying a home should be considered in deciding whether to build. In other words, the first element is to decide whether it is possible to carry the financial burden.

Whom to Consult. Unless the prospective builder knows a contractor in whom he has considerable confidence, the plans and specifications should be drawn up first and then submitted to more than one contractor for competitive bids. The obtaining of several bids will guard against excessive cost. It is not always wise, however, to accept the lowest bid. The reputation of the contractor should play an important part.

Placing a Contract. A contract for a finished house may be placed with a single contractor, who will be responsible for the entire job; or contracts for separate portions of the work may be given to various contractors. The latter plan requires some definite scheme of supervision. Letting one contractor assume responsibility for the entire job is usually considered more satisfactory because it relieves the builder from most of the responsibility of supervision and gives reasonable assurance as to the final cost of the home.

Cautions in Building. Before construction is actually begun, the prospective home builder should make sure:

(a) That the plans are well designed and the finished house will be satisfactory to the entire family.
(b) That the plans meet the requirements of building codes and local restrictions.
(c) That the specifications are complete and that there will be no extra charge for additional work.
(d) That the contractor has a reputation for good work, financial responsibility, and fair dealing.
(e) That the contract specifies clearly the amount of the payments and the conditions under which the payments are to be made.
(f) That the contractor is responsible for loss due to fire or to personal injury during the construction period.
(g) That the property is subject to final inspection before acceptance and final payment.
(h) That all agreements have been approved by a lawyer.

TEXTBOOK QUESTIONS

1. Of the total value of a house and a lot, about what percentage represents the value of the lot?
2. What is a safe ratio between one's annual income and the amount that is paid for a home?
3. What time limit is considered most desirable in paying off a loan on a home?
4. What is a reasonable estimate of the cost of fire insurance based on the cost of a house?
5. What is a safe estimate of the cost of upkeep based on the total value of a home?
6. What are some of the reasons why a person rents a house instead of buying one?
7. According to the information presented in this chapter, how can the financial desirability of buying be compared with that of renting?
8. Point out some guides in obtaining bids on construction.
9. Where can inexpensive plans for small homes be obtained?

DISCUSSION QUESTIONS

1. From the point of view of making an investment in a home, what factors must one consider?
2. A popular slogan is, "Owning a home adds economic security." Explain this statement.
3. Explain how one's budget should be the controlling guide in buying a home.
4. What do you think of the relative desirability of granting a contract to build a home on the basis of (a) a specified predetermined price or (b) the actual cost plus a certain percentage of profit based upon the figures of the contractor?
5. Which consideration in planning for the purchase of a home should come first: (a) the actual selection of the home or (b) the development of a plan for financing the purchase?
6. (a) Why will an agency that lends money to you for use in having a house built be interested in examining your contract with the contractor? (b) Will the agency have any right to see the contract?

Section III

Financing the Home

Sources of Loans. The borrowers in the first group have a more simple problem than those in the other groups. The problem of all borrowers, however, is usually to choose the source from which they can obtain the most satisfactory service and terms on the loan. The sources of loans are principally as follows:

Building and loan associations	Trust companies
Life insurance companies	Mortgage companies
Savings banks	Private investors

Building and Loan Associations. A building and loan association is an organization created for the promotion of thrift and home ownership. Associations of this type use various plans for accumulating funds to be used in lending. The members of an association usually subscribe for shares and make regular payments on their subscriptions until the sum of these installment payments, added to the dividends obtained through the lending operations, equals the matured, or face, value of the shares. Some associations require no subscription but accept deposits of any amount.

Building and loan associations are relatively liberal in their lending. They extend loans for reasonably long periods, usually about twelve years. They frequently appraise property at a value equal to the full market price. First-mortgage loans are sometimes made on property to the extent of from 60 to 80 per cent of the valuation. The liberality in lending depends largely on local and general business conditions and the availability of funds.

Life Insurance Companies. In recent years life insurance companies have invested considerable money in loans on real estate. The loans of such a company are commonly placed through local agents, such as banks, trust companies, mortgage companies, and individuals. The applicant for a loan is required to supply the agent with information as to the risk. Special forms are usually filled out for this purpose. Illustration No. 148 shows a sample form.

ED. 11-29
FORM X-49

APPLICATION FOR LOAN

— TO —

THE WESTERN AND SOUTHERN LIFE INSURANCE COMPANY

OF CINCINNATI, OHIO

M. L. No. 13560 June 1 1940

The undersigned hereby applies to The Western and Southern Life Insurance Co. for a loan of $4,000.00 for a period of 5 years at 5½ per cent interest, and offers as security therefor a first mortgage on the following property:

Location Lot 12, Block 3, Rosedale Subdivision, Cincinnati, Ohio

Size of lot 50 feet front by 130 feet in depth.

Improvements consist of Brick and stucco house and brick garage

When built? 1933

Fee simple: Yes ~~Leasehold, 99 years, renewable forever.~~

Value: Land, $ 1,800.00 Improvements, $ 7,000.00

Tax value, land, $ 1,200.00 Improvements, $ 4,000.00

~~Gross rental?~~ ~~Net income?~~

Amount of Fire Insurance in force? $7,500.00

In whose name is title now? Charles K. Ritchie

If now mortgaged, to whom and in what amounts? None

Purpose of loan To purchase the property

If buying the property, how much is being paid for same? $8,800.00

I agree to pay on account of the principal of this loan 10 % thereof annually, as well as all charges for examination of the title and incidental expenses.

Harold G. Knight

Address 2970 Washington Ave., Cincinnati, Ohio

Business Knight's Grocery, 1250 Main Street

Full name of wife or husband Mary Clark Knight

APPRAISAL

We, the undersigned resident owners of real estate in Hamilton County, State of Ohio certify under oath that we are well acquainted with the property described in the foregoing application, and appraise the same as follows:

Land—exclusive of improvements, $ 1,800.00

Improvements, $ 7,500.00

Total, $ 9,300.00

Name *Edwin S. Summers* Name *M B Dane*

Address 1369 Vine St., Cincinnati Address 1706 Plum St., Cincinnati

State of Ohio County of Hamilton

Sworn to and subscribed before me this first of June, 1940, by Edwin S. Summers and M. B. Dane this first of June 1940.

Walter Gibson

(Notary Public)

Illustration No. 148—An Application for a Loan

The appraiser for an insurance company will usually be very conservative in setting a value as the basis of the loan. This value is frequently less than the price that is being paid for the home. The loans of insurance companies run for periods as long as fifteen years. Interest is charged at the rate prevailing in the locality in which the loan is made, and is usually payable semiannually. In some cases payments on the principal can be made semiannually; in others they can be made monthly. Provision in many cases is made for allowing the borrower to pay off the loan after the third year. The person who wishes to transfer his property after a loan has been made must obtain permission from the insurance company.

Savings Banks. An important source of borrowing on homes is the savings bank. When application is made for a loan, an officer of the bank or a committee usually visits the property and makes an appraisal. The size of the loan that such a bank can make is generally restricted by state law to a certain percentage of the value of the property. In some states this is 50 per cent, but in others it is as high as 60 per cent. State laws do not, however, restrict the banks with respect to making liberal or conservative appraisals. A liberal bank in a state that limits loans to 50 per cent of the property value might lend more than a conservative bank in a state that limits loans to 60 per cent of the property value.

Many of the loans of savings banks extend for only short periods, such as one, three, or five years. The loan periods are, however, gradually being extended. Short-term loans can usually be renewed, but a charge may be made for the privilege of extension. Unless the property has been taken care of satisfactorily, it is difficult to renew the loan.

In some sections of the country, particularly in the East, mutual savings banks are common. A mutual bank is owned by the depositors and is controlled by them or by their elected representatives.

Trust Companies. Trust companies and the trust departments of banks usually have large savings deposits. Some of these funds are available for real-estate loans. The lending policies and methods of trust companies are similar to those of savings banks.

Mortgage Companies. In many large communities mortgage companies are an important factor in home financing. There are two classes of these companies. One class lends on first, or senior, mortgages; and the other lends on second, or junior, mortgages. There is a great lack of uniformity in the policies and the methods of these companies. They are usually not placed under such legal restrictions as are banks, trust companies, and insurance companies. They ordinarily do not lend in excess of 50 per cent of the valuation of the property. When a higher amount is lent, a commission may be charged.

Private Investors. Private investors, who are unorganized, are free to operate as they please so long as they keep within the bounds of state statutes on lending. They usually follow the methods of the lending institutions in their communities. They are frequently willing to lend a higher percentage of the property value than are banks, trust companies, or insurance companies. They do so especially when it is possible for them to get a slightly higher rate.

The person who borrows from a lending institution can usually depend on being able to renew his mortgage if he has been taking care of payments. When he borrows from an individual, however, there is nothing but personal assurance that the loan can be renewed. Such unforeseen circumstances as the death of the lender may cause an embarrassing situation for the borrower.

Second-Mortgage Borrowing. In communities where there are no building and loan associations and in those where such associations and other agencies are unwilling to make loans equal to from 60 to 75 per cent of the value of the home, borrowers in the second group (those who can pay only 25 to 40 per cent of the price) find it necessary to use two loans, a first mortgage and a second mortgage.

The following is an example showing the relation between a first and a second mortgage: A person purchases a house valued at $5,000. He pays $1,000 in cash and is successful in obtaining a first-mortgage loan of $3,000. He obtains the loan by signing a series of notes that will become due at specified intervals. The interest on the notes is 6 per cent. To protect the lender, he gives a real-estate mortgage. If the payments are not made when they become due, the holder of the mortgage has the option of suing for the possession of the property, or of having the property sold to compensate him for the loan. The exact procedure is governed by the laws of each state.

A second-mortgage loan is negotiated for the remainder of the purchase price, $1,000. The borrower signs a series of notes and a second-mortgage contract. The interest on the second mortgage is at a higher rate than the interest on the first mortgage because the holder of the second mortgage has a greater risk of loss. The borrower holds the second-mortgage contract. If the payments are not made when they become due, the first-mortgage holder or the second-mortgage holder, or both, depending upon the laws of the particular state, have the option of suing for the disposal of the property to satisfy the claims against it. The first-mortgage holder has first claim on the proceeds from the sale; the second-mortgage holder has second claim.

Third-Mortgage Borrowing. The third group of borrowers, who can pay only 10 to 15 per cent of the purchase price, can sometimes obtain a second-mortgage loan large enough to bridge the gap between the price and the initial payment plus the amount of the first-mortgage loan. It is frequently necessary, however, to obtain three loans. The seller of the property, as a rule, is the one who must hold the third mortgage. He receives no principal payments on it until the buyer has paid off the second mortgage.

In order to facilitate sales, many builders accept third-mortgage notes as part payment of the purchase price. When they accept these, however, with the purpose of selling them at a discount, they add the discount to the price of the property. The buyer of the property therefore pays more than he would if he were financing the purchase by some more satisfactory method.

Land Contracts. A common form of financing used by home buyers in the third group is the *land contract.* This form is especially popular in the central part of the United States. It is an agreement between the buyer and the seller of the property, under the terms of which the buyer usually makes a small down payment and agrees to pay the full purchase price in installments. The seller does not give the buyer legal ownership of the property, but agrees to convey the title to him when a certain percentage of the purchase price (usually approximately 50 per cent) has been paid. When the title is transferred, the seller usually accepts a first-mortgage note or the buyer either takes care of the unpaid balance or obtains a loan from someone else.

This type of borrowing makes the purchase of a home possible for a large number of people who might be unable to buy in any other way. It is advantageous to real-estate operators because it enables the seller to hold the title of the property until the buyer has invested a sufficient amount in the home to indicate that he can satisfactorily complete payment and assume the obligation of ownership. In case the buyer fails to live up to his agreement, the seller has a better opportunity to take possession of the property.

In some cases the land contract is advantageous to both parties concerned. It is often dangerous for the buyer, however, because it enables a real-estate operator legally to contract to sell property that he does not own, expecting to acquire it before he must transfer the title. The buyer can protect himself against such a contingency by having the title examined. As a land contract is essentially a lease, the buyer has his money invested in the property, but he does not have a title to the property.

Renewing a Mortgage. In obtaining a loan on a home, the borrower should take into consideration what will happen to the mortgage obligation at the time it matures. Sometimes difficulty arises because the loan cannot be paid at maturity. Some mortgages require regular payments of the principal and interest, whereas others require payment of the interest regularly and payment of the entire principal at a specified date.

A mortgage that extends for a long period is safest. If a mortgage extends for only three, four, or five years, the person who borrows the money should obtain some assurance that the mortgage can be renewed or that a new loan can be obtained from some source. Suppose, for example, that a person will require ten years to pay for a home, but that he obtains a loan that will be due in three years. During the three years he will not be able to repay much of the loan. At the end of that period he must either have the loan renewed or obtain a new loan. He otherwise will run the risk of foreclosure on his property. The cost of the renewal of the loan should be predetermined, for this must be considered as part of the cost of financing the home.

Figuring Rates. The final decision in choosing an agency to finance the purchase or the building of a home should be based upon the reputation of the agency and the economy with which the home can be financed. The method of calculating the interest charges and the expenses involved in obtaining the loan should be investigated.

Different types of financial institutions have considerable variation in their plans of charging interest. For instance, some loan companies calculate interest annually; others calculate it semiannually or quarterly. Occasionally the interest is figured on the basis of the original amount of the loan, extended over the entire time during which the loan is being paid off. This method results in the borrower's paying an unusually high rate of interest on the outstanding amount of the loan, provided periodic payments are made. Illustration No. 149 shows how a $1,000 loan at 6 per cent interest is partially retired during the first year by monthly payments of $10 each, the interest being calculated monthly on the unpaid balance. The table in Illustration No. 150 shows how the entire loan is paid during a period of eleven years and seven months.

Concealed Charges. When loans are obtained, special care should be used to detect any concealed charges. Premiums, commissions, and bonuses on loans result in higher interest rates for the borrowers. When a loan is obtained from some sources, the lender charges a commission for grant-

First 12 Months				
MONTH	MONTHLY PAYMENT	PART OF PAYMENT APPLIED TO INTEREST	PART OF PAYMENT APPLIED TO PRINCIPAL	PRINCIPAL DUE AFTER INSTALLMENT PAYMENT
1	$10.00	$ 5.00	$ 5.00	$995.00
2	10.00	4.98	5.02	989.98
3	10.00	4.95	5.05	984.93
4	10.00	4.93	5.07	979.86
5	10.00	4.90	5.10	974.76
6	10.00	4.88	5.12	969.64
7	10.00	4.85	5.15	964.49
8	10.00	4.83	5.17	959.32
9	10.00	4.80	5.20	954.12
10	10.00	4.77	5.23	948.89
11	10.00	4.75	5.25	943.64
12	10.00	4.72	5.28	938.36
		$58.36	$61.64	$938.36

Illustration No. 149—Amortization of a $1,000 Loan During the First Year, Interest at 6 Per Cent Computed Monthly

ing it. If, for example, a $40 commission is charged on a $1,000 loan that will extend for ten years, the actual amount of cash available from the loan is $960. The interest, however, must be paid on the $1,000. The actual rate of interest is therefore greater than the nominal rate.

YEAR	TOTAL OF MONTHLY PAYMENTS	PART OF PAYMENTS APPLIED TO INTEREST	PART OF PAYMENTS APPLIED TO PRINCIPAL	PRINCIPAL DUE AT END OF YEAR
1	$120.00	$58.36	$ 61.64	$938.36
2	120.00	54.56	65.44	872.92
3	120.00	50.55	69.45	803.47
4	120.00	46.25	73.75	729.72
5	120.00	41.71	78.29	651.43
6	120.00	36.89	83.11	568.32
7	120.00	31.76	88.24	480.08
8	120.00	26.32	93.68	386.40
9	120.00	20.52	99.48	286.92
10	120.00	14.40	105.60	181.32
11	120.00	7.89	112.11	69.21
12 (7 months)	70.00	1.44	68.56	.65

Illustration No. 150—Amortization of a $1,000 Loan at 6 Per Cent, Interest Computed Monthly

There are other additional charges that must be considered in obtaining a loan. In some states a tax is levied. In practically every state there is a fee for having the deed recorded. The cost of having the title examined is usually from $15 to $35. The cost of an appraisal should not exceed

$5 or $10. Ordinarily these costs are borne by the person who obtains the loan, but occasionally they are paid by the company granting the loan.

Federal Housing Administration. The Federal Housing Administration is commonly known as the FHA. The FHA provides Federal insurance on loans that are obtained through an approved lending agency. If the FHA approves the loan, the money can be borrowed from the regular lending agency. The lending agency is protected because the FHA insures the loan, guaranteeing its payment. Money may be borrowed for repairing or improving a home, buying or building a new home, buying an existing home, or buying a multiple-family dwelling, such as an apartment building.

Where and How to Apply for FHA Loans. An FHA loan can be obtained for the purchase of an existing home or for the building of a new home. A dealer in building materials, a contractor, an architect, a real-estate agent, a bank, a building and loan association, or other financial institution approved by the FHA will help a prospective home owner to file an application. After the application has been made, no official action will be taken until the loan has been accepted by an approved lending institution and the minimum appraisal fee of $10 has been paid. The lending institution is permitted to charge its usual fees, such as those for examining the title and having the deed recorded.

Charges and Payment Plans of the FHA. A loan obtained under the FHA may be repaid over periods of fifteen, twenty, or twenty-five years. If a new home is being purchased, the minimum down payment is 10 per cent and the mortgage insurance is one fourth of 1 per cent on the decreasing annual balance of the loan. If an existing home is being purchased or refinanced, the minimum cash down payment is 20 per cent and the mortgage insurance charge is one half of 1 per cent on the decreasing annual balance. The interest rate in each case is 5 per cent a year on the decreasing monthly balance. In other words, the monthly payments remain the same, but in each successive month a greater amount is applied to the principal and a lesser amount to interest and mortgage insurance.

Illustration No. 151 is a schedule of typical monthly charges on insured FHA loans on newly constructed homes.

ACCRUED MONTHLY PAYMENTS	$5,000 LOAN			
	15 YEARS	20 YEARS	24 YEARS	25 YEARS
Principal and Interest	$39.55	$33.00	$29.85	$29.25
Mortgage Insurance Premium	.97	1.00	1.01	1.01
Subtotal	40.52	34.00	30.86	30.26
Taxes (Estimated)	7.00	7.00	7.00	7.00
Fire Insurance (Estimated)	1.88	1.88	1.88	1.88
Total	$49.40	$42.88	$39.74	$39.14

Illustration No. 151—Typical Monthly Charges on Insured FHA Loans

Other Federal Agencies. The Home Owners' Loan Corporation and the Farm Credit Administration are of particular interest to the individual who is interested in borrowing money for the financing of a home. The Home Owners' Loan Corporation operates in a manner similar to the Federal Housing Administration, but the money that the borrower obtains is Federal money obtained directly from the Home Owners' Loan Corporation. The primary function of the Home Owners' Loan Corporation is to relieve distressed home owners by extending long-term, low-cost loans to prevent foreclosure. The table provides a brief explanation of the functions of each agency.

TEXTBOOK QUESTIONS

1. (a) What is the purpose of a building and loan association? (b) How much will such an organization usually lend on property?
2. What are the most common sources of loans on real estate?
3. What is usually the maximum percentage of the appraised value of real estate that a savings bank can lend?
4. In financing the purchase of a home, how can a person use a loan that will extend for only three years?
5. Explain the typical policies of mortgage companies in lending on real estate.

6. If a person does not make a sufficient down payment on a home to enable him to obtain the remainder of the price from a bank or a building and loan association, what other sources of borrowing are open to him?
7. Why is a private investor sometimes willing to lend more money on a piece of property than a bank?
8. Explain how money can be borrowed on more than one mortgage on the same piece of property.
9. Which is the safer type of mortgage from the point of view of the mortgagor: (a) a mortgage that extends for a short term of three or four years or (b) one that extends for a long term of from ten to fifteen years? Why?
10. What are some concealed charges that must be paid by the borrower of money?
11. In what way does the FHA serve individuals who wish to borrow money for homes?
12. For what purposes may FHA loans be obtained?
13. Who, other than an FHA representative, can assist a person in obtaining an FHA loan?
14. What is the minimum appraisal fee for FHA loans?
15. Over what period of payment may an FHA loan be extended?
16. What is the minimum down payment under FHA loans?
17. What items, besides payments on principal and of interest, are included in the monthly payments under FHA loans?
18. What two other important Federal agencies serve individuals who wish to borrow money for the financing of homes?

DISCUSSION QUESTIONS

1. Real-estate agents sometimes advertise the sale of a house on easy terms with the statement that the buyer can "pay like rent." (a) Why do they advertise in this manner? (b) Can they sell on these terms at the same price that would be charged if the buyer paid cash in full? Why? (c) Does the buyer necessarily make a poor investment if he "pays like rent"?
2. If you want to borrow the greatest possible amount of money on a particular piece of real estate, from what source would you most likely obtain that amount, assuming that all sources of loans are available to you? Give your reasons.
3. Give the advantages and the disadvantages of second and third mortgages from the point of view of (a) the mortgagor and (b) the mortgagee.
4. Some insurance companies that make loans on real estate include as part of the interest or the service charge an amount that is sufficient to pay for insurance on the life of the mortgagor during the period in which the loan will be

repaid. Can you see any advantages or disadvantages in this plan? Discuss them.

5. If a person has bought a home and has agreed to pay off the mortgage at the rate of $50 a month, (a) can you see any advantage in his paying $60 or $70 a month if this amount is available? (b) Under what circumstances might there be such an advantage?
6. If a person is considering an FHA loan as compared with an ordinary loan from a building and loan association or a bank, what factors in relation to the monthly payments must be taken into consideration to determine which is the more economical method of purchase and which is the more desirable?

PROBLEMS

1. Using the table on page 449 as a guide, compute the first-year cost of financing a home under the following conditions: (a) the value of the house and the lot is $3,750; (b) the first cash payment is $850; (c) a first mortgage is obtained on the balance of the indebtedness at 6 per cent interest, to be charged annually in advance; (d) the monthly payments of the principal and the interest are $30; (e) the taxes are 1.8 per cent of the value of the house and lot; (f) the insurance is .4 per cent of the value of the house ($2,900); (g) the upkeep is 1.5 per cent of the value of the house. Indicate what part of the first-year cost constitutes expense and what part constitutes savings.
2. On the basis of the table on page 449, compute the first-year cost of financing a home under the following conditions: (a) the house and the lot have a value of $2,400; (b) the down payment is $550; (c) annual payments of $240 are to be made; (d) the interest rate is 6 per cent. For the purpose of this problem base the cost of insurance and of upkeep on the entire value of the house and the lot.
3. If interest is chargeable annually in advance, what will be the interest charges for the first year on the following three mortgages on a home: $2,000 at 5 per cent; $1,000 at 7 per cent; and $800 at 8 per cent?
4. On FHA loans, interest at 5 per cent is charged on the decreasing annual balance; and on a new home the mortgage insurance charge is one fourth of 1 per cent on the decreasing annual balance. (a) On the basis of the table on page 464, compute the total amount (principal payments, interest, mortgage, insurance, taxes, and fire insurance) paid on a $5,000 loan covering fifteen years. (b) What is the average monthly expense, not including premium payments and depreciation on the home? (c) How does this amount compare

with the average amount of rent paid per family according to Illustration No. 151 on page 464?

5. Mr. Herbert French owns a house and a lot that cost $5,000. The lot is valued at $800. Assume that, over a period of twenty years, the valuation of the property for assessing taxes will remain at $5,000; the tax rate will stay at 2.1 per cent; the yearly cost of insurance on the house will be .35 per cent of the present value of the house; the annual cost of upkeep will be 1.5 per cent of the present value of the house; the house and the lot will be worth $4,000 at the end of the twenty years (the loss in value to be distributed equally over the twenty years); the money invested in the home would have earned a yearly income of 3.5 per cent if it had been invested in good bonds. Determine whether it is more economical for Mr. French to own his home than it would have been for him to pay a monthly rental of $40. Assume that all other costs of owning the home or of renting are negligible and that the rental rate would have remained the same.

COMMUNITY PROBLEMS AND PROJECTS

1. Investigate the various local sources of loans on real estate. For each type of source find out (a) the percentage of the appraised value of property that will be lent; (b) the rate of interest, (c) the length of time during which a loan may extend, (d) the method of payment, (e) the dates on which interest is computed, and (f) any additional charges in obtaining a loan.
2. Obtain a sample form required by a bank, a building and loan association, or an insurance company for making an application for a loan. Fill out the blank, basing your figures on some particular piece of property, preferably your own home.
3. Analyze the total cost of rent that your family or another is paying. Compare this with the monthly cost of acquiring a home that would fit the requirements of the family. Use an actual piece of property as the basis of your study, and consider the income of the family in making the computations. Use the actual tax rate and the prevailing interest and insurance rates. Make your other computations on the basis of the table shown on page 451.
4. From some institution in your city obtain forms for applying for an FHA loan, and fill out one of these forms for your parents on the basis of some particular type of loan.

CHAPTER XX

LEGAL PROBLEMS OF OBTAINING A HOME

Purpose of the Chapter. Obtaining a piece of property through renting, leasing, or buying involves many legal problems. The average person is not expected to be his own lawyer. He should seek legal advice when it is needed, but he should understand some of the elementary principles of legal relations.

The purpose of this chapter is to point out the legal rights and responsibilities of the landlord, the tenant, the purchaser, the seller, and the borrower.

Relations of Landlord and Tenant. When a person allows his property to be occupied and controlled by another, he is called a *landlord.* The one who occupies the property is the *tenant.* It is assumed, of course, that the tenant occupies the property with the consent of the landlord. The tenant has the possession and control of the property although he acknowledges the superior rights of the landlord. After the expiration of the agreement the landlord has the right to regain possession of the property.

Tenancy. The agreement between the landlord and the tenant is known as a *lease.* The landlord is the *lessor,* and the tenant is the *lessee.* The lease may be oral or written, the form depending upon whether there is a law governing that detail. A written lease is desirable in many cases because it clearly defines the rights of the landlord and of the tenant. As will be seen later, the period of occupancy may be definite or indefinite. In some states the lessor and the lessee must sign their names before a witness, such as a notary public. The formal type of lease usually embodies the following information:

(a) The date
(b) The names of the landlord and the tenant
(c) A description and an identification of the property
(d) The length of the tenancy period

This Lease Witnesseth:

THAT John G. Turner does
HEREBY LEASE TO William F. Goodall
the premises situate in the City *of* Portland *in the County of* Multnomah *and State of* Oregon *described as follows:*

Dwelling House, No. 1229 Melbourne Road, Portland, Oregon

with the appurtenances thereto, for the term of two years *commencing* April 1, *1940, at a rental of* fifty-five *dollars per* month *, payable* monthly.

SAID LESSEE AGREES *to pay said rent, unless said premises shall be destroyed or rendered untenantable by fire or other unavoidable accident; to not commit or suffer waste; to not use said premises for any unlawful purpose; to not assign this lease, or under-let said premises, or any part thereof, or permit the sale of* his *interest herein by legal process, without the written consent of said lessor ; to not use said premises or any part thereof in violation of any law relating to intoxicating liquors; and at the expiration of this lease, to surrender said premises in as good condition as they now are, or may be put by said lessor, reasonable wear and unavoidable casualties, condemnation or appropriation excepted. Upon non-payment of any of said rent for* ten *days, after it shall become due, and without demand made therefore; or the bankruptcy or insolvency of lessee or assigns, or the appointment of a receiver or trustee of the property of lessee or assigns or if this lease pass to any person or persons by operation of law; or the breach of any of the other agreements herein contained, the lessor may terminate this lease and re-enter and re-possess said premises.*

SAID LESSOR AGREES *(said lessee having performed* his *obligations under this lease) that said lessee shall quietly hold and occupy said premises during said term without any hindrance or molestation by said lessor ,* his *heir or any person lawfully claiming under them.*

Signed this first *day of* April *A. D. 1940*

IN PRESENCE OF:

Gene Rainier	John G Turner
Carl Noble	William F Goodall

Illustration No. 152—A Lease

(e) The amount of the payment
(f) The manner of payment
(g) A statement of the conditions and the agreements
(h) The signatures of the tenant and the landlord

The lessor grants the lessee the privilege of using the property for lawful purposes and without interference, provided the terms of the contract are carried out properly. The lease states specifically the rights of each party to the contract. Some of the particular rights of the lessee and the lessor are mentioned later in this chapter.

A tenant may occupy property as (a) a *tenant-for-years,* (b) a *tenant-from-year-to-year,* or (c) a *tenant-at-will.* A tenant-for-years occupies property under an agreement covering a definite period. A tenant-from-year-to-year or a tenant-from-month-to-month occupies property under an agreement covering an indefinite period. A tenant-at-will is one who occupies property for an indefinite period, the agreement being terminable at will by either party. *Renting* is a rather indefinite term that applies to tenancy without a written contract. *Leasing* is a term that applies to obtaining tenancy through the use of a written contract.

Rights and Duties of the Tenant. The tenant of a piece of property is entitled to peaceful possession of it. If he is deprived of that, he may recover damages through a lawsuit. The tenant is also entitled to use the property for any purpose for which it is adapted unless he is forbidden by the agreement. It may not be used for unlawful purposes.

The tenant is under obligation to make minor repairs, but not improvements. He must pay his rent when it is due. Unless the lease states otherwise, the rent is not due until the end of each month. (It is due at the end of each year if the occupant is a tenant-from-year-to-year.)

If the lease is for a definite period of time, the tenant is not obligated to give notice when he vacates the property. The lease may be terminated, however, before the expiration of the period if an agreement is reached with the landlord. If the lease is for an indefinite period of time, the tenant must notify the landlord of his intention to give up the lease. The form and the time of notice are regulated by the customs or the laws of the community in which the tenant is located. The following is an example of a notice:

Auburn, Maine, June 1, 194–

Mr. Harry Becker:

I hereby give you notice that I will quit and deliver possession, July 1, 194–, of the premises at No. 417 Reading Road, in the city of Auburn, Maine, which I now hold as tenant under you.

Robert Mason

Illustration No. 153—A Tenant's Notice of Intention to Terminate a Lease

The tenant should inspect carefully the property that he rents or leases. In the absence of any agreement with the landlord, he accepts the property with the risk of any defects, except hidden defects, that may be present. In most states he is liable for injuries to guests resulting from defects that he should have known and remedied.

Rights and Duties of the Landlord. A landlord does not have the right to enter the premises of a tenant except to do what is necessary to protect the property. He must not interfere with the tenant's right of possession. If the tenant abandons the property, however, the landlord may take possession. At the expiration of the lease the landlord may enter the property and take possession through legal proceedings.

The landlord is entitled to receive the rent as specified in the lease. In some states, through legal proceedings, he may seize personal property of the tenant and have it sold to pay the rent that is in arrears.

In some states the landlord is under no obligation to make repairs or to pay for improvements on the property unless an agreement has been made with the tenant. In most states, however, he is obligated to keep the house in habitable condition. Unless the lease specifies otherwise, taxes and assessments must be paid by the landlord.

When a tenant occupies property for an indefinite period of time, the landlord may obtain possession of it by giving notice. The form and the time of the notice are regulated by local customs or laws. Illustration No. 154 is a typical notice from a landlord.

NOTICE OF LANDLORD

To *Mr. A. L. Harper:*

You are hereby notified that there is now due me the sum of *forty* dollars, being rent for the premises situated in the city of *Hamilton* in the state of *Indiana*, and known and described as follows:

No. 326 Cedar Street

And you are further notified that payment of said sum so due has been and is hereby demanded of you, and that unless payment thereof is made on or before the *first* day of *January,* 194–, your lease of said premises will be terminated.

Dated this *15th* day of *December,* 194–.

Edward Davis
Landlord

Illustration No. 154—A Landlord's Notice Requesting a Tenant to Vacate Property

When the landlord retains control over a part of the property—as in the case of a landlord who leases part of a building to a tenant—he is liable for certain injuries caused by the defective condition of the part of the property over which he has control. For instance, Mr. A owns a two-story building. He lives on the first floor and retains control over the porch and the yard, but he rents the second floor to Mr. B. If Mr. B or a member of his family is injured as a result of the defective condition of the porch or the sidewalk, Mr. A is liable for the injuries. The landlord is also liable, in most cases, for injuries to any friend or guest of the tenant who may have been injured because of defects in the property under the landlord's control.

Improvements and Fixtures. In the absence of an agreement to the contrary, the improvements that are attached to the property become a part of the property and therefore belong to the owner. For instance, if a tenant builds a shed or a garage upon the lot belonging to his landlord, he cannot tear it down or take it away without permission. If a tenant constructs shelves or cupboards in the house that he has rented or leased, he ordinarily cannot take them away when he leaves. In some cases, however, courts have held that such fixtures attached with nails have become a part of the property, whereas fixtures attached with screws may be removed.

Title to Real Estate. The *title* to real estate is the ownership of the property. If a person has a clear title to a piece of real estate, there are no other claims against that property. To establish evidence of a clear title involves an investigation that will prove the true ownership of the property by tracing the history and the legality of the previous transfers of the title. Usually a loan on a piece of property cannot be obtained until the lender is certain that the title is satisfactory. The charge for examining the title is usually added to the loan or is paid as a special charge.

Each legal transfer of the title to a piece of property is recorded in a register of deeds, usually kept in the courthouse. It is therefore advisable to have a competent lawyer examine the records and determine whether there is a clear title to the property. In some states, individuals and companies specialize in the practice of making examinations of the titles to property. A condensation of the information taken from the recorded history of the property is referred to as an *abstract*. The report of the individual or the company making the abstract is called an *opinion of the title*. This report is sometimes, however, referred to as the abstract. It is also possible to obtain a *title-guarantee policy* from such an individual or a company. This policy guarantees that the title is clear and unencumbered.

In order to eliminate uncertainties and to reduce the expense of transferring the titles to property, some states have established a system of registering titles. This is known as the *Torrens System.* For instance, the owner of land applies for a registration of the title to his land. An officer then examines the records, and, if the title is good, he issues a certificate of title. Each time the title is transferred thereafter, a new certificate is issued.

Deeds. There are two general types of deeds: (a) the warranty deed and (b) the quitclaim deed. The *warranty deed* is the more common. It is written evidence of the ownership of a piece of real property and serves as a means of conveying the title from one person to another. The one who transfers the title to the property is called the *grantor* of the deed, and the one to whom the title is transferred is called the *grantee* of the deed. Such a deed not only purports to convey the interest of the grantor to the grantee, but also involves stipulations that certain facts relating to the title are true. A warranty deed is shown in Illustration No. 155 on page 475.

A *quitclaim deed* merely relinquishes the interest that the grantor may have in the property. The grantee assumes the risk that the title may not be good. In some communities a quitclaim deed is used instead of a warranty deed.

Consider this example: Mr. A desires to transfer real estate to Mr. B. He grants a warranty deed as evidence of the transfer of the title. In investigating the title, Mr. B discovers that a former owner, Mr. C, at one time had a claim against the property. Mr. B is therefore not quite sure that the claim has been settled fully. To protect his rights that are granted in the warranty deed, Mr. B gets Mr. C to grant a quitclaim deed relinquishing any rights that the latter may have had in the property.

A deed should be distinguished from a *contract of sale* or a *contract to convey.* A contract of sale or a contract to convey is merely an agreement to transfer property at a specified time and under specified conditions.

Know all men by these presents:

That Joseph Bentley and Marie Bentley, his wife,
in consideration of One thousand Dollars ($1,000)
to them *paid by* Walter Rathburn
the receipt whereof is hereby acknowledged, do ______ *hereby* **Grant, Bargain, Sell and Convey** *to the said* Walter Rathburn, his *heirs and assigns forever:*
Lot sixteen (16) block three (3) in the Avonlea subdivision
and all the **Estate, Title and Interest** *of the said* Grantors
either in Law or Equity, of, in and to the said premises; **Together** *with all the privileges and appurtenances to the same belonging, and all the rents, issues and profits thereof;*
To have and to hold *the same to the only proper use of the said* Grantee
his *heirs and assigns forever.*

And the said Joseph Bentley and Marie Bentley
for themselves *and* their *heirs, executors and administrators,*
do ___ *hereby* **Covenant** *with the said* Walter Rathburn, his *heirs and assigns,*
that they are *the true and lawful owner*s *of the said premises,*
*and ha*ve *full power to convey the same; and that the title so conveyed is* **Clear, Free and Unincumbered; And further,** *That* they **do** ____ **Warrant and Will Defend** *the same against all claim or claims, of all persons whomsoever;*

In Witness Whereof, *The said* Joseph Bentley and Marie Bentley
who hereby release all their *right and expectancy of* **Dower** *in the said premises,*
*ha*ve *hereunto set* their *hands* ______ *this*
fourteenth *day of* October *in the year of our Lord one thousand nine hundred* **forty.**

Signed and acknowledged in presence of—

P. M. Davis

E. R. Hall

Joseph Bentley

Marie Bentley

State of Virginia, **County of** Norfolk, **ss.**

Be it Remembered, *That on this* fourteenth *day of* October *in the year of our Lord one thousand nine hundred* and **forty** *before me, the subscriber, a* Notary Public *in and for said county, personally came* Joseph Bentley and Marie Bentley
*the grantor*s *in the foregoing Deed, and acknowledged the signing thereof to be* their *voluntary act and deed.*

In Testimony Whereof, *I have hereunto subscribed my name and affixed my* official *seal on the day and year last aforesaid.*

E. R. Stern

Notary Public

Illustration No. 155—A Warranty Deed

The important considerations in executing a deed are the description of the property, signature, seal, witnesses, acknowledgment, delivery, and acceptance. The laws in different states vary in some respects. To assure a clear title, the person executing the deed should become familiar with local laws. For instance, the laws in various states differ with regard to the ownership of property by man and wife. Some states require the signatures of both, whereas others require only one signature. In some states the witnesses must sign in the presence of one another, whereas in others they may sign only in the presence of an authorized public officer. Because of the many technicalities the average person should obtain legal advice in granting a deed or taking the title to real estate. It is best to let a lawyer write all the legal papers.

Joint Ownership. In most states a husband and a wife may own real estate with the provision that, when either dies, the survivor will become sole owner of the property. In such a case the survivor is said to become a *tenant by entirety*. In some states the manner in which the title will pass to the survivor must be indicated in the deed. When property is owned under such a condition, the husband and the wife are considered to own it jointly, neither being the owner of any particular part. Our law in this respect is fashioned after the old English law that considers a man and his wife to be one person.

There are laws in most states that grant what is called a *dower right* or *dower interest*. This term means that when a man and a woman marry, each has a legal right to share in the property of the other, including real estate. The laws of most states prohibit a husband or a wife from selling property unless the signatures of both appear on the deed, even though the property may be recorded in the name of only one.

In many states when property that has been owned jointly by a husband and a wife becomes the sole property of the survivor, it is not subject to an inheritance tax or a state tax, for the survivor is not considered to inherit the property.

Mortgages. A written contract that transfers an interest in property as security for the payment of a debt is called a *mortgage*. The one who grants the mortgage is the *mortgagor*, and the one who accepts the mortgage is the *mortgagee*. The mortgage is evidence of the fact that the mortgagee has a claim on the property that has been mortgaged.

Mortgages are not the same in all states, although they have similar characteristics. Every mortgage should be in writing, and usually the signature should be witnessed. The correct wording can be found in statute books, and a special legal form on which to draw up the mortgage can be obtained.

In most transactions involving mortgages, at least two legal papers are required: (a) a mortgage note and (b) a mortgage. In some states a mortgage bond is commonly used instead of a mortgage note. In other states the instrument is referred to as a mortgage contract. Regardless of its title the legal instrument that is used specifies the amount of the indebtedness and the method of payment. The mortgage is given as security for the payment of the debt. In some transactions in which a mortgage is issued, the borrower must sign a series of notes that will become due on certain dates.

The deed should not be confused with the mortgage. The former is written evidence of the transfer of the title, whereas the latter is written evidence of a claim against property. In most states the laws require that, in order to be effective protection against subsequent buyers or mortgagees, a deed or a mortgage must be recorded in the county in which the property is located. This procedure enables other interested people to discover any claims against the property. A deed or a mortgage is recorded under a description of the property. The property involved is described according to its location.

Rights and Duties of the Mortgagor and the Mortgagee. Any person who owns an interest in land, buildings, or even crops raised on land, may mortgage that interest. A mortgage on real estate includes equipment that has become so permanently attached to the real estate that it is considered a part of it. If a piece of land is mortgaged, and a house is later built on the land, the house will be included in the mortgage, for it has become a part of the land.

In the eyes of the law the mortgagor is the owner of the property. The property is merely pledged as security for the payment of a debt. It remains his property to use as he pleases, unless he allows the mortgagee to take possession or he is forced to give up the title to the property through legal procedure. If he fails to perform the agreements specified in the mortgage contract, he can be compelled by the law to relinquish the title to the property.

The mortgagor is under duty to refrain from destroying or damaging the property. The mortgagee must not interfere with the occupancy of the property except through agreement with the mortgagor or through legal procedure.

When the indebtedness is paid, the mortgage is automatically canceled. It is wise, however, for the mortgagor to obtain the mortgage, the mortgage note, and a statement acknowledging the discharge of the obligation. The notice acknowledging the discharge of the obligation should be recorded in the proper place of registration.

If a mortgagee sells a mortgage to a third person, he should give the mortgagor a notice of transfer with the mortgage. When the mortgage indebtedness is paid, the notice of transfer, along with the other legal papers, should be obtained by the mortgagor. The registration of all legal papers of this type provides written evidence of legal obligations.

Mortgage Foreclosure. Although a mortgage contract usually specifies that the mortgagor loses all rights to the mortgaged property if the obligation is not performed at a specified time, the laws in most states permit the mortgagor the privilege of regaining his interest in the property by fulfilling his contract at any time before the *foreclosure* of the mortgage.

If the mortgagor fails to fulfill his obligation, the mortgagee has the right of foreclosing; that is, of bringing a legal suit to obtain possession of the property. Foreclosure may consist in (a) a court order that transfers the title to the property from the mortgagor to the mortgagee, or (b) a court order that requires the property to be sold to pay the mortgagee. The procedure is, however, different in various states.

If the proceeds from the sale of the property exceed the total of the indebtedness and the expenses incident to the sale, the mortgagor gets the difference. If the proceeds are less than the amount of the indebtedness, the mortgagee has a right, in most states, to obtain a judgment against the mortgagor for the difference. This judgment is referred to as a *deficiency judgment.* Because of the possibilities of a deficiency judgment, the mortgagor does not release himself, under the laws of some states, from his obligation merely by giving up his property.

One piece of property may have as many as three mortgages. If it is sold through foreclosure proceedings, the mortgagees must be protected according to the preference given to their respective mortgages. The first mortgage ranks first; the second ranks second; and the third ranks third.

Lien. Any encumbrance, or claim, on real estate that arises from a debt is referred to as a *lien.* A mortgage is one type of lien. A *mechanic's lien* is another. For instance, a contractor who has constructed a building may hold a lien against the property for the payment of the amount due him. A *judgment* rendered by a court as the result of a lawsuit is still another kind of lien. The judgment represents a claim that must be paid by the owner of property.

Things to Investigate. Although an investigation of the title to property discloses all the facts, these facts should be analyzed from the point of view of the original cost and the cost of owning the property. The various claims against the property will affect the value. In purchasing a piece of property, it is important to investigate assessments, taxes, condition of streets, property lines, zoning laws, mortgages, judgments, and other liens. Investigations may disclose that a new street will go through the property or cut off part of the property. New assessments may be planned for grading, sewers, or flood control. In some cities the zoning laws may place property in an undesirable class and may therefore cause its value to decrease.

There should be a thorough understanding of such items as assessments, liens, and unpaid taxes. Unless an agreement to the contrary is made previous to the sale, the new owner must pay the assessments, the liens, and the unpaid taxes. He must also pay any penalty that is assessed because of delinquent taxes. In other words, taxes are claims on the property and not personal claims on the individual.

The prospective buyer should also consider the adjustments that are necessary in relation to the mortgage and the insurance. He may assume the obligation under the old mortgage, or he may have a new mortgage issued. If there is an old mortgage on the property, there should be an agreement as to who must pay the interest between the date of the last payment and the date of the transfer of the real estate. Arrangements should be made to have the fire insurance policy transferred at the time of the sale, or to have the old policy canceled and a new one issued.

Relations with Lawyers and Real-Estate Agents. A person buying real estate may need the services of a lawyer as well as those of a real-estate agent. He should obtain in advance some general idea of what the lawyer will charge. If the real-estate agent is to collect a fee from the purchaser, that fee should be determined in advance. There should be a written contract governing such details.

TEXTBOOK QUESTIONS

1. (a) Who is a landlord? (b) Who is a tenant?
2. (a) Who is a lessor? (b) Who is a lessee?
3. Why is a written lease desirable?
4. What information is usually embodied in a formal lease?
5. (a) Who is a tenant-at-will? (b) Who is a tenant-for-years?
6. May the landlord enter the premises of a tenant any time he wishes?
7. May a tenant use the property for any purposes that he wishes?

8. In the absence of any agreement, when is rent usually due?
9. Under what circumstances must a tenant notify the landlord of his intention to give up the use of the property?
10. Is the landlord or the tenant liable for damages if an invited guest of the tenant is injured on the property?
11. If the tenant fails to pay his rent, what may the landlord do to ensure payment of the amount that is due as rent?
12. Must the landlord make repairs and improvements that are demanded by the tenant?
13. A tenant who intends to move wishes to tear down and take with him any improvements he has made. May he do so?
14. Through what process is it possible to determine who is the legal owner of a piece of real estate and what claims, such as a mortgage, are held against the property?
15. In some states what protection can one obtain against the possibility that the title to a piece of property may not be good?
16. What is the difference between a deed and a contract of sale (or a contract to convey)?
17. (a) What are the two general types of deeds? (b) In what ways do they differ?
18. Is it always true that, if property is recorded only in the name of the husband, he alone has the right to sell it?
19. (a) What is a mortgage? (b) Who is a mortgagor? (c) Who is a mortgagee?
20. If the mortgagor fails to pay the claim against the mortgaged property, what right has the mortgagee?
21. If a mortgage covers a vacant lot, and a house is later built on the lot, does the mortgage cover only the lot or does it also include the house?
22. What is a mechanic's lien?
23. If an assessment, a lien, or unpaid taxes are charged against a piece of property, who must pay these charges: the person who originally incurred them, or the person who owns the property?
24. What are some things that should be investigated at the time of purchasing real estate?

DISCUSSION QUESTIONS

1. (a) Name some of the advantages of a written lease to a lessee. (b) Name some of the disadvantages.
2. (a) Name some of the advantages of a written lease to a lessor. (b) Name some of the disadvantages.
3. How many copies of a lease do you think are desirable?
4. In many states a lease may be registered or recorded to provide evidence of the contract between the lessee and the lessor. What advantages do you see in this procedure?

5. How may a tenant terminate a lease before its expiration?
6. (a) May a tenant change the property that he has leased by making physical alterations? (b) May he repair it without the consent of the owner?
7. When Mr. Brown visits Mr. Cooper, he injures himself on a broken step. Mr. Cooper has rented the house from Mr. Thompson. Who is responsible for the injury?
8. Give some causes that might lead to questions as to whether the title to a piece of real estate is clear.
9. A warranty deed asserts that certain facts stated in the deed are true. In most states the grantee has the privilege of suing the grantor if the facts in the deed do not prove to be true. (a) Do you believe that this protection is adequate? (b) What would you recommend as an additional remedy?
10. (a) Can you give any reason why there are laws of joint ownership in relation to real estate that is owned by a married man or a married woman? (b) How do you think such laws would affect you if you were planning to buy real estate from a married man?
11. Is a refrigerator or a stove considered part of a house or an apartment that is mortgaged? Explain your answer in detail.

PROBLEMS

1. Mr. Woodburn, who has rented a house to Mr. Sears, wants to sell the house. In the absence of the Sears family he unlocks the door and shows the house to a prospective buyer. When Mr. Sears learns what Mr. Woodburn has done, he objects and insists that Mr. Woodburn had no right to enter the house. Mr. Woodburn insists that he did have the right to enter his own house. What is your opinion? Why?
2. Mr. Simmons rents a house to Mr. Baker and later sells the property to Mr. Jackson. Mr. Jackson wants immediate possession of the property. Mr. Baker insists that he has an agreement with Mr. Simmons to the effect that he may stay on the property as long as he wishes. This agreement is, however, not written. (a) Do you think Mr. Jackson can obtain possession of the property? (b) In what way do you think he can obtain possession?
3. Mr. Curry, the lawyer for a bank, investigated the title at the time the bank planned to make a loan on property that Mr. Anderson wished to buy. Mr. Curry charged the bank a fee of $50 for examining the title. Mr. Curry also offered to act as title examiner for Mr. Anderson. He offered, however, to charge a reduced fee of $40 in view of the fact that he had already examined the title. Do you think Mr. Anderson should have accepted Mr. Curry's offer?

4. Mr. J. O. Smith granted a mortgage on a house and lot to Mr. A. G. Merrill. Mr. Merrill insisted that, as he was the holder of the mortgage, he was entitled to the rent derived from the property. What do you think of his claim?
5. The Rice Flakes Company occupied some frame buildings that were leased from the American Realty Company. During the term of tenancy the latter company removed two of the buildings on the property that had been rented to the Rice Flakes Company. Could it do so without incurring a liability?
6. Mr. Duggan granted a mortgage on his house and lot in favor of the Central Building and Loan Association, to which he owed some money. The mortgage was not recorded. Mr. Trees accepted a deed from Mr. Duggan in good faith and without knowing that a mortgage had been granted to the Central Building and Loan Association. The Central Building and Loan Association insisted that it still had a legal claim against the property. Mr. Trees insisted that the property was free from a mortgage. Who was right? Why?

COMMUNITY PROBLEMS AND PROJECTS

1. Obtain copies of your state laws pertaining to the foreclosure of mortgages. Write a report on the legal rights of the mortgagor and the mortgagee. Point out whether there is any possibility of repossessing property after the mortgage has been foreclosed.
2. Obtain samples of the legal papers used in obtaining a loan on a home, and explain their use. If there are options with regard to the use of a particular type of paper, explain the differences.
3. Investigate the procedure in your community for recording a deed, a mortgage, or a lease. Find out the place of recording, the details of procedure, and the fee.
4. Learn what is the common procedure in your community for leasing and renting. Find out whether it is a custom to have leases begin and end in some particular month of the year. Also investigate the customary procedure in giving notices, the forms of leases, and the obligations of tenant and landlord. Try to obtain a sample of a lease form or a complete lease.
5. Obtain copies of the legal forms required in granting a mortgage. Fill out the necessary forms, using an imaginary piece of property, and write an explanation of the procedure and the use of the forms.

CHAPTER XXI

THE CONSUMER CO-OPERATIVE MOVEMENT

Purpose of the Chapter. In some communities consumers attempt to solve their problems by forming consumer co-operatives. In other words, they bind themselves together in a business enterprise for the mutual benefit of the members. Consumer co-operatives are explained in this chapter.

What Is a Co-operative Enterprise? Any organization is a *co-operative* if the members participate in the problems of management, jointly own the enterprise, accept responsibilities for the losses, and share in the profits. Although the co-operative movement began with consumers, there are also producers' and distributors' co-operatives. A co-operative organization may be operated in the same way as a large business enterprise; or it may be operated as a small business, as in the case of a small credit union or a buying club.

A real *consumer co-operative* is one in which the patrons of a particular business are also the owners. Some co-

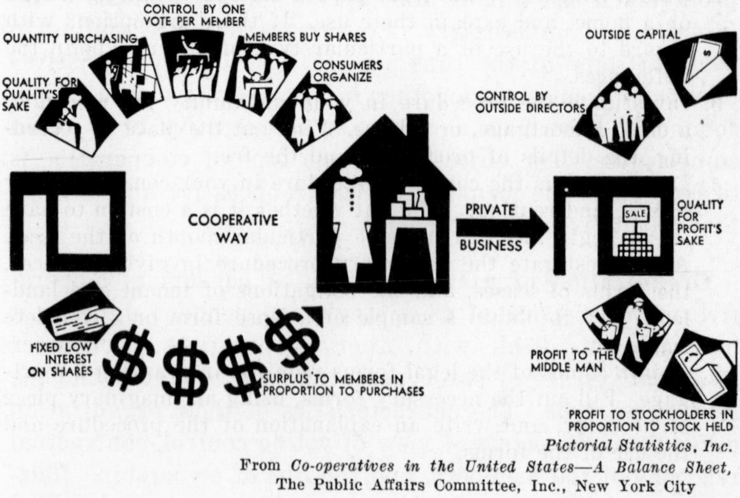

Pictorial Statistics, Inc.

From *Co-operatives in the United States—A Balance Sheet,* The Public Affairs Committee, Inc., New York City

Illustration No. 156—A Consumer Co-operative—A Private Business

operatives, however, also sell to the general public. There are many kinds of consumer co-operatives, although most of them are organized as general retailing establishments. Laundries, banks, restaurants, power plants, and even insurance companies have been and are being operated on a consumer co-operative basis.

Reasons for Consumer Co-operatives. Illustrations Nos. 80 and 81 in Chapter VII show the spread of prices between the individual producer and the final consumer. As every step in the process of distribution adds a cost, the final consumer often pays considerably more than the price at which goods are sold by the original producer. For instance, a producer of oranges may receive five cents a dozen, but the consumer may pay twenty-five cents a dozen. Much of this difference in price is due to the costs of transportation, storage, financing, and other economic functions that are necessary in the process of distribution. Some of it, however, is due to profits that are taken out during the process of distribution. Much of the cost cannot be eliminated because it is impossible to omit the fundamental processes of distribution.

Many consumers believe, however, that the amount of profit taken out during the process of distribution is unjustified and unnecessary. Consumers who are willing to perform some of the functions of distribution themselves may band themselves together in a co-operative association, commonly known as a consumer co-operative or a retail co-operative. The objective of this type of co-operative is to pass on to the members of the co-operative any savings that result from the enterprise.

Organization of a Co-operative. A consumer co-operative may be operated as a single independent unit, or it may associate itself with other co-operatives. Consumer co-operatives are of two types: the *federated type* and the *centralized type*. The characteristics of their organization differ from the points of view of voting control, contractual relations of the members, and the line of ownership. Illustration No. 157 shows how a co-operative may be organized

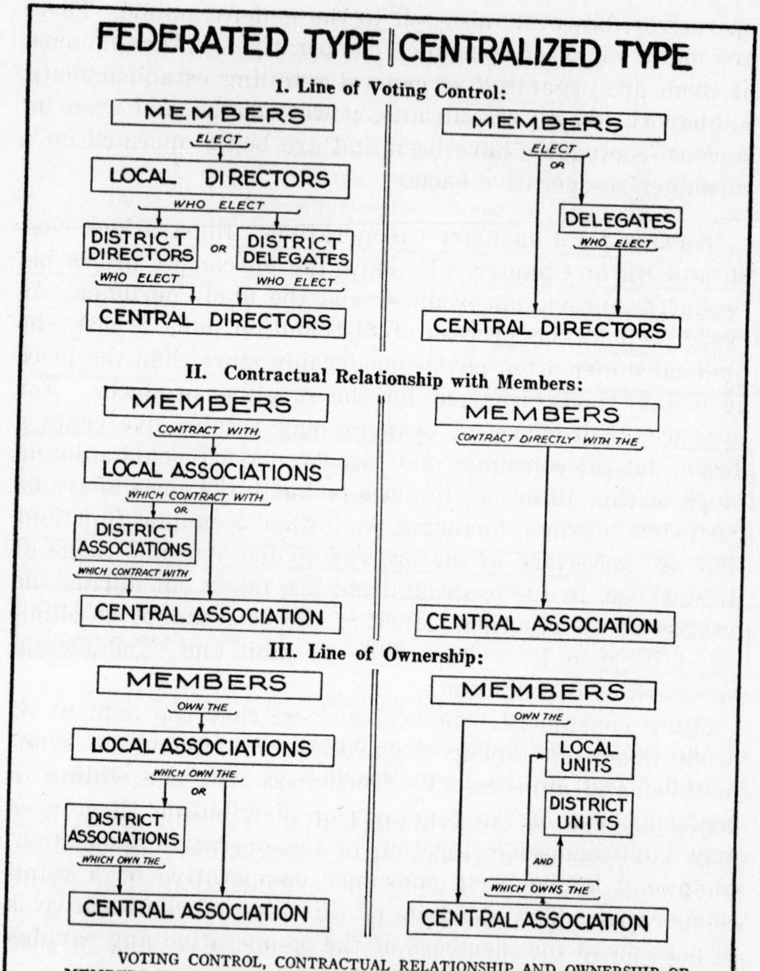

VOTING CONTROL, CONTRACTUAL RELATIONSHIP AND OWNERSHIP OF MEMBERS IN TYPICAL FEDERATED AND CENTRALIZED COOPERATIVE ASSOCIATIONS.

From *Co-operation Principles and Practices,* Extension Service of the College of Agriculture, University of Wisconsin, Madison, Wisconsin

Illustration No. 157—Comparison of the Federated Type and the Centralized Type of Co-operative

under the two fundamental methods if it is associated with other co-operatives. Notice that the members of the federated type own the local associations, which in turn own the central association and the district associations. In the case

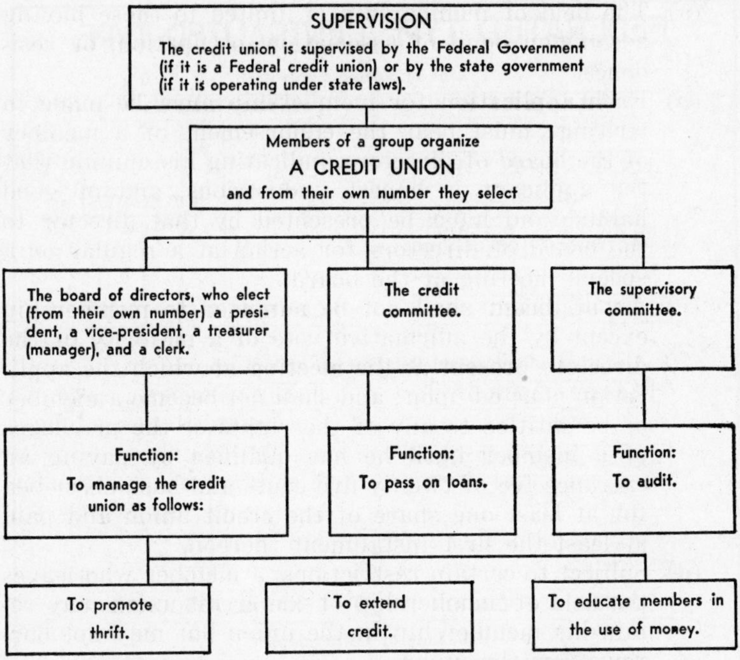

Illustration No. 158—Organization of a Credit Union

of the centralized type the members own the central association, which in turn owns the district and local units.

Organization of Individual Units. A credit union is a good example of a co-operative association. Illustration No. 158 is a chart showing the organization of a credit union. A credit union is designed to encourage thrift and saving and to provide a source of credit at reasonable cost to members of the co-operative. The principle on which a credit union is organized is that any group having a common interest, such as the employees of a single business, may bind themselves together and accumulate their savings for lending to other members of the co-operative. Many states have laws providing for the organization of credit unions. Credit unions may also be organized under Federal laws administered by the Farm Credit Administration. The fundamental principles under which Federal credit unions may be organized are as follows:

(a) The field of membership is limited to those having a common bond of association, occupation, or residence.

(b) Each application for membership must be made in writing; must bear the endorsement of a member of the board of directors, indicating his opinion that the applicant is honest, industrious, and of good habits; and must be presented by that director to the board of directors for action at a regular or a special meeting of the board.

(c) An applicant shall not be admitted to membership except by the affirmative vote of a majority of the directors present at the meeting at which the application is acted upon; and shall not become a member or be entitled to any of the rights or the privileges of a member until he has qualified by paying an entrance fee of twenty-five cents and has subscribed for at least one share of the credit union and paid at least the first installment thereon.

(d) Subject to certain restrictions, a member who leaves the field of membership of the credit union may retain his membership in the union but may not borrow from the union.

(e) The par value of each share shall be five dollars. Subscriptions to shares are payable at the time of subscription, or in equal installments at the rate of twenty-five cents a month on each share subscribed for; but on any day when an installment is due and payable any number of installments may be paid in advance.

(f) The maximum amount of shares that may be held by any one member shall be established from time to time by resolution of the board of directors.

(g) A member failing to pay any installment that is due on shares, unless he has been excused for cause by the board of directors, shall pay a fine amounting to one cent for each full week on each two dollars or fraction thereof of the installment or installments in arrears. In no case, however, shall the fine be less than five cents.

(h) Shares may be transferred only among members by a written instrument in such form as the board of directors may prescribe and upon the payment to the credit union of a fee of twenty-five cents for each transfer.

(i) Money paid on shares, or installments of shares, may be withdrawn on any day when payment for shares may be made; but the board of directors shall have the right, at any time, to require members to give sixty days' notice of the intention to withdraw the whole or any part of the amounts so paid in by them. No member may, however, while he is a borrower from the credit union or an endorser or a guarantor on any loan made by the credit union, withdraw any portion of the money paid on shares or installments of shares, except with the written approval of the credit committee.

(j) Irrespective of the number of shares held by him, no member shall have more than one vote.

(k) A member may not borrow from the credit union when he is not in good standing; nor if he has failed to repay any matured previous loan; nor if he is in arrears in the payment of any current loan or installments on the loan.

(l) Loans shall be made only for provident or productive purposes.

(m) The rates of interest shall be fixed from time to time by the board of directors; and shall in no case exceed 1 per cent a month on unpaid balances, inclusive of all charges incidental to making the loan.

(n) No loan to a director, an officer, or a committee member shall exceed the amount of his holding as represented by his fully paid-in shares. No director, officer, or committee member shall act as endorser or guarantor for borrowers from the credit union.

(o) No loan in excess of fifty dollars shall be made without adequate security. The security may be an assignment of shares, an endorsement of a note, or such other security as the credit committee may, in the given case, deem adequate. No secured loan shall be made to any member in excess of two hundred dollars or 10 per cent, whichever is greater, of the paid-in and unimpaired capital and surplus of the credit union.

Co-operatives in the United States. Although the co-operative movement has had a strong development in European countries, its growth in the United States has been only sporadic. Producers' co-operatives in agriculture have increased rapidly in certain sections. Likewise, farmers have formed many consumer co-operatives to engage in the purchase of farm supplies of various kinds. The rapid development of chain stores has impeded the co-operative movement in the food business because chain stores have tended to lower the cost of distribution. In recent years, however, the encouragement given to co-operatives by the Federal Government and state governments has caused the organization of many new consumer co-operatives.

SALES OF REPORTING DISTRIBUTIVE CO-OPERATIVES
(By Major Types of Business)

MAJOR BUSINESS	NUMBER OF ASSOCIATIONS REPORTING	AMOUNT OF SALES	AVERAGE PER ASSOCIATION
All associations	1,802	$146,153,418	$ 81,106
Store associations	858	71,027,638	82,783
Groceries and meats	259	11,612,935	44,838
General merchandise	194	15,701,165	80,934
Students' supplies	12	1,884,310	157,026
Fuel	56	5,515,885	98,498
Farm supplies	322	35,441,276	110,066
Miscellaneous	15	872,067	58,138
Buying clubs	79	415,991	5,266
Petroleum associations	720	50,781,102	70,529
Distributive departments of marketing associations	132	20,360,534	154,246
Bakeries	6	595,680	99,280
Creameries	4	2,954,121	738,530
Water-supply associations	3	18,352	6,117

Illustration No. 159—Distributive Co-operatives

According to figures available from the Federal Government, there are almost 4,000 co-operative retail associations in the United States, which have approximately 700,000 members and do an annual business of at least 200 million dollars. Illustration No. 159 provides a classification of some of the most common retail distributive co-operatives. This tabulation indicates that co-operatives which distribute petroleum products, farm supplies, and groceries are the most common.

Early Development of Co-operatives. The co-operative movement among consumers was started in an effort to break away from the difficulties involved in the conflicts between laborers, manufacturers, and retailers. The first real co-operative movement was begun in Rochdale, England, in 1844 by a small group of weavers who started their own co-operative store. In certain sections of the United States the Rochdale plan is still in operation. The essence of the Rochdale plan is democratic control; that is, one vote for every member, regardless of the number of shares held. The plan also requires cash sales at prevailing market prices. Dividends are paid to members from profits after the operating expenses have been paid.

TEXTBOOK QUESTIONS

1. What are at least three unavoidable factors causing the difference in the price received by the producer and the price paid by the consumer?
2. What is the contention of many consumers that causes them to organize a retail distributive co-operative?
3. Does a co-operative retail association eliminate any economic functions? Explain.
4. Besides consumer or retail co-operatives, what other types of co-operatives are there?
5. What is a co-operative?
6. Do co-operatives sell to people who are not members?
7. From the point of view of ownership explain the federated type of co-operative organization.
8. From the point of view of ownership explain the centralized type of co-operative.
9. What types of groups may organize a credit union?
10. Besides the board of directors of a credit union, what two important committees are elected?
11. What are the main functions attributed to credit unions?
12. How many votes does a member of a credit union have?
13. Under what two types of laws may a credit union be organized?
14. What is the essence of the democratic control in the Rochdale co-operative plan?

DISCUSSION QUESTIONS

1. Does a consumer's co-operative always assure the customers of getting their merchandise at a saving?

2. In what way is the consumer's co-operative limited in its ability to serve its members?
3. Some people who are opposed to co-operatives contend that the members of a co-operative are not only wage earners but also retailers and investors, and are escaping the normal taxes of other businessmen. Discuss this question.
4. In your opinion could the members of a single community form a credit union? Why?
5. It has been contended that the centralized type of consumer co-operative is comparable to the chain store. What is your opinion?
6. Why, in your opinion, may it be dangerous for a member to have more than one vote in a co-operative?
7. Why is it necessary to place some restriction on persons who may leave the original field of membership of the credit union?
8. What is the purpose of the regulation of Federal credit unions prohibiting a director, an officer, or a committee member from endorsing the note of a borrower?

PROBLEMS

1. Set up a proposed plan for organizing a co-operative book store or candy store in your school. Be sure that the principles are based upon state or Federal regulations.
2. Suppose Mr. J. A. Mason, who is a member of a Federal credit union, borrows $60. He repays the loan at the maximum rate of interest in equal installments of $20 over a period of three months. How much interest does he pay?

COMMUNITY PROBLEMS AND PROJECTS

1. Assume that the members of your class decide to organize a credit union, under either state laws or Federal laws. Set up a tentative organization, establish certain rules and regulations, and make up a chart, similar to that illustrated in this chapter, giving the names of the individuals.
2. If there is a consumer co-operative in your community, investigate it and write a report on the following points: (a) efficiency, (b) convenience, (c) variety of merchandise, (d) stock of merchandise, (e) apparent success or failure, and (f) reason for success or failure.

CHAPTER XXII

DETECTING AND ANALYZING PROPAGANDA

Purpose of the Chapter. In order for consumers to protect themselves as individuals and as a group, they should understand the various influences to which they are subjected. Many of these influences have been previously explained. Propaganda, however, is another form of influence. In simple language, propaganda is influencing people in some manner or another. Some propaganda is good and some is bad. Various forms of propaganda and means of detecting propaganda are explained in this chapter.

Types of Propaganda. Before one is able to detect propaganda, he must have a clear conception of what the word means. Without resorting to a dictionary definition, he can gain such a conception from the following explanation of propaganda:

(a) Influencing people by teaching and *openly disseminating information* that will tend to fix or change ideas, ideals, and standards of conduct
(b) Influencing people by *secretly or subversively disseminating information* that will fix or change ideas, ideals, and standards of conduct

In other words, one form of propaganda is to influence openly by educating, and the other is to influence secretly. In the first case the person who is being influenced is expected to be aware of what is happening. In the second case the person who is practicing the propaganda hopes that he can influence the other person without having that person become aware of what is happening.

In either of the two types the influences may be good or bad. A person should therefore recognize (a) the type of influence that is being used and (b) whether that influence is good or bad. Obviously, one is primarily concerned with the second type of propaganda because that type is more difficult to detect than the other.

Propaganda in Advertising. Much modern advertising contains the two types of propaganda. Many readers of advertising, however, confuse the two types of propaganda and accept all advertisements as being educational truth.

As civilization has become more complicated and competition has become keener, producers have found it necessary to utilize various devices to influence the consumer. Advertising exercises influence over the consumer through one or more of the following ways:

(a) Performing a service by disseminating information that explains the quality of the product, describes the product, explains its uses, gives its price, and specifies the sources from which it can be obtained
(b) Inducing the selection of one class of goods, in contrast to another class, by presenting rational statements appealing to the intelligence of the buyer
(c) Inducing the selection of one class of goods, in contrast to another class, by appealing to the emotions (love, envy, or the like) of the individual
(d) Inducing the selection of a particular brand of goods, in preference to another brand, by presenting rational statements appealing to the intelligence of the buyer
(e) Inducing the selection of a particular brand of goods, in preference to another brand, by appealing to the emotions (love, envy, or the like) of the individual

In preceding chapters there are criteria for determining what is good advertising and what is bad advertising from the point of view of fairness and honesty. Determining what is good and what is bad advertising will, however, depend to a large extent upon one's point of view. In general, advertising that utilizes rational appeals and gives an accurate and truthful description of the product is considered good. An advertisement that resorts to highly emotional appeals, untruths, and paid testimonials is considered undesirable.

Propaganda in Newspapers. In evaluating a newspaper, one should try to determine to what extent the newspaper is openly educating and informing the public, or is secretly influencing the readers. Either procedure will be disclosed by omissions of information or by the substitution of opinions in place of facts; but it is not easy for a reader to distinguish an opinion from a fact or to detect omissions.

Theoretically, newspapers are supposed to report all sides of every question without bias or without prejudice. Readers are supposed, under such circumstances, to be allowed to make up their minds for themselves. Such a situation does not, however, usually exist. In the first place the reporter who collects the original facts may be personally prejudiced, and his prejudice may be reflected in his writing. In the second place the editor who reads the reporter's comments and prepares them for publication may be influenced to the extent that he will add to or delete certain comments in order to make the reporter's facts harmonize with the policy of the newspaper. In the third place the editorial column of the newspaper definitely represents the personal ideas and policies of the management of the newspaper. It should be recognized and evaluated as such.

Furthermore, most newspapers carry what are called feature columns. These are usually syndicated columns containing the personal views of the writers. Some newspapers are rather liberal in permitting various conflicting views of these writers to be published side by side. On the other hand, many newspapers exclude syndicated feature articles that are consistently obnoxious or opposed to the general views of the editors of the newspapers.

One must consider also that a person publishes a newspaper in order to make a living. He derives an income from the readers, who pay a subscription price, and from the advertisers, who pay for the advertising. One should recognize the fact that any editor is human and that he will therefore attempt to please the two classes of his customers. He will try to publish the kind of material that will appeal to the readers and will try to avoid publishing information that will be objectionable to the advertisers. Some newspapers follow a policy of publishing items that are particularly pleasing to the advertisers, but some newspapers do not. This practice helps to sell advertising.

The American Society of Newspaper Editors has adopted a set of ethical rules entitled the Canons of Journalism. In evaluating the propaganda features of newspapers, these canons,[1] partially reprinted below, serve as a guide.

(1) RESPONSIBILITY—The right of a newspaper to attract and hold readers is restricted by nothing but considerations of public welfare. A journalist who uses his power for any selfish or otherwise unworthy purpose is faithless to a high trust.

(2) FREEDOM OF THE PRESS—Freedom of the press is to be guarded as a vital right of mankind.

(3) INDEPENDENCE—Freedom from all obligations except that of fidelity to the public interest is vital.

A. Promotion of any private interest contrary to the general welfare, for whatever reason, is not compatible with honest journalism. So-called news communications from private sources should not be published without public notice of their source or else substantiation of the claims to value as news, both in form and in substance.

B. Partisanship in editorial comment which knowingly departs from the truth does violence to the best spirit of American journalism; in the news columns it is subversive of a fundamental principle of the profession.

(4) SINCERITY, TRUTHFULNESS, ACCURACY—Good faith with the reader is the foundation of all journalism worthy of the name.

A. By every consideration of good faith, a newspaper is constrained to be truthful. It is not to be excused for lack of thoroughness, or accuracy within its control, or failure to obtain command of these essential qualities.

B. Headlines should be fully warranted by the contents of the articles which they surmount.

(5) IMPARTIALITY—Sound practice makes clear distinction between news reports and expressions of opinion. News reports should be free from opinion or bias of any kind. This rule does not apply to so-called special articles unmistakably devoted to advocacy or characterized by a signature authorizing the writer's own conclusions and interpretations.

(6) FAIR PLAY—A newspaper should not publish unofficial charges affecting reputation or moral character, without opportunity given to the accused to be heard; right practice demands the giving of such opportunity in all cases of serious accusation outside judicial proceedings.

A. A newspaper should not invade rights of private feelings without sure warrant of public rights as distinguished from public curiosity.

B. It is the privilege, as it is the duty, of a newspaper to make prompt and complete correction of its own serious mistakes of fact or opinion, whatever their origin.

(7) DECENCY—A newspaper cannot escape conviction of insincerity if, while professing high moral purpose, it supplies incentives to base conduct, such as are to be found in details of crime and vice, publication of which is not demonstrably for the public good.

---

[1] *Editor and Publisher,* January 30, 1937.

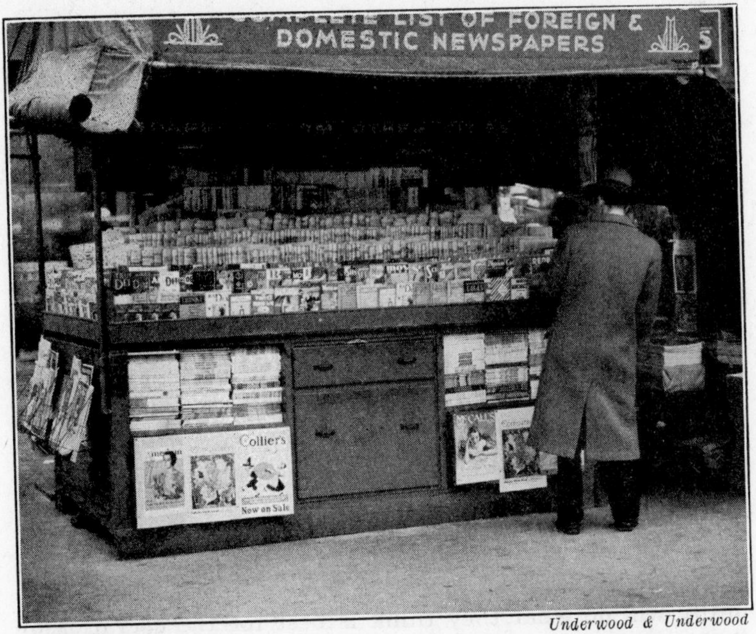

Underwood & Underwood

Illustration No. 160—News, Fiction, and Propaganda

The preceding Canons of Journalism, if followed precisely by editors, would lead to the use of desirable propaganda in most newspapers. Not all editors, however, follow these canons. Bad propaganda in newspapers results from the omission of facts, the complete omission of certain news items, the distortion of facts, the coloring of facts with opinions, and partiality. Not all these are easy to detect, but a good way to detect bad propaganda in newspapers is to read more than one paper and to try to get more than one point of view.

Newspapers and Politics. In some countries newspapers are entirely under the control of the government and are not allowed to publish anything that has not been censored. Such censorship provides the ultimate form of newspaper propaganda and deprives the readers of any opportunity to arrive at their own conclusions in relation to the facts presented. Many facts are entirely withheld.

Even under a democratic form of government, there are constant attempts to influence the editorial policies of newspapers for or against some political theory, some political party, or some general movement.

A later discussion in this chapter points out the fact that governmental agencies attempt to influence public opinion. Part of this influence is asserted through political pressure, and part of it is asserted through a definite program of publicity. For instance, in several of the municipal, state, and Federal agencies, there are publicity directors and public relations directors who serve in fact although sometimes not officially. The function of such individuals is to present the government to the public in a favorable light and to try to disseminate such information as to make the citizens accept and agree with the policies and the acts of the government.

Propaganda Through the Radio and Motion Pictures. The operators of radio stations are human beings. They naturally will do what they think is best for the operation of their stations and will unconsciously or consciously let their own likes and dislikes influence their broadcasting. Some radio operators may attempt to avoid selling broadcasting time because of a dislike for the program or the sponsor of the program. Nevertheless, there is considerable freedom in obtaining the use of broadcasting time. For instance, each political party has an opportunity to buy time on the radio. Various other groups likewise have the same opportunity, but the cost of broadcasting time prevents the use of the radio by some individuals and groups. The Federal Communications Commission maintains control over the character of programs, but that control is exercised primarily to prevent distasteful statements.

One can always turn off his radio and not listen to anything that he does not care to hear, but the fact that there are radios in many homes and that people of all ages listen to programs causes the radio to be an effective instrument of propaganda. Consider, for instance, the various entertainment programs that appeal to children but that have as their primary motive the selling of merchandise to parents.

Various devices are used to encourage children to listen to programs and to get them to enter contests or to send in coupons so that the purchase of the advertised products will be necessary. Sometimes these programs are beneficial in encouraging children to do things that they should do; but, on the other hand, they sometimes cause articles to be purchased as the result of irrational motives.

Motion pictures can spread propaganda by the following means: (a) the themes of entertainment films produced by regular studios; (b) news reels which show only the news events that are acceptable to those sponsoring them; (c) commercial films prepared by manufacturers and distributed through schools, theaters, and clubs; and (d) noncommercial films produced by the Federal Government, state governments, and various societies for the purpose of disseminating propaganda.

Various entertainment films have been produced by regular motion-picture studios with the idea of influencing opinions in favor of one foreign country or another. Some of these films take the opposite view and attempt to create public opinion against some foreign country. Various other films of this type influence people for or against some social or political movement within the United States.

There is no question that motion pictures have influenced style, have molded opinion for or against war, and have caused people to want and to obtain various luxuries. Certainly motion pictures have helped to make women beauty-conscious.

Film producers have been instrumental in encouraging many manufacturers of commercial products to use films in spreading information and propaganda on their products. For instance, a sugar manufacturer produces a film showing the process by which his particular sugar is manufactured. A steel manufacturer may produce an interesting film showing the romance of the steel industry, with the idea of influencing people to think favorably of that industry and his company. Such films often find their way into schools. Some are good, and some serve undesirable purposes. If they are selected properly, however, many of these films are helpful.

Our own Federal Government has been responsible for creating films to spread propaganda on certain programs sponsored by the Government. For instance, the film entitled "The Plow That Broke the Plains" emphasizes the critical problem of the dust bowl. "The River" emphasizes the problem of flood control.

Motion-picture films that are shown in public theaters are censored for (a) political reasons and (b) moral reasons. In some nations they are censored primarily from a political point of view, but also from a moral and racial point of view. For instance, it is common knowledge that England, Italy, or Japan will not allow the showing of certain American films because those films seem to reflect badly on the people of those countries, or seem to promote certain ideas that are objectionable to those people. Certain programs of the "March of Time" and various other news reels have been banned from some foreign countries because their content was considered objectionable. The film censors in the United States ban certain imported films. State boards of censors ban or censor certain films because they feel that such films will have an unfavorable influence on the people of those states. Such censorship may be good or bad, its effect depending upon the motive behind the censorship.

What is good and what is bad in radio programs and motion pictures will depend to a great extent upon one's point of view and one's morals. From the point of view of morals a radio program or a motion picture is bad if it tends to weaken public morals; it is good if it tends to strengthen them. Some programs and pictures are highly educative, while others serve purely for entertainment. Either type may be good or bad according to one's point of view. There is no harm in bringing into the classroom films prepared by manufacturers and governmental agencies if the teacher is fully aware of the purposes of those films. Many of these films are highly educative and serve no other purpose except to build goodwill for the sponsor.

Propaganda in Politics and Government. There is probably no other field of activity in which there is so much propaganda as in politics. Political theories often are contrary to sound economic principles. The politician who can talk the most eloquently is frequently not the one who is best qualified to pass upon legislation, but he is often the one who is elected.

Underwood & Underwood

Illustration No. 161—Politicians Can Be Very Convincing

The politician utilizes the newspaper, the radio, handbill advertising, and personal addresses for spreading his ideas. His entire success in becoming elected depends upon his ability to influence people to believe in his so-called platform. Many politicians believe in promising everything, but they do not fulfill their promises. Some politicians make justifiable attacks on others; but these attacks should be distinguished from "smoke-screen" attacks, which divert unfavorable attention from the attacker and direct unfavorable attention to the one who is being attacked. Some political attacks, while not untruthful, infer untruths.

In a democracy one should, theoretically, vote for the individual rather than for the party, and base his judgment at least partially on the platform that is proposed. A study of the political platform is therefore important, although there is usually no assurance that the platform will be carried out. Some candidates have no intention of carrying out a platform. For instance, a candidate may make promises to one group and make conflicting promises to another group in the hope that the first group will not learn of the promises made to the second. Such promises, however, scarcely represent a platform. They are more deliberately an attempt to mislead.

Nearly every governmental agency in cities, states, and the country has at some time or another utilized the two forms of propaganda. Elected officials make use of propaganda in an attempt to perpetuate their existence in office.

Political parties do likewise. In a democracy a citizen has the right to know what is happening in his government; the use of propaganda for purely educational purposes is therefore justified. One may, however, question the extent to which citizens as taxpayers should pay for secret propaganda disseminated for the purpose of influencing the citizens for or against some political or economic program. Undoubtedly, a certain amount of secret propaganda is necessary in government, but the important point for the individual is to be able to detect such propaganda.

An act of the Federal Congress passed in 1913 forbids the employment of publicity experts by the Government without specific authorization from Congress. Nevertheless, it has been estimated that the Federal Government is spending from thirty to forty million dollars a year to influence voters favorably toward the activities of the Government. In many of the departments of the Federal Government today, there are publicity experts employed under such titles as editorial research assistant, informational service representative, and chief of the Division of Information.

Regardless of the advice that one may be given in relation to political propaganda, he will probably be inclined to believe what he wants to believe and not to believe the things that he does not wish to believe. This fact is true if the person is politically biased. To evaluate political propaganda, one should attempt to separate facts from opinions and to distinguish sound economic policy from political expediency.

Business Propaganda. Almost every group in society uses some form of propaganda. The businessman resorts to the newspaper, the radio, and various other means of advertising for disseminating his ideas. As was mentioned previously, the motion-picture film is coming into common use for such purposes. Chambers of commerce and better business bureaus utilize propaganda to accomplish their objectives. Much of the propaganda of such organizations is socially desirable, but some of their activities can be considered to be socially selfish. Such is also true of the propaganda of almost every group.

For instance, an attempt on the part of a chamber of commerce to influence taxation legislation is socially selfish, but may be entirely sound economically and therefore justifiable. An attack on legislation pertaining to conditions of employment might be socially selfish and economically unsound and therefore not justifiable.

The natural defense of any group or any individual in society is to attempt to justify his existence and his actions. Such is also the case in business. When misunderstanding and strife arise among the workers in an industry, the employers sometimes resort to educating their employees openly or secretly on the operations of the industry, in the hope that an understanding of those operations will cause the employees to have a more favorable opinion of the management. These activities are sometimes delegated to personnel directors, who influence the employees to think favorably of the policies of the management.

The relations of a business organization with the public also require cautious handling because it is necessary to have the goodwill of the public in addition to the goodwill of customers. Many large business organizations have so-called public relations directors, whose work it is to present the organization in a favorable manner to the public. These persons release news items to the newspapers and carefully edit all statements that are issued by the organization. They participate, in many cases, in local civic organizations. For instance, the officials of large businesses often engage in important civic enterprises because of the favorable publicity they obtain from those activities.

There can be no harm in the honest enlightenment of employees and of the public with regard to the plans, policies, functions, and purposes of a business organization. Probably some of the misunderstandings of business can be blamed upon the fact that employees and the public have not known much about business. The propaganda of business organizations is undesirable when it is used in an attempt to gain an unfair advantage.

Specialists in Propaganda. There are individuals and enterprises that make a business of providing publicity or public relations guidance. Foreign countries hire these agencies to influence favorable public opinion in this country, particularly in times of war. The two opponents often have propaganda agents scattered throughout the world to try to develop favorable opinion. Each is trying to influence public opinion in favor of its side of the dispute. In modern times these propaganda agents use newspaper articles, pictures, motion-picture films, books, and speeches. Many of the so-called facts are deliberate falsehoods.

Newspapers, radio sponsors, motion-picture studios, schools, teachers, clergymen, and many others are influenced by this propaganda and often unknowingly take up the battle of the propagandist and help him in his work.

It is quite common for the major political parties of the country to hire expert propagandists or publicity directors. Such persons often write the speeches of the candidates. They supervise or write all statements and literature issued by the party and interview newspaper reporters.

Some of the resort cities employ publicity agents, who are constantly releasing pictures of bathing beauties, various social events, sports events, and other activities that publicize and spread propaganda for the resort and thereby bring new patrons. Contests and stunts are often sponsored by these publicity directors for the same purpose.

Propaganda Devices. The following suggestion for detecting propaganda are offered by the Institute for Propaganda Analysis. The devices through which propaganda is disseminated are:

(a) The name-calling device
(b) The glittering-generalities device
(c) The transfer device
(d) The testimonial device
(e) The plain-folks device
(f) The card-stacking device
(g) The band-wagon device

Most of these devices are used in undesirable propaganda; but some of them, particularly those designated as (b), (c), (d), (e), and (g), are used also in desirable types of propaganda.

Name calling is a device to make a person form a judgment without examining the evidence on which it should be based. The propagandist appeals to hate and fear. He does so by giving bad names to those individuals, groups, nations, races, policies, practices, beliefs, or ideals that he would have one condemn and reject. For instance, one person calls another an "economic royalist," and the latter person in turn calls the other a "Communist."

Glittering generalities is a device by which the propagandist identifies his program with virtue by the use of virtuous words. He appeals to the emotions of love, generosity, and brotherhood. He uses words and terms like *truth, freedom, honor, liberty, social justice, public service, the right to work, loyalty, progress, democracy, the American way, Constitution defender.*

Transfer is a device by which the propagandist carries over the authority, sanction, and prestige of something that the individual respects to something he would have the latter accept. For example, most of us respect and revere our church and our nation. If the propagandist succeeds in getting the church or the nation to approve a campaign in behalf of some program, he thereby transfers its authority, sanction, and prestige to that program. A salesman will often try to get a minister to approve a set of books that he is trying to sell. A political candidate will try to get the sanction of some church group. There are many other similar examples.

The *testimonial* is a device employed to make one accept anything from a patent medicine to a national policy. The propagandist makes use of the testimonials (quite often purchased) of important persons or at least persons who will have some influence upon the people who will read the testimonials.

The device of *plain folks* is used especially by politicians, labor leaders, businessmen, ministers, and educators to win confidence by appearing to be plain or average people. In other words, they want to appear to be "just plain folks among the neighbors." In election years candidates show their devotion to children; they like to have their photographs taken in a home or on a farm or with a group of workers; they go to picnics, attend parties, and even have their photographs taken while they are fishing.

The *card-stacking* device is one in which the propagandist employs the various arts of deception to win support for himself, his group, nation, race, policy, practice, belief, or ideal. He uses underemphasis and overemphasis to avoid issues and to evade facts. He resorts to falsehoods, censorship, and distortion. He frequently omits facts and offers false testimony. He creates a camouflage of clamor by raising a new issue—quite often a sensational one—when he wants an embarrassing matter forgotten. In political campaigns a candidate is often built into an intellectual giant and a great public benefactor. Voters are deliberately misled.

The *band-wagon* device is one that attempts to utilize mass psychology. In other words, the propagandist attempts to get the crowd to follow as a group. He plays upon the idea of "everybody is doing it, you should do it." His tactics are usually quite dramatic and emotional. Mass meetings and parades are utilized. The propagandist appeals to the tendency of people to follow the crowd without any attempt to reason why. An intelligent person should train himself to form his own opinions.

TEXTBOOK QUESTIONS

1. From the point of view of technique in accomplishing the final result, what are the kinds of propaganda?
2. Is all propaganda bad?
3. Give at least two examples of the use of propaganda in commercial advertising.
4. Give ways in which bad propaganda may be used through newspapers.
5. In what respect does the editorial page of a newspaper not always report facts?
6. In what way is the newspaper publisher obliged to favor certain individuals or groups?
7. Name the seven Canons of Journalism.
8. Is it legally permissible for a radio-broadcasting company to show partiality by permitting the broadcast of certain radio propaganda and preventing the dissemination of other propaganda?

9. Through what types of motion pictures is propaganda spread?
10. How does the Federal Government use films for propaganda?
11. On what grounds do motion-picture censors sometimes ban films?
12. Why do politicians always have a so-called platform?
13. Why is the propaganda of government, when used for educational and informative purposes, justifiable?
14. How do governmental agencies sometimes use secret propaganda in a manner that may not be justifiable?
15. Why do many businesses find it necessary to have public relations directors?
16. What is the function of the so-called public relations director?
17. Why are many groups that are interested in spreading propaganda so anxious to contact those in charge of schools and churches?
18. Name the seven devices through which propaganda is spread.
19. (a) What is meant by "name calling"? (b) How is it effective?

DISCUSSION QUESTIONS

1. Give some means of spreading propaganda other than those mentioned in this chapter.
2. Name some types of propaganda that may be considered desirable by one group and undesirable by others.
3. Why is secret propaganda important under a dictatorship?
4. How do you think public officials may use propaganda in order to obtain public and legislative support for themselves?
5. Do you believe that American newspapers in general contain less or more propaganda than the newspapers of many foreign countries? Give examples.
6. Even though a newspaper may report a political speech of an opposing party, how may the report be colored in order to affect the readers?
7. In what way are travel films a form of propaganda?
8. Name some motion pictures that may have propaganda in them.
9. How do the manufacturers of certain products sometimes work propaganda into the ordinary entertainment films seen in theaters?
10. What are some of the functions of the press representatives of many important state and national officials?
11. Give some examples of how propaganda may creep into schools.
12. Why is it desirable for each community to have at least two newspapers published by persons of opposite political affiliations?

13. Give some recent examples of radio propaganda.
14. (a) Why do you think public officials have a right to ban films for political and moral reasons? (b) Are there any dangers in this practice?
15. Justify the use of propaganda by our Federal Government.
16. On what basis would you condemn the use of propaganda by governmental agencies?
17. What is your opinion of a public relations director of a large business organization?
18. Which of the seven devices for spreading propaganda is the most vicious? Why?

PROBLEMS

1. Write a report showing specifically how an editorial in your local newspaper attempted to influence public opinion. Be specific in your comments.
2. Cut out an ordinary news item from your local newspaper. Write a report on it, giving your opinion as to whether the news item is accurate. If it is not accurate, indicate specifically where or why, in your opinion, it is not accurate.
3. From a newspaper or a magazine obtain an advertisement that has as its purpose the selling of a new idea, the acceptance of a new style, the creation of a habit, or the breaking of an old habit.
4. Take one issue of your local newspaper and check it with the Canons of Journalism to see whether it is violating any of these standards. Write a report giving your conclusions.

COMMUNITY PROBLEMS AND PROJECTS

1. Obtain some political literature, political advertisements, or copies of political speeches, and check them with the seven devices for spreading propaganda. Point out the various devices that have been used.
2. Find one good example in a newspaper, a magazine, or some other piece of printed literature that can be classified under one of the seven devices of spreading propaganda. Submit the example with your explanation of how it fits into that classification.
3. Find out what publicity or propaganda agencies exist in your local government, and gather some information on the activities of those agencies.
4. From some popular magazine pick out an example of each of the five different functions of advertising propaganda. Submit the five advertisements with an explanation of your classification of the advertisements.

INDEX

C

D

E

F

J

K

L

M

N

O

P